# Praise for *Teller's War*:

"In clear, nontechnical language, Pulitzer Prize–winning *New York Times* science writer Broad traces the development of the X-ray laser, touted by Edward Teller as the ultimate destroyer of enemy missiles. $25 billion already spent, these overlapping experiments are the costliest military research programs in the nation's history. *Teller's War* is investigative journalism at its finest."

—*Publishers Weekly*

"[A] vivid and disturbing tale of private phantoms and public purposes."

—*Foreign Affairs*

"An absorbing indictment . . . Mr. Broad's presentation is detailed and meticulously sourced."

—*The Economist*

"In *Teller's War*, Broad, *The New York Times* science writer and Pulitzer Prize winner, has provided us with a critical insight into the life of one of this century's most influential and controversial scientists."

—*Arms Control Today*

"As Congress prepares to debate the latest ! Pentagon's $5.43 billion 1993 SDI budge offers a sobering look at the past history o be required reading for every lawmaker."

D0951266

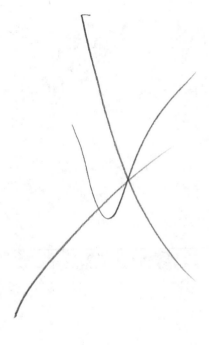

# The Top-Secret Story Behind the Star Wars Deception

A TOUCHSTONE BOOK
Published by Simon & Schuster
*New York* • *London* • *Toronto* • *Sydney* • *Tokyo* • *Singapore*

# TELLER'S
# WAR

WILLIAM J. BROAD

TOUCHSTONE
Simon & Schuster Building
Rockefeller Center
1230 Avenue of the Americas
New York, New York 10020

First Touchstone Edition 1993

TOUCHSTONE and colophon are registered trademarks
of Simon & Schuster Inc.

Designed by Edith Fowler
Manufactured in the United States of America

10   9   8   7   6   5   4   3   2   1

Library of Congress Cataloging-in-Publication Data

Broad, William, date.
  Teller's war: the top-secret story behind the Star
Wars deception / William J. Broad.
      p.      cm.
  Includes bibliographical references and index.
  1. Lasers—Military applications—Research—United
States—History. 2. Teller, Edward, 1908- . 3. Lawrence
Livermore laboratory—History. 4. X-ray lasers—
History. 5. Strategic Defense Initiative—History.
I. Title.
UG486.B76      1992
623.4'46'072073—dc20                              91-34750
                                                      CIP

ISBN 0-671-70106-1
ISBN: 0-671-86738-5 (PBK)

FOR TANYA

# Contents

TWO PHOTOS: LOS ALAMOS NATIONAL LABORATORY

Edward Teller (center), in a turbulent career spanning more than six decades, was constantly driven to achieve more. During the Manhattan Project of World War II, he shunned research on atomic weapons for the bold personal dream of perfecting the hydrogen bomb. Here he holds court among colleagues at a Los Alamos party.

The world's first hydrogen bomb, detonated in 1952, was some 700 times more powerful than the bomb dropped on Hiroshima. Teller eventually became ambivalent about the feat, proud of its intellectual and military aspects but troubled that it caused much of the public to disparage him as a mad scientist fixated on mass destruction. He hated being called the bomb's "father."

Teller used his H-bomb notoriety to lobby for a second nuclear-weapons lab for the nation, which was founded at Livermore, California, in 1952. It amassed thousands of employees and set off hundreds of nuclear explosions. Here he examines a new computer with Harold Brown (center), a Livermore prodigy who eventually became secretary of defense. Such computers aided Teller's goal of designing nuclear warheads for antimissile interceptors.

Teller was the nation's top scientist-politician during the darkest days of the cold war, warning that the West needed greater military strength to challenge communism. He traveled frequently to Washington to court and cajole men of power. Here he makes a point with President Johnson at the White House.

Teller became the nation's top scientific advocate of antimissile arms. In the 1960s, as his Livermore laboratory fashioned warheads for ground-based interceptor rockets, Teller tried to win the nation to the antimissile cause. In 1969 he testified before the Senate Foreign Relations Committee.

In the early 1980s, Teller seized on a top-secret Livermore advance which he believed held promise as a novel weapon that would abolish the threat of enemy missiles, doom the Soviets to inferiority and end the nightmare of mutual assured destruction. The breakthrough team included Lowell Wood (left), Roy Woodruff (bottom left), and Peter Hagelstein (below). Their advance, known as the X-ray laser, channeled the power of an exploding H-bomb into deadly beams that Teller hoped to fire across space.

THREE PHOTOS: LAWRENCE LIVERMORE NATIONAL LABORATORY

Teller threw himself into a campaign to win the Reagan White House to his X-ray vision. Among his early successes was having a young protégé named White House science adviser. Here, physicist George Keyworth greets Reagan. In his White House lobbying, Teller said the X-ray laser promised a new era of assured survival.

The culmination of Teller's two-year effort came on March 23, 1983, when Reagan gave his Star Wars speech, in which he announced a crash antimissile effort. The president made no mention of the X-ray laser, but there had been enough leaks about the secretive project for news organizations to play it prominently in postspeech stories. *Newsweek* put a fanciful image of the would-be weapon on its cover.

Teller was elated after the speech, which he praised in newspaper articles and congressional testimony. His joy was evident in May 1983 as President Reagan awarded him the National Medal of Science, the country's highest and most coveted scientific honor.

The X-ray laser program eventually collapsed, torn by errors, failures and the charges of Roy Woodruff and other Livermore experts that the rudimentary effort had been seriously oversold to federal officials. Even so, Edward Teller retained his influence. He went on to hail a new Star Wars weapon, Brilliant Pebbles, which he unveiled at a 1988 conference attended by President Reagan.

COURTESY OF *HIGH FRONTIER*

Andrei Sakharov, a principal inventor of the Soviet H-bomb and a winner of the Nobel Peace Prize for his advocacy of human rights, warned Teller in late 1988 that Star Wars was so inherently dangerous that its deployment could trigger a nuclear war. Initially shaken, Teller soon regained his confidence and redoubled his antimissile campaign.

LOS ALAMOS NATIONAL LABORATORY

Teller continued to wield enormous influence well into his eighties, advising President Bush, lobbying for Star Wars and urging the United States to deploy space arms. That goal moved closer as the Bush administration made Brilliant Pebbles its antimissile centerpiece. To date, the overall Star Wars effort has cost the nation more than $25 billion.

# TELLER'S
# WAR

# Prologue

AT AGE 70, after a career in which he begat the hydrogen bomb and the most feared laboratory on earth for the design of nuclear arms, using them to battle the Communist bloc for a quarter century, Edward Teller longed for a final accomplishment. His chance came in the 1980s. Filled with determination, at times shaking with excitement, Teller threw himself into a bid for what he was sure would be his ultimate success. The result, however, was no triumph. Over the protests of colleagues, Teller misled the highest officials of the United States government on a critical issue of national security, paving the way for a multibillion-dollar deception in which a dream of peace concealed the most dangerous military program of all time.

The episode was full of riddles. How could Teller, a scientist of outstanding gifts and credentials, a man dedicated to discovering the truth and eminently successful in that regard, end up betraying the central principle of his profession? How could close colleagues fail to save Teller from himself? And how could the federal government, with its ranks of experts and advisers, allow itself to be so completely deceived? Answers to such questions can be found in the uncommon methods of a man who had enormous impact on the twentieth century and whose main attainment late in life was persuading the American government to embrace the deadly folly known as Star Wars.

At first glance, it seemed Teller had no reason to yearn for a

crowning glory. By any measure, he was the most influential scientist of the nuclear era—and perhaps the century. His name was
regularly found alongside such giants of science as Einstein, Bohr
and Fermi. Moreover, his political impact had been nothing short of
enormous. Presidents had come and gone, along with their powerful
aides. Statesmen of science had fallen in and out of favor. But Teller
had been on the center stage for decades, building bombs, testifying
before Congress, advising generals and presidents, fashioning himself into a force that dominated the age. He was given to doom-laden
pronouncements about Communists taking over the earth. He was
tough, bellicose and charismatic. Most important, he was a major
architect of the cold war. With great skill and seemingly boundless
energy, he did more than any other scientist, perhaps any other
individual, to keep its structure intact and evolving.

This short man with huge dark eyebrows began his scientific
career in the 1930s by making basic contributions to physical
chemistry and quantum mechanics. A Jew of Hungarian birth, he
fled Hitler in 1935 for the United States. His political debut came
in the 1940s as a prime mover in the push for the atom bomb,
helping persuade the government to embark on a top-secret effort.
As a senior scientist in the Manhattan Project, he pursued the
weapon high in the mountains of New Mexico at the Los Alamos
laboratory. One night, with remarkable aplomb, he donned suntan
oil and dark glasses to witness the flash from the world's first
atomic blast. After the war, Teller became a strident anticommunist with a particular loathing for the Soviet Union. To challenge
it militarily, he struggled to bring the hydrogen bomb to life and
opposed virtually all arms-control treaties. In the 1950s, at the
height of the cold war, he became the driving force behind the
founding of the Livermore laboratory, a federal center for the design of nuclear arms in California that amassed thousands of employees and set off hundreds of nuclear explosions, many filling
the sky with radioactive fire. The Soviets called it the City of
Death. Always headstrong, Teller was quick to denounce those
who opposed him. In 1954 he launched a calculated assault on the
political and technical judgment of J. Robert Oppenheimer, an
H-bomb skeptic who led the nation's postwar scientists. Teller's
attack brought about Oppenheimer's demise and opened a deep
schism in American science. Perhaps most significantly, Teller's
tireless opposition to a ban on the explosive testing of nuclear arms
helped keep the blasts from ending in the late 1950s and early

1960s, fueling an arms race that, in the end, nearly exhausted the treasuries of the earth's greatest powers.

The influence of Edward Teller was vast. In the East-West conflict that governed the second half of the twentieth century, in an epic as monumental as the superpower struggle, he demonstrated that one man could make a deep and lasting difference. Moreover, his influence was recognized around the world, seeming to diminish another possible reason for careerist longings. If anything, his controversial work had given him an excess of fame and infamy. He was the science hero of the Republican right, which saw him a bulwark in the battle against communism. He was the patron saint of the defense establishment, especially its nuclear arm. He was the seer of conservative businessmen, who sought his advice on investments.

At the same time, liberal politicians assailed him as the mastermind of a ruinous arms race. Left-leaning psychologists ridiculed his communist antipathy as a reaction to childhood traumas. Popular culture cast him as a Dr. Strangelove, a mad scientist fixated on mass destruction. In 1970, students at the University of California at Berkeley declared him a "war criminal" and burned him in effigy a half block from his home.[1]

The clash of opinion was just as great among Teller's peers, whose judgments usually divided along political lines. Eugene P. Wigner, a Hungarian-born Nobel laureate and lifelong friend, called Teller a "great man" of vast imagination and "one of the most thoughtful statesmen of science."[2] Isidor I. Rabi, a Nobel laureate who worked on the Manhattan Project, called him "a danger to all that's important," adding that "it would have been a better world without Teller."[3]

By the time he turned 70, a milestone passed in 1978, Teller had experienced so much conflict and achievement that it seemed there could hardly be room for any more. He also had serious physical ailments. Weariness alone would have seemed enough to slow him down. Even so, Teller's indomitable will fed his ambitions. He behaved like an unruly force of nature, as he had all his life. He could by turns be gentle and charming, dark and brooding, rude and combative, his moods punctuated by outbursts of wry humor and ill temper. He wrote poetry and loved sweets. Restless by nature, he would play the piano for hours in search of emotional solace. At a time of life when most scientists were happy to reflect on the accomplishments of youth, Teller remained driven, yearning for something more.

An opportunity seemed to materialize in 1980 with the demonstration at Livermore of a rudimentary idea that promised a revolution. This was the X-ray laser, a new type of weapon. The name alone was impressive, combining two facets of modern science, X-rays and lasers, that independently conjured up feats of wizardry. The union of the two was to be nothing short of extraordinary. If perfected, the weapon would take the gargantuan power of an exploding H-bomb and channel the blast into intense beams of radiation that flashed across space to knock out up to 100,000 targets. It would be the ultimate destroyer of enemy missiles, heralding their obsolescence as tools of intimidation and war. Less conspicuously, it also promised to intimidate the Soviets, since antimissile arms in space had uses that were anything but defensive.

Coincident with these top-secret musings was a political event of great importance for Teller. This was the arrival at the White House of Ronald Reagan, a former actor whose fierce anticommunism matched Teller's own. The two men had known and respected each other for years. Teller seized the opportunity, visiting the president, writing letters to the White House, bombarding every administration official he could find with news of the X-ray breakthrough. He painted a picture of unremitting progress that promised a peaceful new era. He burst with enthusiasm and vibrated with excitement. Teller's aim was to have the government redouble X-ray funding and deploy the laser as soon as possible.

There was just one problem. The fledgling project was mired in a series of difficulties and setbacks, as Teller's colleagues back at Livermore kept trying to tell him. In the end, what seemed to be one of the greatest strides in the history of nuclear weaponry turned out to be a scientific curiosity of uncertain promise that had no immediate value in the construction of advanced arms.

Undeterred, Teller gathered his energies to hail yet another breakthrough for Star Wars. So deep was his belief, so persuasive his arguments, so powerful his drive, that a new administration led by George Bush caught the fervor, revising the nation's antimissile plan to match Teller's.

This book is about misrepresentations of the truth and how a good scientist who was a great politician used them to lead the nation into fateful decisions that have quietly raised the risk of nuclear war. It also explores the question of how a man who accomplished so much in life could, in his latter years, be compelled to assume such heavy responsibilities.

# ONE

# Atom
# Visionary

Scientists can be divided into two types on the basis of temperament. There are rationalists and romantics. The cool, cerebral types tend to make steady, stepwise advances, often by excelling in experimental technique. The intuitive romantics, on the other hand, tend to push their imaginations in an effort to make large conceptual leaps. Teller clearly fell into the latter category. From the start he was an idea man, a romantic, a visionary. Much of this seemed to be in his blood. Hungarians have a reputation for morose introspection, with associated high suicide rates. Teller had this sullen side to his personality as well as its constructive counterpart, an effervescence of creative thought and action. Moreover, his gift for mental invention was rated by peers as exceptionally great. Some said it had no equal.

Yet, as with most science romantics, the vast majority of Teller's ideas were wrong. There is nothing terribly surprising about this. On the contrary, scientists far and wide recognize that being correct just five percent of the time in the field of theorizing can produce a dazzling career if the insights are important. And Teller's often were. "Teller is one of the smartest people I've ever met," said Alvin M. Weinberg, former director of the Oak Ridge National Laboratory and an atom pioneer. "He's very quick and has an extraordinary physical intuition. That's not to say he isn't wrong a fair amount of the time. He makes proposals that don't pan out. But he's imaginative and original. He invented the whole field of reactor safety."[1]

Ultimately, the secret of Teller's success lay in the sheer volume of his ideas, not simply the quality. He liked to quote the dictum of Niels Bohr, the great Danish physicist, that "An expert is a person who had found by his own painful experience all the mistakes that one can make in a very narrow field." Teller took the motto to heart, producing ideas at an unparalleled rate, making many mistakes and becoming more and more expert in a variety of fields.

His gift, however, had a complication. Teller's ideas were so prolific and audacious that he often needed help from colleagues in separating the good hunches from the bad and in developing true insights. He himself had little or no ability to recognize brilliance among the fantastic, swirling array of concepts he gave the world. "Nine out of ten of Teller's ideas are useless," said physicist Hans A. Bethe, a longtime colleague, adding that he "needs men with more judgment, even if they be less gifted, to select the tenth idea, which is often a stroke of genius."[2]

Teller relied on associates not only for seasoned judgment but also for aid in fundamental aspects of the scientific method, most especially the mathematical calculations underlying a problem. These could be critical in showing whether a proposed solution had promise or was a dead end. Most of Teller's own calculations were inaccurate, not because he lacked respect for precision but because he lacked patience. Endowed with a deep sense of physical intuition, he liked to do "ballpark" calculations in his head and let somebody else work out the details so he could move on to other considerations. Frederic de Hoffmann, a close colleague during the Manhattan Project, gave a vivid example of the process.

"We were coming back from Europe on the *Ile de France*," de Hoffmann recalled. "I was standing in the ship's nightclub when he came up and said, 'Freddie, I think I have an idea.' It was something he'd just thought of about magnetohydrodynamics. I was a bachelor then and I'd located several good-looking girls on the ship, but I knew what I had to do, so I disappeared and started working on the calculations. I'd get something finished and start prowling on the deck again when Edward would turn up out of the night and we'd walk the deck together while he talked and I was the brick wall he was bouncing these things off of. By the end of the trip we had a paper."[3]

Far more complex, and often more turbulent, was the process by which gifted peers would actively sort through Teller's intuitions, trying to sift the good from the bad and to reconcile them with physical reality. For instance, Teller in 1956 led a team of ten experts who gathered to invent a totally safe reactor, meeting in a little red schoolhouse in San Diego. "Nearly every day he came to the schoolhouse with some harebrained new idea," recalled Freeman Dyson, a British physicist. "I used his ideas as starting points for a more systematic analysis of the problem," in the process "demolishing his wilder schemes and squeezing his intuitions down into equations."[4] The profitable result of this process was the world's first inherently safe reactor, which, although small and limited to research, was subsequently built at scores of sites around the world.

Teller was notoriously flighty. His ideas came so fast that he had difficulty seeing them through to completion and working out their implications. He would rapidly move from one idea to the next. With Dyson, new schemes appeared "nearly every day." With de Hoffmann, it was something Teller had "just thought of." Many of his interactions with peers were capricious. "He was so interested in everything," recalled a friend. "His trouble was lack of concentration on any one problem."[5] Enrico Fermi, the great Italian physicist, was heard to remark more than once: "If only he could find one thing to concentrate on!"[6]

Once in a while, Teller did just that. He would be seized by an idea. Then everything changed. It possessed him. It consumed him. He would work it over in his mind, losing sleep, brooding, meditating, seeking a solution. Having wrestled with a concept, conquering it with an almost physical satisfaction, Teller would hold it sacred until he himself or a colleague persuasively shot it down. Moreover, this type of monomania could last not just weeks or months, but years and decades. It took a deep emotional resonance to unite the disparate elements of his spirit. But when an idea took hold, it held on tight.

Two great passions in the field of technology marked his life. The first was finding the secret of fusing atoms together to unleash the energies stored in atomic nuclei. In this he eventually succeeded, as shown by the H-bomb and its numerous offspring. Teller's second passion was the reverse of the first. Rather than aiding destruction, he sought atomic construction. He wanted to harness the atom for social good, championing such things as nuclear reactors for the production of electrical energy. A complex manifestation of both passions was Teller's bid to use nuclear explosives for the destruction of enemy warheads in war.

In all these domains, Teller's need for feedback from gifted colleagues became vital as he moved into areas that lay far beyond his original scientific expertise, which had been developed in the 1920s and 1930s. He sought to do more than science, the aim of which is to understand nature. Increasingly, beginning in the 1940s and 1950s, he wanted to manipulate nature, to build things, to fashion bombs. Here Teller's ideas needed much assessment and refinement by seasoned colleagues. After all, he was no engineer, no systems analyst and no military planner.

Unfortunately, as Teller's career moved forward, peer review of his ideas diminished. The isolation began in 1952 as Teller broke with the community of Oppenheimer-dominated bomb experts to found his own weapons lab. Livermore had few veteran scientists to aid Teller, as demonstrated when several of its bombs failed to explode. The isolation was greatly enhanced by the 1954 Oppenheimer affair, after which Teller was scorned by the majority of his intellectual peers. In response, he increasingly consorted with generals, financiers, industrialists and politicians. His influence rose. He became extraordinarily well connected, often able to enter high councils of government when scientists of lesser note were excluded. But Teller had access to fewer "men with more judgment," as Bethe put it, to help evaluate his scientific ideas. The scientists who ended up surrounding him were an unusual lot, often distinguished by their youth. Some were awed by his stature, some eager to use his influence to advance their own interests, and some prone to the same kind of visions and passions that ruled Teller.

As the isolation from world-class peers grew over the decades, so did Teller's stubbornness and sense of self-importance. He had always been headstrong. But now, possessed by his muse, he could behave as if he were ordained by some supernatural power, promoting ideas and dismissing foes with self-righteous ire. Increasingly, he seemed to be driven from the inside out, not the outside in, just the opposite of how a scientist should operate.

That kind of zeal was clearly evident in the case of the X-ray laser, limiting his reliance on peers, driving him to place unusually great reliance on his intensely personal vision. It was an evolutionary development. A half century had to pass before Teller achieved the passionate isolation that became the hallmark of the X-ray laser disaster.

TELLER was born into a world where science was viewed as the source of nearly all material progress, where this intellectual endeavor had become the religion of educated men and women. As yet there had been no clash of nations made deadly on a frightening new scale by science. In Budapest near the Danube, on January 15, 1908, he was born to Max Teller, a well-to-do lawyer, and his wife, Ilona.

The boy Edward spoke little during his first years, giving rise to worries that he was retarded. Sometime after his third birthday, miraculously it seemed, he proceeded to utter complete sentences.[7] He soon displayed hints of a mathematically rich inner world, making up number games and putting himself to sleep by his own method of counting sheep: "60 seconds in a minute, 3,600 seconds in an hour, 86,400 seconds in a day . . ." By the time he started school at the age of six, Edward was thoroughly familiar with addition, subtraction, multiplication and division.[8]

An affluent family of assimilated Jews, the Tellers stressed Edward's education above all else. While Edward and his older sister, Emma, were growing up, Teller attended the small, private Mellinger School and the famous Minta Gymnasium. He fell in love with learning, eagerly reading all kinds of books for school and himself. Jules Verne, Teller recalled, "carried me into an exciting world. The possibilities of man's improvement seemed unlimited. The achievements of science were fantastic, and they were good."[9]

Edward's mother wanted him to be a concert pianist, as she herself once hoped to be. He was given lessons and showed much promise, becoming devoted to Mozart, Beethoven, Schubert and Brahms. He also excelled at chess, usually playing his father.[10]

Budapest at the turn of the century had a thriving Jewish community and a series of celebrated schools that produced no less than seven of the twentieth century's great scientists. In order of birth, they were Theodor von Karman, George de Hevesy, Michael Polanyi, Leo Szilard, Eugene P. Wigner, John von Neumann and Edward Teller.[11] The city pulsated intellectually, rich in commerce, architecture and opera. As Richard Rhodes has noted, the first subway system on the European continent was dug, not in Paris or Berlin, but in Budapest.[12]

The Hungarian scientists were to have a remarkable impact on science in the United States and were universally seen as visionaries. Szilard, Wigner and Teller played important roles in the push for the atom bomb. Von Neumann was a mathematical genius who helped build giant computers used for H-bomb calculations. Fermi, the Italian physicist, once mused over the number of stars in the universe and its age, saying that if aliens existed they should already have visited earth. Indeed, Szilard joked, "They call themselves Hungarians."[13] Teller also delighted in this notion, applying it to himself with relish. Late in life, after getting to know someone he liked, he would sometimes give the person permission to call him "E.T.," after the movie about a friendly extraterrestrial who visits Earth.

As Teller grew into adolescence, his family went out of their way to nurture his otherworldly feats. "Please don't talk to me—I have a problem," Teller would announce at the dinner table. The "problem," the family knew, was some calculation he was doing in his head for fun. According to Teller's biographers, "Everyone would duly respect his request and isolate him from mundane conversation for the rest of the meal."[14] Edward showed signs of intellectual hunger. As a teenager, he and a close circle of friends would take long walks on summer nights, discussing philosophy and astronomy for hours. One of these friends had a sister who ultimately became Teller's wife.[15]

Teller's childhood was thrown into chaos by the political upheavals that shook Hungary in the wake of World War I, including a brief but brutal Communist revolution and counterrevolution, with riots and bloodshed. The Communists seized power in 1919 while Edward was in his first year at the Minta Gymnasium. As the national economy went to ruin, the Tellers traveled to the countryside to barter with peasants for food. Two soldiers of the Communist revolution were billeted in Max Teller's law offices, adjacent to the Teller apartment, sleeping on couches, urinating on the rubber plant, searching for reserves of the old regime's forbidden currency.[16] Teller, eleven at the time of the counterrevolution, survived the social turmoil. His family suffered no impoverishment. But it made a deep impression on him, planting the seeds of his lifelong hatred of communism. Later on that hatred grew markedly as Teller's parents and sister suffered privations and indignities under the grinding heel of Stalin.

Graduating from the gymnasium in 1925, Teller first attended the nearby University of Budapest to placate his mother and then, from 1926 to 1928, attended the Institute of Technology in the Rhine River city of Karlsruhe in southwestern Germany, the school sponsored by the huge German chemical firm I. G. Farben. There he acceded to his father's wish that he study a practical subject, chemical engineering, although he also took math courses on the sly.

In the field of chemistry, Teller found he had little talent for the outer-directed world of the laboratory scientist, where ideas must be tested and measured against physical reality. "I broke a lot of test tubes, cut my fingers, and nearly put my eye out on one occasion," Teller told his biographers. [17]

Instead, Teller was seduced by the intellectual currents then sweeping Germany. Einstein had already shaken the world of science with his relativity theory and its predictions of bizarre events in the universe. Now the revolution turned inward toward the atom. Quantum mechanics was making surprising progress through a series of paradoxes. Electrons that sped about an atomic nucleus were seen as jumping from one orbit to another without passing through the space in between. Particles of matter were seen simultaneously as discrete objects and as waves of light. By 1928, Teller was so excited by such riddles that he talked his father into letting him join the fray. [18]

After losing a foot in a trolley car accident and learning to walk with a prosthesis, Teller applied to the University of Leipzig, where the leading physicist was Werner Heisenberg, a giant of quantum mechanics. Teller was overjoyed when he was accepted. He quickly fell into the routine, staying up late to study, enjoying the company of Heisenberg's young scholars, even becoming skilled at Ping-Pong despite his artificial foot.

Teller's peers at Leipzig saw glimpses of the passion that would later rule the Hungarian scientist. Isidor I. Rabi, who first met Teller there, recalled that the group's best Ping-Pong player was a Chinese physicist of cool disposition. "Teller would slam and slash the ball," Rabi said, "and the Chinese would just stand there hitting them all back." [19]

At this early stage in his career, Teller displayed another trait that would come to mark his scientific style. He was extremely gregarious, preferring intellectual sparring, jokes, discussion and Ping-Pong games to the drudgery of working long calculations or investigations in private. He was also a night owl, sometimes sleeping until noon before setting upon his daytime routine of socializing and play. "He never came to work before six in the afternoon," recalled Wigner, Teller's Hungarian peer. "He was not tired enough." [20]

In 1930, Teller, 22 years old, obtained his Ph.D. in theoretical physics, having applied quantum mechanics to calculating energy levels in an excited hydrogen molecular ion. Upon graduation, he secured a research post at the University of Göttingen, in a medieval town in Germany then a mecca for physicists.

During this period, Teller began to work collaboratively, avoiding the solitude of many theorists. Between 1930 and 1936, he wrote some thirty papers, with nearly as many different coauthors.[21] These papers were done with peers as well as people he considered teachers, Teller relying on the diverse group to help moderate his fertile imagination and sometimes to do precise calculations. These collaborative sessions were sometimes unpleasant for the young scientist. In 1932, he collaborated on a paper with George Placzek, an experienced, worldly physicist of Czechoslovakian ancestry who grew up in Vienna and spoke eight or nine languages. The topic was the use of spectroscopy for studying the structure of molecules. Placzek dominated Teller, often dismissing his ideas as irrelevant.

"Well, this isn't much, Teller," Placzek would say.[22]

"But it's very important."

"Well," Placzek would reply, "it may be very important but it is wrong."[23]

Ultimately, such friction could be quite creative. The papers Teller and his colleagues produced during this period were generally good to excellent, with only one failing the test of time.[24]

Teller worked at Göttingen from 1931 to 1933, until Hitler was named chancellor of Germany. He soon left the country, worried that growing anti-Semitism would cripple his career. In early 1934 he became a Rockefeller Fellow at the University of Copenhagen, where Niels Bohr, the preeminent elder physicist of the day, served as director of the Institute for Theoretical Physics. The winning of the fellowship put Teller among an elite fraternity of young physicists intent on unraveling the mysteries of the atom. Social gatherings in Copenhagen included a half dozen past and future Nobel Prize winners.[25]

Here, too, the rich and often mercurial nature of Teller's inner world quickly became evident to his peers. One weekend Otto Frisch, an Austrian physicist there, took a train with Teller to Bohr's country house. On the way back, Teller was restless.

"Have you got a problem for me?" Teller asked.[26]

Frisch told him to mentally place eight queens on a chessboard so that none could take the other. Teller was silent for twenty minutes, then called out the answer. Stimulated by this exercise,

Teller asked Frisch to play mental chess. They started, calling out the moves by numbers, but Frisch was unable to keep track of all the pieces. Teller demanded another problem.

"All right," said Frisch. "Tell me the regular polyhedra in four-dimensional geometry." This was a problem Frisch had done for fun when he was sixteen, when he felt his mental powers were at their height. It had taken several months for him to work out the six solutions. Once again, Teller fell silent. Frisch dozed off. When he awoke, Teller had worked out four of the answers.

Teller's stay at Copenhagen gave him sufficient stature to land his first teaching job. In the fall of 1934, he went to the University of London as a lecturer in the chemistry department. Soon, he had two offers to go to the United States: one from Princeton University, offering a lectureship, and the other from George Gamow, a tall, warm, garrulous, imaginative Russian expatriate and friend of Teller's at Copenhagen who had gone on to George Washington University in Washington, D.C. Gamow offered Teller a full professorship, a wonderful career opportunity. The 26-year-old physicist found it hard to resist, despite reservations about moving to America. In August 1935, Teller and his wife, Mici, set sail, destined to live in the United States for the rest of their lives.[27]

Gamow's influence on Teller turned out to be enormous. Up to that point, Teller had been immersed in one of the great revolutions in physics that shook the twentieth century, the quantum one, which tried to fathom the behavior of the electrons around the atom. Gamow nudged Teller deeper, into the heart of the atom, its nucleus, an area from which the most violent revolution in the history of science was about to erupt.

Moreover, at George Washington, Teller's usual role in relation to his peers was reversed. Rather than being the idea man, Teller began a scientific collaboration with Gamow and helped analyze many of the Russian's brilliant, eccentric ideas. As Teller put it: "He relied on me for mathematics and for the corresponding checks on his theories."[28] Physicist Bethe believes Gamow became Teller's ultimate role model, convincing him to develop his imaginative faculties to an even greater extent than he already had. "Gamow seduced him," Bethe said. "He was much impressed by Gamow and wished to be like him in getting a dozen ideas every minute, whether right or wrong."[29]

In pioneering work, Gamow in 1928 had discovered the key to

one type of radioactivity, elucidating a theory of alpha decay. Working with Teller, Gamow now formulated rules for another type of radioactivity known as beta decay, in which an electron or positron is emitted from an atomic nucleus. These became known as the Gamow-Teller selection rules for beta decay.[30]

Most significantly of all, Teller was encouraged by Gamow to ponder the enigma of what powered the sun and stars—a meditation that would ultimately lead to the H-bomb. In 1935, Gamow had begun an annual conference at George Washington to discuss such physics questions. Known as the Washington Conference on Theoretical Physics, it drew an elite group of scientists from across the country and sometimes the world. It was during the fifth annual conference, in January 1939, that news arrived from Europe that threw the assembled group of theoretical physicists into turmoil. Their field, once merely of academic interest, had suddenly taken a dramatic turn.

The startling news was that the atom had been split, in the process releasing a burst of energy. The finding would turn out to be nearly as significant as the discovery of fire. Bohr, visiting from Copenhagen, told the group of fifty-odd physicists that Otto Hahn and Fritz Strassman had bombarded uranium with neutrons and split the element.[31] The question that could only be solved by further experiment was whether a chain reaction was possible. If so, a small amount of fissionable material could be made into a bomb of extraordinary power. It was a question that Teller's Hungarian colleague, Leo Szilard, had pondered privately since 1933, and now, six years later at the Washington conference, it was a question that Teller, according to his biographers, asked aloud. Suppose, he theorized, a split nucleus released more neutrons and might sustain a chain reaction?[32]

That simple question bridged a huge intellectual gulf. Science seeks to understand nature—the orbit of planets, the mysteries of the human cell, or, in the case of fission, the process by which energy is released when an atom is split. Engineering seeks to use science to rearrange nature, to make her conform to the wishes of man. The question that threw Teller and the other scientists into turmoil was ultimately one of engineering, whether nature would allow for the possibility of a chain reaction in a man-made arrangement of heavy metals. It was the kind of question a theoretical physicist might pose, but not be best equipped to answer.

When the conference ended, the scientists rushed off to laboratories to extend the fission experiments and see whether a chain reaction was in theory possible. In March 1939, Teller was at home in Washington playing Mozart on the piano when the answer arrived. It was Szilard on the phone, calling from New York, where he had gone to do experiments at Columbia University. "I have found the neutrons," he told Teller in Hungarian.[33]

The events that followed have often been recounted: the efforts of Szilard, Teller and Wigner to persuade the government to embark on a project to build the atom bomb, Einstein's letter to President Roosevelt on the subject, the start of the Manhattan Project, the camaraderie of the elite scientists at the supersecret Los Alamos laboratory high in the mountains of New Mexico. Their work culminated on July 16, 1945, when the darkness of the New Mexican desert was split by the blinding flash from the world's first atomic explosion.

Strangely, Teller, in his 30s at the time, played a relatively minor role in this venture that turned science abstraction into extraordinary feat. But he was present at every critical juncture. He drove Szilard out to Long Island with a typed copy of the Roosevelt letter, which Einstein signed. He worked on the first reactor in Chicago. He labored three long years at Los Alamos. He even made an important contribution to perfecting implosion, a technique of bomb assembly that was used in the first explosion. But overall, the leaders of Los Alamos often found him more of a hindrance than a help. Rather than working on aspects of the project assigned to him, Teller, a senior physicist at Los Alamos, preferred wide-ranging talks with the project's charismatic leader, J. Robert Oppenheimer, who often found himself pressed for time. Eventually, Teller fell into open conflict with his old friend and then boss, physicist Bethe, who ran the Los Alamos theory section. In the end, Teller was removed from A-bomb work and allowed to speculate on whatever he wanted. Always the visionary, always trying to see ten years ahead of his peers, Teller had decided the atom bomb was a sure thing and unworthy of his attention.[34]

WHAT preoccupied Teller through much of this period was an idea that had haunted him starting in the late 1930s—finding a way to build a hydrogen bomb. The A-bomb worked by splitting atoms apart, the H-bomb by fusing them together. In theory, the materials for the fusion process were more readily accessible and the process itself more efficient, promising a weapon of devastating force. But making an H-bomb posed major hurdles, not the least of which was achieving the tens of millions of degrees of heat needed to spark its ignition. For this reason, the bomb was known as thermonuclear. In contrast, the A-bomb began its detonation at room temperature.

Teller had become intrigued with the H-bomb idea while pondering the riddle of what energized the sun and the stars. The stellar question was taken up by the 1938 annual Washington Conference on Theoretical Physics, which in turn stimulated Bethe to set forth a series of answers that eventually won him the 1967 Nobel Prize in physics. It had long been suspected that stellar fusion involved hydrogen, since hydrogen nuclei are nature's simplest, having the lowest electrical charge (from one proton) and thus the greatest chance of overcoming the electrical repulsion of similarly charged nuclei to achieve fusion. Bethe's work elucidated one of the key ways in which hydrogen fusion powers the stars.[35]

Teller played a minor role in analyzing the celestial aspects of fusion. But he was destined to play a large one in duplicating the process on earth. In 1941, Teller and the Italian physicist Fermi were lunching in New York at the faculty club of Columbia University, musing over challenges old and new. Both were fairly confident the A-bomb could be built. Both knew Bethe's theories about energy production in stars. Both knew that the fusion of atomic nuclei, at least in theory, could liberate more nuclear energy than fission. Strolling across the Columbia campus, Fermi suggested it might be possible to use the intense heat from an exploding A-bomb to trigger fusion reactions in hydrogen, re-creating on earth the energy that lit the heavens. Teller was fascinated. Prophetically, Fermi suggested that fusion would be easier to achieve with deuterium, a heavy form of hydrogen, than with the type of hydrogen found most abundantly in nature.[36]

For weeks, Teller pondered the idea. He liked the simplicity and elegance of trying to mimic what nature does in the heavens. Such a bomb would also be economical, he reasoned. Deuterium could easily be removed from seawater, whereas uranium 235, the isotope needed for the A-bomb, accounted for only 0.7 percent of the uranium found in nature and would be terribly expensive to remove from uranium ore imported from distant lands. But Teller hit what he thought was a roadblock in his rough calculations, becoming convinced that an A-bomb could never be hot enough to ignite the deuterium.

"I told Fermi why I thought it would not work," Teller recalled, "and tried to forget all about the intriguing possibilities."[37]

But he was mistaken about the temperature, as a young colleague soon pointed out. Emil Konopinski was a theoretician at the University of Chicago who, along with Teller, was working on the reactor project that was to be the first practical test of atomic fission. Both had spare time, which they devoted to Teller's H-bomb idea. "Together," Teller's biographers wrote, "they combed through Teller's original calculations and reached a new conclusion—it probably would work after all. Deuterium could, in fact, be ignited by the heat of a nuclear explosion."[38]

By the summer of 1942, Teller was again excited about the H-bomb's prospects. He even had a way to build it. But a spectacular obstacle soon arose. Oppenheimer, recently named scientific head of the Manhattan Project, asked select scientists to meet him at Berkeley that summer to secretly discuss the A-bomb project. The roster included Bethe, Teller, and some of the nation's other senior physicists. After quickly finishing A-bomb issues, the group turned its attention to Teller's H-bomb ideas, the scientists calling the hypothetical weapon "the Super." On a blackboard, Teller wrote out calculations showing how an A-bomb's heat could ignite fusion reactions. Then, in surprise, he noted a grim implication: the bomb might generate enough heat to ignite the nitrogen in the earth's atmosphere (which accounts for 80 percent of its gases) or the deuterium in the world's oceans, setting them afire in fusion reactions.[39] That conclusion stopped the conference cold. The bomb might turn the earth into a new kind of star. Oppenheimer set off to Michigan to discuss the danger with Arthur H. Compton, a senior American physicist who also played an important role in the founding of the Manhattan Project.

"This would be the ultimate catastrophe," Compton said. "Better to accept the slavery of the Nazis than to run a chance of drawing the final curtain on mankind."[40] But by the time Oppenheimer got back to Berkeley, Bethe, with his usual precision, had calculated that there was no danger. "I very soon found some unjustified assumptions in Teller's calculations which made such a result extremely unlikely," Bethe recalled.[41] Teller, having roughly but correctly calculated the heat of the H-bomb, had overlooked certain aspects of heat radiation that diminished the risk of atmospheric ignition.[42]

The scientists became happily excited, experiencing the kind of intellectual agitation that came to characterize the Manhattan

Project. "My theories were strongly criticized by others in the group, but together with new difficulties, new solutions emerged," Teller recalled. "The discussion became fascinating and intense. Facts were questioned, and the questions were answered by still more facts. As our discussions became more and more detailed, the prospects of success changed almost daily. One day the job would look hopeless; the next day someone would have a bright idea that made everything seem easy. But another member of the group invariably asked a question spotlighting some consideration that had been left out, and the explosion of heavy hydrogen again would appear impossible. A spirit of spontaneity, adventure, and surprise prevailed during those weeks in Berkeley, and each member of the group helped move the discussions toward a positive conclusion."[43]

Teller was in his element, being a catalyst for intense discussion and debate among colleagues, who often worked out the details and calculations. Progress was collective. No individual, Teller included, seemed equipped to solve the nettlesome problems.

In Washington, the secret report of the Berkeley group caused startled officials in late August 1942 to calculate that an H-bomb might easily have an energy yield equivalent to 100 million tons of high explosive, thousands of times more powerful than an A-bomb. From that point onward, the Super was firmly on the Manhattan Project agenda. But the H-bomb effort was sidetracked as it became clear that building the A-bomb would be much more difficult than initially envisioned. At Los Alamos, most scientists turned their attention to ensuring the A-bomb's successful development. The main exception was Teller, who repeatedly complained that the thermonuclear work was getting too little attention. Teller was soon replaced at his A-bomb assignment with a team that included Klaus Fuchs, who later turned out to be a Russian spy.[44] Meanwhile, Teller was allowed to pursue the Super idea with anyone who was interested.

Teller's thermonuclear urge mystified many of his colleagues. "While his ideas are always original and often brilliant, they are not always practical or timely," said Rudolf Peierls, a Berlin-born physicist who worked on the Manhattan Project. "He pursues his ideas with great insistence, and this makes him act at times like a prima donna."[45]

THE thousands of deaths caused by the nuclear bombing of Hiroshima on August 6, 1945, filled many of the atomic scientists with moral revulsion for further work on armaments. They urged an intensification of political steps to make future wars impossible. Some felt guilty. All were tired. In any case, the war was over. They wanted to go home. Not Teller.

Today it is difficult to imagine any of the Los Alamos scientists having been eager to stay and work on bigger bombs after so many years in the New Mexican wilderness, isolated from family and friends. Yet this is exactly what Teller wanted to do. When asked to head the laboratory's theoretical division, Teller said he would accept the position only if intensive work could be maintained toward refining atomic explosions or developing the H-bomb. Oppenheimer's successor at Los Alamos, Norris Bradbury, said he could guarantee neither, given the country's mood.

In February 1946, Teller left Los Alamos for research at the University of Chicago. A month later, Freeman Dyson met him there for the first time and found him "bubbling over" with ideas and jokes. "Teller had done many interesting things in physics, but never the same thing for long," the British physicist recalled. "He seemed to do physics for fun rather than glory. I took an instant liking to him." But when Teller started preaching about one of his recent causes, the World Government movement, Dyson's affection for Teller began to cool. "He is a good example of the saying that no man is so dangerous as an idealist," Dyson wrote his family.[46]

Colleagues at the University of Chicago, impressed with Teller's personal energy, jokingly coined the term "Tellers" to describe units of enthusiasm. Subtle degrees of enthusiasm were measured in "micro-Tellers," or millionths of a Teller.[47]

While at Chicago, Teller kept up his H-bomb advocacy, although he had no real base of power from which to press the issue. H-bomb work at Los Alamos went forward fitfully. In July 1949, Teller rejoined Los Alamos to help speed the work. The H-bomb effort got a dramatic boost when the Soviets exploded their first A-bomb in August 1949, creating near panic among American officials as the nation lost its atomic monopoly. In late 1949, Teller made a trip to Washington to redouble his case for pulling ahead of the Russians technically by building a weapon that could be hundreds or thousands of times more powerful than the A-bomb. He met with Paul Nitze, then a State Department official and a third of a century later President Reagan's top arms control adviser. Teller sat Nitze at a blackboard and explained two alternative ideas for igniting a thermonuclear explosion. "Teller was a great expositor of ideas," Nitze recalled, adding that he was much better than Oppenheimer, who seemed to resist the H-bomb for political and humanitarian reasons. "On the question of physics and engineering, Teller had him beaten hands down, because he concentrated on the issue of doable technology."[48]

Teller's rhetorical skills were evidently working well with Nitze, since in 1949 the H-bomb was far from "doable" at that point. Even so, pressures to build the Super soon reached the White House. President Truman on January 31, 1950, announced that H-bomb work would redouble to counter the Soviet menace. Despite the growing clamor, no scientist had the foggiest idea how to build the device. Moreover, many felt the H-bomb was abhorrent on moral grounds and hoped its creation would prove impossible.

At Los Alamos, two parts of the H-bomb problem were undergoing close scrutiny, the first being whether an A-bomb could trigger any fusion reactions at all. Stanislaw M. Ulam, a highly regarded mathematician, went over the calculations that Teller's group had performed between 1944 and 1946 on what was known as the "'classical" Super, in which an A-bomb was to be placed in close proximity to fusion fuel in hopes that great heat would be enough to ignite it. But Ulam found that the design would produce a fizzle. Ulam also predicted a fizzle for the second part of the problem, how well fusion reactions, once ignited, would propagate through the thermonuclear fuel. In short, the key assumptions Teller had made thus far on the viability of the classical Super turned out to be wrong. The program had reached a point of frustrating bafflement, if not paralysis.[49]

"That Ulam's calculations had to be done at all was proof that the H-bomb project was not ready for a 'crash' program when Teller first advocated such a program in the fall of 1949," Bethe, Teller's old boss from the Manhattan Project, recalled. "Nobody will blame Teller because the calculations of 1946 were wrong, especially because adequate computing machines were not then available. But he was blamed at Los Alamos for leading the laboratory, and indeed the whole country, into an adventurous program on the basis of calculations which he himself must have known to have been very incomplete."[50]

The problem was vividly demonstrated by George Gamow at a Los Alamos review meeting. On a table he placed a piece of wood next to a cotton ball. The wood symbolized the fusion fuel, the cotton the A-bomb trigger meant to ignite it. He squirted lighter fluid on the cotton ball and struck a match. The cotton flared and then died out. He passed the piece of wood around the table to the assembled group of scientists. It was petrified wood. And it wasn't even warm. "This is where we are just now in the development of the hydrogen bomb," Gamow said dryly.[51]

The unexpected difficulties made Teller increasingly moody and desperate. Between October 1950 and January 1951, he came up with a number of H-bomb ideas, none of which showed promise and all of which were quickly abandoned. Then came the breakthrough. Ironically, the idea that would revolutionize warfare arose from the field of A-bomb development, which Teller had largely ignored. In December 1950 Ulam proposed a new type of atomic bomb design that used mechanical shock to compress a second atomic bomb core and make it explode, the purpose being to use fissionable materials more efficiently.[52] In February 1951, Ulam took a refinement of the idea to Teller.

"I have a way to make the Super," Ulam said, suggesting that his two-stage idea be applied to making a hydrogen bomb.[53]

Mechanical shock from an atomic bomb, Ulam proposed, could be focused by a special structure to compress the fusion fuel and promote its rapid burning. These were two of the key ideas behind what would prove to be the successful design of the hydrogen bomb—compressing the fuel and arranging the A-bomb trigger and hydrogen bomb fuel in such a way as to achieve that goal. Teller added a third idea, which was also critical. He suggested that radiation from the bomb, rather than mechanical shock, be the basis for compressing the fusion fuel. On March 9, 1951, the two men published a report in which they presented both alternatives. Teller then elaborated on his radiation idea, aided by the extensive mathematical calculations of his colleague de Hoffmann. The paper of Teller and de Hoffmann, published on April 4, became the basis for the success of the nation's hydrogen bomb program.[54]

In terms of Gamow's cotton-wood analogy, the new idea used compression to pulverize the petrified wood into a fine powder that could easily be ignited and burned. The A-bomb trigger no longer acted simply as an igniter for fusion fuel—an approach pursued so zealously and so uselessly by Teller for a decade. Instead, it also served as a catalyst to prepare the fusion fuel for ignition.

The advance was pure Teller. As was usually the case with his work, it had been done in collaboration with another scientist. But this also caused Teller great discomfort, judging from subsequent events. He probably felt proprietary about the breakthrough. After all, he had excitedly and often solitarily pursued the problem for a decade. Whatever the reason, Teller often contradicted himself on the issue of credit, variously acknowledging and denying Ulam's role. The federal government suggested that a patent on the idea be issued jointly to both men. Teller refused to endorse this division of credit, with the result that no patent was ever granted.[55] In a 1955 essay in *Science* magazine, Teller credited Ulam with an "imaginative suggestion."[56] But Teller made no reference to Ulam's positive H-bomb role in his 1962 book, *The Legacy of Hiroshima*, which devoted a lengthy chapter to the breakthrough. Moreover, late in life Teller bluntly told his biographers: "Ulam triggered nothing." The reason for his coolness, they reported, was that Teller felt Ulam had denigrated the chances of the bomb's success even after the emergence of the breakthrough idea.[57]

Public perception was weighted heavily in favor of Teller, the truth buried in layers of government secrecy. *Newsweek* magazine in 1954 hailed Teller as the "mystery man" behind the bomb.[58] The 1954 book *The Hydrogen Bomb*, by James Shepley and Clay Blair, Jr., devoted an admiring chapter to Teller and one minor reference to Ulam.[59] Teller always seemed available for photos and interviews. Magazines of the 1950s are dotted with pictures of Teller, the "father" of the H-bomb, playing the piano or romping with his children.

The first device to test the Ulam-Teller principle was assembled by Los Alamos scientists in 1952 at the government's nuclear test site in the Pacific. It was code-named Mike, the M standing for megatons of high explosive. Erected on the island of Elugelab, the device was essentially a thermos bottle two stories high and six feet in diameter. Its liquid deuterium was cooled by liquid hydrogen, whose temperature was near absolute zero. The device weighed a staggering 65 tons.[60] The whole apparatus of the bomb and its support equipment was the size of a small factory. It was a far cry from the small "dry" H-bombs later developed to fit atop missiles.

History's first hydrogen bomb was detonated on November 1, 1952. The island of Elugelab, a mile in diameter, ceased to exist. The bomb was calculated to have a force of 10.4 megatons, some 700 times more powerful than the bomb dropped on Hiroshima. Teller "watched" the explosion on a seismograph at Berkeley, which measured the bomb's shock wave as it traveled round the world. He wired a three-word telegram to the director of Los Alamos: "It's a boy."[61]

Around this time Teller composed a rhyming atomic alphabet for children that hinted at his ambivalence over the achievement:

> A stands for atom; it is so small
> No one has ever seen it at all.
>
> B stands for bombs; the bombs are much
>     bigger.
> So, brother, do not be too fast on the
>     trigger.
>
> F stands for fission; that is what things
>     do
> When they get wobbly and big and must
>     split in two.
> And just to confound the atomic confu-
> sion
> What fission has done may be undone
>     by fusion.
>
> H has become a most ominous letter;
> It means something bigger, if not
>     something better.[62]

For good or ill, Teller the theoretical physicist, intensely curious about nature and fearful of Russian power, had proven himself a wizard, at least in the eyes of the world. Through an exercise of pure thought and human will, Teller had commanded nature to release the energy of the stars, lifting a million tons of rock into the sky. In the wake of this remarkable success, it was easy to forget the decade of wrong turns, of mistakes, of futile searching, to downplay the importance of ideas other than Teller's own in the genesis of thermonuclear weapons. It was easy to see the Hungarian physicist as a technological prophet whose vision had proven remarkably prescient. For his part, Teller did little to discourage the admiration, in the process making himself less of a scientist who asked questions and more of a politician who gave advice. Increasingly he traveled to Washington. He courted and cajoled men of power. More and more often, he judged people by their ability to listen patiently and ask good questions.

ONE of Teller's first uses of his growing power was to break the Los Alamos monopoly on weapons design and distance himself from its

Oppenheimer loyalists. Ironically, this act helped isolate him from many of the world-class scientists who for so many years had aided his scientific labors. Teller's campaign to found a second weapons lab began soon after the H-bomb ideas of 1951 were conceived and recognized. The move was vigorously opposed by Oppenheimer and the powerful group he led, the General Advisory Committee of the Atomic Energy Commission (AEC), which felt a second laboratory would divert talent and resources from Los Alamos and slow the nation's overall program. The AEC ran the weapons complex. But Teller, arguing that friendly competition helped drive science forward, won allies in the Air Force and soon prevailed.

The new weapons laboratory was established in July 1952 at Livermore, California, in an abandoned World War Two naval air station. The lab's first director was Herbert York, a 29-year-old physicist. Teller, then 44 years old, had veto power over the decisions of its scientific steering committee.[63] Despite great expectations and effort, Livermore's first efforts were flops. The initial project was to make A-bombs with uranium hydride, a substance that promised to substantially reduce the amount of expensive nuclear material needed to create a critical mass. On March 31, 1953, at the government's new testing site in the Nevada desert, some 100 miles northwest of Las Vegas, Livermore conducted its first nuclear test. The hydride device, code-named Ruth, was mounted atop a 300-foot tower. The bomb fizzled. The metal tower, which normally would have been vaporized by the nuclear blast, was merely bent. Laughing Los Alamos scientists scurried for their cameras. Less than two weeks later, a second Livermore shot, code-named Ray, also flopped.[64]

Teller put the best gloss he could on the failure. "The experiment succeeded," he wrote in The Legacy of Hiroshima, "but it brought an unwelcome answer: No. The piece of progress we had hoped for was no progress at all. We had enough data to understand in detail what had happened, and new knowledge in the life of the laboratory—even if that knowledge is disappointing—is most important. But we would have been happier if our first experiment had produced something of immediate value."[65]

Bethe was less charitable. He said extensive calculations of hydride devices had been done during the Manhattan Project, scientists concluding then that hydrogen atoms in the uranium hydride would slow the neutrons needed for a chain reaction. Teller, in his enthusiasm to do something new and different, had apparently forgotten the Los Alamos findings. "He could have thought for an hour and reminded himself," Bethe remarked.[66]

The string of Livermore failures continued in the Pacific, which was reserved for the spectacle of H-bomb tests. In 1954, a series of thermonuclear blasts, the first after the Mike success, were scheduled to consolidate the nation's H-bomb gains. On February 28, scientists from Los Alamos began the series by successfully exploding a "dry" H-bomb based on lithium deuteride instead of liquid deuterium. Its staggering yield, 15 megatons, was much larger than expected. A second test, also by the Los Alamos group, produced a surprisingly large yield of 11 megatons.

Livermore then readied its third nuclear weapon and its first H-bomb. The device was called "Morgenstern" after the medieval club set with spikes that armored knights used to strike each other. It had a predicted yield of 1.5 megatons. But Teller and his aides had forgotten to put a shield around the fusion fuel to block stray radiations until it was ripe for compression.[67] The result, as the countdown reached zero on April 6, was a thermonuclear dud. Plans for a second Livermore H-bomb detonation, code-named Echo, were quickly abandoned and the bomb's parts shipped back home. More than two years would pass before Livermore successfully exploded its first H-bomb, which had a yield of 3.5 megatons.[68] York, the lab's first director, found the failures deeply ironic in view of Teller's earlier denigration of the Los Alamos leadership.[69]

TELLER was undeterred by the difficulties. Moreover, he felt that Oppenheimer's continuing skepticism about the H-bomb, coupled with his vast influence, endangered the nation. The Russians would surely have no qualms about forging ahead with deadly armaments to threaten the West. Teller judged Oppenheimer a risk and was quick to say so. The main forum for his criticism was a hearing before the personnel security board of the Atomic Energy Commission in April and May of 1954, the height of the McCarthy era.

It was a time of widespread hysteria about communism. Fears were heightened by unforeseen Soviet strides in atomic weaponry and the news that some Americans had betrayed their nation to aid these ominous advances. Julius and Ethel Rosenberg were sentenced to death for delivering atomic secrets to the Soviets. Politicians such as Wisconsin Senator Joseph McCarthy saw Communist plots nearly everywhere and assailed individuals who, at any time in their lives, had expressed Communist sympathies. Blacklists were drawn up. Treason was in the air. In this atmosphere, Oppenheimer was quite vulnerable, having dabbled in left-wing politics during the 1930s when many people felt communism was a good alternative to the fascism then spreading across Europe. Oppenheimer, while always stopping short of becoming a party member, had joined groups with Communist ties and had moved in leftist circles. His brother Frank had been a member of the Communist party, as had his former wife, Jackie.

Now, amid the paranoia of the McCarthy era, Oppenheimer was charged with being a Communist agent and blocking H-bomb work for that reason. Teller's testimony to the Federal Bureau of Investigation was important in prompting the hearing in the first place, having led to "a very substantial portion of the charges, certainly most of them related to the H-bomb," recalled Harold P. Green, an AEC lawyer who drafted the accusations.[70] But Teller apparently said little or nothing to federal agents about Communist ties, caring only about Oppenheimer's negative H-bomb views. A week before the hearing, an agitated Teller told an AEC staffer that Oppenheimer's political "machine" had to be crushed and Oppenheimer personally "unfrocked" lest weapon scientists lose their enthusiasm for H-bomb work.[71] During the hearing itself, the H-bomb charges took on added significance since no evidence was presented that showed Oppenheimer had actually given any bomb secrets to the Soviets. His H-bomb actions were taken as the sole sign of disloyalty. On April 28, 1954, Teller testified in Washington against Oppenheimer, speeding the demise of the most famous of the wartime scientists. "If it is a question of wisdom and judgment, as demonstrated by actions since 1945, then I would say one would be wiser not to grant clearance," Teller told the board.[72]

The security clearance was soon permanently revoked. Afterward, many scientists felt Oppenheimer had been punished for personal views that had nothing to do with security and everything to do with policy, over which honorable people always disagreed. Teller, widely seen as Oppenheimer's persecutor, quickly became a pariah, cut off from the nation's intellectual mainstream. Colleagues avoided him. Contacts dried up. One day Teller put out his hand to greet an old friend. The man shot back an icy glance and walked away.

DESPITE intellectual isolation and the poor initial record of the Livermore lab, Teller eventually succeeded in many atomic endeavors, aided by gifted young scientists he was able to recruit. In 1956 at a secret conference, the Navy raised the possibility of building a small warhead with a yield of one megaton that could be fired from a submarine. Many experts at the conference said it was impossible, at least in the near future.[73]

Teller stood up.

"We at Livermore can deliver it in five years," he announced to Navy officials.

Back in California, staff members were distraught, fearing another fiasco was in the works. But soon they started making major strides in reducing the size of hydrogen bombs. In 1960, the first Polaris submarine went to sea, armed with the small Livermore warheads. Teller's optimism had proved even more correct than he imagined. Perfection and delivery of the powerful device had taken four years, not five. With Polaris, Livermore came of age. The lab had opened in 1952 with 75 employees. By 1961 it had 4,300 employees, the Polaris success having played an important role in its growth.[74]

EVEN as Teller's world grew and stabilized, it came under political siege. Public pressure was building to halt the explosive testing of nuclear arms, which would effectively bring the bomb business to an end. Teller fought fire with fire. One episode in the summer of 1957 showed how far he was willing to go in letting his political passions get ahead of the facts. By this time he was extremely powerful and in some respects isolated. Increasingly, his intuitions set the agenda, bereft of the collegial aid that characterized his earlier work.

As apprehension mounted around the globe over the danger of radioactive fallout from the atmospheric detonation of nuclear arms, the Soviet Union, on June 14, 1957, proposed a two- or three-year moratorium on explosive tests. World leaders applauded the action. President Eisenhower was favorably disposed to the idea.[75] But not Teller. On June 24, 1957, the Hungarian physicist and two other scientists met with the president, telling him a ban was foolish. A key argument was that "'clean weapons" could be developed that would produce little or no fallout, diminishing worldwide pressure for limits on nuclear testing in the atmosphere. The idea had intellectual merit, since reduced fallout would cause less environmental damage during peacetime testing and would save untold lives of noncombatants during nuclear war. But it was technically very ambitious. The basic goal was to have H-bombs rely as much as possible on the power of the hydrogen fuel rather than the atomic trigger, since nuclear fusion produced none of the "dirty" fission products like strontium 90 and cobalt 60 whose long radioactive half-lives made fallout so deadly. In large H-bombs, this atomic contamination could be reduced by simply using the smallest and most efficient A-bomb trigger possible. But the effect of this "dirty" trigger became more pronounced as hydrogen bombs became smaller.

Teller told Eisenhower that partly clean weapons had already been developed and that totally clean weapons were a "matter of six or seven years" with continued testing. He noted how they would aid one of the president's great enthusiasms, peaceful atomic projects, making it easier to use H-bombs to explore for oil, to tunnel through mountains, to alter the flow of rivers, "and perhaps even to modify the weather on a broad basis through changing the dust content of the air."[76] News of the meeting quickly reached the press. "U.S. Eliminates 95 Percent of Fall-Out From the H-bomb," said the front-page headline in The New York Times. Actually, the reference in the article was only to giant H-bombs, in which fusion fuel predominated, although the public was given no information about that distinction. Included at the top of page one was a picture of Teller and his two associates talking with AEC Chairman Lewis L. Strauss shortly after the Eisenhower meeting.[77] Eisenhower liked the arguments of the scientists. The day after the meeting, he told an adviser that the "real peaceful use of atomic science depends on their developing clean weapons."[78]

Eisenhower had been familiar with the clean-bomb idea before the meeting and had even talked about it with reporters. But after listening to Teller, he waxed enthusiastic, telling a news conference that in four or five years the nation would produce "an absolutely clean bomb" with "no fallout" to injure "innocent bystanders." Explosive testing had to continue, he stressed, so atomic energy could be used "for the building of a civilization instead of tearing it down." Once again, the story ran on page one of The New York Times.[79]

Beneath these glowing public reports, however, lurked a current of skepticism among weapon scientists and AEC officials. In July 1957 General Alfred D. Starbird of the AEC wrote a secret memorandum to Chairman Strauss, saying there was "a great danger" the public was being misled about how soon clean weapons might appear. In June 1958, a year after Teller met with Eisenhower, Morse Salisbury, director of the AEC's division of information services, said in a memo, "We have made essentially no progress in our attempts to reduce substantially the size of feasible clean weapons." And in August 1958 Commander Harry J. Waters of the Navy wrote an AEC official, "We do not know how to make small nuclear weapons which derive a very small fraction of their yield from the fission process, i.e., the so-called clean tactical weapon."[80]

Teller was undaunted in his public advocacy. In 1958, he stated in his book *Our Nuclear Future*, written with Albert L. Latter, that the clean bomb was "well on its way" to success, having made "notable progress."[81]

Eager to move beyond theory and experiments, Teller launched a campaign for the first civilian use of clean bombs. His target was Alaska. In July 1958, Teller and an entourage from Livermore landed, unannounced, in Juneau to unveil a plan by which bombs were to dig a harbor near Point Hope, some 300 miles north of Nome. Teller told reporters the harbor would be a tremendous economic boon, since it would be located near "the highest quality proven coal deposits in Alaska." It seemed good news to an area troubled by a postwar economic decline and eager for increased federal spending. The first shot could be fired within a year, Teller said. The project would require the detonation of six clean weapons with a total yield of 2.4 megatons, or about 40 percent of all the firepower expended in the Second World War. Some business leaders were skeptical, saying the harbor would be blocked by ice nine months of the year. But Teller, who had secretly been eyeing Alaska for more than a year, showed no hesitancy.[82]

As pressure mounted for a worldwide ban on all nuclear testing and as skepticism over the harbor project grew, Teller became increasingly active in Alaska. He did so despite other pressing business he had as Livermore's director. In June 1959, he made his case in an address to the University of Alaska, sketching a host of uses for atomic engineering. "If your mountain is not in the right place," he quipped, "just drop us a card."[83]

Teller also promoted the Alaska goal to the wider American public in an article he wrote for *Popular Science* that appeared in March 1960. The title was "We're Going to Work Miracles." Teller called the Alaska project a great hope for the future that "will usher in the age of peaceful uses of atomic explosions." In addition to civil construction, he enthused, bombs could generate electricity, stimulate oil and gas production, ready areas for strip mining, and modify the weather. "The dangers from fallout in the weapons-testing program have been greatly exaggerated," Teller wrote, adding that "within a few years we may be able to produce explosives that are completely clean, with no radioactive fallout."[84]

It was not to be. Despite years of planning and promotion, the Alaska project was brought to its knees by people near the site who found it highly objectionable. For three years, neither Teller nor anybody else had explained the project to those it would most affect—the Eskimos of Point Hope, Alaska, some thirty miles from ground zero. AEC representatives finally arrived in March 1960. The Eskimos were unimpressed with the arguments. They had read how nuclear blasts in the South Pacific spewed radioactivity over large areas, endangering the health of local residents. The village council objected to the plan.

"I'm pretty sure you don't like to see your homeland blasted," Kitty Kinneeveauk told the AEC men.[85]

By 1961, the villagers were deep into a letter-writing campaign that included President John F. Kennedy. In 1962, the project was quietly shelved. Its demise was a good thing. In 1966, a study was released showing that the explosions would have contaminated the Eskimos' caribou hunting grounds. It also showed the Eskimos already had more radioactivity in their bodies from fallout than any other people on earth. The problem turned out to be lichen, a rootless tundra plant that derived its mineral nutrients from airborne dust and, as it turned out, from radioactive fallout. The lichen was subsequently eaten by the caribou.[86]

And what of the totally clean bomb? Despite Teller's avid forecast, his successful lobbying of a president and his upbeat articles and talks, the armament failed to materialize—and not just in the course of Teller's "six or seven years" but decades. Moreover, the partially clean bomb turned out to be more of an experimental curiosity than a nuclear weapon. It was more complicated, costly, and massive than a "dirty" bomb, limiting its usefulness. Indeed, Theodore Taylor, for many years a nuclear weapons designer, noted that most nuclear arms have actually gotten dirtier over the years as designers have increased the ratio of the fission yield to the volume of bombs, especially on warheads atop long-range missiles.[87]

But in some respects the '"clean" bomb was a success. To the extent that Teller's promotion of the idea was a public-relations ploy, it achieved much that was dear to him, playing a prominent role in derailing the push for a total ban on the explosive testing of nuclear weapons. The result was that the bomb business was allowed to continue unfettered on its chosen path.

A MORE esoteric goal that remained out of Teller's reach was controlled fusion, with which scientists sought to harness the thermonuclear process to generate usable heat and electricity. At wartime Los Alamos, Teller had become deeply excited about its prospects. Young scientists at a "wild ideas" seminar sponsored by Teller went so far as to sketch out a series of fusion reactors, including ones that used powerful magnetic fields to confine fuels that were so hot they would melt any material container.[88] After the war, magnetic fusion slowly grew into a large national effort, eventually consuming many billions of dollars. Livermore was a main beneficiary of this federal largess. At first Teller was quite optimistic, as were many of his peers, filled with postwar excitement over the dream of harnessing the atom. "I am confident," Teller told a science meeting in 1956, "that controlled thermonuclear reactors will eventually be constructed."[89] A series of setbacks ensued. By 1972 Teller's tone was more cautious. "If one is optimistic," he wrote, "one might hope that within a few years we shall have an apparatus that produces more electricity than it consumes."[90] By the late 1980s, after more than four decades of abortive effort, the goal was still distant, most scientists placing it deep in the twenty-first century. In step with the setbacks, Teller's statements became more restrained. He told a reporter he was "not hopeful" and "not optimistic" that power production with magnetic fusion would be achieved anytime soon. "If you use fission power in the right way, fusion is probably not even needed," Teller said.[91]

A NEW passion seized Teller even as work faltered on clean bombs and controlled fusion. Its intensity rivaled his obsession with bringing the hydrogen bomb to life, and its duration proved to be far greater, which was probably a good thing. After all, the new pursuit, from a technical point of view, made all the others look easy. The roots of the new challenge lay in the fact that the Soviets in the 1950s quickly mastered the making of H-bombs and proceeded to

put them atop long-range missiles. Increasingly worried by the
threat to the United States, Teller quit his post as director of Livermore in July 1960 so he could speak out more freely, urging the
American public to carefully weigh the merits of antimissile arms.
"A retaliatory force is important," he wrote in *The Legacy of Hiroshima*, his 1962 book. "A truly effective active defense system
would be even more desirable. It would be wonderful if we could
shoot down approaching missiles before they could destroy a target
in the United States."[92] In particular, Teller urged the development
of interceptor rockets that could knock out enemy missiles in mid-
flight.

Protecting America was only one of the goals set forth in his
book. Another was fighting communism. He saw antimissile defense
as a way to escape the nuclear status quo, the so-called balance of
terror in which each side could destroy the other with nuclear missiles. This status quo, he felt, gave the Soviets too much room for
aggression. "No matter how often the United States sends strongly
worded diplomatic notes, Russia knows that we will not launch the
first nuclear attack," he wrote in *Legacy*. Russia, he said, thus feels
free to support Communist rebels in such places as the Congo and
Cuba. "Step by step, nation by nation, convert by convert, it will
conquer the world eventually. And this our policy of mutual deterrence does not deter."[93] To fight communism, Teller urged a variety
of military measures, including passive defenses such as bomb shelters, active defenses such as interceptors and even atomic conflict.
"A localized, limited nuclear war will be the answer whenever the
Russian method of ambiguous aggression degenerates to an outright
attack against our allies," he wrote.[94]

If active defenses could be created, he felt, they might ultimately allow America to fight Communist aggression with impu-
nity, freeing the nation from the straitjacket of mutual restraint. But
antimissile defense—in effect hitting a bullet in midair with another
bullet—was impossible in the 1960s. Interceptors were too crude. So
Teller advocated topping them with nuclear arms. In theory, these
would ease the defensive job since an expanding fireball might destroy an enemy warhead even if an interceptor was considerably off
the mark. Even so, such interceptors were so feeble that they were
seen as sufficient mainly to protect small sites on the ground such as
emplacements of offensive missiles, not large areas such as cities and
whole countries.

Despite the limitations, Teller urged exploratory work on defensive arms and warned the West to be watchful lest the needed breakthroughs occur elsewhere. "If the Communists should become certain that their defenses are reliable and at the same time know that ours are insufficient," he wrote, "Soviet conquest of the world would be inevitable."[95] His fear was unstated but clear. An aggressor with a good shield would be free to use his sword, confident he could deflect an opponent's counterattack.

As Teller's 1962 book went to press, his theorizing came to life with explosive force. The United States embarked on a series of high-altitude nuclear blasts in the Pacific to test the feasibility of antimissile arms. The first shot, code-named Starfish Prime, took place on the night of July 9. An interceptor rocket roared aloft from Johnston Island, soaring some 250 miles into space before its nuclear warhead exploded with a force of 1.4 megatons. Thousands of startled people in Hawaii, some eight hundred miles away, saw the night sky turn pink, then orange, then red. Unseen were powerful electromagnetic waves that crippled some of Hawaii's electrical systems. Street lights failed. Burglar alarms went off. Circuit breakers popped open in power lines. The cause, later known as the nuclear electromagnetic pulse, turned out to be a serious impediment to antimissile plans.[96]

The nuclear blasts of 1962 in the Pacific were abandoned as long-running, East-West talks became serious about limits on nuclear testing, the discussions having occurred sporadically since the 1950s. The public was still alarmed about radioactive fallout. And Teller still opposed any cessation. After several false starts, John F. Kennedy and Nikita Khrushchev in August 1963 signed a compromise agreement to ban nuclear testing in space, the atmosphere and the oceans—everywhere except underground. It was a blow to antimissile proponents.

Rumpled and shaggy-haired, his brow furrowed and his voice full of emotion, Teller denounced the treaty before the Senate Foreign Relations Committee. The West needed atmospheric tests, he said, to perfect antimissile arms. "A few years ago I firmly believed that missile defense was hopeless," Teller told the senators on August 20. "I am now convinced that I was wrong." Ominously, Teller claimed the Soviets were far ahead in defensive arms, warning that Khrushchev "now knows how to defend himself."[97]

The majority of Teller's peers felt he was wrong and that he was out of step with the times. "The country needed Edward in the '40s and '50s," a colleague remarked after Teller's testimony. "Without him, we might not have had a hydrogen bomb or its essential delivery system, the missile. But times and needs have changed. Edward hasn't."[98] Underscoring the point, the Joint Chiefs of Staff endorsed the treaty. Harold Brown, then the Pentagon's director of research and engineering and later defense secretary, told the Senate that U.S. antimissile efforts were on a par with those of the Soviets, adding that he doubted an effective system was feasible for either side.[99] On September 24, the Senate ratified the treaty. Teller was despondent.[100]

SURE he was right, Teller took his antimissile efforts underground beneath the Nevada desert, exploding new warheads that he hoped would be more adept at knocking out Soviet missiles. And he became less strident. The battle over the test ban had mellowed him. Asked in 1967 if antimissile arms could be reasonably effective, Teller replied: "The truth is that I don't know. Further, I will tell you the whole truth, and the whole truth is that no one else knows, either. It is for that very reason that I would like to see work stepped up."[101]

And it was stepped up. The Defense Department had long pursued a low level of antimissile research. But now, in the late 1960s, it redoubled its efforts, hoping to build a nationwide system to protect people and cities. In March 1968, amid the palm trees and balmy breezes of the South Pacific, at the Kwajalein testing range, a prototype interceptor known as the Spartan thundered unarmed off the launching pad for the first time. In theory it could hit enemy warheads high above the atmosphere before they wreaked destruction on earth. Also in 1968, Livermore got the go-ahead to develop a big new warhead for the interceptor. In December, Teller's lab conducted a scaled-down test of the bomb beneath the Nevada desert, code-named Benham.[102] It exploded with a force of 1.15 megatons, one of the largest detonations ever to rock the Nevada site.

The blast was a small step toward a truly giant warhead that Teller hoped would suffice for the job of knocking out enemy targets. In theory, the powerful rays from a large bomb could flash spherically across space to destroy anything for scores of miles around. The logic was simple. The more powerful the bomb, the greater its range of destruction. Moreover, the Spartan warhead was to produce more X-rays than nuclear weapons usually did, meaning it would need less accuracy and have a greater range of lethality.

X-rays can travel long distances effortlessly in the vacuum of space, unlike in the earth's atmosphere. They can devastate a warhead and the heat shield meant to protect it during fiery atmospheric reentry. In a split second, the X-rays heat the surface of the reentry vehicle, causing its outer layers to explosively evaporate. An equal and opposite shock wave then rushes inward to crush the warhead.

Teller's vision for the Spartan warhead countered an important trend in the evolution of the nation's nuclear arsenal. Most arms were getting smaller, not larger. Small weapons for battlefield use had proliferated widely. And military planners were reducing the size and power of warheads atop long-range missiles as guidance systems became more accurate, allowing enemy targets to be pinpointed. But in antimissile systems, Teller had found a project that drew deeply on the capabilities inherent in the H-bomb. In this case as no other, bigger was better.

The Spartan warhead's great power and enhanced X-ray production were quite difficult to achieve, however. A Livermore publication called it the most demanding design challenge in the lab's history.[103] As was the case with nearly all hydrogen bombs, the weapon was based on the Ulam-Teller design. The warhead was so powerful that its full-scale testing would be risky at the government's underground site in Nevada, which was too near the homes, casinos and gambling tables of Las Vegas. Instead, plans were made to detonate the full-sized device deep beneath Amchitka Island in the remote Alaskan wilderness. The plan soon came under fire.

By the late 1960s, the nation, deeply divided over the Vietnam War, was also at odds over the idea of building a system of ground-based interceptors that would cost billions and involve scores of sites around the country meant to protect cities and people. To liberals it seemed militarism gone mad. The Nixon administration, which took office in early 1969, pressed ahead with an antimissile system called Safeguard. It was to rely on the Spartan missile to loft Teller's giant warheads high above the earth. However, scores of respected scientific experts said Safeguard would be costly and ineffective, arguing that it should be scrapped.

As debate heated, so did Teller.

"I cannot tell you how much more I would rather shoot at enemy missiles than to suffer attack and then have to shoot at people in return," he told *U.S. News & World Report* in 1969. "I want to repeat—with all possible emphasis—that defense is better than retaliation."[104] He was careful to add a caveat: "I am not claiming that

Safeguard will be foolproof. I am claiming that Safeguard may suc-
ceed and almost certainly will induce very grave doubts in the mind
of any would-be attacker."

IN the wilds of Alaska, some 1,400 miles west-southwest of Anchor-
age in the Aleutian Islands, preparations picked up for the explosive
test of Teller's blockbuster. It posed dangers there, too, despite the
absence of civilization. The uninhabited island of Amchitka was in a
seismologically unstable area prone to earthquakes. Experts feared
the full blast could trigger tremors down the west coast of North
America. So a scaled-down test was planned, less than a quarter of
the ultimate size, to see how the area would hold up. On October 2,
1969, the warhead exploded under the tundra with a force of 1.2
megatons, the shock wave shaking the control center 40 miles away.
The test, code-named Milrow, produced no damaging earthquakes or
tidal waves.[105] Even so, public opposition to further tests soared, the
main explosion being repeatedly delayed as attempts to block it were
made in Congress and the courts. In July 1971, an editorial in *The
New York Times* denounced the impending test as "potentially an
ecological catastrophe" because of the risk of earthquakes and the
radioactive contamination of Alaskan fisheries.[106]

Meanwhile, more than 700 engineers and scientists from Livermore gathered on Amchitka. They dug a mile-deep shaft, placed the
bomb at the bottom, and filled the hole with tons of dirt and gravel.
On the morning before D-Day, gale-force winds drove rain hori-
zontally. Pieces of sheet metal and two-by-fours flew across the
tundra. The power failed. The phones failed. The next day, the
White House hotline on Amchitka rang at 6:30 A.M. The U.S. Su-
preme Court had just ruled, four to three, that the $190 million test,
code-named Cannikin, could proceed. At 11:00 A.M. on November 6,
1971, the bomb flared beneath the tundra. The blast had a force of
5 megatons, some 330 times bigger than the Hiroshima bomb. It was
the most powerful underground explosion in American history. The
shock wave set off 22 minor earthquakes, but no major problems
were reported. Above the blast site, a crater formed in the tundra
that eventually filled with water, creating a lake a mile and a half
wide.[107]

DESPITE the technical strides, political setbacks to Teller's antimissile
efforts came in quick succession during the early 1970s as the cold

war began its first thaw. The majority of Teller's peers had already renounced the idea, dismissing it as costly and futile and instead endorsing the nuclear balance of terror that kept an uneasy peace between the superpowers. Now the government did as well. In 1972 the United States and the Soviet Union, hesitant to get into an expensive race for defensive arms, signed the Antiballistic Missile Treaty. With amendments, it limited the number of defensive missiles on each side to 100, all arranged around one site. Elaborate plans to station Safeguard interceptors all over the country were cut back. Instead, a single emplacement arose near Grand Forks, North Dakota, meant to protect Minuteman offensive missiles rather than cities and people. The system was completed in 1975 at a cost of more than $7 billion. Teller's warheads stood atop 55-foot-long missiles in underground silos, ready to shoot into space.[108]

Another political setback for Teller came with the signing in July 1974 of the Threshold Test Ban Treaty, which sought to limit underground nuclear explosions to a maximum yield of 150 kilotons. That was just 3 percent of the Cannikin blast in Alaska. The treaty was to go into effect in March 1976, giving each side time to conduct some large tests. Time was running out for the free spirits of the weapons world.

TELLER soon had an idea for a weapon of titanic power, igniting a frantic, last-ditch attempt on his part to restore the antimissile goals of the nation to their original, ambitious scope. If successfully tested, Teller felt, this giant bomb might lead to a new class of warheads for Safeguard that would greatly enhance its effectiveness and might give the disputed system a political boost. But the 150-kiloton cutoff was an impediment. Action had to be taken quickly. Teller felt large tests had to be conducted before the imposition of the cutoff and, if possible, the treaty itself should be abandoned, since he felt it was incompatible with the military necessity of seeing where large explosions might lead.[109]

Teller's new weapon idea elaborated not on the Ulam-Teller design but on his original and unsuccessful H-bomb plan, known as the classical Super. It seemed to promise an even bigger blast. The classical Super had never come to life in the 1940s and 1950s, calculations always showing that it would fail. But in the 1970s a young protege of Teller's, Lowell L. Wood, Jr., redid the calculations with

new accuracy, showing it might work and might scale to huge sizes—
not kilotons, or megatons, but gigatons. The prefix "giga" means
billion. A one-gigaton bomb would be equivalent to a billion tons of
high explosive. The destructive power of such a blast is difficult to
visualize. It would be 66,666 times more powerful than the Hiroshima bomb, or 166 times bigger than all the conventional firepower expended in the Second World War.

Exploded in space, such a weapon would radiate a huge sphere
of fire, like a small sun. Its myriad X-rays would streak across
hundreds of miles to destroy nearly anything in their path, including
enemy warheads. Wood called the antimissile idea "Palisades of
Fire," suggesting a wall of fiery destruction. In particular, the
weapon was seen as a way to counter the radical growth in the Soviet
missile threat. In the mid-1970s, the Russians began arming their
rockets with multiple independently targeted reentry vehicles, ensuring that the Safeguard site or any other part of America could be
pummeled with many more nuclear warheads than originally envisioned. In space, the new weapon's unprecedented sweep of destruction was seen as eliminating this advantage and ensuring the
defender's success.

Although everything about the new antimissile idea was top
secret, Wood in an unclassified paper once alluded to the scientific
basis for the gargantuan bomb, saying, "Teller's original thermonuclear explosive concept was successfully demonstrated in detailed
computer simulation."[110] Teller and Wood threw themselves into a
campaign to go further and demonstrate the classical Super in the
kind of explosive test that had already rocked Alaska. Moreover,
Teller decided to take the antimissile idea to Washington, eager to
see if the threshold treaty could be rolled back and if the enhanced
Spartan warhead could move forward. A remarkable set of political
events soon came to his aid.

In August 1974, Nixon resigned in the wake of the Watergate
scandal, replaced by Gerald R. Ford and, soon afterward, his vice
president, Nelson A. Rockefeller. This was a boon for Teller, who
was a good friend of Rockefeller's. As a student, Teller had been a
Rockefeller Fellow at the University of Copenhagen and was deeply
grateful to the family for its generosity. Teller met Nelson Rockefeller in the late 1950s while the millionaire-philanthropist was
governor of New York.[111] They hit it off, sitting on commissions
together and growing close. As governor, Rockefeller was so im-

pressed with Teller's advice on the necessity of fallout shelters that he built a giant one in Albany that could accommodate 700 key officials from state agencies and in theory act as an alternative seat of government during war.[112] Unlike home shelters, the bunker was designed to withstand a nearby nuclear blast as well as radioactive residue. As vice president of the United States, Rockefeller frequently called on Teller for advice. And he publicly lauded the Hungarian scientist. "Once in a while," Vice President Rockefeller told Teller's biographers, "I have encountered an individual of energy, dedication and genius so extraordinary as to mark him indelibly on my memory and leave me eternally in his debt for the services he has rendered mankind. One such person is Henry Kissinger. Another is Dr. Edward Teller."[113]

Teller met with Rockefeller, using his White House connection to press the radical weapon idea on the federal government. Teller's zeal was deeply personal. The idea was not only a bold antimissile proposal, but one that drew upon his own inventiveness from the early days of the nation's H-bomb program. As such, it promised a belated vindication. Ulam, Bethe and Oppenheimer had all criticized his frenzied work on the classical Super, Bethe arguing it had pushed the nation into an "adventurous" program. Now, ironically, Teller was promoting it as a possible path to the nation's salvation.

There was just one problem. Teller's peers, as had so often been the case, had again uncovered a series of difficulties with his idea. They saw the Super design as so demanding and difficult that it would probably fail. The situation was similar to the clean-bomb episode. No one knew for certain whether the new weapon could be perfected and, if so, whether it would take years or decades. In particular, although scientists felt that the fusion fuel of uncompressed deuterium might indeed be made to burn, they saw no realistic way to start its ignition.[114] Moreover, some Livermore experts doubted the weapon, if achieved, would have any military value. The skepticism was especially great in D Division, which had the job of evaluating bomb designs to make sure they were workable and effective. The group's unstated mission was to keep the lab honest, helping forestall charges that the arms scientists had simply turned into bomb peddlers.

Lanky and gregarious, Charles J. Taylor was deputy director of D Division. He was one of the few who knew of the Super idea and the sales pitch in Washington. Taylor talked the lab's director into allowing a detailed study of the Super.[115] In addition to the antimissile idea, the study was to examine a host of other applications that Wood and Teller had suggested for the bomb. Taylor, who had been at the lab from its first days, assembled a team of a dozen scientists to look at the Super proposals. They began to pore over data, running mock battles and computer simulations meant to flesh out the idea's military implications. The study assumed the Super device itself could be perfected and scaled as large as the Livermore enthusiasts wanted.

Teller heard of the study.

"I must know the results," Teller said.

Taylor protested, saying the study was incomplete.

"Nelson has to know."[116]

The name of the vice president was enough to break the logjam. Taylor soon assembled his team in front of Teller and gave an overview of the study's results to date. The bottom line was that the Super had no usefulness in war, even if the device itself could be made to work. "Palisades of Fire" should remain a fancy name rather than a thermonuclear plan to set the heavens ablaze.

Wood was there, growing increasingly angry. He fumed at Taylor, calling him derogatory names. He tore into the analysis, saying it was flawed.

Taylor was shocked at the vehemence of the attack but took it in stride. He stood by his conclusions.

In 1975, the results of Taylor's completed study were published as a top-secret, three-inch-thick report entitled "The Super." He sent a copy to Teller. For a preface, the report quoted from *Die Walküre*, the second of Richard Wagner's music-dramas from his *Ring of the Nibelung*. In the opera, Wotan the god uses an enchantment to punish Brünhilde, placing a ring of fire around her, cutting her off from all suitors. In the end, however, the ring is breached by Siegfried, who takes Brünhilde for his own.[117] The Taylor report looked at myriad ways the Soviets might thwart the antimissile weapon, such as basing their warheads in unexpected places. It also examined the Super's side effects. Just one exploded high above the earth would generate an electromagnetic pulse so powerful that it would shut down the nation's power grid and knock out communications coast to coast. Moreover, its X-rays would threaten not only Soviet warheads but all manner of American satellites hundreds and thousands of miles away in space, damaging or destroying them.

Satellites, by nature, were always more vulnerable than hardened reentry vehicles.[118]

A higher-level clash over the Super subsequently took place between Wood, Teller's right-hand man, and William A. Lokke, the head of Livermore's A Division, which designed all the lab's H-bombs. Lokke was the brains behind the Spartan warhead. He knew weapon design cold and was extremely skeptical of the Teller-Wood plan. Lokke and Wood squared off in front of General Starbird, the high official of the Atomic Energy Commission who had worried the public was being misled about the clean bomb.[119]

Despite Teller's hopes for the Super, the White House found its merits too modest to trigger the renunciation of an East-West treaty. The dubiety of Teller's peers also played a role in its demise. The idea for a nuclear enhancement of Safeguard died as quietly as it had begun, leaving few traces of its existence outside the secretive world of the bomb makers. The 150-kiloton ban took effect on March 31, 1976, after both the United States and the Soviet Union had conducted a series of fairly large underground tests. None was as large as the Alaskan blast. President Ford hailed the new limit as a significant step for arms control.[120] Moreover, the Safeguard antimissile system near Grand Forks, North Dakota, was shut down in early 1976, Congress having decided its upkeep was a waste of money. Teller's warheads were removed from the Spartan missiles and put into storage at Army depots.[121] In short, Teller had been rebuffed twice, the government rejecting both his old and new antimissile ideas, the Spartan and the Super. He had failed in formidable efforts to which he had devoted himself for more than a decade.

THE setbacks of the 1970s in no way cooled Teller's passion. It was frustrated, not exhausted. The theoretical physicist still had a powerful vision whose central tenet revolved around the deployment of antimissile arms. But this vision, and Teller's patience, were destined to be repeatedly tested before he found the ideal vehicle in the nation's capital for the realization of his dreams. Indeed, his Washington influence continued to ebb with the arrival in 1977 of Jimmy Carter. The new president abolished the Foreign Intelligence Advisory Board, a prestigious group on which Teller had served.[122] Moreover, Carter, a deeply religious man of pacifistic leanings, made little effort to consult Teller and his Livermore colleagues for ideas on new kinds of nuclear arms.

Teller nonetheless moved ahead. As he passed his seventieth birthday, he found nonmilitary outlets for many of his energies. Though cut off from much of official Washington, Teller still had a powerful urge to guide America and keep it from what he considered dangerous habits and thoughts. A great opportunity came in 1979 as nuclear power, a cause he had championed for decades, suffered its worst setback. The episode was a particularly vivid example of Teller's visionary spirit at work, his defense of nuclear power being so energetic that it damaged his health. The incident was also revealing because it showed something of Teller's disposition and drive late in life on the eve of the X-ray laser affair.

IT was a winter night. The darkened homes of rural Pennsylvania were filled with people in repose. Nearby on the Susquehanna River, the darkness was cut by the powerful lights of a nuclear power plant, a vast industrial complex rising out of a tree-lined island like something from outer space. Everything was fine at Three Mile Island on the graveyard shift of March 28, 1979. In a control room, six men monitored a futuristic panel of lights, dials, meters and switches. Then, around 4:00 A.M., the men inadvertently cut off one of the water supplies that cooled the 880-megawatt Unit 2 reactor. What followed was a mixture of mechanical failures and operator errors that turned what should have been a harmless accident into a near disaster.

As temperatures and pressures rose in the reactor, a relief valve popped open, as designed. Unfortunately, the valve remained stuck open, causing vital cooling water to drain away. In the control room, the men had no reliable indicator telling of the danger. Indeed, they turned off emergency cooling pumps in the false belief that the reactor was being bathed with cool water. It was more than two hours before they realized the error. By then it was too late. Rising temperatures had started to melt the tons of exotic metals that made up the reactor's core, threatening calamity.[123]

The fear among nuclear experts was the formation of a heavy, white-hot blob of molten metal that would penetrate the reactor wall and melt its way through the plant into the ground, releasing a surge of deadly radioactivity into the environment. Such a scenario was facetiously known as the "China Syndrome," since gravity would cause the molten fuel to head toward China on the opposite side of the earth. More prosaically, it was a meltdown.

Pennsylvania's governor, Richard Thornburgh, called for the evacuation of pregnant women and preschool children within five miles of the crippled plant. In all, more than 140,000 people fled. Meanwhile, hundreds of reporters converged on the site. For five days it was the lead story in newspapers and on television network news programs.

Across the nation, public apprehension about the accident was heightened by the recently released movie *The China Syndrome*. The film's villains were big business and a nuclear reactor. Its heroine was Jane Fonda. She played a smart, ambitious television news reporter who discovered that the plant had suffered a near meltdown. Eerily, the film opened twelve days before the Three Mile Island accident. By the first weekend after the accident, the movie had grossed more than $5 million, making it the biggest nonholiday film in the history of Columbia Pictures, whose officials, uneasy about the bizarre coincidence of a real-life nuclear drama, curtailed publicity to avoid the appearance of exploiting the accident. Producer and star Michael Douglas canceled a scheduled appearance on the Johnny Carson show. Jack Lemmon, who also starred in the film, declined to appear on a CBS News special. But Fonda, long an antinuclear activist, held a press conference four days after the accident to condemn the nuclear power industry, urging that its fate should be an issue in the upcoming presidential campaign.[124]

Through all this, Teller was a whirlwind of pronuclear activity, insisting that Three Mile Island was a crisis of politics, not of technology. Like many of his atomic colleagues, Teller had fervently supported the development of nuclear power ever since the atom's secret was unlocked during the Second World War. In 1948, he became the first chairman of the Atomic Energy Commission's Committee on Reactor Safeguards, the group charged with evaluating the new technology's safety.[125] He was extremely cautious, being among the first to warn of the "catastrophic" dangers of fission reactions and to urge that reactors be sited far from large cities. But his caution turned to strong advocacy over the decades as no serious safety problems emerged and as it became clear that the world's oil reserves would be largely exhausted in the twenty-first century. In the 1970s he wrote *Energy from Heaven and Earth*, a book that among other things sought to rebut every argument ever raised by critics of nuclear power.[126] It appeared in bookstores just weeks after the start of Three Mile Island. Amid the industry's worst crisis, Teller took to the road to defend its record, talking to reporters, speaking at conferences and to groups, telling anyone who would listen that Three Mile Island was a vivid example of how nuclear power technology was basically safe. No one was killed, he stressed. It was not a public health emergency. Although there were equipment failures and operator errors, vital safety systems had worked. There was no meltdown. The amount of radioactive material released into the environment was insignificant. The opponents of nuclear power were exploiting the situation, he said, fanning public fears. The only serious health effects were the fright and trauma stemming from public hysteria.

"It just so happens that the antinuclear movement, lacking a real accident, has latched on to this," he told *Playboy* magazine five days after the start of the emergency.[127]

The field of nuclear power, he told a CBS News program in New York, "has been safer than any other industry," adding that it simply needed better training of technicians. "Operations must be made safer," he said, "and they can, and they will."[128]

Teller was so upset at the public outcry following Three Mile Island that he toyed with the idea of entering national politics to better press his pronuclear stance. He eyed a Republican bid for the seat of Senator Alan D. Cranston, a California Democrat opposed to nuclear power.[129]

The culmination of his efforts came in Washington some six weeks after the accident's start. "Nuclear reactors are not safe," he told the House Science Committee. "But they are incomparably safer than anything else we might have to produce electric energy." Asked if it was possible to develop a reactor with zero risk, Teller replied: "Zero does not exist. I don't expect zero probability from nuclear plants or anything else." He paused and then pointedly contradicted himself. "Zero," Teller snapped, "is the number of proven cases of damage to health due to a nuclear plant in the free world."[130]

The strain on the 71-year-old Teller was too much. The day after his congressional testimony he suffered a heart attack. His recovery was fairly swift, but on doctor's orders his frenetic activity slowed markedly. Teller gave up the idea of running for the Senate. He did, however, manage to pursue his pronuclear advocacy in ways that were less stressful.

"I WAS THE ONLY VICTIM OF THREE MILE ISLAND," cried the headline spread across two pages of *The Wall Street Journal*.[131] From a large portrait, Teller glared down stern and unforgiving, his mouth set firmly, his eyes dark beneath bushy eyebrows. It was an advertisement, signed by Teller, that ran on Tuesday, July 31, 1979, some four months after the accident. In it he blamed Fonda, consumer activist Ralph Nader "and kind" for causing his heart attack. After the accident, he said, he went to Washington "to refute some of the propaganda" of those striving "to frighten people away from nuclear power." To prepare for his congressional testimony, he worked twenty hours a day, he said, overtaxing his heart. "You might say that I was the only one whose health was affected by that reactor near Harrisburg," Teller said. "No," he added, "that would be wrong. It was not the reactor. It was Jane Fonda. Reactors are not dangerous."

The ad went on to predict the consequences for "the survival of a free society" if America turned its back on nuclear power. The problems of gasoline lines, electrical brownouts, and higher prices—which had appeared in the 1970s after the 1973 Arab oil embargo—would seem insignificant, he said. "Politics, law, religion and even humanity may be forgotten," Teller wrote. In the next century his grandson, Eric, would probably live under communism. "There might not be a United States in the twenty-first century," Teller declared.

An editorial in *The New York Times* entitled "Propaganda" later chastised Teller for a factual error and a critical omission. In the ad, Teller claimed that the chance of injury for a person living within fifty miles of a nuclear power plant was "about the same as being hit by a falling meteor." Not so, said *The Times*. "The risk analyses behind this claim have long since been repudiated," it said. The editorial went on to fault Teller for failing to mention that the sponsor of the ad, Dresser Industries, had manufactured the valve that stuck open during the Three Mile Island accident.[132]

Teller was undaunted. In November 1979, recovered from his heart ailment and back on the road, he renewed his attack. "If the environmentalists, the consumers, the small-is-beautiful advocates—whatever you want to call them—win their fight against nuclear power, the U.S. is doomed," Teller told the annual meeting of the Atomic Industrial Forum. "Nuclear power is not an option. It is part of the fight for the survival of freedom." The audience, made up of officials from electric utilities, uranium producers and reactor makers, rose to its feet to give Teller a standing ovation, sure that they and Three Mile Island's only victim could save the nation from ruin.[133]

# TWO

# A Rebellious Aide

WITH THE ARRIVAL of Ronald Reagan in the 1980s, Edward Teller again had a White House connection, this time more powerful than ever. The two men had known each other for years. Now Teller lobbied the White House with great intensity, writing letters, visiting, talking to Reagan and his aides about the X-ray laser and how it promised to end the nuclear balance of terror. Time was running out for Teller. He was getting old, which seemed to increase his sense of urgency. This seemed to be his last chance.

Many of Teller's colleagues at Livermore were skeptical, as they had been about some of his earlier enthusiasms. But Teller had worn them down over the decades. They humored him or did not confront him directly. "Edward," as he was known, was just being himself—stubborn, excited, wildly hopeful and ready to have the nation embark on a new venture that would cost untold billions. Some colleagues seemed ready to turn the other way as he exaggerated the X-ray laser's promise. It was good for the laboratory, after all, and would do little harm to the nation.

But one associate felt the situation had gone awry and was determined to do something about it. His opinion mattered. He had played a major role in bringing the X-ray laser to life and gone on to win complete responsibility for its development. As the head of all nuclear weapons research at Livermore, he was loath to let the X-ray laser be misrepresented, fearing he would be held responsible. Young

65

and idealistic, headstrong and unfamiliar with the corridors of power in the nation's capital, he was ready to join a long tradition of scientific moderation of which he was only partly aware. He was ready to bring the visionary down to earth.

My first encounter with Roy D. Woodruff occurred even as he waged his secret battle with Teller. Although I knew nothing of it at the time, I did learn something about Woodruff as we discussed a range of military issues, some of them sensitive.

It was January 1984. I had been at *The New York Times* for a year as a science reporter and before that at *Science* magazine for five years. In both places I had done a fair amount of defense reporting and learned that government officials often resorted to half-truths or rigid impenetrability when asked about secretive areas of military research. Now I was curious about Star Wars, President Reagan's antimissile plan. Several months earlier, in March 1983, he had called upon "the scientific community who gave us nuclear weapons" to make such arms "impotent and obsolete." If any place could make Reagan's goal a reality, it seemed to be the Lawrence Livermore National Laboratory.

I was escorted to Building 111, the lab's nerve center. Its seven stories dominated the area. Outside lay rural California and the small town of Livermore, located in a dry valley about 40 miles east of San Francisco. The lab itself was a square mile of top-secret research, its hundreds of low buildings and thousands of employees surrounded by barbed wire and armed guards. Visitors were never left unattended in Building 111 because it was open only to employees with "Q clearances," the high-level security pass for atomic energy information. As we entered its lobby through large glass doors, I noticed an elongated drum inside a transparent case. My escort explained it was a seismograph. The paper-covered drum turned slowly while pens twitched over its surface to record earth tremors. Livermore experts watched the pens to estimate the yield of its nuclear explosions beneath the Nevada desert, some 320 miles away.

We rode the elevator to the top of the building, where Woodruff's office was located. His resume suggested a fast rise through the lab. In fifteen years or so he had gone from low-level physicist to associate director for nuclear design. Now, in 1984, he oversaw a budget of $150 million, some 1,000 people and military projects that were among the nation's most sensitive and secretive, including such things as the X-ray laser, which was rumored to be important for Star Wars. He was clearly no dove. I had recently seen an article of his saying nuclear arms were indispensable to the pursuit of American interests. "History indicates that war begins when a tyrant perceives a weakness in an adversary," he had written. U.S. policy, he said, "is to convince the Soviets that they will be successfully opposed at any level of aggression."[1]

Woodruff was 43, just shy of six feet, with thick brown hair and a boyish face. He looked fit. After light conversation, I asked how successful a Star Wars system could be, given the uncertainties of war.

"Because of the inability to test in a realistic environment, with bombs going off and all the electromagnetic effects blinding your sensors, I don't think we're ever going to get a defense that's perfect," he answered. Moreover, he continued, a defensive system, if ever erected, would be insufficient in itself to ensure the nation's safety. "We're going to have to rely on a retaliatory posture with offensive weapons," he said.[2] At the time, it was unusual for government officials to volunteer that America would still need the threat of offensive missiles in the impending age of defense. Instead, they often dwelled on the creation of a leakproof shield that would protect the nation under any circumstances, implying that the nation's nuclear arms would disappear. Woodruff went further, warning of naivete, even for arms experts, in thinking about nuclear war. "It can be awfully easy to fall into this trap of dealing with computers and war games and codes" while losing sight of whether they reveal anything significant about the real world. False confidence, he said, could be dangerous, "especially for politicians." Again, it seemed a subtle putdown of Star Wars.

I decided to press my luck. Signaling the end of the interview, I switched off my tape recorder and mentioned that I had noticed a contradiction in the nation's arms agenda. The Reagan administration had doubled the federal budget for explosive tests of nuclear weapons, I noted. Yet the number of blasts beneath the Nevada desert had been falling.

To my surprise, Woodruff said openly that the government was simply not announcing some of the smaller tests. He added that he had personally fought the action because it made life difficult for weapon designers, since they had to remember which tests were secret and which ones were not. Previously a policy had been in place whereby all nuclear weapons tests were announced. Woodruff then told me it was fine to publish that information as long as it was not attributed to him.

Back at work, I confirmed what Woodruff told me with Energy Department sources and wrote a story. It ran at the top of page one of *The New York Times* on Sunday January 29, 1984, under the headline, "Some Atomic Tests Being Kept Secret by Administration."[3] The article began: "The Reagan Administration has been concealing an unknown number of nuclear explosions at the Government's underground test site in the Nevada desert for about a year, according to Government officials and scientists at Federal laboratories that design nuclear weapons. The tests, never previously disclosed, signify a break with a United States Government policy of announcing all tests."

The story quoted a top official at a federal laboratory for the design of nuclear weapons. "There's been a decision not to announce all the tests," he said. "To me, there's no reason to keep them from the public. In the past we've announced them all." The official, of course, was Woodruff, a man who had impressed me with a talent for taking risks and speaking his mind.

ROY DARR WOODRUFF was born October 15, 1940, in southern California and raised in the towns that ring Los Angeles, the elder of two boys. His father, a staunch Republican, was an electrical engineer by training who had become a successful oil man. In 1947 he formed his own small company to service oil rigs around southern California and moved his family to Arcadia, at the base of the San Gabriel Mountains outside Los Angeles. As a boy, Roy was shy and more interested in music and how things worked than in team sports and the bustling middle-class life of the city. He quit Boy Scouts after a few years. His parents had him join DeMolay, a Masonic organization, but that did not suit him either. Instead, he quietly practiced his violin, becoming good enough to win a seat with the Los Angeles Junior Philharmonic. He also showed a zest for chemistry and was fond of building radios and electronic devices. He could fix almost anything mechanical, although he had a tendency to mislay the parts. His family called him the "absentminded professor."[4]

Woodruff showed no special gift for mathematics or the kind of concentration and mental gymnastics that so excited Teller as a youth. He was fascinated by the worlds of electricity and machinery and making them conform to his will, not by feats of imagination.

During summers in high school, Woodruff worked as a mechanic, building racing engines for cars and boats. With his father's help, he bought a small boat and raced it in Lake Los Angeles, better known as "the puddle." At the lake he won races and gained social confidence. He also rebuilt cars and trucks, his 1953 Ford pickup boasting a bright red paint job and chrome exhaust pipes. The once-shy boy now delighted in drag racing. His friends called him "Woody."

In 1958, Woodruff graduated from Arcadia High School and went to the University of Southern California, where he joined a fraternity, Chi Phi, and had a dismal year. He left before the school could throw him out, his grade point average being 1.5 on a 4-point scale. That summer and fall he worked for his father at the Technical Services Company, analyzing waste water from oil wells. At the age of 18, Woodruff married Sandra Kay Webb, whom he had dated while a student at USC. At the age of 19, he entered the Air Force. By the time he was 22, he had two children, Cynthia Ann and Jonathan Darr. For three years in the Air Force, Woodruff was based with the 682nd Radar Squadron at the Almaden Air Force Station in the Santa Cruz Mountains. There he had a secret clearance and helped maintain a big radar that swept the coast, monitoring air traffic and searching for surprise attack by enemy bombers. It was his first experience with military defense. In 1964 Woodruff left the Air Force with an honorable discharge after four years of service, having achieved the rank of Airman First Class.[5]

A friend of Woodruff's recommended that he apply for work at the nearby weapons lab in Livermore. It had good pay, secure employment and sound science, the friend said. Woodruff applied, having no idea it was a center for the design of nuclear weapons—not that it mattered. He was a Republican, prodefense, and had no objection to weapons work. But by the time Livermore offered him a job, Woodruff had already accepted a post with an electronics firm in San Jose, the just-beginning-to-boom center for electronics eventually known as Silicon Valley. He worked for a company that became part of ITT Semiconductor, doing physics research and working with William Shockley, who won a Nobel Prize for his role in inventing the transistor.

Eager to get an education, Woodruff used the GI bill to go to school, graduating in 1968 with a bachelor of science degree in physics and a minor in math from San Jose State University. Woodruff talked to campus recruiters from several electronics firms. He declined an IBM offer after visiting the company's San Jose facility, where employees wore ties and punched time clocks. The Livermore recruiter had a more tempting offer. Ties were nowhere to be seen at the site, and Woodruff was fascinated by the thought that the lab possessed the fastest computers on earth. He was also attracted by "Teller Tech," the lab's own graduate school, a branch of the University of California, where employees could work toward a Ph.D.[6]

A hint of how headstrong Woodruff could be showed itself during a job interview at the lab. The interviewer, a friend of Teller's, fired a series of tough science questions at the would-be recruit. Woodruff did well but disliked the man, finding him arrogant. Finally, the interviewer posed one of the toughest questions of all, asking Woodruff to mathematically derive the quantum mechanical solution to a harmonic oscillator. Quantum mechanics had been one of Woodruff's favorite courses in college. He went to the blackboard, wrote down a few lines of equations, and then tossed the chalk to the interviewer, suggesting he finish the solution. At first the interviewer looked like he might try. Then he thought better of it.[7]

WOODRUFF got the job at Livermore, then known as the Lawrence Radiation Laboratory, after E. O. Lawrence, Teller's friend who helped found the lab. It was 1968. Woodruff was 27. His application dutifully noted his mixed academic record, all the way from the 1.5 grade point average at USC to a 3.8 average at San Jose State.[8]

The weapons lab was located at one end of a dry, rural valley that was fragrant with eucalyptus and surrounded by rolling California hills. On his way to work, Woodruff drove by cattle grazing on the area's abundant grasses, and here and there a vineyard. The lab itself was a high-technology fortress surrounded by barbed wire and armed guards. Upon acceptance into its ranks, one entered a culture that in many respects was separate from American society. Like the Manhattan Project, the lab had its own factories, planes, and ethos. Secrecy was not only official but self-imposed. After a day at work, a weapon designer was unlikely to tell his neighbors about efforts to build a device that could result in the death of millions of people. Moreover, the lab also had a kind of intellectual solitude that resulted from Teller's famous testimony against Oppenheimer and the fact that many American scientists, most particularly those at Los Alamos, felt a second center for the design of nuclear weapons was unnecessary.

Increasing the sense of isolation, weapons work came under

heavy social fire. As Woodruff entered the lab, the Vietnam War became a divisive issue that helped spawn a generation infatuated with drugs and intent on defying tradition. By the early 1970s, the lab was struck by protests in which thousands of antinuclear marchers would block traffic, hand out leaflets and chant slogans. Amid the growing sense of seclusion, lab workers felt more strongly than ever that their work was a special calling, some regarding themselves as members of a priesthood. The credo of the place was peace through strength. But there were also bouts of black humor, indicating ambivalence about the work. One poster showed a missile with a new type of Livermore warhead heading toward the Soviet Union, the caption parodying the slogan of a greeting card company: "When you care enough to send the very best."

Woodruff rose rapidly through the lab's ranks, making up for a late career start. Although competing against Ph.D.s from some of the nation's top technical schools, Woodruff found he had a knack for turning scientific abstractions into new technologies and weapons, often of terrifying force. He drew on intuition developed during years of work on various kinds of mechanical and electronic devices. He found that a similar kind of reasoning could be applied to computer modeling and computational physics. He had a talent for turning sparse data into sound technical judgments.

One of Woodruff's first tasks was to aid an old Teller cause, the Plowshare project, which, under the Biblical injunction to turn swords into plowshares, had been founded in the 1950s by the Eisenhower administration to explore the peaceful use of nuclear weapons for engineering projects. As a physicist in A Division, which was devoted to the design of thermonuclear devices, Woodruff helped develop a relatively clean, low-radioactive-fallout bomb for digging ditches.[9]

Ready to advance educationally after two years at the lab, Woodruff put in an application to start graduate study at "Teller Tech." But his superiors said no. They wanted him instead to develop yet another Plowshare device, one that could be used to free gas deposits in subterranean rock. In fact, no other bomb designer was interested in the job, since Plowshare in the 1970s was on its last legs. Yet the task had some importance, since the explosion was not to be done anonymously in Nevada but rather in Colorado amid the full glare of public scrutiny, some of it decidedly hostile. There was no room for error. The detonation had to go off without a hitch.

The plan for the Plowshare demonstration was to explode a

string of small bombs deep underground, turning a marginal area into one that in theory could be profitably exploited by gas companies. But many Colorado residents, including Governor John A. Love, worried that the effort would lead to hundreds of similar blasts that could pollute the water table and damage the environment. Geologists estimated that from 5,600 to 12,620 nuclear blasts would be needed to fully develop the deep natural gas fields under Wyoming, Colorado, Utah, Arizona and New Mexico.[10] Teller at the time publicly hailed this type of project, saying oil shale in Colorado and Wyoming could be converted in economical fuel through nuclear blasts, vastly increasing the nation's energy reserves. He told the nation's Republican governors the process could be an economic "jackpot."[11]

Glad for an opportunity to prove himself, Woodruff eagerly went to work designing a small, compact nuclear explosive that would produce reduced amounts of tritium, a radioactive gas that could contaminate the natural gas the scientists wanted to stimulate. The bomb was long and thin, being only 7.7 inches wide so it could fit down a standard oil pipe. In 1972, lab engineers gathered on a high plateau in northwest Colorado near the White River to begin digging a shaft more than a mile deep for the explosive test, codenamed Rio Blanco.[12]

On May 11, 1973, President Nixon gave the go-ahead for the blast, and the national press headed for the site. Three of Woodruff's thin bombs were placed down the hole at various depths. They exploded at 10:00 A.M., on May 17, each with a force of 33 kilotons. The earth shook silently for about five seconds. Small rock slides started and walls cracked. Orange butterflies fluttered off the ground. Cattle and sheep raised their heads briefly, then continued grazing. Dixie Lee Ray, chairman of the Atomic Energy Commission, watched the test from a helicopter, later telling reporters it went perfectly.[13] Despite Teller's hopes for the program, the blast turned out to be the last of some two dozen Plowshare tests conducted over the course of more than a decade. To Teller's chagrin, the public never backed Plowshare and its vision of using nuclear blasts for social betterment.

However, Rio Blanco was a technical success, and as such it gave Woodruff's career a boost. In 1974, he was made associate leader of A Division and its H-bomb efforts. Here, Woodruff led a group of four or five physicists who pondered the problem of how to design a "clean" nuclear weapon for warfare—still an elusive goal some two decades after Teller proposed the idea to President Eisenhower. Woodruff wrote a classified paper, "Clean Warhead Design," that analyzed all previous attempts, showed why they failed, and proposed new research. His ideas were tested in a sequence of explosions, eventually resulting in a warhead design that became the basis for a clean weapon. It was known as MRR, for minimal residual radiation. Despite all the work, however, it never went into the stockpile because it was complex, expensive, and had no unambiguous role in nuclear strategy. For instance, some planners felt a clean bomb conceivably could make nuclear weapons less frightening to use in war, removing old inhibitions that had helped keep the peace.[14]

As Teller searched for potential big tests to conduct before the Threshold Test Ban Treaty took effect in March 1976 and limited blasts to 150 kilotons, he decided some might be needed to perfect a powerful, multimegaton "clean" nuclear explosive for digging a sea-level waterway across Central America as an alternative to the Panama Canal. Woodruff, having proven himself as expert in clean-weapon design, was put on the problem. But his answer irked Teller. Woodruff found that the work was so advanced that if the need ever arose for large peaceful blasts (the treaty making provision for such explosions), a new device could be created from existing designs. No special tests were needed, Woodruff concluded in presentations made over the course of months. Teller initially resisted. But Woodruff's calculations were thorough and convincing. Grudgingly, Teller eventually agreed with the young scientist.[15]

At the age of 36, Woodruff in October 1976 was given his first command position, becoming leader of L Division, which was in charge of designing the complex sensors that sought to measure emanations from underground nuclear blasts. Woodruff managed 70 scientists and could call on some 400 additional personnel for help in particular tests. His annual budget was about $20 million. The group's main job was to build huge instrument-filled canisters that analyzed a bomb's fury for a billionth of a second and flashed their data down wires to distant recording devices, just before the canister and everything else in the blast's vicinity were destroyed by the expanding fireball.[16]

Once a month or so, Woodruff would board the lab's Fairchild F-27 twin-engine plane and fly across the Sierras to the arid expanse of the Nevada desert to inspect nuclear test preparations. He liked the place, which was dotted with mesquite, yucca and Joshua trees and was surrounded by mountains. It was not unusual to see a herd of wild horses on the test site. After a long day, in the cool of the evening, Woodruff would sometimes walk the desert to listen to coyotes and look at the stars.

His job was to make sure things ran smoothly beneath Yucca Flat, which was heavily cratered from decades of bomb blasts and alive with preparations for new ones. Huge trucks lumbered along dusty roads, lights flashing atop their cabs. Drilling rigs dotted the valley floor, boring holes hundreds and thousands of feet deep into which nuclear weapons would be deposited and exploded. Armed guards roamed the site, their standing orders being to "shoot to kill" if someone tried to steal a nuclear weapon.[17]

The pride of Woodruff's group was the cylindrical canisters, often 100 feet long and weighing hundreds of tons, which held the spectroscopes and other sensitive instruments used to measure a weapon's output. Each canister was basically an underground physics laboratory. Preparations for a canister's use could take a year or more and involve hundreds of engineers, scientists, technicians and guards. The first step was to drill the deep vertical hole, which was usually eight or nine feet in diameter. Then a large portable building known as a bogey tower was placed over its top, offering protection from the weather and Soviet spy satellites. The testing equipment was assembled inside the tower. First came the weapon. Atop it went the diagnostic canister, which was bolted firmly in place. Metal tubes running its length carried radiation from the exploding weapon to the sensors. Dozens of long cables ran out its top to recording devices in nearby trailers on the surface of the desert. When everything was ready, the bomb-canister package was lowered by a huge crane into the deep hole, which was then carefully filled with sand and other materials designed to keep radiation and radioactive gases trapped beneath the earth.[18]

In his job, Woodruff wrestled with one of the principal dilemmas faced by the designers of all nuclear arms—uncertainty. The explosions, the most powerful man-made events on earth, were often shrouded in multiple layers of mystery. They took place only underground, so doubts and difficulties often arose about what really happened. Scores of delicate instruments, just a few feet from the bomb, were annihilated an instant after relaying signals along cables to recording devices on the surface. What happened was not unlike having a major physics laboratory at a prestigious university sud-

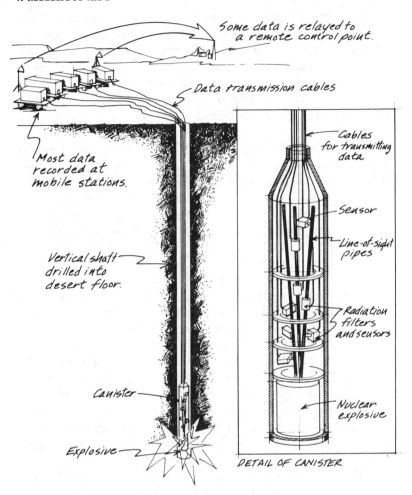

Some data is relayed to a remote control point.

Data transmission cables

Most data recorded at mobile stations.

Vertical shaft drilled into desert floor.

Canister

Explosive

Cables for transmitting data

Sensor

Line-of-sight pipes

Radiation filters and sensors

Nuclear explosive

DETAIL OF CANISTER

Setup for underground nuclear test.

denly vanish at a critical moment. Moreover, underground sensors and instruments were good for only one use. There was no chance to go back and recheck them or a curious reading they had generated. They had no proven reliability. They could not be taken from one test to another to check their calibration. Even in major aboveground laboratories, the reliability and meaning of readings in the fleeting world of physics were often debated for decades. For scientists who deciphered nuclear blasts beneath the earth, the situation could be more daunting.

Nevertheless, Woodruff had a series of successes in his post, overseeing the development of new kinds of instruments and improving the process of taking data from nuclear blasts. He also was handed an unusual challenge that would mark a turning point in his career—to create sensors to measure the output from an entirely new class of nuclear weapon that Livermore scientists were struggling to develop, the X-ray laser.

LASERS are harsh disciplinarians. They force the chaotic forms of energy found in everyday life to move in tight formation and thus to become intense beams of light. Most lasers achieve this organizational feat through a delicate process that revolves around the stimulation of electrons, the tiny, negatively charged particles that orbit the atomic nucleus. Any electron, if properly jostled, will emit a photon of light, also known as a light wave. In an operating laser, trillions of electrons are jostled all at once. This process starts when a significant number of electrons are "pumped" from their ordinary orbits into higher-energy states by an external source of energy. The electrons are briefly held in this excited state, the pause known as a population inversion. When one electron spontaneously decays back to a lower-energy level, it releases a photon of light. A laser becomes a laser when spontaneous photons start to trigger stimulated emissions as well. They trick excited electrons into emitting other photons with exactly the same frequency and in the same direction. That's the beginning of a cascade. What emerges is a very narrow and intense beam of coherent light, its waves in step with one another. In contrast, incoherent light from an electric bulb is composed of helter-skelter waves, like those on a choppy sea.

At Livermore, the art of building lasers rapidly advanced after the first one was demonstrated in 1960. A major challenge was to construct lasers with ever-shorter wavelengths, since these were increasingly powerful. The first lasers fired beams of red light. The goal then shifted to making green, blue, ultraviolet and finally X-ray lasers. At Livermore, the first serious talk of making an X-ray laser occurred in the late 1960s. Its extremely short wavelength would allow it to illuminate very small objects (down to the size of a molecule). The military attraction was that short wavelengths packed more punch. X-rays have 100 to 10,000 times more energy than visible light and react with matter in a very different manner, as demonstrated when medical X-rays penetrate a patient's body. In theory, an X-ray laser would squeeze more power into a thin beam, making it a deadly weapon. Despite nearly a decade of effort, however, no one by the late 1970s had succeeded in making an X-ray laser come to life.

At Livermore, the main person behind the X-ray laser push was George F. Chapline, Jr., an ex-college professor who had an air of happy abstraction. Holding a Ph.D. in physics from the California Institute of Technology, Chapline since the early 1970s had dreamed of powering an X-ray laser with big visible-light lasers, which at Livermore had slowly grown to fill cavernous rooms the size of airport hangars. In 1977, Chapline, then 35, came up with an idea for how to pump an X-ray laser with an energy source many billions of times more powerful than the biggest laboratory laser on earth. He wanted to use a nuclear bomb.[19] If successful, he felt, it might produce a weapon unlike any other, being smaller, cheaper, lighter, more powerful than any other big laser on earth. Most provocative of all, its small size and modest weight meant it would be relatively easy to place in space. However, many Livermore experts were skeptical, viewing the device, if it worked, as an interesting physics experiment but hardly powerful enough to be a weapon. At times when Chapline spoke about the weapons possibility of the X-ray laser, scientific peers would smile behind his back.[20] Chapline nonetheless forged ahead, creating an experimental device to be tested in a nuclear blast beneath the Nevada desert.

Woodruff, challenged by the problem, threw his division into the job of designing new sensors to record whether Chapline's device when tested would indeed produce a laser beam.[21] The work was tricky, since Chapline's idea had been deemed too risky for its own dedicated test, which could cost tens of millions of dollars. Instead, it was to be added to an existing experiment planned by the Pentagon's Defense Nuclear Agency, which had the job of seeing what effect exploding weapons had on military equipment. The agency had no real interest in Chapline's experiment, instead intending to use the raw radiations from the nuclear blast for its own studies. Chapline would be allowed to use some of these radiations as a courtesy.[22]

Woodruff flew to Nevada to oversee the setup of the sensors. The experiment was located deep inside Rainier Mesa in a horizontal tunnel rather than a vertical shaft. A small-gauge train led from the blinding Nevada sunlight into the cold darkness of the mesa's interior. For months, engineers had taken the train back and forth into the mesa, which was honeycombed with more than a dozen miles of tunnels. Inside, the din of jackhammers, drills and welders had been constant. Now there was silence. The finished test apparatus stretched along one tunnel. Scientists and engineers from Woodruff's group went over every detail. At the very back of the tunnel was the bomb. Attached to it was a long, tapered metal pipe that led to a room-size chamber in which the military hardware was to be irradiated. A separate, smaller pipe led from the bomb to Chapline's laser apparatus and the complex sensors meant to relay data to recorders. All the chambers and pipes were pumped free of air, so radiation from the nuclear explosion could move unimpeded. After a last inspection, the whole area was sealed with concrete to keep the blast locked deep inside the mesa.[23]

Unfortunately, before the test could take place, a leak developed in the vacuum pipe leading to Chapline's experiment, ruining the chances for a good measurement. It was impossible to fix the problem without taking apart the whole setup, now sealed in concrete. A decision was made to press ahead, since the principal objective of the nuclear test was still attainable.

On D-Day, September 13, 1978, the mesa's tunnels were cleared of all personnel as the countdown picked up for the test, code-named Diablo Hawk. As the countdown reached zero, the small bomb exploded, sending radiation racing down the large pipe at the speed of light. A fraction of a second later, huge trapdoors in the pipe slammed shut to keep bomb debris from flying into the test chamber. Mock warheads were pounded by radiation, sensors buried in them sending back data about their vulnerability. But Chapline's X-ray experiment failed, as expected. No one had any idea whether or not his innovative idea had produced a beam of coherent X-rays.[24]

THE episode had no negative repercussions for Woodruff, who was judged to be one of the most skilled managers at Livermore. He made tough decisions, changed his mind in light of new evidence and generally inspired confidence in subordinates. At this point in his career, Woodruff was also judged a seasoned hand in the art of nuclear design. He gave lectures in the Livermore in-house course on weapon making, often teaching Ph.D.s. His standing was such that in December 1978 he was appointed head of the premier section in the laboratory, A Division, where he had once worked as both staff physicist and associate leader. Now he assumed responsibility for about 100 scientists and an annual budget of some $70 million, all devoted to the design of hydrogen bombs.[25] It was no small feat for a man with a degree in physics from San Jose State who had joined Livermore a decade earlier.

One dilemma facing Woodruff in his new post was what to do with the X-ray laser. Although fascinated by Chapline's idea and glad to promote a project that was a radical challenge to his staff, he continued to meet resistance from many scientists and officials who felt it was marginally interesting and perhaps doomed to failure. Woodruff thought otherwise. He advocated a dedicated test of Chapline's device beneath the Nevada desert. The bomb meant to pump the laser would be modest, just 7 kilotons.[26] That meant the vertical shaft dug into the desert floor could be quite shallow, saving drilling expenses. Still, the cost of the experiment would be about $10 million, no small sum even for Livermore.

For the national labs, this was a period of declining budgets in weapons work. Livermore's purchasing power dropped 40 percent during the 1970s. East-West detente had cooled the arms race, and the lab instead focused much attention on innovative ways to deal with the energy crisis. For administrators in the weapons program like Woodruff, there was little financial leeway for bold moves and new starts. Moreover, with the arrival of the Carter administration in Washington, a move got under way in the government to negotiate a comprehensive East-West ban on the testing of nuclear weapons. The suspension of explosive testing would have stopped the process by which ideas were turned into arms.

In this atmosphere of political uncertainty and tight budgets, Woodruff vigorously pushed the X-ray laser. As a result, Chapline no longer had to piggyback his experiment onto another shot. He got his own multimillion-dollar test of one of the most innovative—and risky—ideas to emerge in the secretive world of bomb design. Plans went forward. But before they got too far along, another idea for an X-ray laser arose to rival Chapline's.

THE man who was the force behind the new laser idea was Lowell L. Wood, Jr., Teller's protege who had helped resurrect and promote the classical Super as an antimissile weapon. Wood was a large man, bearded and bearlike, brilliant and acerbic. He was about Woodruff's age and at the peak of his professional powers. Wood ran Livermore's "O Group," an eccentric branch of the physics department populated by young scientists who wore blue jeans, drank soft drinks by the case, and entertained themselves with all-night bouts of research. Most were in their 20s. Wood pushed his young recruits hard, being deeply sympathetic to Teller's conservative vision and eager to give it new life.[27]

"Lowell is like another son to Edward," Carl Haussmann, a Livermore veteran, remarked in 1984. "Edward has always been an activist. Ten or twenty years ago he was an activist in detail. Now he relies on other people, people like Lowell."[28]

Wood and Teller first met at the University of California at Los Angeles, where Wood came under the tutelage of Willard F. Libby, a Nobel laureate and politically conservative nuclear chemist who was a good friend of Teller's.[29] Wood was introduced to the famous Hungarian physicist in his sophomore year, and he impressed Teller. When Wood graduated from UCLA with a Ph.D., Teller urged him to join the weapons lab. Wood arrived at Livermore in 1965. He quickly gained a reputation as an iconoclast, at one point shaving his head once or twice a year rather than getting regular haircuts. He also proved to be a bold innovator whose enthusiasms, like Teller's, often put him out on a limb. Wood, for instance, became a driving force in the development of laser fusion, a type of controlled fusion that sought to ignite tiny pellets of thermonuclear fuel with concentrated beams of laser light. Despite his work, his optimistic predictions, and hundreds of millions of dollars in federal funds, the field made only halting progress.[30]

Wood could be courtly, courteous, deferential, and filled with old-world charm to individuals he was trying to influence outside the laboratory, including congressmen and their aides. His attitude was quite different with his "family." Wood's main achievement at the lab was recruiting bright young scientists to O Group, where they worked long hours, sometimes day and night, to pioneer unusual inventions. One was a computer that designed computers. Another was a light detector so sensitive that in theory it could be used on deep-running submarines to receive coded messages from space on beams of laser light. Wood punished and rewarded his crew with a potent mix of kindness and ridicule, most of the young scientists being eager to avoid a tongue lashing. When he got angry, he often accused them of being "brain dead." At such times his whole body became electrified, his eyebrows arching up, his shoulders hunching forward, and his voice taking on an edge. Wood could also show his recruits deep sympathy or join them in pranks. In short, he was the kind of man who tended to inspire either love or hatred in those who knew him.

Most of all, Wood's "family" flourished because he had a vivid imagination, like Teller's, that allowed him to dream up extremely tough projects for his young scientists, and he had the rhetorical skills to make them sound attainable. He was a gung-ho technologist, constantly driving his recruits onward. Perhaps most important, he had an intense sense of mission in which the world (or at least the military side of it) seemed to revolve around his group and its projects, many of which were top secret. Writing one young scientist, Wood promised that joining O Group meant nothing but "hard work, long hours, high risks, low pay, possible fame—and the companionship of some of the heroes of the present age."[31]

In the mid and late 1970s, Wood focused his considerable energies on one of his young scientists, urging him to pioneer the development of an X-ray laser. The device, as with Chapline's early speculations, was to be powered by the laboratory's giant visible-light lasers. It was to be a peaceful achievement. If successful, Wood said, a laboratory X-ray laser would have wide applications in biology and medicine, generating breakthroughs in molecular imaging that would give clues to the riddle of cancer. Dangling the ultimate scientific carrot, Wood suggested that the achievement of the world's first X-ray laser might result in a Nobel Prize.

The target of Wood's salesmanship was Peter L. Hagelstein, a tall, shy, brooding, baby-faced student from the Massachusetts Institute of Technology, who joined O Group in 1975 at the age of 20. Hagelstein hated the thought of working on weapons, avoiding such projects whenever possible. And he fell in love with Wood's lofty X-ray goal, tackling it with superhuman fervor. A reclusive genius, Hagelstein pursued the peaceful X-ray laser idea by writing computer programs to model its envisioned processes late into the night. Eventually, he hoped to try out his X-ray ideas on Livermore's multimillion-dollar lasers. But after years of effort, the shy graduate student seemed no closer to his goal than when he started.[32]

All that was about to change, however. In late 1978 as Chapline's nuclear X-ray laser project advanced toward its own dedicated test, Wood and other lab officials encouraged Hagelstein to go to meetings at which the project was discussed. After all, Hagelstein was one of the best young minds working the X-ray laser field. Millions of dollars were being gambled on Chapline's wild idea, and administrators wanted to make sure the effort would pay off. Hagelstein, loath to aid the nuclear weapons effort, started working nights and sleeping days to avoid design reviews.

On Thanksgiving Day, 1978, a handful of top Livermore officials and scientists were called away from family gatherings and turkey dinners to meet with Teller in his office atop Building 111. When Teller got excited about something, he worked nights or weekends or holidays, whatever it took to make progress. Moreover, he expected his sense of urgency to be shared by those around him. And it was. "The old man," as people at the lab sometimes called Teller, still had a way of imposing his will on others and shaking things up. The call to Teller's meeting was something Hagelstein could not ignore.

The issue under discussion was Chapline's experiment, its promise and any potential problems. Among those present were Teller, Chapline, Wood, Woodruff and Hagelstein. Uneasy at being around Teller and weapons talk, Hagelstein made no real contribution to the meeting. But he did see a mistake in some of Chapline's calculations, saying nothing about it. The next day he felt relieved at the thought that Chapline's experiment would fail. He looked on Chapline as a rival who was threatening to win the X-ray laser race with an unseemly nuclear shortcut. Now it looked like Chapline had accidentally removed himself from the competition.[33]

At two or three in the morning, Wood came by Hagelstein's O Group office, where the young scientist was hard at work on calculations for his peaceful X-ray laser. Wood was immediately aware of Hagelstein's buoyant mood. He pried Chapline's error out of Hagelstein and decided it was easy to fix. At the next review of Chapline's experiment, Wood noted the flaw, crediting its discovery to Hagelstein. It was the young scientist's first contribution to a secret weapons project at Livermore, albeit an inadvertent one.[34]

Nor was it his last. In the summer of 1979, Hagelstein got trapped into going to another review meeting. At the time he was slightly dazed and disoriented from too much work and not enough sleep. In this state, his subconscious seemed to take over. He watched himself make a suggestion for a new kind of X-ray laser. Officials at the meeting were impressed, even though the idea was rough. If feasible, the laser would be more efficient that Chapline's, making it much more than a scientific curiosity. "I had been up twenty hours," Hagelstein recalled. "It had something to do with being stretched out. The mouth just said it."[35] Wood badgered Hagelstein to work on the idea, having told lab officials that calculations behind it were nearly complete when in fact they were rudimentary at best. What was needed was a detailed computer analysis of how different atoms might undergo laser action at X-ray frequencies. Hagelstein, feeling trapped in a bad situation, decided to do calculations on his computer to try to prove his idea wrong. To his chagrin, his computer said that the idea might work. He kept at it, adding new detail to his calculations in the hopes the scheme would fail. Finally it dawned on him that, at least in theory, he had come up with a very good idea.[36]

Hagelstein was now 24 years old. Eventually it became clear he had discovered a way to create a powerful nuclear X-ray laser, an advance eventually hailed by top government officials as the most innovative idea in nuclear weaponry since the hydrogen bomb. One of Hagelstein's realizations was that an exploding bomb could repeatedly pump the electrons of a single metallic atom over and over, producing scores of X-ray photons. Part of his calculational feat was finding which metallic atoms would do this amazing trick. Candidate metals included lead, gold, mercury, platinum and bismuth. The metals had to have atomic numbers between 72 and 95 in the periodic table, Hagelstein calculated. The higher the atomic number, the shorter the wavelength and the more energetic the laser.[37]

Hagelstein found excuses to avoid further work on the idea. Even so, it now had heightened status at the lab, having caught the attention of Teller and other top officials. Woodruff tentatively decided to add it to Chapline's dedicated experiment on the assumption that work would progress one way or another. Besides, Hagelstein's idea was inherently alluring since it promised a laser strong enough to destroy satellites, missiles and warheads across vast reaches of space.

What excited Teller and Livermore's other high officials was the prospect of a weapon that might dramatically improve the antimissile odds. Older, ground-based systems such as Safeguard and its interceptors had the daunting job of working perfectly just seconds before enemy warheads burst over targets. Their range was extremely limited, being largely determined by the relatively slow speed of the interceptor rockets. In contrast, beams from the X-ray laser could flash over long distances of space at the speed of light. In theory, they could reach far across the globe, going beyond Safeguard's "reentry phase" interceptions to try for "midcourse" destruction of warheads and even for "boost-phase" destruction of missiles before they released their warheads. This long-distance reach offered huge leverage. If a single X-ray laser destroyed an enemy missile in boost phase, it might knock a dozen or more warheads out of the battle in a single stroke. Another advantage was increased time. If the battle started with boost-phase interceptions,

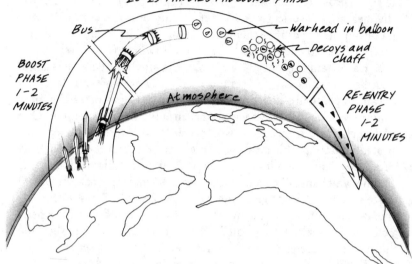

Typical stages of rocket flight.

different "layers" of a defensive system could take independent action. A missile or warhead that slipped through one layer might be caught by another, with old-fashioned interceptors on the ground "mopping up" stray warheads. A battle could be waged over a period of minutes instead of seconds, giving a defender a better chance of destroying all the deadly warheads zooming through space toward his territory. In theory, an X-ray laser could increase odds that an antimissile system might actually work with some degree of reliability.

The idea had another attraction for Teller, the foe of communism. A good antimissile system would scare the Soviets, since its applications could be not only defensive but, less obviously, quite hostile. For instance, an aggressor who launched a surprise nuclear attack could use an antimissile system to brush aside his foe's feeble retaliation, in theory allowing a victor for the first time to emerge from a nuclear war. Teller knew no American president would ever contemplate such aggression. But he also knew a system that gave America that kind of offensive military capability would unnerve the Soviets. Basically, an X-ray advance would give Teller a way of quietly upping the ante in the perilous game of nuclear brinkmanship.

THE pressures on Hagelstein to forge ahead were intense, and eventually he acceded to them. Long afterward, Hagelstein liked to joke about Teller's general influence on people, citing a line out of the movie *Star Wars*: "The Force has a powerful effect on the weak mind."[38] During this period, Hagelstein's pacifist girl friend protested his nuclear labors and eventually broke up with him over the issue. Elusive and brooding, Hagelstein played nothing on his office stereo but the requiems of Brahms, Verdi and Mozart after the breakup, even as Wood kept prodding him on. Grudgingly, Hagelstein kept working.[39]

High atop Building 111, Woodruff had little knowledge of the drama unfolding nearly a mile away in Wood's corner of the lab. All he knew was that a shy young scientist had an interesting idea, that the lab had taken some risk to support it, and that Wood kept promising it would soon be developed to the point where it could be turned into hardware.

Eventually it was. The essence of the idea was to build a long, thin metallic rod that when struck by radiation from an exploding nuclear weapon would fire a beam of coherent X-rays. The "rod" was not really a solid but rather a special foam extracted from plants that was mixed with metallic atoms to form a delicate suspension in which the density of the metallic atoms was about that of gas. This relatively open structure allowed the bomb's radiation to deeply penetrate the rod, triggering the atomic transitions needed for X-ray laser action. A major challenge was to make sure this foam suspension had a uniform density; otherwise the quality of the laser beam would be seriously degraded.[40]

An engineering issue in the development of the X-ray laser was the length of its rods. Usually, lasers had a pair of mirrors, one on each end, that reflected the light back and forth, over and over again, amplifying the beam until it emerged, keeping the vast majority of the photons traveling lengthwise rather than crosswise. But the X-ray laser could have no such apparatus, since X-rays were powerful enough to penetrate most mirrors. The only way to ensure that most stimulated X-rays moved the length of the rod was through its geometry—making it as long as possible. Thus, X-ray photon cascades that started lengthwise down the rod would be highly amplified, whereas sideways ones would be small.[41]

Another important factor bore on the issue of rod width. Laser beams inevitably spread out. In an X-ray laser, this beam divergence could be minimized by making the rod thin, which would optimize

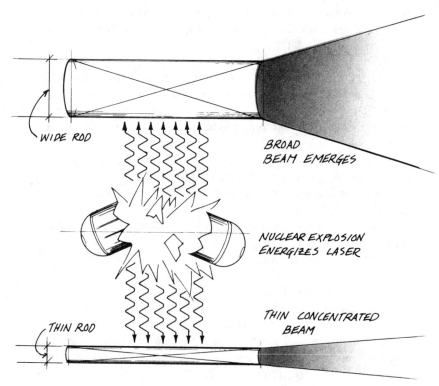

WIDE ROD

BROAD BEAM EMERGES

NUCLEAR EXPLOSION ENERGIZES LASER

THIN ROD

THIN CONCENTRATED BEAM

Geometry favors long, thin rod.

its "optical" features. But if the rod was too thin, another effect, known as diffraction, would start to predominate. This would cause the X-ray beam to break into a less powerful pattern. Keeping all these considerations in mind, Livermore scientists calculated that the optimal width of a laser rod would be about 50 microns, or half the width of a human hair.[42]

However, such an exceptionally thin rod was beyond the lab's fabrication abilities, at least initially. The rods were thus made by cutting a channel in a long block of low-density plastic foam that was about three inches in diameter. The channel was cut by hand. At best, the smallest channel that engineers could cut (and keep extremely uniform) was about one millimeter in diameter, or about the thickness of the wire used in making paper clips. The metallic foam that constituted the X-ray laser "rod" was poured into this tiny channel and protectively covered.[43]

Ideally, the rod should have been quite long, for reasons cited above. But here, too, there was a limitation. The bomb meant to pump the laser would, as any bomb does, radiate in all directions from a central point. A long, straight rod near the bomb would be illuminated unevenly, the middle part irradiated before the end. To minimize this distortion, the rod's length was kept to about a meter.

HAGELSTEIN's fleeting idea was now physically part of a scheduled nuclear test. The event was code-named Dauphin. In November 1980, Wood and Chapline, eager to aid test preparations, flew in a privately chartered twin-engine plane to the Nevada test site, the two scientists having missed the regular flight of the lab's F-27.[44] Hagelstein stayed behind, fretting. As usual during periods of tension, he got no sleep.[45]

On D-Day, Friday, November 14, the test site was cleared of all personnel except a small group of scientists and security guards who drove out to a trailer known as the "red shack" to electronically arm the weapon, which earlier had been placed nearby at the bottom of a 1,050-foot-deep hole and covered with dirt. At the red shack, security was tight, as usual. Two of the scientists carried a special briefcase and a bag of tiny cubes that had numbers painted on their sides. They alternately picked cubes out of the bag and punched the numbers into an "arm enable" device in the briefcase, generating a random code that was sent to the buried weapon on a special electrical cable.[46] The scientists then drove across the desert to the control point in a mountain pass overlooking the test site, joining Wood and Chapline. There, in a high-technology complex surrounded by armed guards and barbed wire, they again opened their briefcase and sent the same random code to the weapon. It was now armed. In the "war room" at the control point, the Energy Department test controller checked with numerous advisers on the state of security and the weather. Winds could not be blowing out of the northwest, lest an accidental leak of radioactive gas drift toward Las Vegas, some 100 miles away.

Everything was ready. The test controller gave the go-ahead and a secret coded signal was sent to the red shack. There was no single "button." Instead, that signal started a computer in the red shack that automatically cycled through a program that ended with the detonation of the weapon.

Radiation flashed from the bomb, hitting both Hagelstein's and Chapline's devices buried with it. Several meters away, sensors in the canisters gathered data and sent it up cables to the surface before being destroyed by the expanding fireball.

At the control point, Wood and Chapline almost immediately saw signs of success in rough data relayed from the bomb. Within a half hour, they were more confident—the X-ray laser experiments had succeeded. The world's first X-ray lasers appeared to have rumbled to life simultaneously in a nuclear blast beneath the Nevada desert. It would take weeks and months to analyze the results and crystallize the nuclear insights, but there was enough there to send shivers of excitement through the scientists. Moreover, Hagelstein's laser appeared to be much more powerful than Chapline's.[47]

Wood and Chapline raced back to Livermore. Aboard the lab's F-27, some senior scientists were annoyed with Wood for touting Hagelstein's results so forcefully, feeling that more analysis was needed before the extent of the success was documented.[48] Back at the lab, Wood excitedly told Teller of the success. He also took Hagelstein and several other members of O Group to the nearby town of Livermore to celebrate, treating them to ice cream at Baskin-Robbins 31 Flavors.[49] Wood's group dubbed the X-ray laser "Excalibur," after King Arthur's sword.

Woodruff was as excited as anyone about the breakthrough. Building 111 was abuzz with talk of the top-secret advance. His administrative gamble, made years earlier, had paid off. It was the biggest coup yet for the young official, now 40 years old. In June 1980, Woodruff had been promoted to become associate director for nuclear design, overseeing the hydrogen bomb work of A Division and the atom bomb work of B Division. His annual budget was about $150 million. He was among the handful of officials who controlled the lab, there being a dozen associate directors. The X-ray laser success did nothing but increase the respect that was accorded the rising young administrator. As one of the most powerful associate directors, he was in a position from which it was conceivable he could wage a campaign to become the lab's director.

Early in 1981, Woodruff set up a new X-ray laser team that reported directly to him. It was known as R Program. Its director was Thomas A. Weaver, an O Group scientist who had played an important role in advancing Hagelstein's X-ray laser idea. Before long, R Program had nearly 100 employees working on X-ray laser design.[50] Its two chief scientists were Chapline and Hagelstein, who despite his deep ambivalence about weapons continued to show a strong interest in refining his idea.

What emerged was an approach to dramatically increase the laser's power. R Program scientists calculated that Hagelstein's one-meter rod had a total output of about 100,000 joules of energy.[51] This was a lot considering that Livermore's biggest conventional laser—a $176 million behemoth known as Nova that covered an area the size of a football field—had roughly the same output. But it was not enough to be an antimissile weapon. The first approach to raising the laser's power was to increase the rod's length. This required careful engineering to ensure its structural integrity. It also required the development of a new kind of nuclear explosive that would distribute its energy in a cylindrical fashion, parallel to the rod, rather than spherically. The plan was to build an advanced hydrogen bomb that had a single fission trigger but two separate assemblies of fusion fuel, one on each side of the trigger, making the device elongated. As usual for new weapons, the development of just this power source was expected to take years.[52]

The other approach was to simply increase the number of rods, bundling them tightly together. R Program scientists envisioned hundreds and even thousands of these extremely thin rods being situated next to one another in a single laser "arm" that could be pointed at a target in space. But the elegant idea posed a major challenge. If no precautions were taken, photons would travel laterally from one rod to another, starting photon cascades in the wrong direction. This short-circuiting of the laser process was known as "fratricide." It would sap much of the laser's energy. The proposed solution was to make the rods out of different metals, so the photon wavelengths would be different and would not trigger action in nearby rods. However, no one knew if all the candidate metals would undergo lasing action at X-ray frequencies, or even if the delicate engineering of the plan would prove practical. In short, bundling had major uncertainties whose resolution would require years of underground explosions.[53]

Until the various advances were made, and the underground tests conducted, all the Livermore scientists had achieved with the Dauphin test of Hagelstein's basic laser was a crude experiment. It nonetheless conjured visions of revolutionary armament. If perfected, Excalibur might have beams with $10^{20}$ joules of energy per steradian, the scientists calculated. The number $10^{20}$ is scientific shorthand for 1 with 20 zeros behind it, or 100,000,000,000,000,000,000. A steradian is a measurement of solid angles. In plain English, it was a lot of energy in a small space. It

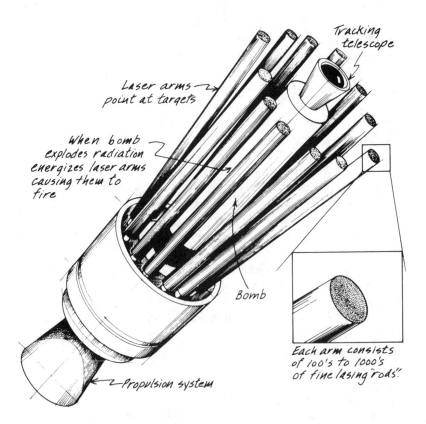

Tracking telescope

Laser arms point at targets

When bomb explodes radiation energizes laser arms causing them to fire

Bomb

Each arm consists of 100's to 1000's of fine lasing "rods".

Propulsion system

X-ray laser weapon.

meant a beam from Excalibur would be a million times brighter than a hydrogen bomb.[54]

An X-ray laser weapon would have clear limitations. Since the earth's atmosphere quickly absorbed X-rays, its usefulness would be restricted to the vacuum of space or to the upper fringes of the atmosphere. But if located in space just above the earth's atmosphere, an Excalibur module of the predicted power might have enough force to damage a satellite in geosynchronous orbit some 22,300 miles away. That kind of reach and destructive power had never been seen in the space age. If achieved, it might rapidly overturn geopolitical rules of the East-West confrontation that had been in place for a third of a century.

THE breakthrough achieved in the Dauphin test—the creation of the world's first X-ray laser—could hardly have come at a more auspicious moment in the history of American politics. Ronald Reagan had just overwhelmed President Carter in an election landslide. Reagan's victory was so complete that Carter began his concession speech before polls closed in several western states. The stunning win extended to the U.S. Congress, where Republicans took control of the Senate and wrested 33 House seats from the Democrats. The nation was about to embark on a trillion-dollar defense buildup.

Teller and Wood decided to go to Washington to promote news of the X-ray advance to congressional leaders. It was the beginning of a new budget cycle, a good time to campaign for new funds. The fledgling effort needed more money if it was to perfect the device in a timely manner. The main expense was underground nuclear tests, which were already seen as so complex that the cost of a single one was expected to rise in the early 1980s from $10 million to more than $50 million. Without major infusions of money, development of the X-ray laser would take many years and, if unexpected problems arose, possibly decades.

Woodruff decided to go along on the planned trip. He was eager to see the program expand. It was his program, carved out of thin air over the objections of key Livermore officials. Its success would be his success. Another reason Woodruff wanted to go was apprehension about Teller and Wood. He knew firsthand how excitable the Hungarian scientist could be, having clashed with him over the perfection of clean bombs. Now, he wanted to keep an eye on them as they headed to Capitol Hill. After all, he was in charge of the program and would ultimately be held responsible for any promises made.[55]

The day Woodruff decided to accompany Teller and Wood coincided with a visit to Livermore by William W. Hoover, an Air Force major general who ran the Energy Department's military programs. Hoover told Woodruff that he was uncomfortable with the idea of a senior Livermore administrator going to lobby Congress. The labs had gotten in trouble for such activity.

"Would you rather have them go alone?" Woodruff asked.

Hoover pondered that for a second, imagining the two biggest visionaries of the weapons world off on a new campaign, unsupervised and unchecked, free to say whatever they wanted as they wandered around Washington.

"Okay," Hoover replied. "Go with them." He added that he wanted to know what transpired.[56]

The X-ray laser, Hoover recalled, "was really being hyped at that time. Roy had some reasonable skepticism. He felt this was not on as fast a track as Teller and Wood believed it to be."

IN February 1981, as Reagan and his California staff settled into the White House, the trio of Livermore scientists flew to Washington to talk to congressional leaders. Teller was 73, Wood 39 and Woodruff 40. They gave briefings on the top-secret device and praised its antimissile potential, saying progress would require more money. Among those who listened was Melvin Price, 76 years old, the powerful chairman of the House Armed Services Committee. Woodruff was satisfied with what was said, in particular that no unrealistic target dates were promised for the laser's perfection.[57]

While still at the Rayburn House office building on Capitol Hill, Woodruff called Hoover, who was happy to hear the briefings had been seemly. As it turned out, however, the elaborate precautions did little good. A magazine soon leaked details of the Dauphin test and reported wildly extravagant claims about the X-ray laser's usefulness in war. It was the public's first glimpse of the top-secret advance and the zealous salesmanship that would come to surround it. The news appeared in the February 23, 1981, issue of *Aviation Week & Space Technology*, a trade publication known in military circles as "Aviation Leak." The information was attributed to anonymous officials in the Defense Department and Congress. The magazine said a secret test in Nevada had resulted in a surprising advance and that Livermore officials the previous week had briefed congressional leaders on it. It also said the laser had radiated at a wavelength of 14 angstroms—a very short frequency that was indisputably in the X-ray region. "X-ray lasers based on the successful Dauphin test," the magazine went on, "are so small that a single payload bay on the space shuttle could carry to orbit a number sufficient to stop a Soviet nuclear weapons attack."[58]

Clearly, the magazine's sources had gone far beyond the experimental results, a leap of faith that would be repeated frequently in the months and years ahead.

WOODRUFF was unable to accompany Teller and Wood on every trip to Washington. And there were others—over the years, many others. In March, Teller continued the Washington sojourns on his own, dropping by the Pentagon to visit Richard D. DeLauer, the newly appointed undersecretary of defense for research and engineering. He was just moving into his office. DeLauer and Teller had known each other for years, DeLauer having worked on nuclear weapons in the 1950s at Los Alamos. Now, Teller exulted over the X-ray laser's potential.

"Edward was Edward," DeLauer recalled dryly, saying he knew Teller well enough to take his enthusiasms with a grain of salt.[59]

Most of the scientific elite in Washington who ran the nation's defense establishment also knew how to judge Teller's claims. These seasoned technocrats were devoted to giving America a technical edge in the seemingly endless cold war against communism. They respected Teller. But most of them also knew something of his track record, of the projects and ideas that had fizzled despite his claims and optimism.

As Teller continued to make the rounds to promote the X-ray laser, he widened the scope of his lobbying, seeing not only congressmen and defense experts but high officials of the Reagan administration. These men knew little of technology and military development but were dazzled by the science hero of the Republican right. For his part, Teller used all the diffident charm and persuasive power at his command to drive home the importance of the X-ray breakthrough.

# THREE

# The Selling
# of Star Wars

AN IMPORTANT FORUM of the 1980s for the discussion of nuclear war was a little-publicized seminar held every August in Erice, Italy, a medieval walled town set atop a steep hill on the coast of Sicily. It was a place out of time. The city was built of ancient stone, often shrouded by mist from the sea. Its streets were too narrow for cars. A half mile above the Mediterranean, at the town's summit, stood a Norman castle with heavily fortified walls and battlements. It was one age's hope for security. The castle commanded a breathtaking view of the countryside and the sea. On a clear day, the coast of Africa was plainly visible in the distance. Though the walled city and its fortress were imposing, their limitations were etched in history. Erice had successfully been invaded many times over the centuries.[1]

Throughout the 1980s a main topic of discussion at the seminar was whether new kinds of defensive arms could achieve security against the preeminent threat of the twentieth century—the intercontinental ballistic missile armed with nuclear warheads. The weeklong seminar, held in a former convent and church, was attended by a handful of elite scientists who had experience in making nuclear arms or developing policies for their use. In sneakers and casual shirts, these men, often bitter intellectual foes, would try to work out their differences around a conference table. A frequent participant was Edward Teller.

At the first Erice conference, held in 1981 during Ronald Reagan's first year in office, Teller gave a remarkably pessimistic forecast on the fate of the East-West struggle. Russia had been expansionist for centuries, he said. Today its "wish for power" was so strong that its leaders were prepared to threaten nuclear war "and quite possibly to carry out their threat."[2] What the Soviet Union still needed, Teller warned, was defensive weapons to hide behind after launching a preemptive nuclear strike.

Teller's statement, which echoed his warning some two decades earlier in *The Legacy of Hiroshima*, was an admission of one of the key military paradoxes of the nuclear era. In earlier times thick walls and towering parapets were unambiguously meant to protect. But now the issue of defensive armament had become murky and ominous. In the wrong hands, Teller said, antimissile arms could ensure deadly success in what had been considered an unwinnable game. This was especially true with the newer class of antimissile arms, envisioned as being based in space, which were meant to protect large areas, even cities and whole nations. By contrast, old-fashioned ground-based systems were good for protecting small sites, usually missiles. In theory, only space systems could totally remove an aggressor's fear of retaliation.

"If the Soviets get this defense, and we do not, then I predict that there will be a nuclear war, and I can predict its outcome," Teller told the group. "The United States will be wiped out by a fraction of the Soviet weapons, and the Soviets will then be able to impose their will on the rest of the world. With their remaining weapons as a threat, they can secure food, machines and labor, and the Kremlin will rule the world." Moreover, Teller said, there was evidence the Soviets were already ahead of the West in forging antimissile arms and might feel "very sure that we cannot retaliate." The best way to preserve peace, Teller argued, was for the West to acquire defensive arms, its moral superiority ensuring they would be used only for protection.

As was often the case, Teller was at odds with a number of his peers on this subject. They saw the large-scale introduction of antimissile arms on either side or both sides as tipping the balance of terror for the first time and possibly triggering nuclear war—not preventing it. These arms would never work well enough to fend off a full-scale attack involving thousands of nuclear warheads, the skeptics said. Antimissile arms would thus be useful only for aggression, for mopping up an enemy's "ragged retaliation" after a disarming first strike. The best way to avoid the temptation, they said, was to ban such weapons altogether. Despite such arguments, Teller insisted the world was already in an antimissile race and said the only hope for the West was to acquire such arms. He also was deeply pessimistic over whether it had the will to pursue that goal.

On the seminar's last day, Teller made a dark prophecy.

"Looking at past developments, looking at the lack of determination and unity in the West, looking at the continuing success of the Soviet Union (not in making its people more content but in extending its power), I predict that the Soviet Union will win."

A stunned silence followed. Teller paused for a moment and then qualified his prediction, saying the West might yet be saved "by several miracles."

One miracle had already occurred, he said—and that was the election of Ronald Reagan.

WRITTEN off by many as the man who learned to love the bomb, Teller was transformed by Ronald Reagan into one of the most prominent scientists in the world again. He became America's number one scientific celebrity. And he loved it. No other figure present at the birth of the atomic age could, after the passage of four decades, claim to still be a key actor in public affairs, much less the nation's most influential scientist.

The bond between Teller and Reagan was a shared distrust of communism and a shared vision of how to oppose it—with military might. But Teller wanted more. Even as he spoke at Erice in 1981, he had begun an aggressive campaign to win the Reagan White House to his particular brand of antimissile defense—one relying on the nuclear X-ray laser. His campaign would ultimately prove successful. On the evening of March 23, 1983, as Reagan gave his Star Wars speech, Teller was an honored guest at the White House. He wore tuxedo and bow tie, and he smiled from ear to ear, ecstatic that he had lived to see another miracle.

REAGAN'S interest in antimissile arms was fueled by a layman's fascination with science and technology that went back to his earliest days. He recalled in an autobiography that as a youth he had listened "with breathless attention" to a primitive radio, "a pair of earphones attached tightly to my head, scratching a crystal with a wire."[3] As an adult, Reagan went into commercial radio and then motion pictures, both of which intrigued him technically.

It might seem portentous now that in his 1940 movie, *Murder in the Air*, Reagan played a secret agent fighting a band of Communist spies out to steal a revolutionary weapon known as the inertia projector. "Well," said Reagan at one point in the film, "it seems the spy ring has designs on the greatest war weapon ever invented, which, by the way, is the exclusive property of Uncle Sam." At the film's end, Reagan turned the ray on the spies, who were fleeing with its blueprints. Their plane stopped in midair, caught fire and crashed to earth.[4]

Reagan had an abiding faith in the notion that Yankee ingenuity could solve nearly any technical problem. For years he was a spokesman for General Electric, whose motto was "Progress Is Our Most Important Product." In eight years, from 1954 to 1962, Reagan visited all of GE's 139 plants, some several times, talking with people on assembly lines and giving upbeat speeches. When he built a home in California overlooking the Pacific, it was filled, he recalled, "with every imaginable electric gadget."[5]

Teller first met Reagan in the fall of 1966. Then 58 and internationally famous, Teller went to see Reagan in Sacramento shortly after the actor was elected governor of California, inviting him to visit the Livermore weapons lab at his earliest convenience. Reagan did so in 1967 on a late winter morning, soon after his inauguration.[6] He was the first governor of California to visit the sprawling lab. Teller gave Reagan a general briefing and took him on a tour of computers, lasers, giant fusion machines, and other wonders no less fantastic than the arms of *Murder in the Air*. "We showed him all the complex projects," Teller told me in 1985. "He listened carefully and interrupted maybe a dozen times. Every one of his questions was to the point. He clearly comprehended the technology. And there was no skimping on time. He came in the morning and stayed over lunch. He quite obviously is one of the really few politicians who takes a detailed interest in technical subjects."[7]

At Livermore, for the first time, Teller also shared with Reagan his vision of protecting the nation from the onslaught of enemy missiles. The physicist explained how a ground-based interceptor known as the Spartan was being built to destroy enemy warheads just above the atmosphere. Teller also told Reagan of the centerpiece of his vision—the giant nuclear bomb atop the interceptor that would simplify the job of destroying an enemy target.[8] "It was Ronald Reagan's first chance to hear about defense weapons," Teller recalled.[9]

That day, as Reagan toured the lab and ate lunch with a dozen Livermore staff members, Teller was taken with the politician's quick grasp of arcane subjects "about which he could not have known a great deal." He was also impressed, as the nation would be one day, by the governor's magnetism. He "got along with everybody," Teller marveled.[10] The admiration was apparently mutual. Governor Reagan subsequently went out of his way to meet with Teller in Sacramento for discussions on a variety of subjects, including politics and how to limit earthquake damage in California. It was, Teller recalled, "a very nice visit."[11] In effect, Teller was becoming one of Reagan's science advisers.

During this period, Reagan, a man of simple beliefs and deep superstitions, became obsessed with the biblical prophecy of Armageddon, the final battle between good and evil at the world's end. He felt it was near and would take the form of a nuclear firestorm. Starting in the late 1960s, Reagan repeatedly voiced his fears in private, saying the Bible foretold many recent events that suggested its approach. In 1971, Governor Reagan startled a banquet companion by asserting that the end was near. "For the first time ever," Reagan confided over cherries jubilee, "everything is in place for the battle of Armageddon and the second coming of Christ." Lou Cannon in his book *President Reagan: The Role of a Lifetime* argues that Reagan's fixation with Armageddon eventually became a driving force in his search for an antimissile shield.[12]

For whatever reasons, Reagan grew increasingly interested in the defensive idea and uneasy with the nuclear status quo. In 1976 during his unsuccessful presidential bid, Reagan often questioned the doctrine of Mutual Assured Destruction, or MAD, saying it was like two men pointing pistols at each other's head, one tightening his finger on the trigger. Another indication of his discomfort came in an impromptu speech made to the 1976 Republican convention in Kansas City, Missouri. Reagan had just lost the nomination and now had an opportunity to outline what he thought were the most pressing issues of the day. He said nothing about the size of the federal government or taxes, instead focusing on nuclear war.

"Horrible missiles of destruction," Reagan told the delegates, stood poised to "destroy virtually the civilized world we live in." He offered no solution other than the party's agenda and having the delegates consider the judgment of their children's children. "They will know whether we met our challenge," he said.[13]

During a 1978 radio speech, Reagan went further, describing

the grim implications of the nation's vulnerability to nuclear attack. "If the Soviets should push the button," Reagan warned, "there is no defense against them—no way to prevent nuclear devastation of their targets here in the United States."[14]

During the presidential campaign of 1979 and 1980, Reagan visited the military site dedicated to warning of nuclear attack, the North American Aerospace Defense Command, or NORAD. A vast city buried inside a hollowed-out mountain in Colorado, NORAD was a top-secret military facility whose mission was to track all objects in space, including missiles or warheads that should suddenly appear on radar screens. Reagan went there with Martin Anderson, one of his campaign aides. "It's an experience," Anderson recalled in an interview. "It's just like the movies. There's a big steel door into the mountain and a huge subterranean complex carved inside. In the war room there's a map of the United States that can show the paths of incoming planes and missiles. We got the full briefing. At the end we went back to the general's office. All day long I had wanted to ask the question. What would happen if they launched just one? The answer was that there was nothing we could do. Reagan joined in and we pressed it further, going into different scenarios. We could do nothing. On the plane coming back, Reagan was clearly struck by the fact that we had spent billions on national defense, with all the weapons, yet we were totally helpless."[15]

Reagan recalled his NORAD visit during the campaign, telling a reporter that it impressed and worried him. "They actually are tracking several thousand objects in space, meaning satellites of ours and everyone else's, even down to the point that they are tracking a glove lost by an astronaut," he said. "I think the thing that struck me was the irony that here, with this great technology of ours, we can do all of this, yet we cannot stop any of the weapons that are coming at us. I don't think there's a time in history when there wasn't a defense against some kind of thrust, even back in the old-fashioned days when we had coast artillery that would stop invading ships."[16]

A possible solution to the dilemma was proposed by Anderson, a senior fellow at Stanford University's Hoover Institution who later became Reagan's assistant for economic and domestic policy at the White House. In August 1979, he wrote "Policy Memorandum No. 3, Reagan for president, Foreign Policy and National Security." The remarkable document was written for Reagan and a dozen top campaign aides, people such as Richard V. Allen, Michael K. Deaver,

Peter Hannaford and Edwin Meese. It listed three campaign options—stick with President Carter's policy of relying on good Soviet intentions ("dangerous folly"), embark on an arms buildup ("apt to frighten as many people as it consoles"), or start to build a system to shoot down enemy missiles ("far more appealing to the American people than the questionable satisfaction of knowing that those who initiated an attack against us were also blown away").[17]

"Of course," Anderson noted, "there is the question of feasibility, especially with the development of multiple entry warheads, but there have apparently been striking advances in missile technology during the past decade or so that would make such a system technically possible." He added that defenses should be constructed "in conjunction with a reasonable buildup in our conventional forces, and an acceleration in development of cruise missiles, and conventional nuclear missiles like the MX."[18]

Anderson's type of solution was generally opposed by the nation's military leaders, who saw little hope of protection from space arms. The Pentagon's top science advisers felt orbiting weapons might eventually be powerful enough to damage thin-skinned satellites but not thousands of enemy missiles and hardened warheads. In early 1979, the Pentagon's Defense Science Board wrote a sober report warning against a "crash" program of antimissile research, while Defense Secretary Harold Brown cautioned against exaggerated space-weapon hopes.[19]

But Reagan got very different advice, and not just from Anderson. As the presidential campaign gained momentum, other advisers sang the praises of antimissile arms. Teller was absent during this early lobbying. After all, he had nothing new to say during the campaign about advanced technologies. In 1979 the X-ray laser was still a dream, coming to life only in late 1980 shortly after the presidential election. In the race to win Reagan's confidence, Teller got a late start and made up for lost time.

THE man with the greatest initial access to Reagan and his entourage was Daniel O. Graham, a short, feisty, cigar-smoking Army lieutenant general who retired from the government in early 1976 as head of the Defense Intelligence Agency. He strongly believed that the rapid growth of the Soviet military was being ignored by the wider intelligence community. As a West Point cadet, Graham had been known as "Little Dog" because of his tenacity. Upon retiring from his Pentagon post, Graham threw himself into redressing what he felt was intelligence shortsightedness, most notably by sitting on a federal panel known as Team B, which attacked the Central Intelligence Agency. He was so hawkish that he raised eyebrows among some staunch conservatives. Amid this intelligence battle, Graham in 1976 had advised the first Reagan presidential campaign. A centerpiece of his advice then was encouraging a national shift to antimissile defense. But the retired general had no explicit plan for achieving the goal. After being asked in late 1979 to again advise Reagan's campaign, he got "really busy" on finding a way, he recalled.[20]

What Graham found was a plan developed in the 1950s during the Eisenhower administration to destroy Soviet missiles early in flight with Ballistic Missile Boost Intercepts, or BAMBI. It was never tested in space. But in theory, BAMBI was to consist of hundreds of space-based battle stations, each housing several small rocket interceptors that would flash to life, track the fiery exhaust of rising enemy missiles with infrared sensors, and smash into them. To increase the odds of a direct hit, the BAMBI interceptor upon nearing a missile would unfurl a 60-foot rotating wire net known as a "spinning spider web" that was laced with steel pellets. After extensive study involving thousands of pages of documentation, BAMBI was canceled by the Kennedy administration after being found costly and unworkable.[21]

Convinced that technical strides had changed all that, Graham worked to update BAMBI. The advent of more accurate guidance systems, which could pinpoint targets, would end the need for the "spider web," he decided. And miniaturization would allow more interceptors to be put in each battle station, increasing the system's power. He called the refined idea Global Ballistic Missile Defense, or GBMD.

In February 1980, General Graham briefed Reagan on the plan. The meeting occurred in Nashua, New Hampshire, just before a key debate among presidential candidates. Reagan's campaign was in turmoil at that point, riven by staff disagreements and reeling at having just lost the Iowa caucuses. Iowa, which Reagan considered a second home because of his days in Davenport and Des Moines as a radio broadcaster, had been considered a sure thing. In New Hampshire, Reagan and his advisers were under enormous pressure. It had to be the turning point. They would take the state or sink out of sight. Into this cauldron came Graham. Reagan and his advisers were sitting around a table in a motel room when the retired general laid out the antimissile idea.

"Mr. Reagan was very interested," Graham recalled. "He took out his cards and began writing notes to himself. At this point a few of my colleagues became a little irritated with me because I was taking more time than I was supposed to—not because I wanted to, but because he did."[22]

The key selling point for General Graham's GBMD idea was that the technology was rather simple, "off the shelf," as he liked to say, although that was stretching it. However, many Reagan advisers favored a more exotic approach that required further research—lasers, whose intense beams promised, years and decades hence, to dance across the heavens at the speed of light to knock out enemy missiles. Unlike General Graham's rocket interceptors, each one of which could knock out one missile, a laser in theory could be fired repeatedly, enhancing its powers of destruction.

An important laser advocate was Senator Malcolm A. Wallop, Republican of Wyoming, a balding, fiery conservative who had embraced the defensive idea and urged it on Reagan. During the summer of 1979, Wallop sent the candidate-to-be a typewritten draft of an antimissile article for the journal *Strategic Review*. Reagan returned it with notations.[23] In the finished article, which ran in the fall 1979 issue of the magazine, Wallop asserted that "technology is rendering the 'balance of terror' obsolete," foreshadowing the "impotent and obsolete" line of Reagan's Star Wars speech. Wallop described how enemy missiles could be zapped by chemical lasers, giant devices that got their energy by explosively combining fuels similar to those used in rockets. The first laser battle station could be in space by the mid-1980s, he wrote. A fleet of twenty-four, each with enough fuel for a thousand "shots," could give birth to a new defensive era. "If an all-out effort on the scale of the Manhattan Project were mounted," Wallop argued, "a full-fledged defense could materialize well before the close of the 1980s."[24]

That summer while grilling steaks at a barbecue near Lake Tahoe, Reagan and Wallop discussed the coming campaign, with Wallop urging that space-based defenses be a major theme. "Reagan said he was going to make a big issue of it," Angelo M. Codevilla, a Wallop aide, recalled. "Later I was asked to give Deaver some material on it, but he turned out to be very unenthusiastic, to put it mildly."[25] Indeed, Reagan's top managers, despite their candidate's growing personal enthusiasm for antimissile defense, had decided it would be political suicide to flaunt the issue in public given its reputation as a cause of the far right. "The political people prevailed," Anderson recalled. "And I think they were right. Even as president, the roof fell in when he announced the goal. As a candidate, it would have been worse."[26]

But in the towering glass edifice of the Renaissance Center, carefully isolated from the urban decay of Detroit, Reagan quietly approved an antimissile item in the Republican platform during the party's convention in July 1980. It called for "vigorous research and development of an effective antiballistic-missile system, such as is already at hand in the Soviet Union, as well as more modern ABM technologies." The platform also called for a new round of nuclear weapons and missiles, the ultimate goal being "overall military and technological superiority over the Soviet Union."[27] As planned, antimissile defense never emerged as a major issue in the presidential campaign or debates between candidates.

Soon after his landslide victory of November 1980, Reagan showed increasing interest in antimissile arms. In December, the president-elect questioned Republican Senator Harrison H. Schmitt—chairman of the Senate Subcommittee on Science, Technology and Space and a former astronaut—about the feasibility of modern antimissile technologies, particularly lasers. "The meeting lasted about twenty minutes," Schmitt recalled. "We were talking about science and technology in general. Then, about halfway through the session, he made a statement that he was concerned that we could not just keep building nuclear missiles forever—that ultimately their proliferation would get us into serious trouble. He asked what I thought about the possibility of strategic defense, especially with lasers. We spent half the conversation talking about it. When I later heard his speech, the phrases sounded very familiar. The words had the same ring."[28]

BETWEEN his inauguration in January 1981 and the Star Wars speech in March 1983, Reagan's talks with his technical advisers were dominated by the question of feasibility. The president himself, the oldest man ever sworn in to the office, needed no convincing. He was morally committed to defense. He admired "this great technology of ours" and personally thought the goal of strategic defense could probably be achieved. The question was whether reputable experts agreed. "Reagan had embraced it in a philosophical sense," said former aide Anderson, who left the White House during Reagan's first term. "The main question was technological, can it be done, and then questions of economic and political feasibility."[29]

With Reagan generally committed, various groups and advisers, including General Graham and Senator Wallop, stepped up efforts in 1981 and 1982 to win presidential approval of their antimissile plans. So did Teller. After all, he now had a breakthrough to talk about, the X-ray laser.

THE Hungarian physicist staged a coup in the administration's first days, using his White House contacts to have a young protege named as President Reagan's science adviser. This was another of the "miracles." It came by a strangely circuitous route, after the White House in early 1981 had initially expressed doubts that a science adviser was needed at all. Finally, the administration said one would be appointed but he would have a smaller staff and budget than his predecessor—and less access to the president. The coolness arose from the fact that Reagan aides felt science advising had degenerated into special-interest pleading for more research funds. They wanted personal loyalty to the president put above ties to the scientific community. In fact, the new administration's overall terms were so unappealing that more than a dozen prominent scientists and engineers turned down the post.[30]

Into this vacuum came Teller touting the virtues of George A. (Jay) Keyworth II, a little-known, boyishly enthusiastic 41-year-old nuclear physicist from Los Alamos. In the 1970s Keyworth had played an important role in Teller's reintroduction at Los Alamos, where, after decades of bitter absence, the Hungarian physicist returned to consult and lecture. Keyworth had no power base in Washington other than that provided by Teller. In May 1981 he was named Reagan's science adviser.

"Bluntly," Keyworth later recalled, "the reason I was in that office is because Edward first proposed me, and the president very much admires Edward."[31]

Keyworth was born in Boston, son of a New England furniture factory president. Educated at Yale and Duke, he was an Ivy Leaguer who acquired an affection for the West while working in New Mexico. He was affable, even impish, with an easygoing style. He often wore western belt buckles and padded around his White House office in stocking feet. He drove a Porsche. Since he had little experience in national science policy or the complexities of the federal budget process, it was feared in some quarters that he would simply be a Teller surrogate. Indeed, Keyworth was typical of the bright young scientists that had long been groomed for positions of power by

Teller. In Washington, the young science adviser told new friends he looked on Teller as a father figure. It came as no surprise that Keyworth appointed Teller to the White House Science Council, a group of seasoned experts who were to advise the new science adviser.[32]

As it turned out, Keyworth would need all the advice he could get. During his first meeting with Reagan, in August 1981, the president quickly turned a casual conversation about families into a discussion of attitudes about nuclear arms. "He felt extremely uncomfortable in an ethical sense, in a stability sense, from the point of view of the man who controls the button," Keyworth recalled. "He said it sent shivers up his spine."[33] With the president eager for expert advice on antimissile systems, Keyworth spent much time during his first year in office learning about the field and critiquing various proposals, especially those he considered risky and irresponsible.

TELLER, already a force in the formal process of advising the White House, penetrated an even more important center of power—a highly organized group of Reagan friends, most of them millionaires, who wanted the president to adopt the antimissile goal. Remarkably, Teller succeeded in having this group promote his ideas even though it initially allied itself with his competition, General Graham.

The group was formed in May 1981 by Karl R. Bendetsen, undersecretary of the army for President Truman and later chairman of the board of the Champion International Corporation, a forest products company. Tall and patrician, with piercing dark eyes, Bendetsen had been raised on the West Coast, graduated from Stanford University Law School, and served extensively in the military. As an Army colonel in World War II, he directed the internment of 110,000 people of Japanese origin. Very successful in private life, he championed conservative causes and backed them financially. Bendetsen was a founding member of the Committee on the Present Danger, started in 1976 to publicize the "the Soviet drive for dominance." In 1981, he approached General Graham after hearing him give a speech on antimissile defense at the Army-Navy Club in Washington, offering to help raise money for the founding of a lobbying group.[34]

Soon recruited to Bendetsen's effort were such members of the president's "kitchen cabinet" as brewer Joseph Coors, oilman William A. Wilson, and food magnate Jacquelin Hume. Bendetsen had gotten to know Hume through the Bohemian Club of San Francisco, whose all-male membership included a number of prominent national figures. Bendetsen wanted Hume on the panel because he was a good friend of Edwin Meese's; Meese was a member of the Bohemian Club who had become Reagan's powerful White House counselor. Through this circuit, Bendetsen felt he would be assured direct access to the president.[35]

To this group of wealthy industrialists, who were in their 60s and 70s, Bendetsen added a sole scientist—Teller, whom he first met in the 1940s and subsequently befriended at the Hoover Institution, where Bendetsen was an overseer and Teller a fellow.[36] The official White House liaison to the panel was science adviser Keyworth, although Bendetsen eventually communicated just as extensively on antimissile topics with Meese, Keyworth's immediate boss. The group decided it needed $250,000 to conduct a study. Meese at the White House agreed to help raise money, making telephone calls to a series of wealthy conservatives.[37]

Giving itself the name High Frontier, the group agreed to try to influence government policy by producing a detailed antimissile report. Once the report was completed—to which end Graham employed some two dozen consultants, including those refining Global Ballistic Missile Defense as well as Wood, Teller's protege—it would be presented to the president, hopefully by the end of 1981. The group's plan for a new government antimissile policy was known as the "Reagan Initiative."[38]

On Saturday, September 5, 1981, the group held its first formal meeting. It occurred in Washington. Among the topics was the need to keep the work secret. As Bendetsen said in a memo, the group wanted no credit for influencing the White House and was eager to avoid tipping off potential critics in and out of government. Most especially, there were to be no press reports about the group or the interest of high federal officials.[39]

Meanwhile at the White House, the antimissile issue, abandoned for strategic reasons during the campaign, was being quietly resurrected. It came to life during daily national policy meetings in the office of Meese, counselor to the president, which were attended by national security adviser Richard V. Allen and domestic policy aide Anderson. "We all shared a strong commitment to missile defense and used every opportunity to further the concept," Anderson recalled.[40] Keyworth was recruited to this small group, if only because he was seen as Teller's man. "Since Keyworth regarded Edward Teller—the most distinguished, well-known proponent of missile defense outside of government—with awe, we were not surprised to find Keyworth generally supportive of missile defense," said Anderson.[41]

THE first formal White House meeting on antimissile defense occurred in Meese's office on Monday, September 14, 1981. Several members of High Frontier were present, including Teller.[42] Meese, as chairman of the meeting, sat at the head of a small, dining-room-sized table, his back to windows that overlooked Pennsylvania Avenue. To his right sat Bendetsen, General Graham and science adviser Keyworth. To his left sat Teller, Anderson and a Meese aide. The main item on the agenda was whether there was enough justification to redouble the nation's research on antimissile arms. The group was filled with a sense of optimism. The X-ray laser showed promise, as did General Graham's idea for rocket interceptors based in space. Great leaps of technology were clearly possible, as had been demonstrated that April during the maiden flight of the world's first reusable spaceship, the winged space shuttle. Its success was seen as a portent of bigger things to come.

"I felt a rising sense of excitement," Anderson recalled. "It became clear that not only did everyone feel we should pursue the idea of missile defense, but they also deeply believed it could be done. There was also general agreement that a major part of a missile defense effort would probably be based in space, far above the earth's surface."[43] The group talked of using space arms to shield MX missiles on the ground, for which the Pentagon was then struggling to find a secure basing mode. But Teller insisted this goal was only a start. Defenses, he told the White House officials, should eventually be strong enough to protect not only missiles, but cities and allies as well. The goal, Teller stressed, should be "assured survival" rather than assured destruction.[44]

The meeting was of considerable moment. Not only was the occasion significant, it being the first time in the Reagan presidency that Teller had formally shared his vision with the White House, but more important, Teller, in uttering the words "assured survival," had begun a pattern of bold advocacy he would pursue with great intensity during the coming months as he sought government approval for the antimissile goal. He pushed the rhetorical limits. As had often been the case in past endeavors, Teller during his first White House presentation had quickly moved beyond his colleagues, proposing a goal that was extraordinarily ambitious. "Assured survival" conjured up visions of a shield that was virtually leakproof, since only one enemy warhead would have to slip through an antimissile system in order to reduce Washington, New York or any other major city to rubble. The feasibility of "assured survival," despite its vast challenge, despite what many experts would describe as its patent impossibility, would be vigorously promoted by Teller in and around the White House, eventually with Reagan himself.[45]

THE High Frontier group continued to meet that fall, often on weekends when there were fewer scheduling conflicts. All group members received security clearances so they could learn about and discuss the secret details of the new technologies and weapons. Soon, the group moved its meetings to the Heritage Foundation, a conservative think tank that General Graham won to the antimissile cause.

The group's initial harmony did not last, however. General Graham and Teller were soon attacking each other's proposals. Teller charged that Graham's idea was expensive, antiquated and impotent—that it would fail to stop a significant number of the more than 1,000 missiles the Soviets could hurl at America in a nuclear attack. Graham countered that an orbiting X-ray laser had a "fundamental flaw"—that it was particularly vulnerable to enemy attack. While other weapons could protect themselves, an X-ray laser waiting in orbit for an enemy attack would have to destroy itself in order to fire a beam at the attacker in self-defense.[46] At the group's next meeting, Teller and protege Wood proposed a solution. American X-ray lasers would be based on the ground, perhaps in submarines, and "popped up" into space at the first sign of trouble, ready to wage war. This kind of deployment got around the problem of space vulnerability, they argued.[47] Their plan for "pop-up" deployment from the ground eventually became a centerpiece of the X-ray laser program and distinguished it from all other Star Wars weapons, most of which were to be based in space.

General Graham continued to criticize the X-ray laser, saying it was a bad idea no matter what. The public would never accept the placing of nuclear weapons in space, he said. Moreover, the X-ray laser would take years and possibly decades to develop, whereas his proposal was ready to go. In the end, General Graham felt Teller's adherence to a nuclear concept was motivated by deep personal needs. "The man is carrying a load and has taken a lot of abuse as the 'father' of the H-bomb," Graham told me in 1985. "He wants to see nuclear technology turn out to be the answer in the opposite direction, to save the Western world."[48]

While opposing Teller and the X-ray laser, General Graham sought wider approval for his system of Global Ballistic Missile Defense, briefing both State Department and Defense Department officials. There it came under heavy fire, although Graham became aware of the rejection only slowly. Various federal analysts found his antimissile idea unrealistic and unworkable, saying it had "substantial risks" and "serious technical and economic shortcomings."[49]

At a second White House staff meeting on October 12 in Meese's office, Graham breezily said support for his plan was growing throughout the government, including the Department of Defense. White House aide Anderson, present at the meeting, recalled that the status report of Graham and Bendetsen was "glowing." Toward the end of the meeting, the small White House group considered naming a crash program to develop antimissile arms Global Ballistic Missile Defense, after the High Frontier study.[50]

No such thing came to pass. For a number of reasons, Graham's fortunes continued to fall. More important, those of Teller and Wood rose rapidly as they applied increasing pressure and eloquence in championing the X-ray laser. Their powers of persuasion were so great that the High Frontier panel took the unusual step of asking the White House to intervene in the fate of the fledgling technology.

On October 20, 1981, Bendetsen wrote Meese a remarkable letter to hail the X-ray laser and recommend that it get an immediate financial boost. The letter was noteworthy for its optimistic forecasts and precise technical detail, being laced with secret data. Bendetsen started the letter by noting that the High Frontier panel had reviewed the X-ray laser in "classified briefings and discussions, and has assessed its potential impact on defense of the Nation against Soviet ballistic missile attack." Because of the "urgency" of the panel's findings, he wrote, "we are communicating them at this time, in advance of our full report."[51]

The device, Bendetsen wrote, directed a small fraction of the total explosive yield of a hydrogen bomb "into one or more tightly focused and independently aimable beams. Each of these beams has about a million times the brightness of the bomb's undirected energy, so that the lethal range of a sub-megaton bomb can readily be extended to distances of thousands of miles." Although not labeled as such, that statement was clearly a goal rather than an accomplishment. Livermore's crude Dauphin experiment had nothing to do with demonstrating a millionfold increase in a bomb's brightness, nor had it shown such an impressive range of destruction in space.

Continuing his letter, Bendetsen said Livermore had proposed to deliver "a fully weaponized" X-ray laser "for ballistic missile defense on a five year time scale." This schedule was totally unrealistic. Such a brief period would be unusual for the development of an ordinary nuclear weapon in the 1980s, much less one meant to push into a new realm of physics.

Bendetsen then discussed its aid to war. "This initial technology," he wrote, "would be useful against Soviet reentry vehicles as they reentered the atmosphere, against all Soviet satellites, and against ballistic missiles themselves as they are launched from Soviet submarines off the U.S. coast." His statement implied the laser would be too weak to reach all the way to the Soviet Union and the most menacing threats of all. But he quickly addressed the point, saying a stronger version of the device was on the horizon. "Second generation X-ray laser technology, which is expected to become available three years subsequently, will permit attack of Soviet boosters as they enter space from central Asian silos or from Soviet submarines in distant oceans."

The overall vision was sweeping— a first-generation device by 1986 and a second-generation one by 1989 that would fire "tightly focused and independently aimable beams" to destroy enemy missiles over long distances. In particular, the idea of multiple beams was revolutionary. Heretofore antimissile lasers had been seen as having one beam. Multiple beams firing in unison would act quickly, saving minutes and seconds, a precious commodity during antimissile war.

"The Panel therefore concludes," Bendetsen wrote, "that X-ray lasers may represent the largest advance in strategic warfare since the hydrogen bomb itself." It was a statement sure to give any reader pause, and to make General Graham's ideas or any other antimissile proposal seem quite crude in comparison.

Bendetsen closed the letter by saying the panel "strongly" urged the administration to increase the device's funding. A rise of just $50 million over two years, he wrote, would result in a "fifteen month reduction in the time before this possibly pivotal technology can be deployed to defend our country from attack from space." In other words, the first X-ray lasers might be available for deployment as soon as 1985, just four years hence.

The Bendetsen letter contained no caveats and no explanation of the vision's basis. There was no mention of the single explosive test, no mention of the evolutionary process needed to achieve desired energy levels, and no mention of possible pitfalls.

General Graham recalled that he was annoyed by the letter and the fact that Teller had succeeded in getting the panel to intercede on behalf of the Livermore effort. But there was nothing he could do. Bendetsen "had the greatest respect for Ed Teller, as everybody did," Graham remarked, "so the panel went along with Teller's funding proposal."[52]

Significantly, the glowing promotion of the X-ray laser to the White House, and the commitment of the Livermore lab to an extremely ambitious plan for its perfection, had been done without the knowledge of Woodruff, the man ostensibly in charge of the secret program.[53]

As Teller's vision was praised within High Frontier and the White House, Keyworth, the president's science adviser, took several steps to challenge Teller's rivals. In September 1981 he hired an antimissile skeptic, Victor H. Reis, to help him analyze weapon systems. Reis had engineering degrees from the Rensselaer Polytechnic Institute, Yale and Princeton. He had worked at the Massachusetts Institute of Technology. In government he had specialized in sober analysis of exotic military projects. Before Keyworth hired him, he had written a Pentagon study that challenged Senator Wallop's *Strategic Review* article, saying that up to 1,444 space lasers would be needed to stop Soviet missiles, not 24, and that the system would fail in any event because enemy missiles could be protected from lasers by a simple layer of cork.[54]

From his new position in the White House as deputy to the science adviser, Reis and his aides went to High Frontier meetings and studied other antimissile plans.[55] What got most of his attention was not General Graham's idea for Global Ballistic Missile Defense, which seemed to be self-destructing on its own. Rather it was an effort outside High Frontier—Wallop's push for giant lasers powered by chemical reactions, prototypes of which had been studied by the Pentagon and were gaining vocal support on Capitol Hill. Congressional advocates were known as the "Laser Lobby." They included Senator Wallop, who had shared his manuscript with candidate Reagan, and Senator Schmitt, the former astronaut who had talked with the president-elect. They wanted to quickly deploy such lasers in space. The Laser Lobby had rallied around a laser known as Alpha. Proposed in the Carter administration, Alpha was seen by the government as an exotic test to understand the limits of laser technology. But the Laser Lobby wanted to place dozens of them in space as working weapons to fire at enemy missiles. Keyworth was strongly opposed to the idea.[56]

Keyworth and Reis ultimately fought the Laser Lobby with a subtle technical argument. They said the current generation of chemical lasers, including Alpha, had wavelengths that were too long. This meant their optics would be gigantic and their beams only mildly concentrated. A decade or more in the future, they said, exotic lasers with smaller wavelengths would be much better at focusing an intense beam of light on a speeding missile thousands of miles away in space. The shorter a laser's wavelength, the more destructive energy it could pour onto a target.

Politically, the logic of wavelength gave Keyworth a way to divert the congressional push for rapid deployment into long-range research that was relatively harmless. And he pursued it with fervor. After all, a paranoid enemy might interpret the vast, expensive job of deploying antimissile arms as an act of war. The diversionary tactic would prove increasingly popular with scientific moderates in the Reagan administration and Congress. In late 1981, Keyworth gained a powerful ally in the form of Anthony Battista, a Democratic staffer on the House Armed Services Committee. Together they agreed to try to scrap Alpha and to champion lasers of shorter wavelength.[57]

The war of the wavelength also had salutary repercussions for Teller. As was well known in Washington at this time, even among those without top-secret security clearances, the laser with the shortest wavelength of all was the X-ray laser.

As Keyworth fought the Laser Lobby, he went out of his way to aid his mentor in ways that were quite down to earth. On November 2, 1981, he made his White House offices available to Teller so the Hungarian physicist could give the High Frontier panel yet another secret briefing. Those in attendance included Bendetsen, Coors and Hume.[58] At the meeting, Teller hailed not just the X-ray laser but a whole new class of nuclear arms he said were coming into existence. He called them the "third-generation" weapons. The first and second generations were seen as the atomic and hydrogen bombs, which radiated their energy spherically. In contrast, the third generation was to send its energy into beams. Teller told the High Frontier panel that the X-ray laser was furthest along of the third-generation ideas but that others were on the horizon, including microwave and particle-beam weapons.[59]

The crude experiment in the Nevada desert had now given birth, at least in theory, to a whole new family of nuclear arms. This mounting wave of newness dazzled members of the Bendetsen panel and soon overwhelmed all antimissile rivals, paving the way for Teller's conquest of the White House.

IN December 1981, the rivalry that had marked High Frontier meetings came to an end as the group split in two. Bendetsen, Teller and the kitchen cabinet separated into a small group to quietly lobby the White House for advanced antimissile arms that needed a period of gestation, including the X-ray laser and its exotic cousins. General Graham and his consultants moved in a different direction, keeping the name High Frontier to publicly promote his system of small, "off-the-shelf" interceptor rockets. Graham was convinced that if the antimissile baby were not laid before the public, the federal bureaucracy would strangle it in its cradle.[60]

For Teller, the split was a personal triumph. He had come from behind to take the lead in the intellectual race for a persuasive antimissile plan. Moreover, his victory had vast implications in terms of presidential access. Bendetsen and the kitchen cabinet could visit the White House with relative ease. General Graham could not.

THE American economy was on its knees early in 1982, mired in one of the worst recessions of modern times. Unemployment was up. The gross national product was down. The prime interest rate stood at an all-time high, stifling growth. Soup lines appeared around the country. On Friday, January 8, 1982, the Bureau of Labor Statistics reported that the nation's unemployment rate had risen to 8.9 percent, the second highest monthly level since the start of World War Two. At the White House, Reagan told reporters the news was tragic.[61]

That same day, Reagan took a break from the sometimes bleak job of being president to engage in a bit of research about one of his favorite topics. He met with Bendetsen and his panel to hear their antimissile report and to discuss the feasibility of defense against the Soviet threat. It was the first such gathering at the White House. Given the secretive nature of the enterprise, the meeting was kept off the president's official schedule. It started at 2:00 P.M. Originally planned for the Oval Office, the meeting was moved across the hall to the Roosevelt Room, where a larger group could assemble around a large mahogany conference table that could comfortably seat twenty.[62]

White House aides in attendance included Anderson, Keyworth, Meese, and William P. Clark, who had recently become the president's national security adviser. Clark would eventually play a pivotal role in the birth of Star Wars. Tall and lanky, he was one of Reagan's most trusted advisers, a long-time associate who served as chief of staff when Reagan was governor of California. Around the White House, Clark often wore a dark blue suit, white shirt and hand-tooled, black cowboy boots.[63] Outside advisers at the meeting included Bendetsen, Hume, Coors and, by several accounts, Teller. No less an authority than Bendetsen himself recalled that the Hungarian physicist was present. Others disagree.[64] In any case, whether Teller was there personally is of little importance, since his spiritual presence dominated the gathering.

Reagan greeted his old friends and listened as Bendetsen summarized the panel's findings. The president then asked questions. The discussion was lively. The meeting had been scheduled to last fifteen minutes but went on for nearly an hour. The group said advances in intercepting enemy missiles made the field more promising than ever before. It recommended that the nation embark on a program of advanced research rather than trying to actually build defenses with General Graham's off-the-shelf rockets or the current generation of big lasers.

"The president expressed great interest," Bendetsen told me. The conversation, he said, focused on directed-energy weapons that might be used to destroy aircraft as well as missiles. There was much talk of lasers. "Our little committee frankly told the president that the Pentagon was experimenting with lasers that might have only limited capacity because the wavelengths were too long," Bendetsen said, adding that as an alternative "we talked about the X-ray laser."[65] In conclusion, the group said the time was ripe for the president to make a speech announcing the start of a crash program of antimissile research similar to the Manhattan Project that produced the world's first atomic bomb.

Bendetsen gave Reagan a two-page written summary. It said the Soviet missile threat was increasing and foreseeably could not be matched, and that the Soviets were apparently about to deploy "powerful directed energy weapons" in space. These, the report said, would allow the Russians to "militarily dominate both space and the earth, conclusively altering the world balance of power." In response, the report called on America to abandon the current strategy of Mutual Assured Destruction for one of Assured Survival that relied on defense. That phrase was identical to the one Teller had championed months earlier, implying that the nation's goal should be the creation of a shield that was virtually leakproof. The Bendetsen report said nothing of General Graham's more modest antimissile ideas. Instead it called on the nation's "directed energy efforts" to be "greatly intensified" with "urgent action." It noted the average time for the Pentagon to select and acquire weapons was thirteen years. "We cannot survive such delays," the report warned darkly.[66]

White House aide Anderson saw the meeting as a turning point in the history of the Reagan presidency. "As I left the Roosevelt Room," he recalled, "I was personally convinced that President Reagan was going ahead with missile defense. How and when I didn't know. But I did know that whenever he decided to move forward on such an important policy path he rarely looked back or changed his mind."[67]

Bendetsen told me: "I don't want to claim credit, but I think we were the ones who convinced him to go forward."[68]

After the meeting, President Reagan wrote Bendetsen to thank him for the panel's service. He also predicted action. "You can be sure," Reagan said, "that we will be moving ahead rapidly with the next phase of this effort."[69]

GENERAL GRAHAM heard about the meeting only after it occurred. He was furious. His resentment was fueled by his personal exclusion, by the neglect of his rocket-interceptor idea, and by the news, recounted by Bendetsen, that the White House wanted to avoid any kind of public advocacy by his team.

"I told him that I had already gone public," Graham said. "The document was going to be on the streets."[70]

His bid for presidential access denied, General Graham in March 1982 publicly unveiled his idea, despite continuing protests from Bendetsen and other panel members. *High Frontier: A New National Strategy* was a 175-page book filled with a detailed description of Graham's vision as well as futuristic drawings of battles in space. It made no mention of the original High Frontier panel or its kitchen-cabinet members, instead crediting the work to his team of consultants. In a foreword, Graham frankly noted the system's limits, saying it might only stop a fraction of an enemy's missiles. But, he argued, even such limited protection could save the nation's offensive missile forces from "a disarming first strike."[71]

At the White House, the situation in early 1982 proceeded to become quite delicate for science adviser Keyworth as he was asked by White House officials to give his assessment of the ideas of his mentor Teller and the Bendetsen group. On one level, Keyworth had expressed enthusiasm to Bendetsen about his group's work and had lent aid in small ways that meant a lot. In a letter to Bendetsen on White House stationery, Keyworth praised the group's "collective skill and experience," adding "I laud your efforts."[72] Bendetsen was sure he had secured Keyworth's firm support, telling his colleagues he was "confident" the science adviser "thinks well of our proposals."[73]

But in the privacy of a White House staff meeting in early 1982, Keyworth expressed misgivings about the Bendetsen plan, saying it had "very difficult technical aspects."[74] In a small way, he was exercising his own judgment and apparently trying to distance himself from the unqualified zeal of his mentor. At Meese's suggestion, Keyworth established a team from his White House Science Council to assess the ideas, and had his deputy Reis lay out the ground rules.[75] Keyworth bent over backward to get his mentor on the study team. But its chairman, Edward A. Frieman, vice president of Science Applications, Inc., a defense consulting firm, objected strongly, saying the aged physicist was too ardent an antimissile advocate. So Teller was dropped.[76]

Excluded from the panel's top-secret deliberations, Teller nonetheless monitored them closely throughout 1982 and pressed his case on chairman Frieman whenever the two scientists saw each other at full meetings of the White House Science Council. Teller's message was always the same. And it was consistent with the one conveyed in Bendetsen's October 1981 letter to the White House—the X-ray laser could be available in four or five years and could become the centerpiece of an antimissile revolution.[77] Teller was sure. The change was coming.

Teller was extremely wary of the White House study, fearing its findings would undercut his stance or at least be less enthusiastic than he felt the situation warranted. He was also mildly frustrated by the Bendetsen group, which had embraced his ideas but communicated them to the White House in its own way and at its own pace. So Teller repeatedly asked Keyworth for a private audience with the president, eager to recount the revolutionary details directly to the commander in chief. It was the kind of situation White House officials avoided at all costs. The president was too impressionable. Reagan was a man of great charm and warmth. A personal bond meant everything and could result in almost anything. His aides therefore made sure virtually no visitor saw the president alone, especially one as controversial as Teller. Moreover, Keyworth was struggling to be his own man. He did not want to carry water for Teller or anyone else. As a relatively junior member of the White House team, he had already experienced how difficult it could be to see the president, much less arrange a private audience for an outsider. He had little enthusiasm for discovering new limitations on his personal power. So the science adviser dodged the issue whenever his mentor brought it up.[78]

Teller was undeterred, going public to complain. The incident occurred on June 15, 1982, while Teller was being taped for a segment of the *Firing Line* television program, hosted by William F. Buckley, Jr., the influential conservative. Teller said lack of funds was inhibiting work on antimissile weapons and warned that in such areas the Soviet Union was forging ahead.[79]

Buckley: "Are you telling me that the Soviet Union is currently engaged in defensive work of the same kind that you recommend to America, which would have the effect of making it safe for them to launch a first strike?"

Teller: "I am not telling you that. I am only telling you that I have reason to suspect it. I have strong reason to suspect it."

Later in the show, Buckley suggested Teller make an urgent message on antimissile matters to President Reagan, drawing a parallel to the warning Einstein took Roosevelt in 1939 about the danger of Nazi Germany developing the atom bomb.

Teller: "May I tell you one little secret which is not classified? From the time that President Reagan has been nominated I had not a single occasion to talk to him."

Buckley: "Have you sought out such an occasion?"

Teller: "I have talked to people to whom I am close and who in turn are close to the president. I have tried what seemed to be reasonable to get action on these things. I may have been clumsy in one way or the other, but I am deeply grateful for any opportunity to speak about these things. I have lived through two world wars. I don't want to live through a third one."

I ONCE asked Teller about his antimissile meetings with President Reagan, saying the first I knew of was the one in January 1982 that Bendetsen told me about.

"Look," Teller replied, "if Bendetsen says something, fine. I have the feeling if I participate in such affairs that they are not covered by secrecy but by something very much stronger, namely privacy."

I said I was curious because on *Firing Line* he had said he had no opportunity to see the president.

Teller paused. "Aaaaah, I said that on *Firing Line*—and I will not contradict myself."

I pressed Teller on the point, saying Bendetsen had insisted that Teller and the kitchen cabinet first talked to the president in January 1982. (Years later, Reagan aide Anderson, in his book *Revolution*, reported the same thing.)

"Look," Teller said, "I'm not going to confirm or contradict what Bendetsen says. He is a very wonderful man. He is a good friend. If he says something, it is probably so. In fact, I trust Bendetsen. But that is he speaking, not I."[80]

TELLER'S wish for a private audience was granted, Reagan having watched the *Firing Line* program.[81] On September 14, 1982, he met with the president in the Oval Office. The physicist was 74, Reagan 71. Teller had been accompanied to the White House by his protege Wood, who waited outside. Several White House aides were present at the meeting.

"Mr. President," Teller said as he shook Reagan's hand, "third generation, third generation."[82]

Reagan looked confused, as if Teller was unexpectedly preparing to talk about his relatives. Then Teller explained his nuclear vision as the two men sat down on either side of the fireplace. It was a dramatic start. Teller, with his usual theatric flair, had set a powerful theme he then expanded upon in the course of the meeting.

Two generations of nuclear weapons had been developed, Teller said. Now there was a third one that promised a revolution in strategic affairs. Beams flashing from these new weapons had the potential to destroy enemy missiles, Teller assured the president. He used no notes and no charts. And he spoke with conviction. Teller also said there was evidence the Soviets were making strides in the same areas.[83]

Reagan asked if an American antimissile system could really be made to work.

"We have good evidence that it would," Teller replied.[84]

Present at the meeting was national security adviser Clark, clad in his cowboy boots. He indicated doubt, and questioned Teller closely on the third-generation idea.[85] Teller elaborated in some detail and went on to appeal for a dramatic increase in funds for X-ray laser and other antimissile research at Livermore.[86] Altogether, the meeting lasted a half hour.

At the end, Reagan seemed receptive to the idea, comparing it to an earlier military feat. "When the submarine was first proposed, nobody believed it," Reagan remarked.[87]

Teller's visit made a vivid impression on Ray Pollock, a National Security Council staffer present at the encounter. It was Pollock's first meeting with the president, the experience clearly etched in his memory. "The whole thing was quite relaxed," he recalled. "It seemed to me that Teller had talked to Reagan before."[88]

A week after Teller's visit, *Aviation Week & Space Technology*, read widely in Washington's military circles, announced that Teller had met with Reagan at the White House. It cited no source. The magazine said Teller asked for increases in X-ray laser funding of $200 million a year "over the next several years."[89]

The White House meeting was a personal coup for Teller, who used it as leverage to continue his campaign. On September 25, he wrote a follow-up letter to Reagan, going into details of the X-ray laser research and again appealing for a funding rise. "The limitations in budget," Teller wrote, called for "immediate corrective action." In closing, Teller said, "I dare to look forward to a decision both timely and favorable regarding American exploration of 'Third Generation' nuclear weapons technology at a pace commensurate with its promise for replacing Mutual Assured Destruction with assured survival."[90]

Then, Teller went out of his way to quietly advertise his advice to the president, sending copies of the Reagan letter to several administration officials. Those who received copies included Vice President George Bush, national security adviser William Clark, Energy Secretary James Edwards, science adviser George Keyworth, presidential counselor Edwin Meese and Defense Secretary Caspar Weinberger.

TELLER was prepared to do much more than advise Reagan and his White House aides. He went so far as to draft a presidential speech—an announcement to the nation of a crash antimissile program, meant to be included in Reagan's State of the Union Address that January. On December 29, 1982, Teller sent Bendetsen a draft of the proposed insert.[91] It was a shortened and modified version of a text that had been prepared by members of the Bendetsen panel.[92]

Teller's draft started by hailing all kinds of breakthroughs in high technology, especially computers. It then noted the swift success of the Manhattan A-bomb Project and the Apollo moon landing, the former achieved in less than four years and the latter in less than six. The nation, it said, was now ready to exploit "new and revolutionary" ideas for defense, and would start to do so immediately. The first goal of the antimissile effort would be to defend the MX missile, ultimately spreading the protective shield to "our people and our cities," Teller wrote. This passage had two important implications. First, since the MX missile was then nearing completion, it suggested that a rudimentary antimissile system could be available quite quickly. Reagan in his Star Wars speech would propose nothing so immediate. Second, in promising protection for "our people and our cities," Teller was again envisioning an antimissile defense that was virtually perfect. Most knowledgeable experts considered this a pipe dream. General Graham in his High Frontier report had been satisfied to thwart a fraction of incoming enemy missiles. Even Reagan in his Star Wars speech would promise nothing so impenetrable, although he hinted at that goal.

In closing, Teller dismissed an anticipated wave of criticism from skeptics. The nation had a duty to prove them wrong, he wrote, and to free not only the nation "but also the world" from the danger of nuclear war.

The insert went nowhere, despite the obvious time and effort taken in its preparation. Reagan's aides decided the nation was unprepared for such a bold move. But the idea of a speech in itself was prescient. Events were fast conspiring to elevate the status of the antimissile issue, with Reagan soon turning his long-term interest into a personal crusade.

THE year 1982 was a time of intellectual turmoil over the proper role of nuclear armament in American policy. The Reagan administration's arms buildup and strident anticommunist rhetoric, abetted by occasional statements about the feasibility of fighting and winning a nuclear war, had fostered an unusual level of domestic discontent. Reaction was sharp. Substantial gains were made by the nuclear freeze movement, which sought a halt in the testing, production and deployment of nuclear arms. Protests grew, reaching new heights in June when an antinuclear rally in New York City's Central Park drew a half million people, far more than any demonstration during the antiwar movement of the early 1970s.[93] Intellectual ferment soared. In 1982, Jonathan Schell published the best-seller *The Fate of the Earth*, which pictured nuclear war as so ruinous to the earth's environment that it was seen as challenging the basis of nuclear deterrence.[94]

Public dissatisfaction gained a new kind of moral credibility when the American Catholic Bishops drafted a Pastoral Letter on War and Peace that echoed the nation's growing antinuclear sentiment. "We fear that our world and nation are headed in the wrong direction," the Bishops wrote. "More weapons with greater destructive potential are produced every day. More and more nations are seeking to become nuclear powers. In our quest for more and more security we fear we are actually becoming less and less secure."[95]

Late that year the antinuclear mood peaked as Congress dealt a stunning blow to the centerpiece of the administration's strategic modernization program, the ten-warhead MX missile. In December, the House rejected the president's request for $988 million to produce the first five MX missiles for deployment, following widespread debate about the wisdom of placing them in closely spaced silos. According to White House aides, this vote drove home to Reagan how difficult it would be to get funds to continue a major buildup of offensive land-based missiles.[96] While a totalitarian state like the Soviet Union easily produced one type of missile after another, the United States had the mixed blessing of democracy, ensuring no simple consensus on something as controversial as nuclear arms. The missile gap gnawed at the president and his men.

By all accounts, Reagan was fairly desperate to make a positive contribution to the nation's security at this point. The traditional means seemed to have reached an impasse. Moreover, his advisers were growing eager to try something, anything, to help overcome the political liabilities that arose from the perception of Reagan as a hard-line cold warrior, as long as it did not alienate the conservative constituencies that had helped bring the president to power. What they needed was a bold move that challenged the Soviets, diverted attention from the military buildup, and could be seen as inherently peaceful. Now, in late 1982, Reagan took the first, hesitant step in that direction, beginning to grope toward the option that had long been recommended by Teller, by Meese, by Anderson and by his closest California friends. Just as important, political pragmatists in the White House decided the time was right to aid the president's exploration. The process began at a December meeting between the president and the Joint Chiefs of Staff. There Reagan asked a single, pregnant question.

"What if we begin to move away from our total reliance on offense to deter a nuclear attack and moved toward a relatively greater reliance on defense?"[97]

Bells began to go off in the minds of the Joint Chiefs. Later, one of them asked national security adviser Clark if they were being told to take a hard look at the question.

"Yes," Clark replied.

Clark also mobilized his own staff, telling Robert C. McFarlane, the deputy national security adviser, to explore every nuance of the antimissile issue.[98] McFarlane was a short, slight Marine lieutenant colonel with an earnest nature and a methodical approach to his work. He quickly made the antimissile issue his own.

ONE of the Chiefs most troubled by the nation's nuclear turmoil was Admiral James D. Watkins, Chief of Naval Operations. A devout Catholic who attended Mass daily, he was deeply attentive when the Bishops said nuclear weapons were immoral. Admiral Watkins took such matters quite seriously. His staff called him "Hamlet" because of his propensity to brood over decisions with moral implications. Twice a month, Admiral Watkins and the other service chiefs met for a prayer breakfast, eventually discussing the Bishops' letter. "Most of us agreed that we had never approached our responsibilities from what you might call a moral direction," he told a reporter, adding that he personally decided to go back to ethics fundamentals, not the "Soviet threat," in forming a stance on nuclear arms. This meditation reinforced long-held doubts. "Mutual assured destruction has never been a concept that I could understand," he said. "I don't think it's morally sound."[99]

In addition to the ethical dilemma prompted by the Bishops' letter, Watkins faced one that was quite practical. He was disturbed to learn in late 1982 that officers and enlisted men were beginning to leave the Navy in response to the Bishops' stance.[100]

As Watkins searched his soul and looked for ways to answer the president's antimissile query, he arranged to meet Teller, whose proposals were the talk in Washington among individuals with top-secret security clearances. "I am inadequate in my understanding of where we are technologically," Watkins recalled himself as thinking. "I've got to talk to a visionary."[101]

On January 20, 1983, a Thursday, Teller and Watkins met in the admiral's Pentagon office for an hour, Teller talking incessantly, Watkins asking only an occasional question. American X-ray lasers could be based in submarines, Teller told the Navy man, and popped up into space at the first sign of trouble. Teller also described other emerging antimissile technologies, including ground-based lasers whose beams could be bounced off mirrors in space toward enemy missiles. The Hungarian physicist was emphatic in stressing that the defensive goal was coming within grasp for the first time. As he spoke, Teller shook with excitement, reminding Watkins, an engineer, of a reed vibrating at its resonant frequency. Teller told Watkins he felt a great personal frustration, similar to what he experienced decades earlier in trying to convince U.S. leaders it was necessary to develop the H-bomb. The two men adjourned to the flag mess hall and continued their discussion over lunch.[102]

"He cross-examined me carefully about one specific defensive measure, the X-ray laser," Teller recalled.[103]

The admiral was moved by Teller's optimism and his vision of a world in which the East-West race for offensive nuclear arms had come to an end. The secret revelations and Teller's allusion to the circumstances surrounding the birth of the H-bomb only contributed to the sense that epochal events were at hand.

"I will tell the president," Watkins said at the end of the session.[104]

While no physicist, Watkins was technically literate and had long been a nuclear enthusiast. He had received a master's degree in mechanical engineering from the Naval Postgraduate School in Monterey, California, and had helped Hyman Rickover build the nuclear navy. Watkins served in the Navy's nuclear submarine program. Then he commanded the Navy's first nuclear-powered cruiser, the USS Long Beach. He was a true believer in the potential goodness of nuclear technology for both military and civilian uses. Moreover, his technical opinion mattered in Washington circles because of his long service and expertise. During the Bush administration, he became secretary of the Department of Energy, the successor agency to the Atomic Energy Commission.

Fortified by Teller's antimissile vision, Admiral Watkins began to proselytize on its behalf. In late January 1983, he met with Mc-Farlane and his deputy, John Poindexter. The trio sat in the sunlight on the porch of the Tingey House in the Washington Navy Yard, where Watkins lived. There, McFarlane recalled, they agreed that "advances warranted a new look" at the antimissile question.[105] McFarlane and Poindexter encouraged Watkins to discuss his views with the other Chiefs, and if possible to form a consensus on the issue.

McFarlane, more so than national security adviser Clark, understood in detail the makeup of the nation's nuclear arsenal and was deeply worried by the political difficulties in matching Moscow's. "The more I thought about it, the more I was convinced that we had to change our investment strategy," McFarlane told me.[106] "We had to stop trying to compete on their terms—ICBM for ICBM—and change our strategy to emphasize what we did best, high technology." McFarlane said he had little of the moral enthusiasm of Watkins or the technical zeal of Teller. He saw a program of enhanced antimissile research not necessarily as an end in itself but as a way to get Moscow's attention by exposing "the woeful inferiority of the Soviet technology base." The program could be a "bargaining chip," McFarlane felt, to press for negotiated reductions in the growing arsenal of Soviet missiles.

Significantly, his views turned out to be quite different from those of the president.[107]

THE Joint Chiefs of Staff were scheduled to meet with President Reagan in February 1983 to address the strategic missile situation in the wake of the MX setback in Congress. At a dress rehearsal for this meeting, held on Saturday, February 5, Admiral Watkins laid out the rationale for embarking on an enhanced program of antimissile research, cautioning that conventional deterrence based on offensive arms, no matter how abhorrent morally, should not be scrapped immediately but simply that a new option should be explored. The Chiefs agreed to adopt Watkins' position as their own and to bring it up with the president.[108]

Friday, February 11, dawned cold and snowy. By noon, the weather was so bad and the roads so clogged that the Chiefs had to use four-wheel-drive vehicles to get to the White House. The group met in the Roosevelt Room. The Joint Chiefs told the president the MX was in trouble and that, with luck, it might be the last major missile system to get through Congress. Finally, the topic of antimissile defense came up. General John W. Vessey, Jr., chairman of the Joint Chiefs, laid out Watkins' logic and said the Chiefs felt it was time to take another look at antimissile defense.[109]

"Do you all feel that way?" the president asked.

Silence filled the room. Reagan looked at each Chief one by one. And they endorsed the idea one by one. General E. C. Meyer of the Army said the historic balance between offense and defense had gotten "out of kilter—whether you're talking about defense against tanks, defense against aircraft, or defense against missiles."[110]

Watkins took the floor, telling the president he had learned of rapid advances that were being made in antimissile research.

"Wait a minute," McFarlane interrupted. "Are you saying that you think it is possible, not probable but possible, that we might be able to develop an effective defense against ballistic missiles?"

"Yes," Watkins replied, "that's exactly what I'm saying."[111]

"Mr. President," McFarlane said, "the implications of this are very, very far-reaching. If it were feasible to find an alternative basis for maintaining our security against nuclear ballistic missile weapons, that would be a substantial change, obviously."

Reagan nodded. "I understand that."[112]

Watkins, after elaborating on the possibility of building a defensive shield, asked a rhetorical question. "Would it not be better if we could develop a system that would protect, rather than avenge, our people?"[113] Implicit in the question was the idea of near-perfect defense, the hope Teller had raised so frequently in advising the White House and high government officials.

"Exactly," said Reagan.[114] Sensitive to politically effective rhetoric, he added: "Don't lose those words."[115]

Despite Reagan's expressions of interest in the subject, the Joint Chiefs were vague in their recommendation. The Pentagon, they said, should step up its investigation of the long-range possibilities of antimissile defense—something it was already doing, albeit in a limited way. But there was no talk of deployment or even of a crash program of research—or, for that matter, of whether the Chiefs were advocating a total switch in strategy to defend the nation's cities against missiles or the more limited goal of defending the nation's force of silo-based missiles. To a man, the Chiefs later said they were surprised by the Star Wars speech.[116]

To Reagan, however, his meetings with the Chiefs in December 1982 and February 1983 were a turning point. "I asked them, 'Is it worthwhile to see if we could not develop a weapon that could perhaps take out, as they left their silos, those nuclear missiles?' " Reagan recalled. "And when they did not look aghast at the idea and instead said yes, they believed that such a thing offered a possibility and should be researched, I said, 'Go.' "[117]

Reagan left the February meeting exhilarated. His aides found him suddenly talking about a utopian plan to "render nuclear weapons obsolete." National security adviser Clark encouraged Reagan to move rapidly on the idea, while McFarlane was more cautious, wanting to seek a bipartisan approach with Congress. Reagan sided with Clark, who ordered McFarlane to develop the plan in great secrecy.[118]

Among those who worked on it was Ray Pollock, the National Security Council aide who witnessed Teller's meeting with Reagan in the Oval Office. Pollock was a scientist-technocrat, having previously worked at the Energy Department and Los Alamos. He knew nuclear weapons cold. As far as he was concerned, the X-ray laser was "a sideshow," a nascent technology that might or might not play a critical antimissile role. It was just one of many options being studied. Moreover, like DeLauer, the Pentagon official visited by Teller, Pollock was intimately aware of the old physicist's track record. But in recalling those feverish days leading up to the Star Wars speech, Pollock felt the X-ray might have represented much more to those with less arms expertise and less familiarity with Teller. He noted the "nontechnical nature" of the National Security Council staff at the time and how it was consumed by the general question, "Can technology bail us out?" In that atmosphere, Pollock recalled, the X-ray laser was probably seen by some of the president's men as "a silver bullet."[119]

TELLER, unaware of the depth of the political currents he had helped set in motion, was still enthusiastically promoting the X-ray laser. Significantly, at this juncture he began to seek the approval of some of his academic and scientific peers—Bethe in particular, his onetime friend turned foe after the Oppenheimer affair. It was as if Teller, knowing his need for intellectual aid, wanted to turn back the clock and have the bright idea blessed by a seasoned colleague, just as had occurred in decades past. Bethe was a good choice, having more or less founded the field of atomic physics. In February 1983, he arrived at Livermore for a secret, two-day briefing on the X-ray laser, curious about its promise. Although impressed with its scientific novelty, Bethe went away highly skeptical it would contribute anything to the nation's defense. [120]

DOUBTS about the X-ray laser were also troubling a small but significant corner of the White House—the science adviser's office. For some time, unbeknownst to the majority of the president's men, Keyworth's team had been raising serious questions about the X-ray laser's ability to alter the East-West balance anytime soon. The secret storehouse of misgivings accumulated even as the device was hailed in Washington as a wonder weapon and as White House strategists rushed to draft an antimissile plan for the president.

Throughout 1982 the Frieman panel of the White House Science Council, formed at Meese's request after Reagan's meeting with the Bendetsen group, had investigated whether any emerging technology could affect the administration's plans for strategic modernization. On June 23, 1982, the panel held its first X-ray laser review, gathering in La Jolla, California, at the headquarters of Science Applications, Inc., where the panel's chairman, Frieman, was an official. There scientists from Livermore's R Program briefed the panel. But their assessment was far less optimistic than Teller's. There was no talk of having it available in four or five years to wage antimissile war. Instead Tom Weaver, head of R Program, sketched out a development plan in which the laser's perfection might take as long as decades. Overseeing the Livermore presentation was the man responsible for the weapon, Roy Woodruff. [121]

A major tenet of the presentation was that X-ray laser work could be accelerated if its funding were increased. This approach had first been broached in Bendetsen's 1981 letter to Meese, which suggested that an extra $50 million could speed the weapon's appearance by more than a year. That logic was now applied to the X-ray laser program as a whole. Weaver spoke of work at a "technology-limited pace," rather than one determined by the amount of available funds. In essence, he assumed a federal spending spree in which the X-ray laser program would receive anywhere from $150 million to $200 million in additional funds each year. [122] With this kind of money, Weaver told the panel, the series of underground nuclear tests needed to perfect the boosting of the laser's brightness could be held frequently. All told, there were to be ten laser development tests, labeled LD-1 to LD-10. With the extra funding, these underground

blasts could be accomplished in as little as six years, by 1988. At the
end of the series, Weaver said, the laser should be a million times
brighter than a regular bomb.[123]

But after achieving proof of scientific feasibility, more work
would be needed to transform the prototype into a weapon. The
delicate laser apparatus would have to be made strong enough to bear
the vibration, buffeting and acceleration that a speeding rocket would
impose as it carried the weapon into space. Perhaps even more daunting was the creation of a complex apparatus to locate enemy missiles
and aim the laser's arms with great accuracy. The extent of the
needed work was suggested by the Energy Department's standard
plan for making a warhead. Its seven phases were concept study,
scientific feasibility, development engineering, production engineering, first production, quantity production and retirement.[124] Weaver's six-year, billion-dollar plan would take the X-ray laser only to
scientific feasibility, the second of the seven steps. Then it would
take years, perhaps a decade, to do the engineering. And even if
some of this work could be done in parallel with the push for scientific feasibility, a laser weapon would debut no earlier than the
mid-1990s. Moreover, if the extra funds failed to materialize, the
project might go well into the twenty-first century. That was a far
cry from the Teller-Bendetsen report to the White House saying the
"pivotal technology can be deployed to defend our country" as soon
as 1985.

The La Jolla briefing piqued the interest of the White House
Science Council panel in the X-ray laser. It was new, exciting and
ambitious. But the panel saw nothing in the idea that would quickly
change the nation's military structure. The laser was "blue sky,"
something off in the distance that might or might not become a
powerful weapon. In the late autumn of 1982, the panel wrote a draft
of its findings. No antimissile technology it examined, including the
X-ray laser, was seen as affecting military affairs in the near future.
In short, no silver bullet.[125]

Teller had a fit when he heard of the panel's findings, becoming
"unglued," one panel member recalled.[126] The panel had received
bad information, Teller told Frieman. The real situation was different. The laser could be ready in five years. A more comprehensive
presentation by Livermore would show the X-ray laser's quick feasibility and application to warfare. The panel had to have another
Livermore briefing, Teller insisted. If not, he would resign altogether from the White House Science Council—an act sure to send

shock waves through the administration's constituency of ardent conservatives.[127]

The gambit worked. Another panel meeting was scheduled at which Livermore would be allowed to make another presentation.

During this period, Teller tried to get Woodruff to adopt a more optimistic view of the X-ray laser, insisting that the laboratory could perfect the device in five years. Woodruff resisted the pressures. Though unaware of Teller's machinations in Washington, he knew that as Livermore's director of nuclear design he would be held responsible for any extravagant promises. The situation came to a head in December 1982.

"SHIT," said Woodruff as he hung up the phone, having been abruptly pulled from a Livermore meeting by Teller and ordered to appear in his office. Woodruff was unhappy with the clash over the X-ray timetable but was ready to do battle.[128] On foot he headed for Building 111, the lab's nerve center, going through its glass doors and up the elevator. Teller's office was on the fifth floor, next to the director's.

"Roy, I may never speak to you again," Teller snapped as Woodruff came through the door. "If I do, it certainly won't be this year."

That was it. The confrontation was over before it began. Teller dismissed Woodruff with a wave of his hand, satisfied with the demonstration of displeasure. Woodruff felt relieved, having no fear as he walked away, confident his position on the X-ray laser was correct.

That afternoon, Teller's secretary called. Woodruff's invitation to a party marking Teller's seventy-fifth birthday was being rescinded. It was to be an intimate affair, just a few close friends and top managers from the lab gathering at the home of Teller's personal aide. The disinvitation was clearly an escalation in the war. But Woodruff held firm.

Mysteriously, Teller relented a few days later, reinviting Woodruff to the party. There had been no compromise, no change in Woodruff's position. But Woodruff was back in the old man's graces as suddenly as he had left them.

The aide's house was just north of the lab, near wintry farmland. Woodruff and his wife brought a gift. Teller was his festive self at the party, charming and playful. The confrontation was forgotten. Teller loved being the center of attention. One of the gifts he received was a bright yellow toy duck on a stick. Smiling, Teller moved around the party with the duck, making its wings flap, laughing at his own silliness.[129]

TRYING to ease tensions with Teller, Woodruff did take one step. He agreed that a new study could be conducted on how an X-ray laser, if weaponized, might be used in war. This study was initiated at Livermore and performed by the Martin Marietta Aerospace Corporation.[130] It was to be ammunition that Teller could fire at the panel of the White House Science Council.

On February 17, 1983, Frieman's team met at the Naval Air Station in San Diego to review for a second time prospects for the X-ray laser. This time, Woodruff himself made the presentation, carefully going through the development plan. Rather than tilting in Teller's direction, Woodruff went the other way. At the technology-limited pace, his date for scientific feasibility was 1989, the schedule having become slightly more conservative since Weaver's presentation. And engineering the novel warhead remained as formidable as ever.[131]

In the afternoon, Woodruff turned the program over to the Martin Marietta people, who described what an X-ray weapon might do in war. Their depiction had nothing in common with the vision shared by Reagan and Watkins days earlier in which Americans were protected rather than avenged. Instead, the presentation showed that, at best, the X-ray laser might destroy only enemy missiles launched close to the United States, such as those from Soviet submarines. This short range was due to the laser's limited power and the curvature of the earth. In addition, the Martin Marietta people spelled out all the additional equipment needed to achieve the mission—including submarines to carry the weapons, rockets to fire them into space, early-warning satellites to track targets, and satellites to relay data throughout the defensive armada. In conclusion, the Martin Marietta officials gave an estimate of how long it might take to prepare all this extra equipment, saying five years was "stressing but feasible."[132]

The study, meant to appease Teller, actually suggested another layer of work that had to be done before the laser could flash to life in war. To some members of the White House Science Council panel, the second Livermore briefing only pushed the X-ray laser farther into the future.

Nonetheless, the panel's final report underwent a minor change.

In deference to Teller, and probably in a bid to forestall another outburst, Frieman and the panel added a sentence about the scientific feasibility of the X-ray laser. But the report's gist was exactly the same. No technology was seen as likely to change the military balance. "Edward had a fuss," a participant said, recalling the events of 1982 and 1983. "We went back and did it again, and it came out exactly the same way."[133]

As it turned out, the panel's report was dead on arrival. By the time science adviser Keyworth sent it to Meese, the White House was on the verge of making public its antimissile vision. No gloomy report by a panel of experts, overseen by a junior member of the White House team, was about to stop that.

ON Friday, March 18, 1983, President Reagan went to Camp David, where he conferred with McFarlane and security adviser Clark. The trio decided the time was right for the antimissile announcement, which was to be tacked onto a speech warning about the growing Soviet missile threat.[134] Their decision came just days after Reagan had attacked communism as "the focus of evil in the modern world."

The next day, Saturday, Keyworth was called into McFarlane's office and told of the "insert." The science adviser says he was "surprised, shocked, even stunned," but reacted cautiously.[135] McFarlane clearly wanted Keyworth's blessing. Even so, Gilbert D. Rye, an Air Force colonel on the National Security Council who worked on the insert, said McFarlane's request to Keyworth was almost an afterthought. "He wasn't part of the core group of people who were helping the president in terms of addressing the issue and understanding the implications," Rye recalled.[136]

McFarlane's request put the science adviser on the spot. Clearly, Keyworth had good reason to be skeptical. Many of his scientific peers and assistants had serious doubts about antimissile defense, seeing it as costly and futile for protection and dangerously destabilizing. During the past 18 months, he and his deputy Reis had vigorously fought the antimissile proposals of General Graham and Senator Wallop. Most recently, his White House Science Council had reinforced his misgivings, saying there was no technology on the horizon to alter the status quo, including that of his mentor. Yet Keyworth was hesitant to take a negative stance on an issue that seemed to be rushing forward with the president's strong approval. He had been on the losing side of too many battles within the administration, including acid rain (which he found worrisome) and

Reagan's plan for a space station (which he attacked as a costly "motel in the sky"). He was apparently tired of being a naysayer in an administration famed for its optimism. Moreover, he knew the whole basis for his hiring as White House science adviser had been to back the president. Finally, there was the issue of what Teller would think, and possibly do, if an attempt were made to block the antimissile initiative. Teller was a loaded gun. There was no telling where a stray bullet might land.

During the next few hours and days, Keyworth underwent a conversion. Reis said his boss "felt very strongly about the need to support the president on things the president felt strongly about."[137] Indeed, Keyworth in the end became one of the administration's most ardent antimissile advocates.[138]

That Saturday, Keyworth told McFarlane the time could be considered ripe to embark on a stepped-up program of antimissile research. As Keyworth worked on the president's speech during the next few days, he fought to dissuade those who wanted to quickly deploy antimissile weapons in space, as advocated by General Graham and Senator Wallop, and seriously considered by White House aides Anderson and Meese.[139] The success of Keyworth and his allies was reflected in the speech, which made no mention of deployment but spoke only of a stepped-up program of research. This was a happy outcome for both Keyworth and his mentor, Teller, for entirely different reasons. Teller wanted the X-ray laser perfected. That would take time. Keyworth also wanted time, but mainly to postpone the complex, dangerous issue of what kind of weapons, if any, the nation should place in space.

TELLER was dropped off at the southwest gate of the White House by a limousine, having only a vague idea of why he had been summoned from California. It was Wednesday, March 23, 1983, around six in the evening. There was a slight chill in the air. Teller limped up the staircase to the Blue Room, where some three dozen chairs had been set up for guests that included many of the nation's top scientists. Greeting them were Poindexter and Keyworth, who informed the assembled group that a historic change in national defense policy was to be announced by the president in a televised address at 8:00 P.M. Teller broke into a grin.[140]

The president shared his vision with the nation that evening, asking, "Would it not be better to save lives than to avenge them?"—a phrase borrowed from Watkins.[141] Reagan went on, saying that after "careful consultation with my advisers, including the Joint Chiefs of Staff," he had decided the time was ripe for the nation to "embark on a program to counter the awesome Soviet missile threat with measures that are defensive." Reagan outlined "a formidable technical task" that "may not be accomplished before the end of this century. Yet, current technology has attained a level of sophistication where it is reasonable for us to begin this effort." At the end of the speech, he called on "the scientific community who gave us nuclear weapons" to find a way to render them "impotent and obsolete."[142] It was a passage that aides say he wrote himself, seemingly in reference to Teller and his ranks of scientists at Livermore.

Teller was ecstatic. Another miracle had occurred. Yet his elation soon turned to worry as skepticism arose around him. Minutes after the speech, Secretary of State Shultz asked Teller if any system could stop 99.9 percent of incoming missiles. It was a disarmingly simple question, but one that had seldom arisen in the months and years of antimissile lobbying in and around the White House.

"No," Teller replied, instantly deflating his own rhetoric about assured survival, adding there was no guarantee such protection could be achieved.[143]

As the evening wore on, Teller became increasingly subdued and preoccupied with the obstacles ahead. When he called Livermore that night, he reported that several White House attendees had already rejected the president's summons by declaring themselves opposed to antimissile defense.[144] Among the skeptics was Bethe, who believed that East-West negotiations, not armaments in space, were the best way to secure peace.

Bethe was worried that an antimissile system would, for the first time, make possible the successful waging of nuclear war, since it could be used to block the threat of retaliation. It was the same dark paradox Teller had raised at Erice. But while Teller had pictured this danger in relation to the Soviet Union, Bethe turned it around. What, he asked White House officials that evening, would keep an American antimissile system from being viewed as an aid to offensive attacks? No matter that it was meant solely for protection, wouldn't its mere existence be seen as aggressive, undermining the balance of terror and possibly provoking a nuclear war?

White House aides evaded the question, Bethe recalled. Their answer, he said, was "so empty that I don't remember it."[145]

Indeed, the president in his speech had also dodged the issue. "I clearly recognize that defensive systems have limitations and raise certain problems and ambiguities," Reagan had said. "If paired with offensive systems, they can be viewed as fostering an aggressive policy, and no one wants that."[146] This phraseology was significant, since it seemed to imply that Reagan wanted to completely eliminate the need for an American force of retaliatory arms.

Teller regained enough of his confidence in the days following the announcement to pen an op-ed article for *The New York Times*, entitled "Reagan's Courage." In it he hailed the president's decision as a turning point in world history, saying it was made after careful inquiry into the state of research on antimissile defenses. "Mr. Reagan did not lightly accept the idea that these can be made to work," Teller said. "He wanted to know a vast number of details. He asked questions of his science adviser, George Keyworth, and of many other scientists, myself included. He then decided that something must and can be done."[147]

Teller went on to make a veiled reference to Livermore's X-ray wizards, praising the president for learning of their work. "He made sure that the novel defense-oriented ideas proposed by an ingenious group of young scientists had a way of reaching him," Teller said, adding that Reagan's action "may save us from a future war."

TELLER had succeeded to an extraordinary degree in his campaign to win the White House. The victory came despite his slow start, despite the tentative nature of the X-ray laser, despite attacks from antimissile rivals, despite the stubborn resistance of the program's head at Livermore, despite the apathy of his own hand-picked presidential science adviser, despite the disparagement of an expert panel, and despite the deadly ambiguities inherent in the whole notion of antimissile defense—ambiguities that Teller himself repeatedly warned about in relation to the Soviet Union.

The achievement stemmed in no small part from Teller's forceful personality and persuasive lobbying of high administration officials. They were fascinated by his top-secret disclosures about the X-ray laser, clearly the most revolutionary in the emerging antimissile arsenal. On several scores it had no rival. Of the competing ideas, only it had actually been tested, albeit in a single crude experiment under the Nevada desert. And it far outdistanced the rivals in terms of expected performance. General Graham's orbiting interceptors were primitive, harking back to the 1950s. Senator Wallop's lasers were interesting but fraught with problems, not the least of which was how to get the giant devices into space. In contrast, Teller's X-ray laser was seen as small, compact and vastly more powerful. Perhaps most important, it was top secret, giving it a seductive aura. Always described in hushed tones, it had dazzled Bendetsen and the kitchen cabinet, White House aides Anderson and Meese, Chief of Naval Operations Watkins and, most important, President Reagan himself.

After the speech, science adviser Keyworth often cited a different technology as evidence of antimissile progress, pointing to advances in optics. These, he said, might allow conventional ground-based lasers to fire through the earth's turbulent atmosphere without distortion. While the technology was indeed interesting, White House insiders felt that Keyworth's singling it out was essentially an attempt to distance himself publicly from the X-ray laser and his mentor.[148]

Technically, the most attractive part of Teller's vision was that the X-ray laser might simultaneously fire multiple beams, perhaps a dozen or more. That had big implications. A single X-ray laser firing at a group of rising Soviet SS-18 missiles, each carrying ten weapons, might instantly knock out 120 or more nuclear warheads. It was breathtaking leverage. Many other antimissile weapons were seen as destroying a single warhead or a single missile. The overwhelming firepower of the X-ray laser suggested that, for the first time in the nuclear era, the strategic balance might tip from offense to defense.

The primacy of Teller's laser was clearly understood by news organizations, which knew of it through information leaks to the technical press. *Newsweek*, in its issue on Reagan's Star Wars speech, devoted its cover to just one item—an artist's rendering of an X-ray laser in action, the device bristling with rods firing at enemy missiles.[149]

Would the Star Wars program have gotten under way without the X-ray laser? It seems unlikely. No other weapon had the allure. It and it alone suggested the field had reached a new level of maturity. Whether the silver bullet would actually save America was immaterial. What was important was what it symbolized—that the nation, after decades of work and an investment of many billions of dollars, had entered an entirely new phase of antimissile research, one that promised, for the first time, to end the nightmare of Mutual Assured Destruction. General Graham was happy to have his interceptors destroy a small fraction of Soviet missiles so American military forces could survive the attack. But that was just a bid to enhance deterrence. Teller said he wanted it overthrown.

Would the Star Wars program have materialized without Teller? This too seems unlikely, though Reagan has implied that Teller played no real role in its genesis. In his 1990 autobiography, *An American Life*, Reagan belittled the notion that the antimissile program was conceived by outsiders, calling it a myth. Instead, he stressed that the origins of the endeavor lay in his own aversion to the nuclear status quo and his personal search for a new strategy. Reagan made no mention of the antimissile advocacy of Anderson, Graham, Wallop, Schmitt, Bendetsen, Hume, Coors, Wilson, Watkins, or Teller.[150]

Reagan's analysis is surely correct as far as it goes. There is no doubt he was favorably disposed to the antimissile idea when he arrived at the White House and went out of his way to pursue that interest during his first years in office. But Reagan errs in neglecting the key role played by advisers who gave substance to his fuzzy intuitions and bestowed their blessing on the antimissile goal. And no adviser was more important than Teller.

First and foremost, Teller was trusted. He had been involved in the game longer than anybody else. Of the advocates, only he was a scientist and only he had actually designed and built antimissile arms. All the others were basically armchair experts. Teller intimately knew the field's ups and downs, its promise and problems. Reagan automatically looked to Teller as the leading authority in the field. After all, it was Teller who first briefed Reagan on antimissile systems in the 1960s. And nearly two decades later, it was Teller who was celebrated in the Reagan White House as the most distinguished proponent of antimissile defense, as Anderson put it. No one else had that kind of stature, expertise and familiarity with Reagan.

If Teller was the president's most trusted antimissile adviser, he was also the most zealous. Perhaps his major contribution to the volatile mix of ideas circulating in and around the White House was a sense of vision and urgency. The impossible could be done and done soon, Teller insisted. Committees of experts would have had the X-ray laser appearing, maybe, with luck, in the twenty-first century, and then performing only limited missions. The Frieman panel said as much. But Teller was incessant in his assurances. The weapon could be ready—soon—and would do wonders. "He was a charismatic individual who had the reputation of his earlier successes working for him," recalled Hoover, head of the Energy Department's military programs. "His view carried a lot of weight."[151]

In the end, it was probably Teller's sheer excitement, his mantra "third generation, third generation," his bold assertions about "assured survival," as much as anything else that convinced Reagan and his White House staff that the time was ripe to move forward.

"Teller clearly did have great influence with President Reagan and, to the extent that Teller always focused on the X-ray laser, it is fair to say it was a factor" in the genesis of the Star Wars program, McFarlane told me. But the critical part of the equation, McFarlane stressed, "was Edward Teller—who could have been talking about anything." Teller's enthusiasm and credibility, McFarlane said, were far more important "than the technology he explained, which Reagan grasped only superficially."[152]

Evidence of Teller's influence comes from Reagan himself. After leaving the White House, Reagan, a man wary of nuclear Armageddon, a onetime G.E. spokesman in awe of the nation's technical powers, a former actor hooked on heroes and villains and happy endings, described the goal that motivated his drive for space arms. He used no technical terms, saying nothing of lasers or wavelengths or military strategy or the aim of sowing doubts in the mind of would-be attackers. He made no mention of any kind of political calculus or a desire to intensify the economic competition between East and West. Instead, he used two words to describe his "dream," as he put it, two words that epitomized his optimistic outlook on life and resonated with rhetorical power, if little else. His dream, he said, was to give America the gift of assured survival.[153]

# FOUR

# Cracks in the Shield

T HE FEDERAL PROGRAM of antimissile research that grew out of President Reagan's initiative had no real focus. It was basically a scientific free-for-all, a license to spend tens of billions of dollars as creatively as possible. Nearly any idea that seemed to show a hint of antimissile promise was appraised by Pentagon planners and often lavishly funded. No concept seemed too wild. Considerable sums were spent investigating antimatter arms, which years earlier had emerged as wonder weapons in the pages of science fiction. And despite their ambiguous status in the origins of Star Wars, chemical lasers (Senator Wallop's idea) and kinetic-energy arms (General Graham's) were heavily funded. All told, federal experts probed the practicality of hundreds of would-be weapons.

In California, center of the nation's aerospace and electronics industries, antimissile defense became a hot new business. Scores of companies won big contracts, including such giants as Hughes Aircraft Company, Lockheed Missiles & Space Company, Rockwell International, and TRW, Inc. In New Mexico, plans took shape for a $1 billion laser meant to stretch across miles of desert, its beams dancing into space and bouncing off orbiting mirrors toward enemy missiles. Just cooling the laser was seen as requiring more than 450 million gallons of water a year, a considerable amount in such an arid region.[1]

In Seattle, Boeing began work on a 767 jet meant to carry a

giant, 5.5-ton sensor for tracking warheads in space. To house the sensor and its support equipment, an 86-foot-long cupola was welded atop the plane. The mammoth project ended up costing more than $600 million.[2]

At the University of Texas in Austin, researchers working in a cavernous seven-story lab started to build a 130-foot experimental rail gun named "Jedi," after the characters in the movie *Star Wars*. The device was to use powerful magnetic fields to speed small projectiles. For war, the researchers foresaw space-based rail guns firing tiny, smart, homing interceptors toward enemy missiles.[3]

The space shuttle became the focus of some of the most elaborate plans drawn up by the Strategic Defense Initiative, as the Pentagon called its antimissile program. The winged spaceship was to carry dozens of experiments into orbit. Near the shuttle's launching pad in Florida, military planners set up a center for handling Star Wars payloads. The facility included a laboratory for visiting scientists, a training area for astronauts and a "clean room" for payload assembly, checkout and storage.[4]

Around the world, allies of the United States joined in the antimissile effort, lining up for contracts even while some of them publicly belittled Star Wars as a naive dream. In West Germany, Defense Minister Manfred Worner said the plan would lead not to stability, but just the opposite.[5] In Britain, Sir Geoffrey Howe, the British foreign secretary, made a major speech in which he listed a host of questions about the antimissile effort and said answers to them could prove disappointing.[6] Despite widespread skepticism, international agreements were eventually struck with the governments of Israel, Italy, Japan, West Germany, the United Kingdom and the Netherlands. Hundreds of millions of dollars flowed overseas in this program, the largest sums going to Israel. Among other things, Israel attempted to perfect a ground-based interceptor that would destroy missiles flying over relatively short distances.[7]

Amid this whirlwind of activity, the federal government was notably cool to the most exotic antimissile idea of all—the X-ray laser. It was funded, but at levels far below the hopes of Teller and his cohorts. The government's reservations about the would-be weapon were due to a host of X-ray laser liabilities that had largely escaped notice before the Star Wars speech. The ambivalence became clear as President Reagan and his top aides, whenever speaking publicly of the antimissile plan, took pains to emphasize that it was nonnuclear.

This rejection brought no admission of defeat from Teller. Sometimes he sulked. Other times he railed against what he called the government's antinuclear bias. More than a year after the president's speech, in September 1984, Teller met with Bendetsen, Wood and several other colleagues, denouncing the government's antimissile program as nonsense. Lofty goals had been corrupted by special interests and pork-barrel politics. Moreover, Teller said, the program was haunted by a prejudice against the X-ray laser that threatened to doom the whole enterprise. "The key point is that nuclear explosives are an essential ingredient," Teller said. Their rejection had to be reversed, he declared, "even clandestinely." Until then, "the program is in very deep trouble."[8]

After months of brooding, Teller took action. He felt he knew the promise of the X-ray laser better than anybody in Washington, and furiously sought ways to realize its potential. Eventually Teller found what he thought was the perfect solution—a way to vastly increase the laser's power so it could destroy enemy missiles more effectively than ever, perhaps so much that a single laser would simultaneously zap 100,000 targets. He rushed news of the breakthrough to the White House. As it turned out, however, Teller's enthusiasm was premature.

FROM the moment that President Reagan made his antimissile dream public, the X-ray laser was in trouble.

"Is it a bomb?" Defense Secretary Weinberger asked as he rushed to brief Congress on the antimissile program, right after Reagan's Star Wars speech in March 1983.

"That's how you get the X-ray," explained Richard D. De-Lauer, the Pentagon's head of research and engineering. "You're going to have to detonate a nuclear device in space."

"But it's not a bomb, is it?" Weinberger repeated, looking for a semantic loophole.

Amazed at the display of high-level ignorance, DeLauer offered Weinberger a euphemism. "No, it's not a bomb," he said. "It would be a nuclear event."[9]

The X-ray opposition that emerged within the government was based partly on the perception that the device had serious political shortcomings. Most fundamentally, the laser, powered by a nuclear blast, was seen as contradicting the Star Wars ethic. President Reagan wanted to make nuclear weapons "impotent and obsolete." But the X-ray laser would simply make them more versatile. On a more practical level, policy makers felt the public would oppose the placement of nuclear weapons in space. It was a point General Graham had argued during the Bendetsen panel's deliberations of 1981, and now it rose to prominence as the president's initiative was subjected to close scrutiny.

The risk of public opposition was seen as "a significant problem," recalled Gilbert D. Rye, an aide on the National Security Council. "The X-ray laser involved a nuclear explosion, and that was a new ball game. Teller never addressed that. He waved it off as a nonissue."[10]

Another early trouble that emerged was technical in nature. It had nothing to do with the X-ray laser's brightness or power but with the more fundamental problem of getting any readings out of the apparatus at all. The episode, more embarrassment than major setback, was nonetheless a bad omen.

On Wednesday, March 23, 1983, the day of Reagan's speech, the Energy Department announced that the largest underground nuclear test of the year would be held in two days. It was code-named Cabra. The bomb was to be detonated 1,780 feet beneath Pahute Mesa, a volcanic plateau in the Nevada desert, the blast nearing 150 kilotons, equal to 150,000 tons of high explosive. That was the upper limit allowed by East-West treaty. A spokesman for the Energy Department told reporters that earth motion might be felt outside the boundaries of the Nevada test site, especially by people in Las Vegas high-rise buildings some hundred miles away. Workmen in Las Vegas were warned not to be in precarious positions at the time of the explosion, which was set for 7:00 A.M. Friday morning.[11] While a simple annoyance for office workers, the tremor might cause a construction worker to slip and fall to his death.

What the Energy Department omitted to say publicly was that Cabra was another test of the X-ray laser. So far, despite all Teller's lobbying and the interest it sparked in Washington, Livermore had previously conducted only one successful test, the 1980 Dauphin shot. And even that accomplishment was under fire from skeptics who felt the Dauphin data were ambiguous.

As D-Day approached, the Energy Department delayed the Cabra shot at least 24 hours because of bad weather. The wind at ground zero was blowing directly toward Las Vegas, threatening to send any leakage of radiation toward the city. Underground blasts were routinely postponed until the wind changed direction. Early on Saturday morning, March 26, the winds were still unfavorable as

7:00 A.M. came and went. Late that morning things improved. Although more people in Las Vegas were up and active, Energy Department officials judged there was little or no risk for the city dwellers. At 12:20 P.M. the bomb exploded, the shock wave moving rapidly past scientists at the control point toward Las Vegas, where it caused few problems.[12]

As Livermore scientists scrutinized the results, they were greatly disappointed. A quick glance told them the test had failed. New sensors that were to give an improved reading of the laser's output had instead produced a cacophony of meaningless electronic noise. While some of the data might be salvageable, it was clear that the $60 million test was largely a loss. Most important, it provided no information that would help persuade skeptics that the X-ray laser really existed—much less that the device had the power to end the uneasy standoff that had dominated superpower relations for a third of a century.[13]

For Woodruff, Livermore's associate director for nuclear design, the man ultimately responsible for the development of the X-ray laser, the Cabra failure coupled with Teller's unmitigated enthusiasm was a personal test of integrity. It was not unusual to have a technical setback in a program so new and risky. But the political environment was very unusual. Teller's lobbying had created high expectations in Washington. It had also created enormous pressure within the nuclear arms establishment to forge ahead, to quickly write off the Cabra test and press onward to LD-1, the first official step in the series of planned nuclear blasts meant to speed research into boosting the laser's brightness. Advocates of such a move—including Teller's protege, Wood, as well as Weaver, head of R Program—held that the Cabra results would have been interesting but were unimportant for long-term success. Woodruff felt otherwise. He said the test had to be redone. Livermore scientists had identified the problems and knew how to solve them, Woodruff said. All that was needed was time and money.[14]

Woodruff took firm steps. But he also tried to cast the situation in the best light possible. At the White House and Energy Department, he argued that Cabra had been a successful test of a new nuclear bomb specially designed to pump the X-ray laser, which was true. Known as SD-1, for source development, this aspect of Cabra was part of an effort meant to perfect large bombs for pumping X-ray lasers with exactly the right kind of radiation.[15] But Woodruff also said Cabra was a clear failure of the laser's sensors itself and that the experiment needed to be redone. The Energy Department agreed. Woodruff then took it upon himself to find money for the new test, working with the Livermore's financial controller, Mary E. Tuszka, to squeeze funds out of the existing budget. After much work, the plan was approved. A new test, code-named Romano, was scheduled for later that year.[16]

Under Woodruff's direction, the X-ray laser juggernaut was moving forward, albeit in fits and starts. But the turbulent state of research in the fledgling field bore no likeness to the rhetoric that marked its continued promotion in Washington.

"A GREAT change in the national defense situation is impending," Teller told the research and development subcommittee of the House Armed Services Committee in April 1983. "The initiative for this change does not come from me. It comes from younger people, such as my very good friend Dr. Lowell Wood, and my friend Dr. Tom Weaver, who is in charge of the development of one of the most important of these new systems." The two physicists were at Teller's side, watching the master testify.

"I am talking about a third generation of nuclear weapons," Teller said. "What counts is no longer the big size of nuclear explosions. What counts is no longer their enormous destructive power. I no longer can, should, or will emphasize the balance of terror because the balance has become tragically unbalanced. I will talk about defense using the enormous concentrations of energy and temperature of nuclear weapons." Making no mention of how underground blasts such as Cabra could rock the state of Nevada, Teller testified that the nuclear explosions meant to power the new arms "can be relatively small." Thus, he said, the new weapons could be used "to destroy very specific targets such as offensive weapons in action" rather than for purposes of "mass destruction."[17]

Teller then opened fire on rival antimissile plans that envisioned weapons in orbit about the earth, such as the chemical lasers championed by Senator Wallop and the rocket interceptors of General Graham. "To develop great battle stations for use in space is an outlandish idea," Teller said, warning that an enemy would have plenty of time to find, attack and destroy them. In contrast, he said, the new generation of nuclear arms, which would be compact and lightweight, could be kept safely on the ground and shot into space only when needed at the outbreak of war. "I am talking," he said, of weapons "that pop up into space when the time to use them has come." With this line of reasoning, Teller was setting himself in opposition to the vast bulk of Star Wars, which in the popular imagination was mainly lasers pre-deployed in space that zapped bombs. He had originally adopted pop-up in 1981 as a counter to General Graham's criticisms that the X-ray was unable to defend itself in space, since it would have to blow itself up to do so. But now, in a clever twist, pop-up had become the basis for Teller's critique of virtually all other antimissile plans. Only the X-ray laser, powered by the titanic energies of a nuclear bomb, was small and light enough to be kept on the ground until just before battle. Its small size meant it could, in theory, be shot into space only when needed. In contrast, the space-based arms and power sources envisioned for Star Wars were usually so massive and complicated that their deployment, assembly and testing in orbits hundreds of miles above the earth would have to be done months and years in advance of any anti-missile battle.

In closing, Teller appealed to the congressmen for a dramatic boost in funding for the new generation of nuclear arms, concluding that the nation was on the verge of a new era. "We are talking about defense not just of the United States but of the free world."[18]

A few weeks later, on May 23, 1983, Teller, Bendetsen, Coors and Wilson met with Reagan at the White House to urge rapid action on the president's antimissile goals. Much of the discussion centered on bypassing the federal bureaucracy to achieve swift progress.[19] The next day, President Reagan, standing in the East Room of the White House, awarded Teller the National Medal of Science, the country's highest scientific honor. Teller wore a carnation in his lapel and a broad smile on his lips. The citation that accompanied the award hailed Teller for "his outstanding contributions" and "leadership in science and technology."[20]

THE X-ray laser program soon suffered a secretive intellectual blow that left it reeling. The source of the jolt was a large Defense Department study that President Reagan ordered after his Star Wars speech. Directed by James C. Fletcher, former head of the National Aeronautics and Space Administration, the group was known officially as the Defensive Technologies Study Team, informally as the Fletcher panel. It consisted of sixty-seven top scientists from the nation's military-industrial complex, including such organizations as Livermore, Los Alamos and the Sandia weapons lab in Albuquerque, New Mexico. The head of the subpanel that examined the X-ray

laser and other directed-energy weapons was Gerold Yonas, a physicist from Sandia who was widely respected for his intelligence and
wit. After the Fletcher study, Yonas would be named the first chief
scientist of the Strategic Defense Initiative. For his X-ray analysis,
Yonas drew on testimony from Livermore itself. The Fletcher panel
worked through the spring and summer of 1983 and delivered its
report to the White House that October. In all, it recommended that
up to $26 billion be spent on antimissile research during the remain-
der of the 1980s. Moreover, it called on the government to spend
nearly $1 billion of that money on the X-ray laser alone—more than
it recommended for any other single antimissile technology uncovered in its search.[21]

Superficially it looked like a ringing endorsement of the X-ray
laser. But the seven-volume study was actually a major indictment.
Most basically, the weapon was found to be largely futile for defense. Soviet missiles could outwit the X-ray laser and its deadly
rays simply by using the earth's atmosphere as a protective blanket,
the panel concluded. An X-ray laser, "popped" into space atop a
rocket, would have to shoot over the atmosphere to hit rising Soviet
missiles, since its beam had no power to significantly penetrate the
earth's gaseous shell. It had to operate in space where X-rays could
travel unimpeded. To foil the X-ray laser, all the Soviets had to do
was put engines on their missiles that were more powerful. So
equipped, the missiles would finish firing, not far out into space, but
amid the upper fringes of the atmosphere, where they would then
deploy hardened warheads. Or in the case of Soviet submarines close
to America's shores, all the missiles had to do was follow what was
known as a depressed trajectory. In either instance, the earth's blanket of air would protect the missiles from the X-ray laser.

"We looked at the problem of pop-up, but the time-line was
very stressing, especially for the responsive threat," Yonas told me,
referring to possible Soviet countermeasures. "Fast-burn boosters
would outwit it. The X-ray lasers could never get there in time—
period."[22] However, there was still a slim chance the weapon might
have an antimissile role. What it needed was greater power. The
beams of Excalibur, the basic X-ray laser weapon, were meant to be
a million times brighter than a regular nuclear bomb. But Livermore
was also trying to increase the brightness, possibly by as much as a
billion. This design was known as Excalibur Plus. Its more powerful
beams would be able to burn through some the earth's atmosphere,
in theory allowing them to zap enemy missiles. But it was a big "if,"

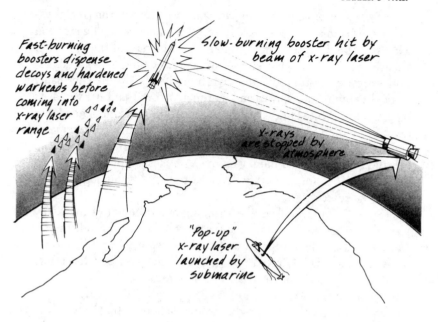

Fast-burning boosters dispense decoys and hardened warheads before coming into x-ray laser range

Slow-burning booster hit by beam of x-ray laser

X-rays are stopped by atmosphere

"Pop-up" x-ray laser launched by submarine

Fast rockets can evade X-ray laser.

given the multiple layers of uncertainty surrounding the would-be weapon.

The Fletcher panel largely wrote off the X-ray laser for antimissile defense in the role touted by Teller—attacking missiles that were boosting warheads into space. So why spend nearly $1 billion? Mainly out of fear or perhaps, to put it more positively, the need to know what an enemy might do.

The logic went like this: The X-ray laser could undoubtedly destroy satellites, as Bendetsen had noted in his 1981 letter to the White House. What became clear only on further reflection was that its beams were so strong they also could destroy all kinds of antimissile arms in space. It was seen as ideal for this job. The logic became alarming when the lasers were pictured in Russian hands. Soviet X-ray lasers could knock out nearly any American antimissile system, including not only weapons but the host of satellites and sensors needed to track missiles and aid communications during a fast-paced battle. For instance, the beam from a Soviet X-ray laser could easily smash the delicate mirrors and optics that made up a space-based chemical laser such as Alpha, even if the two objects were quite far apart. An even easier target would be giant rocket interceptors. Also vulnerable were American X-ray lasers. These could be attacked by Soviet X-ray lasers in the upper atmosphere that fired upward, their concentrated beams easily cutting through the thin air to smash anything in space. But the reverse was not true. The beam coming down from a defensive American X-ray laser farther out in space would have spread too much and become too weak to penetrate the atmosphere and destroy a Soviet aggressor.

In short, the X-ray laser threatened to end the Star Wars vision. Contrary to everything Teller had ever said, the device promised to hurt the antimissile goal, not help it. The Fletcher scientists felt the nation needed to quickly know if the weapon could be successfully developed so as to judge whether the Soviets might deploy one. "It is important to determine the ultimate limits of nuclear-driven X-ray laser performance," the panel wrote, "because of their potential as a major threat to our space-based assets."[23] The work had to be done rapidly, the panel said.

Of the host of weapons it reviewed, only the X-ray laser was recommended for priority funding. Such urgency was seen as quite reasonable. After all, the Russians might use X-ray lasers to destroy any antimissile system that America chose to erect in space, annihilating many billions of dollars worth of military investments and ending whatever immunity the nation thought it possessed to nuclear destruction.

EVEN as the Fletcher panel worried that the X-ray laser might shatter Star Wars, Teller wrote the president to assure him just the opposite in terms so sweeping they would give almost anyone pause. Advances in nuclear-powered weapons, Teller wrote on July 23, "by converting hydrogen bombs into hitherto unprecedented forms and then directing these in highly effective fashions against enemy targets would end the MAD era and commence a period of assured survival on terms favorable to the Western alliance."[24]

A FEW Fletcher panel members knew of Teller's high-level interventions in Washington but were unable to do anything about them. Teller was too powerful. Privately, some complained that Teller's advocacy represented an overzealous scientist operating far beyond his expertise.

"I can see how Edward was attracted to all this," a panel member, who had long known and respected Teller, told me. "The X-ray laser was elegant. It was beautiful and elegant. It was technically

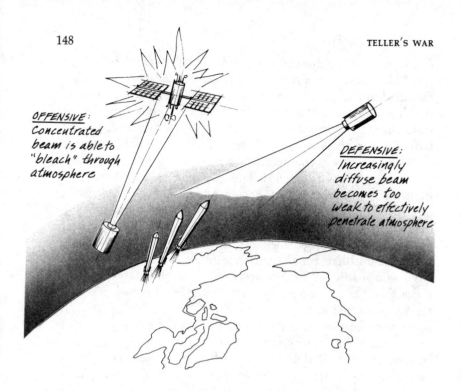

OFFENSIVE:
Concentrated
beam is able to
"bleach" through
atmosphere

DEFENSIVE:
Increasingly
diffuse beam
becomes too
weak to effectively
penetrate atmosphere

X-ray laser offense is far easier than defense.

sweet, just like Oppenheimer said. But is Edward an engineer? No.
Is he a systems designer? No. Is he a military planner? No. He was
enthralled with the principle and rightly so. The principle is in fact
that beautiful. But he is not the kind of guy who ever got hooked on
building things. His first H-bomb was the size of an apartment
house. Edward is a physicist with a fantastic creative mind. He
understands the beauty of a piece of music. But for God's sake, don't
ask him to design a trumpet."[25]

   For his part, Teller dismissed the findings of the Fletcher panel
and belittled the overall report as "weak."[26]

THE Fletcher panel knew the technical score. It was not good, especially in relation to the X-ray laser and other possible Soviet countermeasures. But within the top ranks of the panel, political
pressures mounted to keep the bad news from the public. And it was
dutifully buried. The seventh volume of the secret report—possible

Soviet countermeasures, including how an X-ray laser in Russian hands could knock out Star Wars—was left out of the overall antimissile assessment. By all accounts, this was a critical omission. "If you read volume seven first, you wouldn't bother reading the rest of the report," said Theodore Postol, then a scientific aide to Navy Chief of Staff Watkins. "It presents an overwhelming case against the possibility of a hope of mounting something useful. It quite unambiguously indicates the problem was insolvable unless certain things were solved that no one even knew how to address."[27]

Moreover, the panel's top-secret report was prefaced by an enthusiastic introduction. Asked about this years later, Fletcher said it had been written by no one on the committee. By whom then? "Someone in the White House," he replied.[28]

Clearly, the White House by this time had gnawing doubts about the X-ray laser, fanned by the Fletcher report and the realization of the weapon's political liabilities. Its coolness was codified in National Security Decision Directive 119, which said SDI was to be nonnuclear if at all possible.[29] But the powers that be wanted no general disparagement of Star Wars. Indeed, the disinformation campaign about the Fletcher report was aided by a chorus of praise from White House and Pentagon officials, who, despite more than a few private doubts, knew the antimissile plan had become a test of loyalty to the president. As a result, most news accounts represented the Fletcher report as a warm endorsement of the antimissile vision and the X-ray laser as the best way of getting there. *Aviation Week & Space Technology* quoted a high-level Defense Department official as saying the Fletcher panel "provided a report far more positive and enthusiastic on directed-energy weapons development than any of us expected."[30] In listing the antimissile weapons found promising by the panel, the magazine's first reference was to the X-ray laser.[31] Following the magazine's lead, *The New York Times* reported that "the Fletcher panel report placed great emphasis on X-ray lasers as perhaps the most promising future technology to block hostile missiles."[32] Months later, in summarizing the Fletcher report, Defense Secretary Weinberger told the National Press Club: "They have found the dream to be indeed possible."[33]

Deep within the government, key officials at the Pentagon and White House knew the real score. Yonas, after all, soon became the chief scientist of the SDI program after having spent a good part of 1983 chipping away at X-ray laser rhetoric. But the weapon's failings and the danger it posed to the antimissile program remained highly classified secrets, unknown to most of the government and all of the American public.

AT this point, Teller belatedly took steps to ascertain for himself the real status of the X-ray laser. His own intuitions, joined by the enthusiastic pronouncements of O Group, were not enough. He needed an independent evaluation. So Teller did as he had done for decades, soliciting advice from respected colleagues. Though now largely cut off from the world's top scientists outside the weapons lab, Teller was able to assemble an informal group of trusted Livermore experts in mid-1983 to advise him. They included Abraham Szoke, a Hungarian physicist and close friend; Duane C. Sewell, a longtime Livermore manager; and Ray E. Kidder, a lab veteran and scientific maverick. Their advice was not always to Teller's liking. Kidder soon filed a secret report saying that, among other problems, even the most humble brightness goal would probably be impossible to achieve. "I was a skunk at their picnic," Kidder recalled. "I could see it wasn't going to work. But Teller figured there had to be some way to get around the problem."[34]

TELLER'S natural optimism was reinforced as the X-ray laser moved forward technically in a minor way. The advance did nothing to resolve the dangers documented by the Fletcher panel or to raise the laser's brightness. But his reaction was nonetheless dramatic. Teller exploded in a burst of enthusiasm that was immediately communicated to the White House. His depiction of the X-ray advance was so extravagant that it prompted a struggle with Woodruff over whether the record should be corrected.

The episode began on Friday, December 16, 1983, at 10:30 A.M., as a nuclear blast shook the Nevada desert. It was Romano, the experiment meant to correct the Cabra failure. Once again, it was a large explosion, the Energy Department having warned workers in high-rise Las Vegas buildings to avoid precarious positions at the time of the blast.[35] Romano was the fourth test for Livermore's X-ray laser program, the earlier ones having been Cabra, Dauphin and Diablo Hawk, the 1978 test of Chapline's laser that had been marred by an equipment breakdown. Despite more than five years of explosive testing, Romano was the first experiment in which there was unambiguous evidence that an X-ray laser had indeed come to life far beneath the sand and sagebrush of the Nevada desert.

The test was specifically designed to prove X-ray lasing. It consisted of multiple laser rods that got longer and longer. During the explosion, there was to be an amplification of X-ray energy along the length of the rods ("laser" being an acronym for "light amplification by stimulated emission of radiation"). So increased output was expected as the rods got longer. For instance, if the rods were one, two and three meters long, the output should grow exponentially—creating 10, 100 and 1,000 units of laser energy. And so it was. For the first time in the history of the X-ray laser program, Romano gave Livermore scientists "gain versus length" measurements that proved beyond a doubt that the X-ray laser was real. No other phenomenon could account for the increasingly bright spots produced by the laser rods.[36]

Late Friday, the day of the test, Wood and Tom Weaver, the head of R Program, arrived breathlessly at Livermore, having flown from Nevada with photocopies of the first results. A meeting was quickly called in the Coronet Room high atop Building 111, next to the director's office. There Wood, Weaver, Teller and Woodruff pored over the data, which was quite crude at that stage. It would be weeks before the complex readings, which included coded signals to mark time intervals, could be processed. But the experiment's general outcome was clear. "We knew we had a tremendously successful experiment," recalled Woodruff.[37]

Teller was ecstatic. Of course, the success did nothing to dispel the various doubts surrounding the laser or to boost its suitability for waging antimissile war. But at least it proved the device was no mirage.

Less than a week after the test, on Thursday, December 22, 1983, Teller sent a letter to George Keyworth, hailing the results. Years later, in recalling the episode, Teller said he had been especially eager to win over the president's science adviser, who he felt was "rather doubtful, not only of the usefulness, but even of the very existence of an X-ray laser."[38] Teller's letter was typed on Livermore stationery, "SECRET" cut in large letters across its top and bottom.[39] Despite the sober format, it was alive with happy informality. "Dear Jay," it began. "Merry Christmas! This may be the first classified Christmas greeting you have received," Teller wrote, adding that his Christmas present for Keyworth was news of the first proof of the existence of the X-ray laser. Three parameters measured in the test, Teller wrote, were in "essentially quantitative agreement" with predictions, showing that X-ray scientists understood the physical principles underlying the laser's action.[40] Most compelling were the length-versus-gain signals, he wrote. "There is no other theory except that of the laser which could explain these results." Teller hailed the data as validating his optimistic approach to the X-ray laser. "What our results may mean is not that we are geniuses at Livermore," he wrote, "but that too many people may have overestimated the difficulty of the job."[41]

Teller also appealed for a rise in X-ray laser funding, since the money recommended by the Fletcher panel had so far failed to materialize. "I agree that science cannot be sped up by throwing money at it," he wrote. "But we are now entering the engineering phase of X-ray lasers where the situation is different."[42] The words "engineering phase" were pregnant with meaning, implying that basic research was complete. In the Energy Department's seven phases for the life of a nuclear weapon, the start of engineering began in phase three, known as development engineering.[43] Emphasizing the point, Teller said: "We have also developed the diagnostics by which to judge every step of engineering progress." Again, the phraseology implied certitude. The phase of scientific doubt, characterized more by failures than successes, was over. Now it was just a matter of time and money before the weapon itself was in hand. To speed the process, Teller said, Livermore needed $50 million more in funding for the current fiscal year, and an additional $100 million for the next one.[44]

He then moved to the big picture. The X-ray laser, Teller said, gave the nation's antimissile quest a unique reason for hope. His message was remarkable because it made no mention of the dilemma documented by the Fletcher panel, that the laser could doom the search for a defensive shield. "I do not believe that the X-ray laser is clearly the only means, the best means, or even the most urgent means for defense," Teller wrote. "It is clear, however, that it is in this field that the first clear-cut scientific breakthrough has occurred. It is necessary to draw all the possible consequences from this fact." In closing the letter, Teller again stressed "we are now in the stage where money talks."[45]

The letter was sent. But in contrast to the one he wrote Reagan in 1982, Teller made no copies of it for other Livermore officials. This time his communication with the White House was meant to be very private.

Woodruff nonetheless learned of it. His informant was Robert E. Budwine, a Teller aide who helped the aged physicist write letters and papers. Unlike Woodruff, Budwine was knowledgeable about many of Teller's dealings in Washington. This one disturbed him.

"Roy, the old man's gone and done it this time," Budwine said, handing Woodruff a copy of the letter.[46]

Woodruff was aghast. He believed the letter was premature at best, a serious distortion of the truth at worst. As far as Woodruff knew, Teller's promotion of the X-ray laser had heretofore been optimistic generalities—and little more, since there was so little hard data. But now Teller was imposing his interpretative framework on the detailed physics of the experimental program and conveying that fantasy-as-fact to the highest science official in the land.

Woodruff stormed out of his office high atop Building 111 and raced down two floors to Teller's office. There he objected in strong terms. The so-called engineering phase was years away, if feasible at all. There were too many scientific uncertainties. Even the raw Romano data, while seeming to be encouraging, had to undergo more analysis and could end up less auspicious. Given the Cabra failure, it was best to be cautious. Most important, Woodruff said, it was wrong to assert there was quantitative agreement between laboratory predictions and critical measurements in the field. Woodruff felt it was a key point and that Teller's claim was misleading.[47]

At the core of Woodruff's final objection was a fundamental distinction about the nature of experimental data. In general, weapon scientists used computer models of atomic processes to make predictions about underground tests. If results agreed with those predictions, the scientists concluded they understood aspects of the X-ray laser, that they had "quantitative" proof they were on the right conceptual track. *Quan*titative agreement meant data were closely in line with predictions. It dealt in quantities. In contrast, *quali*tative agreement meant the presence of something had been detected but not measured. It dealt in qualities. The difference between the two was like the gap between precision of numbers and the nebulosity of colors. They were worlds apart. Quantitative understanding was hard-edged and precise. Qualitative was fuzzy, reflecting much ignorance about what was really happening beneath the desert. Woodruff objected to the letter in part because he felt the Romano data were qualitative, not quantitative.

Teller, caught off guard, agreed that parts of the letter were wrong but stubbornly refused to send a follow-up letter of clarification.

"No, I cannot," Teller is reputed to have said in his Hungarian drawl. "My reputation would be ruined."[48]

The aged physicist went on to argue that such a letter would damage attempts to win additional funding for the X-ray laser. He also objected to Woodruff sending a follow-up letter. At an obvious impasse, Woodruff left, saying he would discuss the situation later that day with the laboratory's director, Roger E. Batzel.

Back in his office, Woodruff drafted a "Dear Jay" letter of correction to be sent to Keyworth. "As the leader" of X-ray laser research, he wrote, he wanted to mitigate "premature conclusions by Edward."[49] Instead of quantitative agreement between predictions and results, Woodruff suggested there was "qualitative agreement." Emphasizing the point, Woodruff said the program had no "solid predictive ability" for X-ray results. The implications were stark. It meant the Livermore scientists had a laser but the cause of its action was still largely a mystery.

Woodruff also wrote that despite the demonstration of lasing in Romano, the program had failed to show that the beam could be made bright enough to be militarily useful. While the program could use a dramatic boost in funding, Woodruff wrote, it was because there were so many nagging questions about the laser's basic physics—not because Livermore scientists were on the verge of a weapon. "The X-ray laser is nowhere near the engineering phase at this time," he emphasized. In closing, Woodruff assured Keyworth that the program had "unequivocally demonstrated an X-ray laser" in Romano and "our enthusiasm, as well as the need for accelerating this research, continues to grow. Let me also caution, however, that it is premature to extrapolate present successes to the conclusion that a viable weapons system is possible in the near term."

By the time Woodruff could schedule a meeting with Batzel later in the day, Teller had already discussed the situation with the laboratory director, who told Woodruff to scrap the idea of a corrective letter. Woodruff reluctantly did so. "At that point it was not a fall-on-your-sword kind of issue," Woodruff recalled.[50] For one thing, Keyworth was an X-ray skeptic who was unlikely to be swept off his feet by a single underground test. For another, Keyworth undoubtedly knew Teller's penchant for technical optimism and inflated expectations. Woodruff did, however, decide he would circulate to Keyworth the "results" letter that normally went to military officials after a nuclear test, and made plans to visit the science adviser in person to emphasize the real state of affairs.

While meeting with director Batzel, Woodruff also extracted a promise that he thought would help keep Teller in line. Senior Livermore officials had decided to promote Woodruff to a newly created position, associate director for defense systems. This post would include not only Woodruff's old turf in the field of nuclear weapon design, but also allied areas such as underground testing and the lab's weaponization program, which turned experimental arms into ones ready for mass production. He would control nearly half the 8,000-person laboratory and be responsible for $300 million in programs. Woodruff told Batzel that a condition of his accepting the post would be the promise of greater rein on Teller, who at the time held the title of lab director emeritus. If anything like the Keyworth episode came up, Batzel would encourage Teller and Woodruff to interact. That was it—just the promise of keeping Teller in closer contact with the man in charge of the X-ray laser. But Woodruff, even as he made the proposal, had doubts about its effectiveness. He feared Teller had decided to circumvent them all. After all, Teller had routed no copies of the Keyworth letter to senior lab officials, which would have been standard practice.[51]

On January 13, 1984, nearly a month after Romano, Woodruff mailed off the secret "results" letter, the complex process of analyzing the data having finally been finished. This letter went to Department of Energy and Department of Defense officials as well as to Keyworth. In it, with fully analyzed data at his command, Woodruff was more sanguine than in his proposed letter of correction, where he had warned that Teller's conclusions were premature. Two of three parameters measured in the test—the laser beam's color and shape—had been found to be in "excellent quantitative agreement with predictions," he wrote. But the third measure, the laser's brightness, the most important parameter of all, was merely in qualitative agreement.[52]

Woodruff also alluded to the revelations of the Fletcher panel, calling for more study of the dangers of an X-ray laser "in the hands of the Soviets." In closing, Woodruff emphasized that many more tests had to be done. In his opinion, he said, they would show the X-ray laser could become an effective weapon. "But until the experiments do show this, the issue remains a matter of speculation."[53]

A month later, on February 15, Woodruff met briefly in Washington with Keyworth, who was effusive with praise about the Romano success. Woodruff detailed how the lab was sure it was the

first proof of lasing and, referring to Teller's letter, sketched out
some of the program's uncertainties.[54]

BACK in California, one of the best scientists in the X-ray laser
program gave a technical talk at Livermore that same day in which
he elaborated on the message Woodruff was delivering to Keyworth,
speculating about a key uncertainty that would come to haunt the
X-ray effort.[55] George Maenchen was a heavy-set man with a full
beard and round face, looking almost elfin as he puffed on his pipe.
He was an old-world craftsman, bringing a precision and thorough-
ness to everything he did. Now that Romano had finally proved
X-ray lasing, he did something that was very simple and very astute.
He searched for weak links in the chain of scientific logic. One that
intrigued him was whether the sensors deep beneath the desert were
interacting with the powerful laser beam, giving it a false brightness.
He was especially suspicious of reflectors used to bounce radiation
from beam pipes to sensors mounted off to the side. These might be
glowing under the impact of the intense radiation, he told a group of
Livermore scientists. "It was a simple question," Maenchen recalled.
"How was the sensor working?"[56]

Maenchen's apprehension struck at the heart of the program. If
correct, it would dash Teller's claims and the assertion, made to
Keyworth, that the program had "developed the diagnostics by
which to judge every step of engineering progress." Woodruff
clearly had good reason to tread lightly in advertising the X-ray
laser. Scientists at the core of his program, even while making
strides, had serious reservations about the overall health of the secretive endeavor.

TELLER and Wood still had what seemed to be unqualified enthusiasm for the X-ray laser at this point. Their fervor went far beyond
the White House and high administration officials. Amid the intellectual crisis caused by the Fletcher panel and the onset of technical
X-ray wariness, they shared it with me, a science and technology
reporter for *The New York Times*.

I had become interested in the top-secret laser and its developers
as I read vague references to their work in technical journals after the
Star Wars speech. The whole thing seemed undoable. But I was a
reporter in a field where I knew conventions were easily overturned
by the march of knowledge. Most of all, I was curious.

When I first saw Wood he was staring into space. He was

heavy, maybe 220 pounds, and over six feet tall, with sandy brown hair spilling over his shirt collar. His beard was full. He had a crumpled nose and breathed in a slightly labored way. Most noticeably, he had a quick smile. As we moved through the O Group offices, located in ramshackle trailers, I was struck by the extreme youth of the scientists, who were often sitting on office floors, talking quietly with one another. Their offices were filled with plants and books, and looked more like a college dormitory than a hotbed of weapons research. One room was filled with cases of Coke in 16-ounce bottles. There was also a stand-up freezer stocked with ice cream.

As we sat at a conference-room table, Wood explained the essence of the vision. Not only would the X-ray laser shoot down enemy missiles, but it would do so at a fraction of the cost of offense.

"Let's say you spend $2 million for an X-ray laser that can kill a $100 million booster," he said. "And suppose, for purposes of discussion, that a bomb can create 10 or 100 lasers and each can be pointed at a booster. Now you get into a situation where a single bomb with X-ray lasers around it can kill a large fraction of the total number of boosters in existence. If a single bomb can kill 100 of them, then it takes only 10 or so bombs to sweep the field clean. Being conservative, let's say it costs $10 million for something that can kill 100 boosters. So $10 million can knock out $10 billion of investment. That puts numbers on it and explains why it might be interesting."[57]

"The crucial thing," Wood stressed, "is that defense is now cheaper than offense—not by a factor of two or three, which was the sort of thing that was argued ten years ago, but maybe by a factor of 10, or 100, or 1,000. Now the balance really tips sharply in favor of defense."

Not only were the numbers impressive, but the fact that Wood was citing them to a reporter was nothing short of extraordinary. He was arguing fine points, and even alluding to one of the laser's most secretive aspects—how many independent beams might flash across space. On the other hand, he said nothing of the Fletcher panel's reservations about the laser, instead couching his argument only in terms of antimissile success.

During our talk, Wood praised his mentor as an intuitive genius who was eager to shake up the status quo. "He is not quick," Wood said. "He never was, and I've known him for a quarter century. He has an exceedingly well informed physical intuition. It is good at guessing the size of something. He understands how the world works. He can solve calculations slowly. He is not a Hans Bethe type. Bethe is much faster. Teller, however, has this capability to guess the answer. And he wants things to happen. He will not hesitate to use a cattle prod when a gentle tap on the shoulder doesn't suffice."

I flew back to New York and wrote an X-ray laser story based on my Livermore interviews. I aimed for balance, quoting not only Wood but experts highly critical of the device. But I knew nothing of the Fletcher panel's secret findings that the X-ray laser would shoot down Star Wars, and thereby unknowingly aided the disinformation campaign.[58]

By early 1984, my interest in the X-ray laser and its creators had grown so great that I decided to write a book on the subject. Apparently eager for publicity, Wood, whom I had interviewed on two occasions by this time, agreed to let me spend a week in May with him and his young recruits, working among them and observing their lives close up. The book was to be entitled *Star Warriors*.[59]

Early during my visit, Wood arranged for me to meet with Teller before he left on a business trip. The old scientist's office, adjacent to the lab director's, was dominated by a large wooden conference table. Its back wall was covered with framed photographs and documents. A photo of Wood, wearing a fierce expression, stood out. So did a mushroom cloud that appeared to be from the first H-bomb explosion.

To the left of Teller's desk was a large safe for top-secret documents, its top covered with African violets and a rubber plant. Nearby on a shelf were a number of books, *Real Peace* by Richard M. Nixon among them. Above his desk hung a testament to his fascination with the atom, a multicolored scientific chart. Its tables detailed the sequence of the nuclides, the various species of the chemical elements known to man.

Teller himself was wearing an old-fashioned herringbone suit of fine weave and a wide tie. The physicist, then 76, also wore a pair of black cowboy boots. His thick eyebrows were a wild tangle of gray hairs.

"Well," he said in his famous, slow Hungarian drawl, "what can I do for you?"[60]

I asked whether an antimissile system would really work.

"I would say the chances are good," he replied, adding that he was familiar with several ideas for weapons that were much better than anything ever before devised. "On the other hand, defense is *not* easy"—the "not" exploded out of his mouth. "It needs ideas. The fact that a great many American scientists, perhaps the majority, are against it puzzles me, disturbs me.

"I believe that my young friend, Lowell Wood, is a first-rate scientist. And I know that he has an extraordinary knack for getting talented young people interested in the topic and making them work hard and willingly on it—not like a chain gang but like a football team. Still, this is a small fraction of the talent there is in America. And almost necessarily it is much less than the talent the Soviets can deploy in the same field. If we had worked during the Second World War in the same way, if the *scientists* had behaved in the same way, Hitler would have won."

Teller went on to complain at length about Star Wars critics, especially elder scientists who were veterans of the Manhattan Project and the early postwar battles over the bomb. "The majority of these people opposed the H-bomb because it was too terrible," he said. "Now, they are opposing defense because it is apt to make a nuclear war less terrible and therefore more probable. Somehow I don't feel they can be right both times. I feel they are even wrong on the basis of simple logic.

"Anybody who has any feel for technology will not look at the future with blinders on their eyes. I see new ideas. These new ideas give me hope. But a lot of ingenuity is needed, and we just don't have enough talent. The number of people who could make contributions and exhaust themselves in fabricating objections is legion."

THE critics Teller complained about in 1984 were starting to make points similar to those of the Fletcher panel, not with the same authority, perhaps, but at least in public. One of the most pointed critiques was by Ashton B. Carter, a physicist then at the Massachusetts Institute of Technology and later at Harvard. In a report for the Congressional Office of Technology Assessment, Carter noted that fast-burn boosters would "severely compromise the effectiveness of X-ray lasers."[61] He also said X-ray lasers by nature tended to favor offense, noting that one high in the earth's atmosphere could fire into space to cripple man-made devices there. The reverse, he said, was not true. An X-ray laser in space would be unable to hit one high in the earth's atmosphere. "This fact bodes ill for defensive space-based X-ray lasers attacked by similar lasers (or even weaker ones) launched from the ground by the offense," he wrote.[62]

Even Livermore scientists began to address the point publicly. Kidder, the lab veteran who gave Teller independent X-ray advice, drove it home in a short paper issued in July 1984. "If we can develop the X-ray laser," Kidder wrote, "so can the Russians. Each side will then be able to destroy the other's defensive umbrella."[63] Appearing on an NBC News special, "The Real Star Wars," Kidder took the point a step further. The X-ray laser, he said, was an "incentive for banning weapons in space."[64]

One of the most detailed analyses of this period appeared in the July 19, 1984, issue of *Nature*, the prestigious British science journal. It dwelled on how limits in the laser's brightness made it largely futile for antimissile defense. Edward W. Walbridge, a physicist at the Argonne National Laboratory in Illinois, calculated that the laser beam would spread greatly over long distances in space like a flashlight beam, becoming weaker. For instance, Walbridge found that over a distance of 1,240 miles, the X-ray laser beam would spread from a pencil-thin ray into a cylinder some 200 feet wide. The device could destroy missiles, Walbridge wrote, only if its own nuclear bomb was titanic, unleashing up to 3.7 megatons of explosive energy—what he called a "disturbingly" large blast, conjuring a vision of apocalyptic forces at work in the heavens.[65]

As public critics took aim at the X-ray program, it was torn by growing internal doubts of a different nature. George Maenchen, the old-world craftsman of R Program, had concluded that the brightness measurements of all X-ray laser tests were indeed flawed. Just how defective was uncertain. Moreover, his R Program colleagues were divided on the issue, some seeing other explanations for his data. But Maenchen was sure he had established the existence of a flaw. In April 1984 he wrote an 11-page secret Livermore memo that outlined the problem, concluding that "it may, however, be difficult to correct the rosy impression left by earlier exuberant claims."[66] Maenchen kept refining the analysis, making it deeper and more pointed. In August 1984, he published a top-secret internal Livermore report, "Romano Power Measurements," its 76 pages warning of the brightness problem in great detail and calling for corrective actions. Among the 87 recipients of this report were Teller and Wood.[67]

Maenchen's theory got a boost after scientists from Los Alamos in New Mexico conducted their own X-ray laser experiment beneath the Nevada desert. The blast, code-named Correo, took place on

August 2, 1984. At first it seemed a success. But the laser's signals
were very unusual and prompted a bout of intense analysis, the Los
Alamos scientists going so far as to confer with their Livermore
rivals. It turned out that the sensors deep beneath the desert had
been tricked by the bomb's own radiations. Maenchen was right.
False brightness was a real danger. With a wave of his analytical
wand, he had turned one success into a failure. The question that
now troubled many analysts was whether the overall X-ray laser
program was threatened by similar illusions.[68]

DESPITE the emerging problem, the two top promoters of the X-ray
laser by this point were ready to go on the offensive, at least against
some of the objections raised by the Fletcher panel. They had finally
come up with what they saw as a technical solution that would
silence critics and pave the way for the laser's success. Wood called
Walbridge at Argonne, criticizing his *Nature* paper. "He was aggressive and hostile," Walbridge recalled. "He said I messed up
some of the basic physics and assured me that the X-ray laser was
fine."[69] Wood could offer no evidence to back up his assertion,
however. It was classified top secret.

Hints of the solution nonetheless soon appeared in open congressional testimony, part of the pattern of X-ray information leaks.
The testimony came from Robert Jastrow, a space scientist who
taught at Dartmouth and was a staunch defender of Star Wars. His
book *How to Make Nuclear Weapons Obsolete* was one of the first
to expound on President Reagan's plan.[70] His confidants in the antimissile community included Teller and Wood. On August 9, 1984,
toward the end of a hot, muggy summer in Washington, Jastrow
testified before the House Republican Study Committee, which was
preparing issues for the 1984 presidential campaign. Jastrow said the
*Nature* article had no technical validity. It was the victim of flawed
assumptions, he said. "The scientist who wrote the *Nature* article
assumed that X-rays cannot be focused, and therefore the spreading
out of the X-ray laser beam cannot be controlled," Jastrow said. The
assumption seemed sound, he said, because X-rays tended to penetrate mirrors rather than being reflected by them. But Jastrow noted
that space telescopes were routinely able to focus X-rays from distant stars, and that while such methods might be unsuitable for
harnessing the output of a nuclear blast, "any physicist can think of
other methods that might do the job."[71]

In fact, no physicist without a top-secret clearance had any idea

what Jastrow was talking about. It was one thing to bend a few stray
X-rays from a star located many light-years from the earth, and
another to focus trillions of X-rays from a nearby nuclear bomb that
was in the process of exploding.

At Livermore, scientists had been trying to advance the laser
ever since the Fletcher panel's revelations. In theory, the best solution was to boost the laser's brightness so its beams could cut deep
into the atmosphere to destroy rising energy missiles. There were
three ways to achieve the goal of higher brightness—increase the
size of the bomb (the solution identified by Walbridge), increase
the laser's efficiency (a goal limited by physical constraints), or focus
the beams so they packed more punch (the goal identified by Jastrow). The lab was already working to increase the bomb's size. So
in 1984, Wood and the young recruits of O Group pursued the most
daunting approach of all, focusing.

The basic X-ray laser design, Excalibur, was to have beams a
million times brighter than raw radiations from the bomb. The more
advanced design, Excalibur Plus, was to have beams a billion times
brighter. But Jastrow's excitement and that of the Livermore physicists centered on the most radical design of all—Super Excalibur,
which if perfected would have beams a trillion times brighter than
the bomb. Moreover, there would be hundreds and perhaps thousands of beams, vastly increasing the laser's powers of destruction.
Super Excalibur was the perfect solution to a pressing problem. This
feat of American technology was seen as finally heralding the triumph of antimissile defense, the powerful beams of the weapon
flashing much farther through space and cutting deep into the atmosphere to zap enemy missiles.

Super Excalibur was seen as having such stupendous firepower
as to defeat nearly any fast-burn booster—especially if the laser was
placed in orbit rather than being popped into space. When popped
up, Super Excalibur would still have to cut through much of the
earth's atmosphere, blasting parallel to the horizon to reach distant
targets. To be really effective, an X-ray laser had to shoot straight
down from a stable orbit, a geometry that shortened the beam's path
through the atmosphere. This logic applied not only to Super Excalibur but to Excalibur Plus as well. However, the latter's limited
powers meant it would have to orbit fairly close to the earth. In
contrast, Super Excalibur was seen as so powerful that it could be
based in geosynchronous orbit—the point 22,300 miles above the
equator where orbiting satellites move as fast as the earth rotates,

making them stationary relative to the ground. From this distant point in space its powerful beams could dig deep into the atmosphere to zap even fast-burn boosters. Moreover, geosynchronous orbit had a number of other advantages. From that great height, a single laser would have an exceptionally wide field of view, firing on missiles rising from nearly any part of the Soviet Union. An X-ray battle station in geostationary orbit would also sit motionless over its targets. In contrast, X-ray lasers in lower orbits would constantly move over the earth's surface, in and out of range. This meant there would have to be huge swarms of them to ensure that enough would be near Soviet targets at the start of a nuclear attack.[72]

But there were problems in all this as well. First, the placing of nuclear weapons in space was formally prohibited by the 1967 Outer Space Treaty, which the United States had promoted and sworn to abide by. For this and other reasons, the proposal raised the possibility of public opposition and a political uproar. But Super Excalibur advocates felt even this objection would fade if the device was placed in geosynchronous orbit. At such a distance, it was hard to envision the bomb swooping back to earth to be used offensively. Another problem was the new weapon's vulnerability. Teller and Wood had invented pop-up to keep X-ray lasers from being sitting ducks in space. While orbital basing was inherently unsafe, its dangers were seen as lessened for objects in the remoteness of geosynchronous orbit. They would be difficult to locate and destroy, especially if decoys were also deployed. In another precaution, heavy shielding was seen as protecting X-ray battle stations in geosynchronous orbit.[73]

A final problem was the most fundamental of all. Super Excalibur had no reality apart from a few paper studies. It was more hope than invention.

After months of incubation, in the fall of 1984 the idea seemed to burst forth at Livermore in full glory. The basic paper that outlined the plan was the work of an O Group team including Peter Hagelstein, Rod Hyde, Tom Weaver and Larry West.[74] On September 21, 1984, Wood and Hyde, a bearded math prodigy, wrote Teller a top-secret memorandum describing the idea. They detailed the physics and battle strategies for the proposed device.[75]

Teller was clearly delighted. In October he spoke to a group at SRI International in California, saying America now had the wherewithal to learn to defend itself against a massive attack of Soviet missiles. As autograph seekers surrounded him after the talk, one earnest young man asked for more details about the defensive arms.

"I wish I could tell you how ingenious they are," Teller replied, "how promising."

The young man nodded, saying he recalled a test in which an interceptor rocket had destroyed a warhead.

Teller waved his hand impatiently.

"One missile is nothing," he growled. "Anything can stop one missile. When the attack comes there will be 5,000 missiles and 300,000 decoys." The implication was clear. There were antimissile wonders to behold, if only Teller could speak of them.[76]

On October 15, Wood presented the vision of Super Excalibur to the head of the Pentagon's Star Wars program, Lieutenant General James A. Abrahamson. This marked the start of a hectic period in which Wood began to meet frequently with Abrahamson and other federal officials to inform them of X-ray laser progress. During 1985, he would travel to Washington at least fourteen times to promote Super Excalibur and other X-ray ideas.

THE stage was set for chaos. The X-ray laser program at this point was torn by extremes, with Maenchen and company arguing that the device tested in the desert was much dimmer than generally believed, and Teller and Wood arguing that the laser was not only dazzling but on the verge of an advance that would make it a trillion times brighter than a hydrogen bomb. Both claims could not be correct. Conceivably, the program might have reconciled these contradictory assertions through a process of quiet study. But that was not to be. Teller and Wood were intent on charging ahead, with little time for reflection, dialogue or revised goals. Moreover, a political factor was about to emerge nationally that caused Teller to redouble the pace of his White House lobbying, driving him to actions that caused the internal tensions of the X-ray laser program to multiply and explode.

ON November 6, 1984, Ronald Reagan was reelected for a second term in a landslide victory. Republicans won an all-time high of 525 electoral votes. The message heard at the weapons labs was resounding. Star Wars would have a chance. It was very good news for the thousands of scientists around the country who were struggling to make the dream come alive.

As in 1980, Republican strategists had tried to downplay the antimissile question during the campaign, viewing it as too controversial for public display. Neither Reagan nor his vice president, George Bush, pressed the issue during the race. The tacit understanding among Star Wars advocates was that if the president was reelected, he would push for Star Wars with all his political will and personal persuasiveness. The Republicans generally succeeded in their low-key strategy, despite Democratic attempts to make Star Wars a liability.

Paradoxically, the Republican win also held a vague antimissile threat. During the campaign, Reagan had launched a peace offensive. At the United Nations on September 24, he eschewed talk of the evil empire to appeal for "a better working relationship" with the Soviet Union.[77] In a dramatic gesture, he proposed establishing a new Soviet-American negotiating framework to chart the course of arms-control talks for the next twenty years. The move made headlines around the world and drew praise from allies long worried by the administration's saber rattling.

On November 22, the United States and Soviet Union announced that Secretary of State George P. Shultz and Foreign Minister Andrei A. Gromyko would meet in Geneva in January to negotiate an agenda for talks on limiting nuclear arms. It was the start of the most comprehensive arms talks ever, including, at the insistence of the Soviets, a set of negotiations aimed at blocking the development of space weapons. The administration, of course, had no plans to constrain Star Wars. But the space-weapons talks were a compromise made to get the Soviets to the table. The suspicion among some Star Wars advocates was that the talks were a dangerous gambit that would inevitably lead to other compromises and concessions.

TELLER was deeply upset by the administration's moves, fearing an arms agreement might thwart his newly energized antimissile hopes. In December 1984, on Livermore stationery, he wrote key government officials to tell them of Super Excalibur and urge them to avoid any East-West agreements that might block its development and eventual deployment. The move was unusually bold. First, it was again done without the knowledge of Woodruff, the program's head. Second, it was done even though Super Excalibur had undergone little hardware development and no underground testing at all.

On Friday, December 28, just after Christmas, Teller phoned Paul H. Nitze, the senior arms-control adviser to the State Department and to President Reagan and the man Teller had impressed a third of a century earlier with his H-bomb assessment. Teller said he had important news that would be conveyed in a letter carried by his close colleague Lowell Wood, who would be glad to answer any follow-up questions in person.[78]

Teller's letter, dated December 28, was stamped "SECRET," top and bottom. It started by reviewing the basic concept of the X-ray laser and the program's progress to date.[79] The current work, he said, showed the feasibility of generating an X-ray laser beam a million times brighter than the bomb. "One example of its utility would be the ability to kill a target at a distance of 10,000 km which would not be killed unless it were no more than 10 km from the bomb itself," Teller wrote. "Another would be the ability to kill 100 such targets at distances of 1,000 km." The logic behind such scenarios was straightforward. For destruction at great distances, all the laser's arms had to be aimed at one target so its power could be concentrated. Over shorter distances, the arms could focus on individual targets. Teller's suggestion that Excalibur could have 100 arms was the extreme upper limit of what was envisioned, the scenarios more often centering on a dozen or so arms.

"We expect," Teller wrote, "to be able to realize this advance in this decade even though our pace is severely resource-limited and we have received meager additional funding to pursue it." This statement was pointedly at odds with the official program estimates at the time, which put the demonstration of Excalibur's scientific feasibility in the 1990s or later and, with greatly increased funding, perhaps in the late 1980s. And even then, the device would require years of engineering. Teller's claim of being "able to realize this advance in this decade," after having just sketched out battle plans, clearly seemed to imply the appearance of a working weapon.

Teller then explained how the Soviets had been the world's leaders in unclassified X-ray laser research before their stream of publications suddenly dried up in 1977. The implication, he said, was that the Soviets were far ahead of the United States in such work, an ominous assertion that suggested military danger. However, Teller made no mention of the Fletcher panel's worries that, in the hands of the Soviets, an X-ray laser might spell the end of Star Wars.

Finally, Teller came to the news, saying he would not have communicated "in so urgent a manner" unless there had been "a final consideration which is very little known in Washington." Wood's team, he said, had made a breakthrough that promised "a real prospect of increasing the brightness" of the laser. "The overall military effectiveness of X-ray lasers relative to the hydrogen bombs which energize them may thus be as large as a trillion," he wrote. "This is an exceedingly large gain, and even if it cannot be fully realized, this approach seems likely to make X-ray lasers a really telling strategic defense technology. For instance, a single X-ray laser module the size of an executive desk which applied this technology could potentially shoot down the entire Soviet land-based missile force, if it were to be launched into the module's field-of-view. Such a module might be pre-emplaced in space, popped-up in an attack-suppressing mode, or popped-up as the Soviet attack commenced. A handful of such modules could similarly suppress or shoot down the entire Soviet submarine-based missile force, if it were to be salvo-launched."

Teller had envisioned an incredible feat. He was saying a single laser might destroy more than a thousand speeding missiles. But he went on to describe an even more fantastic accomplishment for the laser, saying it might be "devastatingly effective" against the tens of thousands of warheads and hundreds of thousands of decoys that emerged from missiles to speed through space. "It might be possible to generate as many as 100,000 independently aimable beams from a single X-ray laser module," he said, "each of which could be lethal even to a distant hardened object in flight." Stressing the laser's vast potential, Teller said its beams would flash not only through the void of space but would be strong enough to penetrate deep into the atmosphere, hitting targets as low as 30 kilometers from the earth's surface. This clearly would eliminate any problem of fast-burn Soviet boosters.

Teller's vision had important implications for one of Nitze's main areas of interest, the cost of antimissile defense. For years Nitze had argued that having the power to destroy a certain number of enemy missiles was not enough. An adversary could simply add more, overwhelming any defense. The only hope lay in cost effectiveness. If defense could be made cheaper than adding a new round of offensive armament, there was a chance the East-West balance would slowly shift toward antimissile arms. If not, defense would always be doomed by relatively cheap countermeasures. Nitze had laid out this logic in the 1960s during the nation's first great antimissile debate. In the 1980s, he refined it and championed its adoption by the federal bureaucracy, the principle becoming known as "the Nitze criteria."[80] National Security Decision Directive 172, adopted in 1985, eventually turned the Nitze criteria into national policy. No antimissile system would be adopted unless it could be shown to have an economic advantage over offense.[81]

Teller's vision spoke to this point in vivid terms. The super-powerful laser would be far cheaper than any offensive response the Soviets could possibly mount. Redoubling a force of missiles or warheads would be much more costly than generating a few more X-ray beams. The economical nature of Super Excalibur was also evident when it was compared with the emerging arsenal of American antimissile arms. The laser ("the size of an executive desk") would be incredibly light and cheap. In contrast, the other weapons, sensors and power sources being investigated by the Pentagon's Strategic Defense Initiative were gargantuan. Some of its lasers, such as variants on Alpha, were seen as nearly the size of a football field. Just lofting the thousands of weapons and sensors needed for antimissile war would cost as much as $1 trillion, according to the Congressional Research Service.[82] By contrast, Teller conjured up visions of a single, small X-ray laser destroying all Soviet land-based missiles. The implications went far beyond the Nitze criteria. Critics publicly railed that Star Wars would be so expensive it would bankrupt the nation. But Teller was assuring Nitze the venture might be not only doable in a military sense but also eminently affordable.

In closing, Teller told Nitze, "I felt that you should be aware of the possibilities of such striking advances, both the ones already in hand and the even more impressive ones in reasonable near-term prospect, before you go to Geneva," the site of the impending East-West talks. "You may wish to reflect on not only what they could mean to the United States, but of what significance they could have for the Soviet Union, particularly when the Soviet half-decade lead is taken into account."

Teller sent copies of the letter to director Batzel and Wood, but not Woodruff.

On December 28, the same day Teller drafted the Nitze letter, he wrote a shorter note to Robert C. McFarlane, who had become the president's national security adviser. Again, it was marked "SE-CRET," top and bottom. Teller opened the letter by saying he had news "of urgent importance," and noted that he had briefed President Reagan on the X-ray laser in late 1982. He then sketched the advances since then. The millionfold enhancement of Excalibur over a hydrogen bomb, he wrote, now had "some solid experimental foundation." Moreover, "theoretical calculations indicate that beams can be directed even more precisely, giving rise locally to an additional billionfold enhancement, giving rise to a seemingly impossible trillionfold enhancement."[83]

Given "moderate support" and "considerable luck," Teller wrote, the trillionfold enhancement "might be accomplished in principle in as little as three years." Again, this forecast was strikingly at odds with the official program, which had so little confidence in Super Excalibur that the idea was never even given a projected date for proof of scientific feasibility. Teller's prediction was also significant in that it meant the revolutionary idea might become fact before Reagan left office.

Boldly, Teller acknowledged that his motive was "to try to prevent the inadvertent appearance in any possible forthcoming agreement with the Soviets of limitations that might impede our work, though they could be secretly violated by the Soviets." In closing the letter, Teller said that any follow-up questions about the secret research would gladly be answered by the letter's courier, Wood, "who is primarily responsible for these developments."

Again, copies of this letter went to director Batzel and Wood. And again, Woodruff was left out of the loop.

BACK at Livermore, the two letters caused apprehension for at least one member of the extremely select group of individuals who knew of them—Budwine, Teller's assistant. He gave copies of them to Woodruff, asking what the head of the X-ray laser program was going to do about them.[84]

Woodruff was amazed. The earlier letter to Keyworth had at least been prompted by a successful experiment. But now Teller was touting a hypothetical nuclear device that had yet to be explosively tested and was doing so for reasons he acknowledged to be purely political. With Budwine's aid, Woodruff drafted a proposed letter of "clarification" to Nitze. Dated January 31, 1985, it said Teller and Wood were "overly optimistic" about the feasibility of an X-ray laser weapon. Woodruff noted that hoped-for increases in brightness had so far been "substantially lower" than expected and that its usefulness as a weapon remained "a matter of speculation" until a number of underground experiments could be conducted.[85]

Woodruff then took strong exception to Teller's contention that Livermore expected to "realize this advance in this decade." Instead, he said, at the current level of funding, Excalibur would not be proven scientifically until the twenty-first century.[86] A funding increase of $150 million a year could considerably speed up that schedule, Woodruff added. However, even if the research phase was successful in this century, then the development and engineering of an X-ray laser weapon would require an additional five to ten years and "several billion dollars." Moreover, contrary to Teller's 100 possible beams demolishing as many targets, Woodruff said the laser might strike "tens of objects."

Woodruff also downplayed Excalibur's antimissile role, saying a "more likely" use would be to destroy satellites and other spacecraft at ranges up to geosynchronous orbit. He also noted the findings of the Fletcher study and the reason it called for increased X-ray laser funding.

As for Super Excalibur, Woodruff agreed with Teller that in theory it was possible to "enhance the output of an X-ray laser weapon." But he warned that Teller was far too optimistic about the chances of doing so, especially of achieving a trillionfold rise in brightness that would allow a laser to shoot down the entire force of Soviet land-based missiles. "Will we ever develop a weapon close to the characteristics described?" Woodruff asked rhetorically. "Not impossible, but very unlikely." Eager to drive home his point, Woodruff said the odds of success were similar to the likelihood that a group of Soviet missiles would be struck down by a meteor shower. But Budwine removed that analogy from the final draft.[87]

In closing, Woodruff said it was "prudent" to assume the Soviets were at work on X-ray lasers, warning that "it could be very dangerous if they are successful first."

At this point, the letter was only proposed. Woodruff, wary because of his experience with the Keyworth letter, wanted to get official reaction before he went on to write one to McFarlane. He went to see Batzel, the lab's director, to tell of his planned response. But as before, Batzel blocked him, saying there was nothing in Teller's letters that violated the laws of physics. In addition, Teller had identified Super Excalibur as a concept "in principle" and had used many qualifiers.[88] Besides, Batzel said, the federal system would discount Teller's enthusiasm. Nitze and McFarlane undoubtedly knew that what seemed to be an easy technical goal to Teller might appear far more challenging to other scientists. Teller was a visionary. And the federal establishment knew his visionary zeal had to be taken with a grain of salt, Batzel said.[89]

Woodruff disagreed. Teller's letters were on Livermore letterhead and implied the laboratory's endorsement. "We" did this, "we" did that, Teller had reported. Furthermore, neither Nitze nor McFarlane had an independent basis to judge Teller's remarks on Super Excalibur. As Teller had said, few in Washington even knew of the plan's existence, while Teller touted it as a potential breakthrough that could make Star Wars more real than anyone ever imagined.

Batzel held firm. Woodruff could visit Nitze if he wanted, but there was to be no follow-up letter on Livermore letterhead, copies of which would circulate through official Washington as a rebuke to Teller.

WOODRUFF arrived in Washington on a cold winter's day in February 1985, the nation's capital snarled by ice storms. President Reagan had given the State of the Union Address the night before in which he had celebrated the start of his second term. A prominent part of Reagan's speech hailed the antimissile plan, calling it "a better way of eliminating the threat of nuclear war" than the balance of terror. "It is the most hopeful possibility of the nuclear age," Reagan enthused, adding that its goal was "aimed ultimately at finding a non-nuclear defense."[90]

Woodruff met Nitze in his State Department office. They talked for two hours, sitting on the couch in Nitze's office. The situation was worse than Woodruff expected. It turned out that Wood, in delivering Teller's letter, had come equipped with viewgraphs and given Nitze a full briefing. Now Woodruff stressed that Super Excalibur was basically a fantasy. Nitze, familiar with Teller's history, seemed ready to accept Woodruff's as an honest assessment.[91] "He had real doubts about whether the project was worthwhile," Nitze recalled, adding that he was "impressed" by Woodruff and took his reservations seriously. "I thought he was a bright guy. It's always good to get a bright, skeptical mind on a problem. I would have known less about it if he hadn't come out, so I appreciated his visit a great deal."

HAVING failed to subdue Teller, Woodruff was now engaged in damage control. But that exercise was arduous at best. Batzel, the lab director, was clearly siding with the stubborn old scientist and seemed ready to let him have his way on any issue, no matter that he was rapidly moving away from the technical reality of the X-ray laser program toward fantastic schemes. It was a bad situation. For Woodruff there was no reliable way of knowing who in Washington had been told what, no reliable way of judging how much damage had been done, no reliable way of making sure that the record had been set straight.

# FIVE

# The Collapse

SOCIAL PSYCHOLOGIST Leon Festinger and colleagues in the 1950s conducted an influential study on the behavioral effects of deeply held beliefs. They published their findings in *When Prophecy Fails*, a book about UFO cultists who thought they would be saved by aliens shortly before the earth's demise.[1] The cult's leader, Mrs. Marian Keech, had discovered that while writing she could telepathically transcribe messages from extraterrestrial beings. She learned that the spacemen had superior intelligence, wisdom, skill and machinery. They dwelled on the planets Clarion and Cerus. Soon Mrs. Keech and a select group of followers were told, through her writing, that the spacemen were planning to rescue them with flying saucers just before the destruction of the earth by an enormous flood. The group prepared to meet their saviors. Following exact instructions from the spacemen, group members removed every scrap of metal from their persons, including coins, watches, keys, zippers, bobby pins, belt buckles, buttons with metal backing, tinfoil around sticks of gum and brassieres with metal clasps. They waited patiently in Mrs. Keech's home as the predicted time of the pickup came and went. When it became clear that no spacecraft was about to materialize in the backyard, the group decided, after some discussion, that the episode had been a drill. Another message came, with a new time of rendezvous. The group eagerly waited in Mrs. Keech's backyard. It was winter, in the dead of night, with snow coming down. The cultists shivered and stomped their feet and did calisthenics to keep warm. Finally, they gave up. In the days and weeks that followed, the cycle of disappointments was repeated.

Surprisingly, the setbacks in no way caused the dissolution of the group. Instead, the believers rationalized the difficulties away, becoming more firmly set in their convictions than ever. Moreover, they began to proselytize among those who were curious about the affair. They lectured visitors. They called in reporters, eager to publicize the story of the compassionate spacemen. They sent out news releases. Eventually, the police were called in after a crowd of some two hundred unruly spectators converged on the Keech home. A warrant was issued for Mrs. Keech's arrest. Ultimately the cult broke up, many of its members still convinced they had been in contact with benevolent beings from outer space.

Festinger and colleagues concluded that the episode illustrated a general truth. "When people are committed to a belief and a course of action," they wrote, "clear disconfirming evidence may simply result in deepened conviction and increased proselyting."[2] The reason, they wrote, was that disconfirmation of deep beliefs resulted in "cognitive dissonance" and psychological stress. Rationalization could reduce some of the tension. But for a deeper sense of consolation, the researchers said, a believer needed to win support from new people to make the rationalization seem really correct. "If the proselyting proves successful, then by gathering more adherents and effectively surrounding himself with supporters, the believer reduces dissonance to the point where he can live with it."

To a degree, this kind of analysis can be applied to Teller and the saga of the X-ray laser, especially in its later stages. The atomic situation was clearly more complex than the episode with the UFO cultists. Nonetheless, Teller had all the markings of a prophet preaching a gospel of nuclear salvation. And, like Mrs. Keech and her group of UFO believers, his faith was to be sorely tested.

EARLY in 1985, Teller's aides at Livermore were doing everything in their power to bring his nuclear vision to life in the form of Super Excalibur. The technical exuberance of the team was evident in a memorandum Wood wrote an engineer in January 1985. At its top was the ubiquitous "Re:" of business memos. But instead of a bland reference to the subject matter, there was a single word in capital letters that evoked the start of a military campaign: "CHARGE!"[3]

In breathless prose, Wood said lab director Batzel had "provisionally" decided to feature Super Excalibur in the upcoming round of congressional budget hearings and urged that no effort be spared to advance the novel device. The work, he wrote, "needs to be accelerated to the maximum extent practicable." In closing, Wood referred to the O Group team that invented Super Excalibur, calling it the "High Brightness Conspiracy." It was clearly a cabal, a select group of believers working on a radical plan in great secrecy. But the period of incubation was over. Super Excalibur was now being advertised as an important new goal for the 8,000-person laboratory. The memo was sent not only to the engineer but to twenty-eight other Livermore scientists and officials, including director Batzel, Teller and Woodruff. It was a cross between a coming-out announcement and a declaration of war.

The zeal of O Group and Teller for Super Excalibur was largely a local phenomenon at this point. Woodruff vacillated between deep skepticism and cautious interest, as did much of the Livermore staff that knew of the idea and Wood's track record. The situation with other American scientists was much less ambiguous. Experts at Los Alamos felt that the claims and passions of Teller and Wood had become laughable and sometimes dangerous. After all, their own X-ray laser success in the Correo event had, like a mirage, vanished upon close inspection. Perhaps Livermore's data were illusory as well. Top Los Alamos officials were ready to communicate their skepticism, as Woodruff found out that January.

The tense confrontation took place on the evening of Monday, January 28, 1985, during a first-ever summit meeting between high officials of the rival laboratories. It occurred on the neutral ground of the Nevada test site, where both laboratories maintained offices and facilities in the federal town of Mercury. After a day of talks, the handful of top Livermore and Los Alamos officials had gone to the Energy Department's steak house, where their dining was abetted by a considerable amount of wine. The usual tension gave way to laughter. After dinner, the group went back to the Los Alamos dormitory area for social drinking. It was late. The two directors of the laboratories sat down opposite each other. The cordiality was about to vanish. Donald M. Kerr of Los Alamos was a headstrong, hard-driving manager in his mid-40s who was trying to shake up and revitalize his own laboratory. Sitting on a bed, sipping brandy, he turned his energies on Livermore director Batzel, saying one issue still troubled him. Teller, he said, was wildly overstating the merits of the X-ray laser.[4]

"We fired him when he was a group leader at Los Alamos," Kerr lashed out, "and you, sir, rehired him!"

Batzel, surprised by the outburst and never comfortable with confrontations, froze. Woodruff, standing behind him, asked sarcastically how old Kerr was during the Manhattan Project.

Kerr raged on, saying it was unconscionable that Batzel allowed Teller and Wood to go all over the government misrepresenting Livermore's work on the X-ray laser.

"I would fire Lowell Wood for what he has said," Kerr continued, adding that Teller should go as well.

Woodruff jumped in, saying what Kerr really meant was that he'd put restraints on the pair.

"No," Kerr shot back. "They should be fired."

Now Woodruff found himself defending Teller and Wood. There was a place for them, he said. Their creativity was an asset to the nation's security programs. He noted that Wood had succeeded in attracting talented young scientists to the laboratory who had made major technical strides. But he also expressed some concern about X-ray overselling and, trying to make peace, said further discussion was clearly warranted.

People started to drift away, embarrassed at the display of emotion. The Livermore team walked to the Mercury bowling alley, director Batzel having decided he wanted a beer. They got in the door just as the place was closing.

Batzel went to the bar.

"We're closed," said the man behind the counter.

"What do you mean you're closed? I'm the director of the Lawrence Livermore National Laboratory. I want a beer."

"I don't care who you are. We're closed!"

The dispirited Livermore team called it a night, stung by criticism that it was unable to restrain its own scientists and chagrined that it was unable to prevail over a barkeep. The next day, nursing hangovers, the officials flew back by commercial jet to California.

AT Livermore, Wood continued to press the bureaucracy to back Super Excalibur, increasing the forcefulness and detail of his presentations. The push worried Woodruff even as it drew praise from Teller, who told top lab officials that the fledgling idea should be accelerated with a lobbying campaign in Washington and a substantial rise in funding.

This division in perspective was exemplified by an episode that took place on Wednesday, January 30, 1985, two days after the Nevada summit. It occurred at a formal review of Livermore's physics department attended by all the lab's senior officials, including Teller, Woodruff and director Batzel, as well as two senior scientists from outside the lab. Wood was there because he headed O Group, an arm of the physics department. For the assembled group he unveiled a glossy artist's rendering of what Super Excalibur might look like in action, myriad beams radiating from an exploding bomb to destroy enemy missiles. Wood urged that work be accelerated in a crash program to a "technology-limited pace," rather than one limited by funds. The billions of dollars needed to turn the artwork into arms could come from two places, Wood said. Initially, some $100 million a year could be taken from "Whitney" funds, the code name for Livermore monies dedicated to basic nuclear weapons research, including work on safety and reliability. The rest of the money, Wood said, might be won from the government after the Super Excalibur advance was disclosed to Congress, the Pentagon (with its Star Wars program), the office of the Secretary of Defense and the National Security Council.[5]

Wood's estimate of when Super Excalibur might appear was less optimistic than Teller's, who told McFarlane in 1984 that it might be "accomplished in principle in as little as three years," or 1987. In contrast, Wood told the gathered lab officials that the program, if accelerated with the aid of large sums of money, might not establish the scientific principles until 1990—and only then could a firm commitment be made to a prototype weapon and work begin on serious research and development. The "baseline" weapon, he said, would have 1,000 beams.[6]

Teller was delighted with the presentation. He asked for no assessment from the assembled group of top scientists and administrators. Instead, he gave what amounted to orders for the idea's advancement. "These are very real possibilities pointed out by Lowell," Teller told the group. "The X-ray laser has produced entirely unexpected results. There is no reason to believe that further surprises are impossible. This work should be supported at much higher levels. The amount of money [currently being spent], compared to past less important programs, is preposterous. It is not hopeless to get more money on it, and this we should do. What has been done is astonishing, and we can go to Washington and talk about what's been done. On this we should agree. There can be no argument among us."[7]

Woodruff listened with growing apprehension, the Los Alamos denunciation of Teller and Wood still ringing in his ears. He had no control over Wood and his domain in the physics department. That was a place of dreamers and theoreticians. The area he did govern, the lab's making of nuclear arms, was a down-to-earth endeavor that carried a grave responsibility for sobriety and caution, if only because of the great costs involved. Now he was hearing details of a radical plan that would rock the Excalibur program he had successfully built. Super Excalibur was a good idea. But no matter how good, it had to be pursued with care lest it damage the more pragmatic parts of the X-ray effort already under way. Super Excalibur was so speculative it could easily fail. Its design was so vague that the normal prerequisite of a computer investigation of its feasibility had yet to be completed. The more tenable work had to survive and prosper. Woodruff resolved to move cautiously in aiding the revolution—and to do so with authority. After all, Wood had no real responsibility for the development of the X-ray laser.[8]

As Woodruff listened to the presentation, he was called out of the room for a phone call from Washington. It was Major General G. Kenneth Withers of the Army, who had succeeded Hoover as director of the office of military applications at the Energy Department. Withers, the federal official most closely associated with oversight of the weapons labs, was, in effect, Woodruff's boss in Washington. In military fashion, Withers chewed Woodruff out, saying too little money was being spent on the X-ray laser program. Echoing Wood's presentation, General Withers ordered that money be transferred from the laboratory's core weapons program to the X-ray laser effort.[9]

Woodruff objected. It was one thing to receive new monies for the project, a goal Woodruff strongly supported. It was another to raid the core program, the bedrock of the lab's efforts to improve the safety and reliability of nuclear arms. The tense conversation ended on a sour note with no resolution. Woodruff thought it was likely that the lobbying of Teller and Wood in Washington had provoked the confrontation. In any case, he intended to do something about it. At the time Woodruff was already working on his proposed letter of correction to Nitze in an attempt to counter X-ray misinformation in the nation's capital. Now he planned to send a letter to General Withers as well.[10]

Late that afternoon at the review meeting, senior Livermore

officials went into executive session to evaluate the day's activities. Woodruff, angered at the X-ray threat to the lab's core weapons program, lashed out at Wood and Super Excalibur. Wood, he said, was "heading off on a divisive path. If he pushes too much harder he'll lose the support of the people in A Division," the group that designed hydrogen bombs and supplied much of the expertise for the X-ray laser's development. Wood's plan could wreak havoc, Woodruff warned. "There's a dark side to him that needs to be kept under control."[11]

The general tenor of the meeting, however, seemed to go in other directions. Carl Haussmann, a craggy lab veteran who was an associate director at large, said the trouble came down to money. "Edward was right on when he observed that the real crux is that X-ray lasers deserve grossly more funding than they're getting. This is an example of the malaise that's present today in this country. I think we should collectively address how to remedy that situation."[12] Michael M. May, another associate director at large, observed that the problem was perhaps the "antinuclear feeling" among Washington officials who ran the SDI program.

Teller, who the previous year had expressed exactly the same opinion, now dismissed it. The old scientist was inspired by a new vision and filled with new confidence. Nothing, it seemed, could stand in his way or that of the would-be weapon. "The distinction is not nuclear versus antinuclear but rather mass destruction versus defense," Teller snapped. "The whole point is whether defense can be more economical than the offsetting measures"— a veiled reference to the hope that Super Excalibur would have vastly increased powers of destruction.

May voiced quick agreement.

"That's the rational approach," he said. "What's been imposed on SDI is a lot of other things."[13]

TELLER, the authoritarian side of his personality in full expression, had clearly communicated his opinion on Super Excalibur to the lab's top officials. With this endorsement in mind, they met two days later, on Friday, February 1, to discuss the lab's future agenda. Batzel, May and Haussmann were joined by Mary E. Tuszka, the lab's financial controller who had been promoted to the post of associate director for administration. Woodruff was not present. The key topic was Super Excalibur. The few hesitations that were voiced mostly came from Tuszka, a nonscientist who felt a campaign to pursue the idea was premature. The consensus was to press ahead, seeking significant new funds.[14]

Meanwhile, Woodruff worried that the Excalibur push was already distorting the lab's nuclear weapons work and that things would grow worse as pressure mounted for Super Excalibur progress. On Monday, February 4, he wrote a seven-page letter to the lab's top seven officials, stressing grim facts and calling for a major X-ray laser review similar to the one just conducted for the physics department. The letter contained a substantial amount of cold water. "Notwithstanding all the recent rhetoric," Woodruff wrote, "the last data taken are from the Romano test over a year ago." New analysis of that data, he said, showed the laser's efficiency was "substantially lower than expected" and the beam's brightness "considerably lower than expected." Progress with Super Excalibur, he added, would be even more uncertain. "I am concerned we still need some inventions," Woodruff wrote. "Much work and many experiments need to be done before we will know if this idea is viable," adding it was "too early to sell" as anything more than a concept. "However, it is a very good idea and we should and will proceed to develop it as rapidly as possible."[15]

Two days later, on Wednesday, February 6, Woodruff wrote General Withers to warn of dangers to the lab arising just from the Excalibur work, much less an expensive push for a far more ambitious X-ray venture. He elaborated on his fears, expressed on the phone, that Excalibur's privileged funding had already distorted the lab's weapons program to "the bounds of tolerance" and cautioned that further diversion would have "effects of major proportion." For instance, several lab facilities would have to be closed and work scrapped on other ideas for advanced nuclear arms. "The long-term consequence of such actions are, in my view, life-threatening to this institution," Woodruff wrote. He sent copies of the letter to several Energy Department officials and a dozen top Livermore administrators.[16]

Woodruff eventually won the point of contention. General Withers and the Energy Department backed down, ruling that no more X-ray laser funds were to come from Livermore's core weapons program. For Woodruff, it was not only a sensible solution but a clear victory over Wood.

Despite rising pressure for the promotion of Super Excalibur, Woodruff continued to soft-pedal the idea. While calling it a very good concept, he strictly avoided the sweeping claims made by Teller and Wood. On February 13, 1985, Woodruff briefed the Senate Strategic Defense Initiative Working Group, a coalition of congressional aides who followed Star Wars. On a chart, he listed the lab's various X-ray laser ideas and their "concept validation date" in a program that was "technology-limited," rather than one with constrained funding. Excalibur, whose beams were to be a million times brighter than a bomb, was listed as 1992. Excalibur Plus, with beams a billion times brighter, was 1995 followed by a question mark to show the estimate was tentative. Super Excalibur, with its trillion-fold enhancement, had no date at all—just a question mark.[17]

And privately, Woodruff tore into Wood and his Super Excalibur push. In a February 19 memorandum to the lab's top four officials, he wrote: "This High Brightness Conspiracy must be put to rest." He stressed that exaggerated claims threatened to damage the lab's credibility within the defense community and to alienate Livermore's own scientific staff. "I'm not sure how to stop or mitigate Lowell, but I know we must try and I am asking for your assistance."[18]

THE X-ray laser at this point started to regain some of its luster, at least in Washington's eyes. Thanks largely to Super Excalibur, Wood's salesmanship and Teller's influence, it was again seen as a potential Star Wars weapon—despite the Fletcher report, the internal doubts at Livermore and the Reagan administration's own "nonnuclear" stance.

"A new kind of nuclear-driven defensive weapon is in fact very much in the DOD's thinking as one of the options we would like to develop for the SDI," Richard L. Wagner, Jr., the Pentagon's top nuclear official, told Congress in February 1985.[19]

The point was driven home in a policy statement signed toward the end of February by Defense Secretary Weinberger and Energy Secretary John S. Herrington. The statement said its purpose was to "clarify the role of nuclear research" in Star Wars. While the antimissile program had a long-term "nonnuclear" goal, it said, nuclear-powered beam weapons were also under study for two reasons—to learn what "an adversary may develop for use against future U.S. surveillance and defensive systems," a reference to the Fletcher panel's fears, and to "explore nuclear directed-energy options as SDI possibilities."[20]

INFLUENTIAL skeptics were still leery of the X-ray laser, despite the rising excitement over Super Excalibur and the renewed push to promote the would-be weapon in Washington. Significantly, their doubts were conveyed directly to Teller. Ray Kidder, the lab veteran and maverick, published a Livermore report on March 14, 1985, that said no significant enhancement of the brightness of the X-ray laser was likely to be achieved. The technical difficulties, Kidder said, were too great. The first person on the paper's distribution list was Teller.[21]

A more important event took place a week later, on March 21, when two world-class scientists arrived at Livermore for an X-ray briefing. They had been invited by Teller, who was still eager for the approbation of the kind of eminent researchers he had known in his early days. The two were Hans A. Bethe and Sidney D. Drell, both of whom had secret clearances. Bethe was an emeritus professor of physics at Cornell University. Drell was head of theoretical physics at the Stanford Linear Accelerator Center. Both men had long advised the government on military issues. Moreover, both were widely respected for integrity, their opinions carrying great weight in scientific circles.

Teller, 77 years old, spared no trouble in trying to inform and entertain his guests. He had his best young scientists give summaries of their X-ray work, including Wood, Tom Weaver and such O Group luminaries as Peter Hagelstein, Larry West and Rod Hyde. In all, more than a dozen scientists made presentations.[22]

"Well," Teller effused at the briefing's end, "do you think we are ready for engineering?"

"Absolutely not," Drell replied. "You still have basic science to do."[23]

BUT Teller was undeterred. His technical excitement over Super Excalibur culminated a few days later as the idea underwent its first attempt at experimental verification during a nuclear explosion at the Nevada test site. The aim was to achieve some degree of X-ray focusing by means of two different techniques.[24]

The focusing part of the test was a late addition to what was already an extraordinarily complex series of experiments known collectively as LD-1. The goal of LD-1 was to advance the baseline X-ray laser program, Excalibur, and to evaluate a host of new sensors. In the main experiment, four rods made of different metals were bundled together in close proximity. The hope was that all would fire at once, making a single beam of great power. It was to be a small step on the road to bundling hundreds and possibly thousands of rods. In an additional move of major significance, one of many sensors on the test apparatus had undergone modification in order to explore Maenchen's fears about false brightness. The change was cursory, since the time between the elaboration of his thesis and the building of the hardware had been too short for wide modification. It nonetheless marked the start of Livermore's attempt to grapple with the difficulty.[25]

In general, the underground test was one of the most elaborate in the forty-year history of the American program of nuclear explosions. More important, its diversity hinted at growing X-ray discord. Focusing would raise brightness, while a revision of sensor readings would lower it. The test in some respects was a manifestation of the philosophical clash between Livermore's conflicting blocs.

The underground blast, code-named Cottage, took place on Saturday, March 23—the second anniversary of President Reagan's Star Wars speech. Wood was in Nevada to get the X-ray laser results firsthand. In an unusual move, so was Teller.[26]

The two scientists viewed Cottage as an extraordinary success for focusing, paving the way for the triumph of Super Excalibur. When the lab's plane flew into the Livermore airport on Sunday, disembarking scientists were greeted with champagne. On the Monday after the test, March 25, Wood briefed SDI officials in Washington on the X-ray achievement. Teller, too, went to Washington that week, telling the Energy Department that the advance called for a rise in X-ray laser funding.[27]

Teller also described the success to the nation's new Energy Secretary during a secret Livermore briefing on April 2. John S. Herrington, 45, was a lawyer and longtime member of the Reagan team who had been White House personnel chief before being tapped for the Energy post. An efficient administrator, Herrington had no experience in energy or nuclear weapons and had never before served in a cabinet. At Livermore, he listened patiently as Woodruff tried to give the standard X-ray laser overview. But Teller kept interrupting, talking excitedly about Super Excalibur, the Cottage test, and the overall promise of the X-ray laser. Woodruff would put up a chart and start to talk, then Teller would interrupt and go on for five or ten minutes. Woodruff got through only about a third of his presentation.[28]

Later, the group went on a tour of the top-secret vault where

Livermore kept models of its nuclear weapons, including cutaways that showed how the bombs were put together. The vault held some of the nation's most closely guarded secrets. As they toured its depths, Herrington spoke in hushed tones with Woodruff, saying he sympathized with the difficulties that evidently came in working with Teller.[29]

Irrepressible, Teller the next day hailed the X-ray laser in an open public forum. On April 3 in a speech at the University of California, Irvine, he spoke to an overflow crowd of five hundred. X-ray lasers, Teller said, would be highly accurate in hitting and destroying enemy targets. Moreover, he said, they now existed "not on paper" but in reality.[30]

AROUND this time, I too encountered some of this effervescence. My mail at *The New York Times* brought a note and an invitation to an April 20 party. "Dear Bill," wrote Wood, who proceeded to tiptoe around the classification laws: "Find a fast-breaking science story, grab a plane to the Coast, and join us to celebrate that which we cannot discuss with the unsanctified but are *exceedingly pleased with*, nonetheless. We'll throw in an interview with ET."[31]

The invitation read:

O Group's

HIGH BRIGHTNESS CONSPIRACY

Invites *You*
to a Gala Celebration
of

HIGH BRIGHTNESS EVENTS

Coinciding with the second
anniversary of President Ronald Reagan's

STRATEGIC DEFENSE SPEECH

of 23 March 1983,

said celebration convening at
1800 Hours, 20 April 1985
at

*The Sty in the Sky*

The "Sty in the Sky" was Wood's wry name for his own home, a rambling, two-story structure made of logs that sat atop a ridge near the laboratory. I was amazed to get his note and the invitation, since they seemed to press the limits of what could be discussed publicly. As soon as Wood's missive reached me at *The Times*, I phoned a series of sources at Livermore and other places and wrote a story that in May 1985 ran at the top of the front page.[32]

"Gains Reported on Use of Laser for Space Arms," read the headline. "What appears," said the story, "to be an important advance in developing an X-ray laser space weapon powered by a nuclear bomb has been made by scientists at the Lawrence Livermore National Laboratory, Federal scientists said yesterday. According to these scientists and others familiar with the top-secret research, the advance has increased the brightness and thus the power of the X-ray device by focusing its rays."

For me, the article was a paradoxical and somewhat troubling exclusive. Though far from being convinced that Star Wars could work, I had nonetheless worked myself so deeply into the confidence of the antimissile advocates that I had become the focus of leaks of classified information. I was proud of my reportorial skills and even-handedness, but, in truth, the Pentagon could have had no better coverage of another Star Wars "advance" if it had put out a press release—not that it wanted publicity in this particular case. Quite the contrary. My article touched off probes by the Federal Bureau of Investigation and the Energy Department, which sought the source of the leaks. The public release of atomic secrets was a federal offense that could bring the loss of security clearances or the imposition of jail sentences. However, in this case no charges were ever brought.

FOR all its seeming accomplishments, its leaks to the press, and its blandishments about the nation's capital, the X-ray laser program was at a public relations disadvantage compared with other elements of the Strategic Defense Initiative. The top-secret successes of the X-ray laser program were abstractions. When a bomb exploded beneath the Nevada desert and a laser fired, the only evidence of its action was the twitch of recording devices. By contrast, the advances of the broader SDI program were often played as public extravaganzas, especially during 1985. The showy demonstrations were meant to increase public interest in antimissile defenses and boost funding now that President Reagan had won reelection. These shows, which had Pentagon approval, had the code name Beacon, for Bold Experiment to Advance Confidence. Examples included bouncing a low-powered laser beam off the space shuttle and firing a chemical laser at a stationary missile in New Mexico, the events being hailed by Pentagon officials as evidence of great headway. Critics disparaged such displays as political stunts structured to promote the illusion of technical progress.[33]

After years of ups and downs, the X-ray laser program now seemed to be on a roll—and Wood intended to keep it that way. In the wake of the Cottage success, he proposed a Beacon-type nuclear test at the Nevada test site. The idea was to fire an X-ray laser beam from deep beneath the earth into a chamber on the desert floor where a mock missile would be shattered. In promoting the idea, Wood bypassed both Woodruff's office and the Energy Department, which sponsored the X-ray laser research and explosive tests. Instead, he took it to the Star Wars program of the Pentagon, which was more political and far more influential, having good connections with the White House.

On Friday, April 19, 1985, Wood described the proposed test to General Abrahamson, director of the Strategic Defense Initiative. Wood's briefing was entitled "Pillars of Fire in the Valley of the Giant Mushrooms." The "pillar of fire" was the X-ray laser beam, while the "giant mushroom" harked back to the days when atmospheric nuclear blasts rocked the Nevada test site to produce towering radioactive clouds. Wood outlined several goals. The X-ray beam could fire upon "realistic retrievable samples," including reentry vehicle shields and missile parts. It could also plow through the earth's atmosphere, helping verify how far a beam might propagate through air. Most important, the experiment could influence the next "congressional budget cycle" if done in a timely manner, Wood wrote in a document that summarized the briefing. "Irradiated targets" and movies of the experiment, he said, would emphasize the weapon's "reality."[34]

Wood's attempt to promote this idea was a serious trespass on Woodruff's turf. It was one thing to propose ideas inside Livermore, or even to advertise them around Washington. But now Wood was urging a radical change in the nation's program of underground testing, and doing so outside normal channels at Livermore and the Energy Department. It seemed to be a bureaucratic end run meant to push a controversial idea. Wood never publicly stated his motive or defended his actions. But he seemed intent on following in the footsteps of Teller and shaking things up.

TIRELESSLY, Wood zigzagged his way across the country as he pro-moted the laser and celebrated its success. Back in California the day after the Abrahamson briefing, a Saturday, he threw his "Gala Celebration of High Brightness Events" to toast the advance. O Group was there in force. I did not attend. Woodruff was not invited.

On Tuesday, April 23, Wood was back in Washington, this time to deliver the good news about Super Excalibur to Central Intelligence Agency director William Casey, the rich conservative and longtime Reagan confidant who went on, after his death, to be at the center of the Iran-Contra controversy. Wood's briefing was entitled "Soviet and American X-ray Laser Efforts: A Technological Race for the Prize of a Planet."[35] As Teller had done with Nitze, Wood described Super Excalibur as having "as many as 100,000 independently aimable beams." Unlike Teller, he also included a glossy artist's drawing of the laser in action. The briefing said the Cottage test had achieved not only focusing but also "weapon-level" brightness.[36] Wood also reviewed possible Soviet X-ray work, saying the devices, if perfected, "offer the prospect of drastically altering the geopolitical balance." Wood sent copies of the briefing to the Energy Department, the Defense Department and the White House.

WOODRUFF was furious when he found out about Wood's briefings to Abrahamson and Casey. He and his deputy, George H. Miller, flew to Washington to tell SDI personnel that Wood's estimates for "Pillars of Fire" were hopelessly unrealistic. The experiment would cost more, take longer to field and have a laser substantially dimmer than Wood advertised. In May, Woodruff asked Miller to write him a memo as a "sanity check," just to see if Miller's perceptions of Wood were anywhere close to his.[37]

Miller's memo said R Program scientists felt Wood consistently oversold the program, creating a "serious" problem. "It is [not] as easy as Lowell states, our current capabilities are not as significant as he states, and the time scales are not nearly as short as he states. This conflict of views is in large part due to Lowell's verbal style in which he contends that anything which he believes is possible is likewise easy. He does not ever mention the inventions which are required, the new knowledge which must be gained or the real difficulties which must be overcome."[38]

Ironically, Miller noted that the overselling occurred even as Wood denigrated and harassed those who were supposed to produce the needed breakthroughs. "An explosion of personal resentment may be imminent with an attendant loss of manpower and consequent failure of the program," he wrote. "The problem is that his style is absolutely monolithic, uncompromising and frequently abusive personally to the other scientists in the program. He has little toleration for those less brilliant and less well-spoken than he."

FOR Teller, the political climax of the Super Excalibur push came in June 1985 when he again visited the White House. The Hungarian scientist told Reagan of the success in the desert and lobbied for more funds. Impressed with news of a breakthrough, the president promised Teller a quick $100 million infusion for the X-ray laser program.[39] While at the White House, Teller stopped by the office of McFarlane, the national security adviser. It was McFarlane's first meeting with the famous physicist, his impression being somewhat unfavorable. "He was very excited about the experiment and made very extravagant claims," McFarlane recalled. "He said with additional infusions of money, we could demonstrate the feasibility of it [Super Excalibur] in high-earth orbit. My instinctive reaction was that he was not an impartial analyst. He was an advocate."[40]

Teller's salesmanship, coupled with Wood's efforts and the sheer technical allure of Super Excalibur, had a profound impact on the administration's plans for the overall X-ray laser program, despite the skepticism of McFarlane and many others. Its budget was slated to swell. In fiscal 1985, the Energy Department's program to develop third-generation weapons had received $215 million, the bulk of it for the X-ray laser. In fiscal 1986, the funding was to jump to $270 million—plus the additional $100 million Teller secured by lobbying Reagan. From then on it was to skyrocket. The fiscal 1987 budget was to be $536 million. Fiscal 1988 was to be $700 million, and so on, the projections going through 1991. Altogether, from 1985 to 1991, research on the X-ray laser and its less mature cousins was to receive $3.7 billion.[41]

Livermore itself was to benefit greatly from this federal largess, its research budgets soaring. So, too, plans were laid for a $62.5 million, 121,000-square-foot complex that would have large new laboratories and help house the hundreds of new scientists who would work on the project.[42] The planned expansion of the X-ray laser program was especially timely, since the lab's traditional work, the design of conventional nuclear arms, was entering a period of decline. To a large extent, the X-ray laser was seen as the lab's financial savior.

THE downfall of the X-ray laser began even as Teller's lobbying over Super Excalibur reached its apex. Politically, a key force behind its demise was Los Alamos, which had long been skeptical of Livermore's alleged breakthrough. The rivalry between the two weapons labs had gone on for more than a quarter century at this point, deepening over the years. Los Alamos scientists still prominently displayed photos of a nearly undamaged bomb tower from one of Livermore's early nuclear fizzles. Now Livermore was unilaterally proclaiming a new era based on a different kind of bomb. Los Alamos management was deeply suspicious, the more so after its own 1984 underground test of the X-ray laser failed in the Correo event. Management had decided the idea was unworthy of serious attention. "We felt there were more important things to do," recalled Donald Kerr, the Los Alamos director.[43] The lab's growing distrust had been evident in Kerr's late-night harangue against Teller and Wood in early 1985, but at that point he had no firm evidence to back his complaint, only a hunch. Now the New Mexico lab launched a bold assault based on a host of facts and calculations.

Los Alamos scientists applied Maenchen's analysis of sensor ambiguity to Livermore's own work, much as the Livermore scientists had done with the 1984 Correo shot. They did so with a vengeance, some claiming not only that the Livermore brightnesses were false but that no true laser had ever been observed in Cottage or any other X-ray laser tests. Other Los Alamos scientists said the signals had simply been exaggerated. In either case, the charges were momentous.[44]

The Los Alamos analysis centered on reflectors made of beryllium, which were standard equipment in the evacuated pipes that carried radiation away from an exploding bomb to sensors. Beryllium is a hard, rare metal. A small beryllium reflector, placed at a 45-degree angle in a pipe, was used in the Romano and other X-ray tests to bounce some of the bomb's radiation to a sensor located just outside. Such a reflector was handy for two reasons. First, it kept a delicate sensor from having to look directly into the blast. Second, it allowed a single bomb pipe to feed many sensors. A half-dozen or so reflectors could be spaced along the end of a pipe, scattering radiation to numerous sensors that measured different aspects of a bomb's radiations.[45]

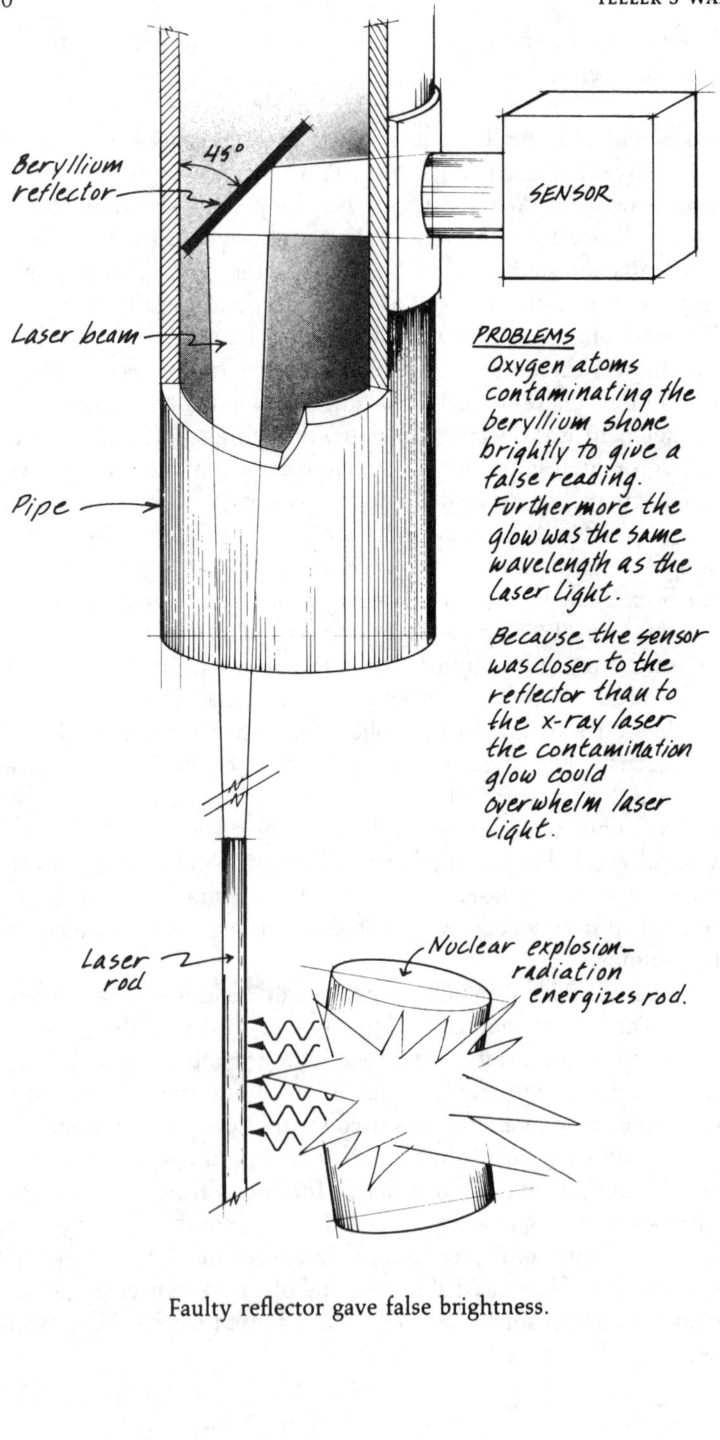

Beryllium reflector

45°

SENSOR

Laser beam

Pipe

PROBLEMS
Oxygen atoms contaminating the beryllium shone brightly to give a false reading. Furthermore the glow was the same wavelength as the laser light.

Because the sensor was closer to the reflector than to the x-ray laser the contamination glow could overwhelm laser light.

Laser rod

Nuclear explosion—radiation energizes rod.

Faulty reflector gave false brightness.

What Los Alamos scientists found was that, at the very least, Livermore's X-ray laser beams were probably causing the beryllium reflectors to glow, exaggerating their brightness. The problem was tiny atoms of oxygen that inevitably contaminated the beryllium. When excited, the oxygen would shine quite brightly. Moreover, the glow was exactly the same wavelength as the laser light, making the two virtually indistinguishable. A final complication was that the glowing reflectors were located quite close to the sensors—just inches away—whereas radiation from the X-ray laser had started many meters away. The setup meant that contamination glow would easily overwhelm laser light, skewing readings. Some of the criticisms were more aggressive. At times, Los Alamos scientists and officials argued that the reflectors had simply been excited by stray radiations from the nuclear blast, meaning the X-ray laser had never existed.[46]

The first internal Los Alamos report on the overall topic was dated June 10, 1985, and authored by Gottfried T. Schappert and Donald E. Casperson. Soon, Los Alamos officials raised the issue in Washington, asking pointed questions not only about the Cottage test but suggesting that all brightness readings from Livermore's program were flawed at the very least. After all, they noted, beryllium reflectors had been used from the earliest days of Livermore's X-ray laser program, all the way back to the 1980 Dauphin test. They urged that the situation be investigated and corrected, noting that it would seriously delay the X-ray effort.[47]

Unruffled by the growing tempest, Livermore managers told Washington they already knew of brightness problems from Maenchen's work and had been in the process of giving the issue a thorough exploration. As evidence, they noted that one corrective step had already been taken. On Cottage, for the first time, at Maenchen's urging, a new sensor configuration had been tested. Hydrogen gas, the simplest and least reactive of all the elements, had been substituted for the usual type of reflector. The aim was to scatter the laser's radiation into sensors without introducing any distortions. The results of this test were far from unambiguous, the novel technique needing to be refined as well as the interpretation of its data. But the results nonetheless hinted that serious brightness revisions had to be made.[48]

Livermore managers, including Woodruff, looked at the Los Alamos analysis as simply a detailed confirmation of Maenchen's method. Livermore was far ahead of Los Alamos in understanding the dimensions of the flaw, they told colleagues. The charges were nonetheless a political bombshell, coming as they did from the lab's arch rival and having been fired with deadly intent and skill. In the depths of the X-ray laser program, many scientists, long absorbed in their own part of the laser challenge, had been only dimly aware of Maenchen's fears. Now the issue struck home with a force that was both painful and embarrassing. Livermore scientists were confident the Romano blast had decisively demonstrated the existence of the laser. But it was now clear that no one had a good idea of its real brightness. Their work, representing many years of intense effort and an investment of hundreds of millions of dollars, had been thrown into doubt.

A crash effort to resolve the issue got under way. On June 27, weeks after the initial Los Alamos salvos, Joseph M. Nilsen, a young scientist in R Program, filed a report that concluded the Los Alamos scientists were on the mark. In July, Livermore held a large meeting to decide what to do technically. In the end, it was decided that all the beryllium reflectors had to be replaced by vials of hydrogen gas. On July 30, Livermore scientists gave Energy Department officials a tentative new estimate of the Cottage test's output, greatly lowering the laser's brightness.[49]

DESPITE the setback, the X-ray laser still seemed to grow in stature, publicly at least, thanks to news leaks that were confidently upbeat. Under the headline "Birthday Blowout," the July issue of *Scientific American* reported that a Super Excalibur test had occurred on the second anniversary of the Star Wars speech. It said the brightness of the X-ray laser beam had been increased "by six orders of magnitude," a technical detail no publication had previously disclosed. Translated into English, "six orders of magnitude" stood for the number one followed by six zeros—in other words, an enhancement of one million. If true, the test was a phenomenal success. The figure implied that lethal X-ray laser battle stations were around the corner. The magazine did not attribute the news to any source, instead making assertions about Livermore "workers" and "investigators." The article concluded that the brightness advance had solved one of the "technical challenges that may need to be met if the president's goal is to be realized."[50]

News of the X-ray focusing "breakthrough" also caught the attention of the Russians, who privately said they were worried. On July 29, Soviet leader Mikhail S. Gorbachev announced the Soviet Union would suspend the testing of nuclear weapons for five months and asked the United States to join the moratorium, which he said could be extended indefinitely if America too halted its nuclear blasts.[51] American experts saw the move as part of the Soviet campaign to halt Star Wars. Reagan administration officials, rejecting the Soviet proposal, were quoted as saying that continued underground testing was needed, among other things, to perfect the X-ray laser.[52]

TELLER still moved in his own world at this point, wielding vast power within the federal establishment despite the emergence of the brightness flaws. That influence was demonstrated with extreme clarity on September 6, 1985, in a meeting of two dozen or so federal science officials, including Woodruff, in the office of Star Wars director General Abrahamson. The topic was the transfer of $100 million from the Defense Department to the Energy Department to accelerate research on the X-ray laser and other third-generation ideas. It was an increase Woodruff and everybody else in the X-ray laser program had long advocated. Three national laboratories—Livermore, Los Alamos, and the Sandia National Laboratory in Albuquerque—were now competing for a piece of the pie. Before the meeting, Woodruff and officials from the other labs tentatively agreed on a division of the money that would give Livermore $60 million, Los Alamos $30 million and Sandia $10 million. In light of their rivalries and competing interests, it was a fragile consensus.[53]

At the gathering, the officials discussed the situation and eventually reiterated the agreed-on division. A half hour into the meeting, General Abrahamson went to a display board to write down the division of the money. Just as he raised his pen, Teller walked in.

All smiles, General Abrahamson seated Teller in a high-backed blue chair at an imposing desk. Teller, a small man, settled down so that only his head could be seen. Teller said he wanted the entire $100 million to go to Livermore, for two reasons. First, the X-ray laser was the most deserving project. It was the newest idea, championed by bright, creative young people. In contrast, he said, the competing idea from Los Alamos was much older and less likely to produce a breakthrough. The Los Alamos project was known as Prometheus, using a nuclear blast to fire small pellets. The second reason, Teller said, was more important.

He paused.

"President Reagan told me I could have it."

No one in the room stirred.

"Do you really want to challenge someone who says he's talked to the president?" an official later recalled.[54]

General Abrahamson thanked Teller for his remarks and said he was just about to write down the division. The lab names were already on the display board. Next to Livermore, General Abrahamson wrote $100 million.

Woodruff, sitting on a couch, was poked in the ribs by a Los Alamos official next to him. "So this is how you're in charge of the weapons program at Livermore," the official whispered. Embarrassed, Woodruff sank into the couch. It was the first he had heard of the president's promise to Teller of $100 million.

General Abrahamson continued writing, putting $30 million by Los Alamos and $10 million by Sandia. He joked that he was not as bright as Teller, but it was obvious that this division of the money failed to add up to $100 million. Yet $100 million was all the Strategic Defense Initiative could contribute. Turning to an Energy Department official, General Abrahamson said he was sure that the agency could find an extra $40 million in its $6 billion annual budget. With that, the meeting ended.

WOODRUFF felt he had been humiliated in front of his peers. He already knew all about his loss of influence over Teller, about his inability to respond with any bureaucratic effectiveness to the Keyworth, Nitze and McFarlane letters. Now his predicament was on public display. Moreover, Teller's move represented an escalation in the battle, involving not just ideas and influence but money. Woodruff was philosophically at odds with Teller's approach. In theory, a $100 million boost for the X-ray laser was fine. Early on, Woodruff himself had called for up to an extra $200 million a year. But Teller's move was likely to sow dissension. In the proposed division, Woodruff had worked hard to balance the competing interests of the other weapons labs and their officials, whom he worked with regularly. Now he had lost their respect.[55]

Woodruff was already deeply involved in damage control on "Pillars of Fire." Now here was another case of excessive zeal to deal with. But the options for action were few. There was little chance of telling the president it was all an illusion, little hope that Teller would admit his error or change his ways. More and more frequently, Woodruff toyed with the idea of quitting his job.[56]

Back at Livermore, Woodruff's deputy, Miller, expressed some of the bureaucratic frustrations that grew out of the episode. His memo was written two weeks after the Pentagon meeting, on September 23, 1985, and was sent to several midlevel managers at Livermore. "We are viewed as petulant, arrogant, uncompromising children who want the whole candy store," he wrote. "I'm not sure at this time if the relations can be repaired." Miller said Sandia was withdrawing some of its support of Livermore's X-ray laser program, especially in the area of advanced materials. "Feelings were particularly bitter since they had provided significant near-term effort voluntarily," he wrote. In talks with Sandia, Miller suggested the laser's promise had to be explored or else "there would be no work for any of us." But that argument and others, he wrote, "seemed to fall on deaf ears."[57]

TOP scientists slowly began to leave the X-ray laser program at this point, upset at the gap between the idea's humble technical status and its grandiose promotion. One who left in September was W. Lowell Morgan. He had joined the X-ray laser program in 1981 while in his early 30s, eager to work on what was clearly the most exciting thing to emerge in the world of nuclear weapons in decades. Morgan rose rapidly to become head of R Program's atomic modeling group, which used powerful computers to predict the conditions under which materials might produce coherent X-rays. But he grew increasingly upset with the exaggerations of the mid-1980s. "Basically we knew very little," Morgan recalled. "It wasn't like they made it seem."[58]

As he left the program, Morgan publicly declared his antipathy to the politicizing of science in an interview with a reporter for *The Los Angeles Times*. "The public holds scientists in awe and has implicit trust in them," Morgan was quoted as saying. "Scientists, consequently, have an obligation to level with the public. To lie to the public because we know that the public doesn't understand all this technical stuff brings us down to the level of hawkers of snake oil, miracle cleaners and Veg-O-Matics."[59] By the time the article appeared, Morgan had transferred from the X-ray laser program to what he considered a more respectable job at Livermore.

Another who left was Stephen M. Younger, widely seen as one of Livermore's best and brightest. He had led the R Program team that devised the various X-ray laser designs. But the exaggerations became too much for him as well. He tendered his resignation during this period, although he was persuaded to stay on until after the next nuclear test. He was in his early 30s and bitter about misrepresentations of his team's work on the laser. "It's fantastically complicated," he recalled. "It's one of the most difficult engineering challenges ever attempted. I have never seen people work so hard. They would sleep in assembly rooms for days, not seeing their families. Many times I saw people with tears running down their face because they had worked so hard. It was a source of considerable frustration that our work was many orders of magnitude short of the advertisements. Talk is cheap. It's a different thing to make it happen. It was a period of considerable frustration for the people trying to make it happen."[60]

FOR Woodruff, pressures continued to mount, as did evidence of his declining influence over Teller and Wood. On October 10, 1985, General Abrahamson of the Strategic Defense Initiative came to Livermore for a series of briefings. Wood gave him a report entitled "Concerning the Vulnerability of Objects in Space to Attack by Ground-Based Laser Systems." It was an assault on space-based weapons and sensors, arguing that they could be blasted out of the sky by Soviet lasers. The X-ray laser, Wood maintained, kept either on the ground for pop-up or in geosynchronous orbit with shields and decoys, would be much safer. "The need to reassess the survivability of space assets," Wood wrote, "seems compelling."[61]

Late that day, General Abrahamson asked Woodruff if he had seen Wood's study and whether he thought it was any good.

"No," Woodruff responded, he had not laid eyes on it.[62]

Wood's efforts at marketing the X-ray laser were soon meant to pick up speed with the publication in October of my book, *Star Warriors*, which was an O Group profile based on a weeklong visit with the young scientists. Wood had hoped for a glowing account. But the book depicted him as a headstrong visionary making extravagant claims and his subordinates as far more candid about the X-ray laser's weaknesses. "Broad argues that the researchers are paying lip service to President Reagan's goal of a perfect defense," reported a Livermore newspaper. The article appeared on Saturday, October 19.[63]

That same day, Woodruff vented his growing frustrations with the whole X-ray affair, saving his venom especially for Wood, who he felt was the engine of many of Teller's excesses. In a four-page letter to director Batzel, he charged Wood with overselling the X-ray laser to Congress and a host of White House officials. "Do I remain relatively silent and allow Lowell to continue to potentially mislead the highest levels of leadership in our country?" he asked. "That would certainly be the easy course of action as you have made it clear on numerous occasions that your preference is for me to do nothing."[64] The usual rationale behind such inaction, Woodruff wrote, was that the weapons establishment had Wood "calibrated," knowing him as a gifted maverick on the X-ray effort's edge and seeing through his exaggerations. But the zealous salesmanship was actually being taken seriously and had greatly expanded Wood's influence and credibility beyond the lab. As evidence, Woodruff pointed to a chart I had drawn in *Star Warriors* that upended the lab's bureaucracy, putting Wood on top. This topsy-turvy order, he said, was how the lab was increasingly viewed by much of the outside world.

Woodruff went on to cite specific examples of X-ray misrepresentation, noting Teller's letters to Keyworth, McFarlane and Nitze. "In all cases Lowell assisted with the drafting of these letters and in no instance was I asked to review them for accuracy," he wrote, even though "responsibility for attempting to meet the programmatic goals called for in these letters would clearly fall to me." Woodruff noted that after the Keyworth letter, Batzel had assured him such an incident would never happen again. "Well," he wrote, "it did! [for both] the Nitze and McFarlane letters, and I am concerned there may be others."

The exaggerations had to cease, Woodruff said. "It is simply unacceptable to allow the continued selling of the X-ray laser. And believe me, it has not stopped." As examples of hyperbole he cited Wood's briefings of Abrahamson and Casey, his zealous pronouncements in *Star Warriors* and his attack on other antimissile options in the laser vulnerability study. "The crux of the issue is how much credibility does the outside world give to Lowell Wood? Does the organization of the lab as reflected by W. Broad prevail or does the 'system' have Lowell in proper perspective? And given the risk, can we afford to be wrong?" In closing, Woodruff called for measures "to bring Lowell under control."

He did not send the letter. In the course of writing it, in venting his anger over the contradictions, the exaggerations, the broken promises on the part of the director, Woodruff had come to the conclusion that the situation was beyond repair.[65]

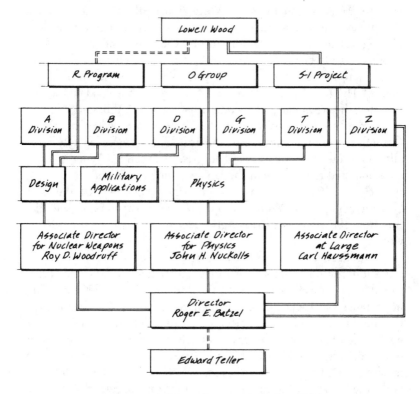

Livermore's hierarchy upended, circa 1984.

WOODRUFF, 45 years old, a 17-year Livermore veteran, began to plan his resignation, his resolve strengthened by a new sense of emotional well-being. His marriage of 25 years had broken up in April, the last five years having felt like a forced march. He moved into an apartment. Soon after, Woodruff had started to date Mary E. Tuszka, the lab's associate director for administration who played a key role in finding the money to redo the failed Cabra test. Tuszka was cast in much the same mold as Woodruff—a skilled manager who was tough, fair and straightforward. Born on a dairy farm in Wisconsin in 1946, with blue eyes and blond hair, she had graduated Phi Beta Kappa from the University of Wisconsin at Madison and gone on to rise rapidly in the federal bureaucracy. By the end of the Carter administration, she was director of the Energy Department's budget office, presiding over billions in federal funds. Tuszka arrived at Livermore in 1983 and proceeded to work closely with Woodruff.

She, too, had grown wary of the X-ray laser, having witnessed the clash in Nevada between the directors of Livermore and Los Alamos as well as the continuous salesmanship of Teller and Wood. She was an intellectual ally. In July 1985, some three months after they started dating, Tuszka and Woodruff became engaged. Both were bruised by failed marriages. Both were delighted to make a fresh start.[66]

As Woodruff prepared to leave his high Livermore post, the laser was sinking deeper into inter-lab controversy. At the end of October, Livermore hosted the annual "Nuclear Explosive Design Physics Conference" held by the nation's nuclear weapons labs. These conferences alternated each year between Livermore and Los Alamos. This year Woodruff was the keynote speaker. At the meeting, Los Alamos scientists Jack C. Comly, Donald E. Casperson, Nelson M. Hoffman and Gottfried T. Schappert told how beryllium reflectors had exaggerated the brightness readings of the X-ray laser. Their report, "Modeling of Diagnostics Foil Behavior with a Non-LTE Atomic Kinetics Code," could hardly seem more innocuous. But it was explosive. Elaborating on the false-brightness problem, it said the oxygen contaminant had played an "important role" in the emission of spurious radiation.[67]

The brightness failure was the talk of the conference, among both staff scientists and high officials. On Tuesday, October 29, C. Paul Robinson, head of weapons research at Los Alamos, handed a caustic letter to Miller, Woodruff's deputy, saying Los Alamos doubted that the existence of the X-ray laser had been demonstrated and that Livermore managers were losing their credibility because of their failure to stand up to Teller and Wood.[68]

To Woodruff, the incident symbolized how far things had deteriorated. He had done his best to cure the program of the schizophrenia of conflicting claims, with false-brightness adherents on one side and Teller and Wood on the other. And he had failed. The disease was too much for him. For days he had been drafting his letter of resignation. Now he finished it, working late into the night. The next day, Wednesday, October 30, 1985, he handed director Batzel the letter, along with several documents and the unsent letter of October 19 in which he had complained so bitterly about Wood.

"For god's sake read this," said Woodruff, afraid Batzel would simply sweep the whole thing under the rug.[69]

In the four-page resignation letter, Woodruff spoke of being at an impasse after two years of friction with Batzel. Once again, he zeroed in on Wood rather than Teller, seeing the younger scientist as the force behind much of the trouble. Wood's X-ray misrepresentations had potentially misled the nation's top leaders and had clearly damaged both Livermore's credibility and his own. Indeed, Woodruff wrote, peers had recently questioned his effectiveness and that of his deputy, George Miller, "because we 'won't publicly stand up to Lowell.' It does not help to respond with the fact that Lowell Wood does not report to either George or me."[70] Clearly, this Catch-22 was the nub of much of the conflict. Wood kept making extravagant claims and promises for the X-ray laser, even though, as a member of the physics department, he had no real authority over that program. It was Woodruff, head of all Livermore work on nuclear weapons, who had the authority and would be held responsible for false promises. Yet he had no control over Wood.

Woodruff then criticized Batzel, saying he encouraged Wood's excesses by never disciplining him. For instance, Wood had recently attacked a colleague as "brain damaged" in front of General Abrahamson, Batzel, several associate directors and key members of the staff. "No one corrected him other than myself," Woodruff wrote. "For the Director to allow such a comment to go unchallenged does a disservice to the Program by potentially giving a false impression to a high level visitor. Moreover, it is extremely debilitating to the staff who are present." This incident, he wrote, was but one of many instances where Wood's excesses had gone unchecked. "Roger, the bottom line with regard to Lowell is that you, as the Director of the Laboratory, have an obligation to the Laboratory staff and the Nation to be accountable for his professional conduct." Woodruff then proposed a lab reorganization that would help solve the problem. All weapons work and related fields, including physics, should be put under one person holding a new post of deputy director for weapons, he wrote. This would unify the lab's warring camps.

In closing, Woodruff said he had unsuccessfully discussed these issues with Batzel many times before. "Your repeated assurances that you will moderate Lowell Wood have been unfulfilled or unsuccessful, to the detriment of our national security." The situation demanded leadership, Woodruff wrote. Instead there was a vacuum at the top. "I can no longer support you as Director," he wrote. "Thus, I ask to be relieved of my assignment as Associate Director for Defense Systems."

While writing the letter, Woodruff and Tuszka had discussed the possibility that Batzel might create the new post Woodruff recommended and offer it to him. But Woodruff decided to turn it down, having lost any desire to work directly for Batzel. The job was for someone else. In any case, Batzel made no job offer to Woodruff nor any move to reorganize the lab along the lines suggested.[71]

The resignation was announced at Livermore the next day, Thursday, October 31, during a short meeting held at 2:00 P.M. and attended by the lab's top hundred managers and officials. In the front of the room, Batzel and Woodruff explained that they had irreconcilable differences and that Woodruff had resigned. No details were given. Later that day, Woodruff got calls from officials at Livermore and throughout the country expressing shock and disappointment. There were no communications from Wood or Teller.

Woodruff avoided the press. At that point it was forbidden to even utter the words "Super Excalibur" to the uninitiated. Moreover, he feared that public knowledge of the affair would damage the lab. In talking with reporters, the lab's public affairs office echoed an agreed statement that Woodruff and Batzel had worked out—that Woodruff had requested to be relieved of his duties in order to pursue his own studies. "After 17 years of nuclear weapons research, five of which were in a leadership position, he was ready for a change," Mike Ross, a Livermore spokesman, told the Associated Press.[72]

People in the Teller camp rejected the idea that Woodruff had resigned as a matter of principle, instead viewing the move as driven by a mix of personal pain and ambition. There was much talk of a "midlife crisis" centering on Woodruff's divorce. There was also talk of a failed power play. Woodruff, they felt, had been using Wood as an excuse to try to acquire more laboratory turf. They also felt Woodruff had simply become jealous of the good access Teller and Wood had to high administration officials, and of their visits to the White House.[73] But neither Teller nor Wood would ever publicly say so or discuss the matter in that kind of detail.

Among the general Livermore staff, few scientists were sure why Woodruff had quit. Only Batzel and a few others had seen the Teller letters to federal officials, although many staffers were aware of Woodruff's attempts to moderate the excesses of Teller and Wood. Many were deeply upset by the resignation, fearing it boded ill for the lab. "It came as a thunderbolt to people in the program," recalled Younger, the R Program scientist. "We felt he had been leading us in the right direction. He was one of the best technical managers I have ever seen in operation. He could get people to do incredible things, just by making a suggestion. He was respected. He was strong and decisive."[74]

One of the many notes Woodruff received was from Christopher Hendrickson, a computer expert. "I'm sure you've heard this many times by now, but as one who has followed your career over the past few years, I felt shock, dismay, and a good deal of anger Thursday when you announced your resignation. While folks like me may never know the real reasons behind it, I have known you well enough over the years to know that it had to be a matter of principle—that you refused to give, and that it cost you your job. In addition to your obvious competence, the trait I respected you most for was your unwillingness to play games with people. I admired your determination to be straightforward and honest in an atmosphere that often discourages these qualities. To be perfectly candid, my faith in the laboratory management has been seriously shaken. I'm sure I'll survive, but it's been a real shock to see someone of your ability removed from a position he was doing so well."[75]

Woodruff had hoped to take a year of professional leave at the arms-control program of nearby Stanford University. But no position there was immediately open. So instead he transferred to Livermore's Z Division, the secretive group of scientists that helped the nation's intelligence agencies ponder what foreign governments do in the development of nuclear weapons and other kinds of arms. Woodruff was still at the laboratory. He stayed because he was loath to leave the place in which he had invested so much energy and because his skills were too specialized to market easily outside the government's network of weapons labs. And Livermore acquiesced, more or less. Even though Batzel, director of the entire laboratory, undoubtedly wanted Woodruff off the premises altogether after the strong criticism, senior lab personnel had contracts that protected them from indiscriminate firing. So Woodruff stayed. But he had no regular contact with Batzel or the upper echelons of lab management. He had no personal staff. He no longer had control over half the weapons lab and a budget of $300 million. He no longer had anything to do with being an official, having renounced the turbulent world of lab politics for quiet research.

As Woodruff settled into relative obscurity, the X-ray laser burst into headlines around the nation as some of its flaws became public for the first time. The initial report was carried in *Science*, the weekly journal of the American Association for the Advancement of Science. In early November 1985 the magazine reported "growing skepticism" about the X-ray laser "in the wake of several disappointing tests." The Cottage test, at first thought to have demonstrated a dramatic increase in brightness (as reported in my May article and the July *Scientific American*), was subsequently found to have been seriously flawed, it reported. "Lab researchers discovered that key monitoring equipment had been improperly calibrated," it said. As was often the case with the public release of secret information, the magazine made no mention of its information sources.[76]

News of the setback was carried forward by *The Los Angeles Times*, which reported that Livermore scientists were preparing to carry out a new test of the X-ray laser despite the unresolved flaws. The paper said the impending test, code-named Goldstone, was being pushed forward over the objections of experts at both Livermore and Los Alamos. "A design error in a key measuring device used in all past tests has caused it to give false readings," *The Times* reported. "Los Alamos scientists urged Livermore to develop a new mechanism to measure the laser, which would have caused an estimated delay of six months to a year in the program."[77]

The trouble was disparaged by a chorus of Washington officials. "It's one group of scientists arguing with another group of scientists on how you measure the intensity of a light beam," said Energy Secretary Herrington, who once sympathized with Woodruff over Teller's excesses. "There's disagreement but it's nothing more than a small blip in the program."[78]

High in the Reagan administration, reports of X-ray setbacks seemed to have little or no impact on the status of the laser or its backers. Teller, exercising his extraordinary White House access, again met with President Reagan in November 1985 to discuss Star Wars.[79] Most surprising of all, Keyworth, Reagan's science adviser, in December reportedly echoed Teller's most enthusiastic forecasts. "A single X-ray laser would defend against the U.S.S.R.'s entire offensive forces," he was quoted as telling five hundred laser scientists at a conference in Las Vegas.[80] Actually, this claim went beyond even Teller, who in his letter to Nitze had referred only to the single laser's destruction of land-based Soviet missiles, not arms fired from submarines and other offensive weapons as well.

One place the X-ray setbacks did produce a strong reaction was on Capitol Hill, where Democrats had grown quite wary of Star

Wars. On Wednesday, December 4, 1985, Representative Edward J. Markey of Massachusetts, a young, brash critic of the nation's arms establishment, entered the recent news articles into the *Congressional Record* and called for action. "The Administration should delay the planned Goldstone test until it has rectified these technical problems," he said. "It should not be rushing to continue expensive X-ray laser tests that may yield little useful data."[81] On Friday, December 6, thirty congressmen wrote Defense Secretary Weinberger to call for Goldstone's delay, saying the test was seriously flawed.[82] But Weinberger replied that the test would move ahead as planned. Upset, the congressmen asked the General Accounting Office to investigate the X-ray laser program.

Neither Weinberger nor any other administration official informed the congressmen that the impending test, just days away, had been struck by a new, unpublicized problem. In Goldstone, as was standard practice, a nuclear bomb had been attached to the bottom of a boxcar-sized canister filled with instruments, and the whole apparatus had been lowered to the bottom of a 1,800-foot hole in the Nevada desert. The hole was then refilled with gravel and epoxy glue. This process usually worked without a hitch. But this time, the canister had been bent while the hole was filled. Livermore scientists, testing the sensor instruments of the buried device, knew they had problems with laser alignment. But a decision was made to press ahead despite the problems.[83]

On December 27, during the Christmas holidays, a team of top government officials arrived at Livermore in limousines. Among them were General Abrahamson, the Star Wars director, as well as Secretary of State George P. Shultz and his chief arms-control adviser, Paul Nitze. The officials were given a daylong secret briefing on the lab's Star Wars projects, including the X-ray laser and the Goldstone test. Nitze asked about Woodruff, whose briefing in Washington had been a sober counterpoint to the excitement of Wood and Teller. Nitze was told Woodruff was unavailable.[84]

The next day, Saturday, December 28, the Goldstone device was detonated, causing the desert to shudder. As usual, the government had warned people in high-rise Las Vegas buildings to avoid precarious positions during the blast.

Because of the bent canister, only three of the ten or so X-ray laser experiments produced useful data. An added limitation was that Livermore's tight production schedules meant there had been time to replace only a few of the beryllium reflectors with tubes of hydrogen gas. But the data's message was sobering. For the first time in the history of the X-ray laser program, which had conducted explosive tests for seven years, Livermore scientists now had a fairly good idea of the laser's brightness. All the top-secret hoopla about the various forms of Excalibur eventually being a million, a billion or a trillion times brighter than a hydrogen bomb had been dealt a devastating blow. Teller's claims to the White House now seemed almost comical. The simple fact revealed by Goldstone was that the laser's brightness was about ten times less than previously believed. In short, the laser was extremely inefficient. It was relatively dim.

For one of the experiments, a gold rod was predicted to have a strength of 400 kilojoules of energy but turned out to produce only about 40 kilojoules of energy. It was like the owner of a new car suddenly discovering that his engine produced 10 horsepower instead of the 100 advertised by the dealer. After reviewing the Goldstone data, some Livermore scientists decided the X-ray laser was so weak it could never be turned into a weapon.[85]

The false-brightness episode was reported rather delicately in the General Accounting Office probe requested by Congress, which described what it called "a research program with many unresolved issues." It said Livermore scientists were justified in conducting the Goldstone test. Several past blasts, the report said, had problems with sensors that were serious enough to generate false impressions of the laser's performance. "Absolute power calculation inaccuracies occurred," it said. But some of the test equipment was "reconfigured" for Goldstone, so improving the situation that "these unexpected uncertainties are now much better understood."[86]

HIGH in the mountains of New Mexico, Los Alamos scientists were elated. Laughing happily, a group of them told me in early 1986 that perfecting the X-ray laser might require 100 or 200 tests—which was as good as saying it might not materialize for a century or two. "This is a very new thing," said Robert W. Selden, head of theoretical and computational physics at Los Alamos. "The physics processes we're looking at are far more complicated than anything we've looked at before."[87]

As Livermore's program caved in, top scientists continued to leave. In 1986, at the age of 32, Peter Hagelstein, the inspiration behind several X-ray laser advances, resigned after eleven years at the laboratory. After announcing his decision, Hagelstein was called into

Teller's office. There the Hungarian sage pressured him to stay, hinting that his resignation was treasonous. Teller recounted a story about how, during the Manhattan Project, some young physicists decided to leave, with Teller objecting. "His basic argument," Hagelstein recalled, "was that strong principles were involved—that Hitler and the Nazis were horrible in terrifying ways, that a decision had to be made: Do you hold your ground and fight? Do you team up against the bad in the world and do what you can to fight it— annihilate it, or crush it into rubble? One or more of these physicists had decided to take the easy way out and go into pharmacy, where they could remove themselves from the battle and lead lives analogous to sheep. At the end of our discussion, Teller summarized his opinion of me in the most devastating metaphor he could think of at the time. He accused me of being a pharmacist."[88]

THE brightness failure made focusing even more important. In theory, a weak beam still might be strengthened by being made more concentrated, though hardly to the point of having the vast destructive powers once envisioned for Super Excalibur. Livermore officials were cautiously optimistic about the focusing effort but now, in the wake of the program's overall collapse, were also careful to disassociate themselves from the wilder claims. Batzel, having just been accused of authorizing the exaggeration of the X-ray laser's powers, in February 1986 flatly denied there was any reality to the notion that a single Super Excalibur module could knock out all the Soviet Union's land-based missiles. "There are no data at this stage of the game which would support that," he told Congress.[89]

As usual, Teller was quite optimistic, hammering away on the promise of focusing. In May 1986 he told a Senate subcommittee that it had been successfully "established" in nuclear tests, paving the way for incredibly narrow X-ray laser beams that could speed across 1,000 miles of space while spreading no more than five feet.[90] In contrast, Walbridge had said a beam traveling that distance would spread more than 200 feet. In the press, fanciful extrapolations of Teller's claim conjured up antimissile visions that were as incandescent as any. "This degree of focusing," said a glowing report of Teller's testimony, "means that a single X-ray laser device could destroy upwards of tens of thousands of nuclear warheads and missiles at any stage of their trajectory."[91]

In fact, Teller's pronouncement was premature at best. Rather than being firmly "established," focusing soon suffered a crisis, the victim of difficulties in trying to fathom what was happening deep beneath the desert. Focusing had first been attempted in the Cottage test of March 1985. In Goldstone that December, no reliable focusing data had been obtained because the bent canister threw that experiment out of alignment. The next nuclear test, code-named Labquark, was held in September 1986. Its focusing experiment seemed to work. Then, in April 1987, Livermore scientists conducted Delamar, which sought to consolidate and extend the focusing gains. But instead of making strides, that test revealed what seemed to be another serious blunder in the interpretation of earlier test data.[92]

Focusing is indicated by a narrowing of a laser beam and a decrease in the size of the spot it projects on a flat surface. The beam's energy is thus concentrated into a smaller area. This is what Livermore scientists thought they had achieved for the X-ray laser, starting with Cottage. But Delamar had a more elaborate set of sensors to measure the spot's size. It showed that, instead of a smaller spot, the scientists had actually measured the edge of an annulus, or a doughnut-shaped ring. With Delamar, the realization came when the area around the "spot" was more carefully scrutinized. Further work on the problem convinced Livermore scientists that focusing still had merit and had been achieved to some degree. But at the very least, the episode showed that the ambitious goal was surrounded by as much uncertainty and interpretational difficulty as had bedeviled the readings of laser brightness.[93]

The net result of all this was that Super Excalibur, pursued so vigorously by Teller and Wood to save the X-ray laser program, steadfastly remained a fantasy. The wonder weapon failed to materialize—despite the enthusiasm, the optimistic leaks to the press, the upbeat letters to administration officials, the pep talks at the White House and all the expensive tests. The revelation of false brightness in 1985 threw the X-ray laser project into disarray, and the fear of false focusing in 1987 redoubled its sense of caution and wariness. What remained was a program that moved in fits and starts toward Excalibur, which if ever realized would threaten, not aid, Star Wars.

On a national level, the Pentagon's antimissile program had always tried to develop a variety of antimissile arms, the chief ones being directed-energy weapons such as lasers. But in late 1985 and early 1986, it started to switch its emphasis toward more rudimen-

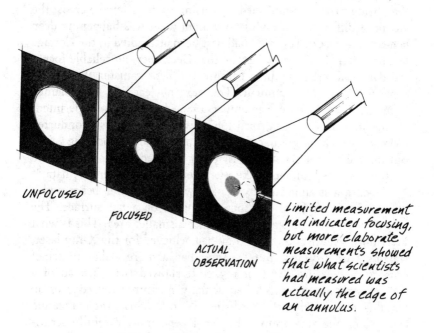

UNFOCUSED

FOCUSED

ACTUAL
OBSERVATION

*Limited measurement had indicated focusing, but more elaborate measurements showed that what scientists had measured was actually the edge of an annulus.*

Focusing was feared to be an illusion.

tary weapons such as rocket interceptors that would zero in on targets and destroy them by force of impact. It was like tossing rocks at bottles. Indeed, the interceptors were often called "smart rocks." This change in emphasis was brought about by several factors, including the desire of the Reagan White House to deploy something in space as soon as possible and the discovery that directed-energy arms, including the X-ray laser, were turning out to be far more difficult to perfect than federal officials had ever imagined.

The decline of the X-ray laser was reflected in its shrinking budget. Bureaucratic momentum carried the program to a funding increase in 1987, but thereafter it went steadily downhill. The Energy Department's outlays for nuclear directed-energy weapons fell from $349 million in 1987, to $279 million in 1988, to $255 million in 1989, to $220 million in 1990. In its budget request for fiscal 1991, the department asked for a mere $192 million, the smallest amount since it started releasing figures on the program.[94] That figure was less than a third of the 1991 budget originally projected in the first hectic days of Super Excalibur. Moreover, Congress dealt the program a near-fatal blow in October 1990 when House and Senate negotiators voted to end X-ray laser financing as a separate item in the federal budget, beginning in fiscal 1991.[95] The action eliminated all federal funds other than internal research money that the Energy Department chose to spend on the laser. Department officials said these might amount to tens of millions of dollars and, for fiscal 1991, possibly as much as $90 million. In the end, Livermore got a mere $28 million. (R Program was disbanded in late 1990 and residual X-ray laser research moved elsewhere in the lab.) The overall message was clear. The laser was to limp along as a low-level research effort rather than a robust program to develop a weapon. In short, the billions that Teller so eagerly sought for the X-ray laser failed to appear. The decade-long quest had come to an unceremonious end.

Troy E. Wade II, the Energy Department's acting assistant secretary for defense programs, dryly summed up the situation in 1988. "To get from the understanding of physics to a weapon," he told Congress, "is perhaps a much bigger job than Dr. Teller thought."[96]

THROUGHOUT the collapse, Teller continued to be optimistic, his public advocacy frequent and at times strident. In articles, speeches, television appearances and a book, he continued to hail the promise of the X-ray laser and antimissile defense. It can be argued that the scientist never had a good grip on the real state of X-ray advances, any data he saw being instantly overwhelmed by fervent hopes. In any case, he seemed totally unaware of the bad news. During this period he apparently made no public acknowledgment that the X-ray laser, the device he had promoted so zealously for so long to so many high government officials, was doing anything but making rapid progress. Moreover, his upbeat declarations were remarkably public. The secretive X-ray consultations, which played such an important role in the birth of Star Wars, were over. Teller's accolades were now made to an increasingly wide audience, as he hailed the laser and the vast military program it helped bring into existence.

In October 1985 as the revelation of brightness flaws threw Livermore into disarray, Teller in *The Washington Times* called the X-ray laser "a remarkable feat" that promised "an immense step forward in our ability to defend ourselves." Teller ended the article with an extended metaphor. "The atomic Genie existed during the unmeasured depth of time in the dark bottle of ignorance," he said. "Neither through technology nor through our fervent wishes can we put the Genie back into that bottle. But technology can provide something of a solution. The Genie should contribute to the shield. The Genie can make the shield stronger than the sword."[97]

In December 1985, as Congress tried to stop the X-ray testing program, Teller wrote *The New York Times* to praise the "young American physicists" who had developed the "amazing new device." The X-ray laser, he said, promised to make "significant contributions in stopping rockets carrying weapons of mass destruction."[98]

At the University of Colorado in October 1986, he addressed a packed auditorium with evangelical fervor, saying the Star Wars program had "made progress in rockets, in lasers, in particle-beam weapons, in kinetic-energy weapons, in all kinds of peculiar things. And whenever we tried—in every case—we found the answers easier than we expected them, not easy, but easier."[99]

Teller's 1987 book, *Better a Shield Than a Sword*, struck a similar note, praising the "remarkable" X-ray laser and "my young friends" behind the advance. Like his talks and articles, it said nothing of the X-ray setbacks or the scientists leaving the program, instead painting a picture of unremitting progress. "Today there is increasing evidence that modern technology can produce successful defense measures," he wrote. In the book's acknowledgments, Teller singled out Wood for praise, applauding his antimissile ideas and saying "his record is equal to that of the best I knew in the Manhattan Project."[100]

In October 1987, Teller appeared on *Firing Line* to promote his book and praise SDI, saying he had "more and more hope that it actually will work." He also upbraided critics, including a group skeptical of the X-ray laser. "They are pessimists," he growled.[101]

"The X-ray laser works," Teller assured reporters in December 1987. "The X-ray laser is a fundamental, new and wonderful discovery."[102] Six days later he told the California Commonwealth Club that the United States had succeeded in developing an X-ray laser that could fire very intense beams of radiation. "It works," he said, adding that government secrecy laws kept him from revealing the "intensities we have achieved."[103]

TELLER continued to campaign on behalf of SDI and the laser wherever there was a receptive audience. Though wrong about the quickness with which the X-ray laser might appear and its suitability for waging antimissile war, he suffered no ill effects for his failed prophecy. Woodruff, on the other hand, suffered much. His sense of caution about the X-ray laser had proven more correct than he ever imagined. He was intellectually vindicated. But in his three-year battle to keep the program honest, Woodruff had challenged a number of powerful Livermore figures. After the resignation, his plan was to renew himself, to celebrate a new relationship with the laboratory. But now he found himself sinking ever deeper into a state of alienation.

# SIX

# Assignation
# of Blame

ORGANIZATIONAL CHARTS and bureaucratic titles gave few indications of Teller's power at Livermore. He was retired. He had no status as a regular employee, instead being retained as a consultant and using the titles of director emeritus or, at times, rather ambiguously, associate director emeritus. He visited his Livermore office irregularly, almost on whim. He lived an hour's drive from the lab. His home was located across San Francisco Bay in Palo Alto on the edge of the Stanford University campus, where he kept an office at the Hoover Institution. He traveled widely outside California, going frequently to Washington, consulting in Israel and giving talks around the world. One year Teller made forty-four trips. He did this while in his 70s, against his doctor's advice, while fighting a number of infirmities and seemingly on the verge of physical exhaustion.[1]

An observer might have assumed that Teller's role at Livermore was largely honorary and had no direct bearing on its policy and day-to-day operations. But that would be incorrect. Teller in fact ruled the 8,000-person laboratory. He did so in the same way he exercised power in national affairs—through personal relationships with high-level policy makers rather than through official positions or panels. At Livermore his influence was informal and pervasive, moving in hidden channels. Its breadth and depth, though perhaps unexpected, were not that surprising. After all, Teller had been a force in the lab's founding, had been its second director, and for decades had known and worked closely with the people who ran the place.

First and foremost, Teller's power came from his ability to make or break key appointments, including that of director. No official got his post without Teller's approval. Up until the 1970s, Teller even interviewed candidates for high-level scientific jobs at Livermore, deciding whether or not they were up to his standards. In the case of laboratory directors, the University of California regents ostensibly had the power of choice. But here, too, Teller's network of friends among the regents ensured that his candidates won. And woe to the director who irritated Teller, as Batzel once did in the late 1970s. Teller turned on him, threatening to have him removed, and came within an inch of doing so. Batzel appeared to have learned his lesson.

So, too, program leaders at Livermore were on pins and needles when Teller reviewed their work. The grizzled scientist, walking stick in hand, would ask pointed questions and make quick judgments about future directions they might pursue. With a nod, Teller could send millions of dollars into or away from a laboratory program. His blessing was viewed as crucial in the race for "resources," as scientists put it. For this reason, Teller was courted by a large contingent of Livermore officials and scientists who went out of their way to dine with him or be at his beck and call. One of Teller's frequent requests was simply to have questions answered. Even into his late 70s and early 80s, he had lost none of his intellectual curiosity.

It went like this. A scientist would be hard at work when the phone would ring. It was a secretary, saying Dr. Teller was arriving in his lab office at 2:00 P.M. and would like a briefing about the latest findings on the plasma instabilities of controlled thermonuclear fusion, or whatever. The scientist might know little of the subject, since Teller's solicitations were based more on a person's availability than his expertise. The scientist would drop everything and run to the library to review the field. He then would brief Teller in Teller's office atop Building 111. Altogether, six or seven briefers might gather there, informing Teller of what was new and answering his questions. Sometimes the scientists would get together afterward to puzzle over the session, trying to discover a common thread in Teller's curiosity. Usually there was none.[2] The sessions were just a manifestation of his uncanny ability to generate and absorb a vast array of ideas. In some respects the sessions were an extension of his mercurial interaction with Otto Frisch a half century earlier when Teller kept asking, "Do you have another problem for me?"

A Livermore scientist could back out of this role of intellectual servitude by claiming pressing "appointments" and it would not be resented. But scientists who, like director Batzel, crossed Teller or actively opposed him could find their careers in ruins. Teller's comment to Woodruff, "Roy, I may never speak to you again," was no idle threat. To be shunned by Teller was a serious problem. And not just because of Teller's own ire. Livermore's top officials, eager for approval, were known to anticipate what they saw as the old man's wishes and try to carry them out. Ultimately, being on Teller's bad side too long meant there would be pressure to leave.

Hugh E. DeWitt was a Livermore physicist who in the 1970s and 1980s publicly questioned many of the lab's activities, saying they aided a needless arms race. Eventually he had a series of confrontations with lab officials, including Teller. After one tense session with DeWitt, Teller wrote the director: "I can respect his opinions, even when they are in clear conflict with the interests of the Laboratory, as soon as he is outside the Laboratory, but not as long as he is a member of this organization."[3] The implication was not hard to see. A lab employee could be in Teller's good graces only by supporting his view of the lab's interests. DeWitt repeatedly violated this dictum, eventually suffering a series of setbacks. He was subjected to a lengthy security investigation after my focusing article, even though it was laughable to think that DeWitt, an outspoken Star Wars critic, was the source of the optimistic leak. He later came under unusually harsh job review, and was threatened with dismissal. In the late 1980s DeWitt left Livermore on professional leave, eager to escape the pressure.

An anecdote told by DeWitt illustrates the enmity Teller could hold against someone he considered disloyal. After a bitter argument one day, Teller dismissed DeWitt from his office, clearly expecting never to see him again even if DeWitt stayed at the lab. Some time later, two Russian scientists came to a science conference near Livermore that DeWitt helped organize. Teller was eager to meet with the Russians and invited them to his home. The session was quite pleasant. Unbeknown to Teller, DeWitt was scheduled to pick up the Russians. Teller opened the front door, appalled at the sight of the heretic.

"He glared and turned purple," DeWitt recalled.[4]

DeWitt sat quietly on a couch as Teller bid farewell to the Russians. The senior of the two, Vladimir Fortov, pulled a camera out of his pocket and asked Teller for permission to photograph the small party, including DeWitt.

"No!" Teller exploded, shooing them out the door.[5]

Teller later told associates he was comfortable being photographed with the Russians, but there was no way he would have his picture taken with DeWitt, a known nuclear dissident.

TELLER's rule was especially autocratic in the mid-1980s after Reagan was reelected. Already at the pinnacle of Livermore's power structure, and now having the ear of the White House during a two-term Republican presidency, Teller was untouchable—and he knew it.

It was during this period that Woodruff's long conflict with Teller and his protege Wood came to a head, resulting in Woodruff's resignation from his high post. It did not end there, however. Woodruff in effect had called Teller a liar and Batzel, Livermore's director, a coward. These acts had not gone unnoticed. It mattered little that Woodruff had been right about a technical matter that led to one of the most embarrassing episodes in Livermore history. In fact, it probably aggravated matters. Teller, while acknowledging no technical problems in the X-ray laser program, was clearly upset with the man who bore ill tidings. Teller's displeasure with Woodruff was voiced pointedly in private meetings with aides and, to a lesser extent, in public.

"I don't want to have anything to do with him," Teller snapped at a local reporter in his first public comment on Woodruff.[6]

On a radio talk show in San Francisco, Teller said Woodruff was "not as constructive a member of the team as I hoped" and deplored ever recommending him for a high position. "That was a case of poor judgment on my part," Teller added.[7]

On a segment broadcast by 60 Minutes, Teller became so upset when Woodruff's name was mentioned that he tore off his microphone and stomped off the set.[8]

FROM the start, Woodruff was an outcast. He naively expected that as a former associate director he would be included in program reviews and in the general intellectual life of the laboratory, would be part of the informal group of former officials who acted as Livermore's brain trust. But he was not. In late 1985 and early 1986, as he settled into his new job, he became aware that he had been largely cut off from meaningful commerce with Livermore programs, except for the work he had begun in Z Division. "It was like I died," he recalled. "I was never invited back into the mainstream. People would visit the laboratory and ask for me, but management would say I was unavailable that day."[9]

Behind the scenes, Livermore officials were taking steps to convey that same message in a very important place—Woodruff's paycheck. On February 5, 1986, Batzel wrote the University of California, which loosely supervised the nation's two nuclear design laboratories for the Energy Department, to say Woodruff's salary was being cut. His annual salary had been $105,000 when he ran a $300 million weapons program, but now, Batzel wrote, "I have decided that a salary of $100,000 appropriately recognizes Roy's major contributions as Associate Director while beginning to vector his salary toward the appropriate peer group."[10]

While this happened out of view, Woodruff heard rumors that top Livermore managers were still telling subordinates his resignation was prompted by a midlife crisis or, in another version, that they would never know why he quit. Harold Weaver, chairman of a university group that helped oversee the weapons labs, was told the same thing. "We were bamboozled," Weaver recalled.[11]

In such circumstances, a more compliant Livermore employee might have seen the writing on the wall and been content to do his own quiet research or else leave the lab altogether. But not Woodruff. He was furious. On March 20, 1986, he wrote Batzel a four-page letter, telling him to cease and desist. "Malicious innuendo" had the "potential to seriously impact my future earning power," he said. Woodruff noted that Batzel had previously agreed to accurately portray his reasons for quitting in private conversations with members of the defense and university communities, telling them "that you and I disagreed on a number of key issues and I could no longer support you as the Director."[12]

As the university became curious about the real reasons for Woodruff's resignation, it invited him to testify before a special board set up to review the quality of Batzel's leadership. On June 16, 1986, Woodruff appeared before the board, telling them in detail of his rift with Teller and Batzel.[13]

Worried about Teller's continuing influence on national affairs, and the possible distortion of American policy, Woodruff also warned William Frazer, a senior vice president at the University of

California, that President Reagan might rely on information that had come from Teller when the president met Soviet leader Mikhail Gorbachev in Reykjavik, Iceland.[14] Frazer took no action.

Whatever the reason, the Reykjavik meeting, which began on October 11, 1986, turned into an extraordinary spectacle of dashed hopes. At the summit, the Soviets, after intense negotiations, offered a grand compromise—the elimination within ten years of all offensive strategic arms, including ballistic missiles, bombers and cruise missiles. In exchange, they wanted SDI limited to the laboratory. But Reagan refused, eager to deploy the system in space. It was one of the most dramatic moments in the history of East-West arms control, holding out the hope of dismantling the weapons that for so long had kept the world poised on the brink of nuclear annihilation. But it passed, unfulfilled, because of Reagan's tenacious grip on his vision.[15]

After the summit, the new leader of Livermore's nuclear arms program, George H. Miller, Woodruff's former deputy, tried his best to bring the antimissile discussion down to earth. The X-ray laser's threat to any Star Wars system was "underrecognized," he told the annual meeting of the American Association for the Advancement of Science, adding that a "much different question" was whether exotic nuclear weapons could ever be perfected for the more taxing job of shooting down missiles.[16]

In December 1986, Woodruff's worries over his own plight intensified when he learned for the first time that his salary had been capped and was scheduled to be cut, treatment he felt had been accorded no other former associate director. He also discovered he had been permanently assigned to Z Division. While he enjoyed his first year there, the place now felt like a prison. Woodruff's office, like all of the Z Division building, had been especially constructed to thwart spies. It had no windows. Moreover, Woodruff had no assignments other than ones he generated for himself. Increasingly his small room seemed like a cell.[17]

After protesting his situation to Livermore officials, Woodruff received a curt note from Batzel, who told him to pipe down and suggested that the real reasons for his resignation were a failed power play and contempt for his directorship. Batzel went on to say he believed Woodruff had called for his removal before the university's special review board. "You are entitled to your opinion," Batzel wrote, adding, however, that the strain between them was such that there was no possibility of Woodruff's movement to a higher Livermore job. Woodruff was to remain in Z Division, he wrote, probably with a salary loss.[18]

Irate, Woodruff fired back a long letter. First, he contested Batzel's interpretation of the resignation, saying he clearly wanted someone to take control of the lab but never asked for a higher post. "As you well know, the reason I left my position was your refusal to challenge or allow to be challenged the over-optimistic, and in my view seriously damaging, representation of the X-ray laser program." Further, he assailed Batzel's move to "unilaterally circumscribe for me an assignment which is wholly inappropriate, contrary to Laboratory and University policy and practice."[19]

In March 1987, Woodruff got some satisfaction when it was announced that Batzel was to retire. Rumors at the lab linked the retirement to an unfavorable finding in the university's review. For Woodruff, the development was interesting but offered no immediate resolution to the conflict, since there would be a long search for a new director, with Batzel keeping the reins of power for another year or more.[20]

At this point, Woodruff took action. He appealed informally to the university for help but got none. So he took a series of administrative steps, aided by his wife. In early April 1987, he filed a formal grievance with the university, alleging that Batzel had taken illegal reprisals for his X-ray challenges. From 1983 to 1985, Woodruff wrote, Teller and Wood had conveyed both orally and in writing "overly optimistic, technically incorrect statements regarding this research to the nation's highest policy makers." In late April, Woodruff filed a second grievance alleging that Miller, the new associate director for defense systems, had denied him a job because of the Batzel dispute. In this grievance, Woodruff cited an April letter from Miller. "I have concluded," Miller had written, "that it is not appropriate for me to act as an arbitrator in the settlement of the issues which exist between you and the Director," adding that "were the circumstances different I would be excited by the potential of bringing your exceptional talents and background back into the Weapons Program."

The university rejected the first grievance as dealing with issues that were too old, but proceeded to take action on the second one. A panel of three Livermore managers was appointed to hear the grievance. On September 17, 1987, the panel ruled unanimously in Woodruff's favor, saying he clearly had been denied a reasonable job because of his dispute with Batzel. The panel called the situation

"extraordinary." The picture that emerged, it wrote, was "of a senior employee unable to communicate with the Director despite
considerable evidence of effort, and who consequently becomes isolated with no remedy available (e.g., relocation within the Laboratory, etc.) because of the lack of communication. The creation of
such an 'unperson' status is unacceptable in an organization that
endorses the principle of accountability for actions."[21]

For a remedy, the panel called on the University of California to
ensure that Woodruff got an "appropriate position" at the lab, and
that the salaries of former associate directors be investigated "to
provide guidance" for setting Woodruff's. More than a month later,
on October 20, the university accepted the findings and sent Livermore a letter telling it to find Woodruff a new job.[22]

At this point, October 20, 1987, nobody except a handful of
laboratory and university officials knew of Woodruff's five-year battle with Teller, Wood and Batzel. At Livermore, no details had ever
been disclosed. At the university, the grievances and hearing process
had all been secret. Even Woodruff had no idea he had won his
second grievance at this point. The letter was still in the mail. But
things were about to change, and change dramatically. Woodruff's
charges soon burst into public view, with the world for the first time
learning of Woodruff's long fight over the misrepresentation of the
X-ray laser. In his new public role, Woodruff would lose the cloak of
anonymity he had worn for so many years as a federal servant
working on highly sensitive matters of national security. Reluctantly at first, then with growing boldness, he took his battle public.
To some he became a hero, to others a villain.

THE unveiling began when someone at the university leaked a copy
of Woodruff's first grievance to the Southern California Federation
of Scientists, a private group long opposed to Star Wars. It was the
grievance charging that Teller and Wood had made "overly optimistic, technically incorrect statements." On Wednesday, October 21,
1987, the Federation held a noisy news conference at the Los Angeles
press club at which it released the grievance and denounced what it
called "evidence of fraud" in a multibillion-dollar program of federal
research on nuclear weapons.[23]

The news made headlines around the nation. "Teller Gave
Flawed Data on X-ray Laser," said *The Los Angeles Times*.[24] "Dispute on Star Wars Device Erupts," said *The New York Times* in an
article I wrote. The story quoted Woodruff as being "outraged" by

the group's release of the confidential papers. He also said he still strongly supported X-ray laser research but added, "It has to be responsibly portrayed to the nation's senior policy makers."[25]

When the news broke, Woodruff was in the mountains of New Mexico for the annual "Nuclear Explosives Design Physics Conference," held in 1987 at Los Alamos. At such conferences, in addition to talks, an area was set aside where scientists could hang "posters" that gave an overview of their work. It was a place for top-secret browsing. Now the Los Alamos scientists sprang into action, creating a poster that bore a giant likeness of Teller and a blowup of the article from the *Albuquerque Tribune* on Woodruff's charges. "An Uninvited Paper on SDI," read the poster's title. Scores of scientists signed the bottom of the poster, some writing comments such as "Go get 'em, Roy."[26]

As Woodruff walked to the podium to give a paper at the conference, the audience broke into applause.

That same day, Woodruff got a call from the staff of Representative George E. Brown, Jr., a California Democrat and senior member of the House Science Committee, asking him to come to Washington to discuss the charges with Congressmen Brown and Les Aspin, the Wisconsin Democrat who chaired the House Armed Services Committee. The next day, Thursday, October 22, Woodruff learned from his wife, Mary, that he had won the second grievance. He was elated at his vindication. The pall over his career seemed to be lifting.[27]

On Friday, Woodruff, now in Washington, told the congressmen about the X-ray episode. After hearing the details, Representative Brown told reporters that he would call for an investigation of the charges by the General Accounting Office.[28] Brown, a portly, gray-haired man who liked nothing better than a good cigar, was a powerful ally. A liberal devoted to environmental protection and alternative energy development, Brown had received his undergraduate degree in physics from UCLA, had been an early opponent of the Vietnam War and for nearly two decades had helped set science policy on Capitol Hill. He had a reputation for being unintimidated by scientific minutiae and for pursuing exotic issues with tenacity.

Director Batzel of Livermore issued a statement of denial on Friday, October 23, as Woodruff told his story in Washington. He dismissed the charges, saying he felt "senior people in Government were correctly informed" about the X-ray laser from lab briefings and testimony. "Further," said Batzel, "my policy is that when individual scientists wish to speak out with differing points of view on technical issues, the Laboratory does not intervene."[29] Clearly, that characterization seemed to ignore the repeated instances in which Woodruff was told to refrain from writing letters of correction to top government officials.

The Energy Department in Washington issued a statement that same Friday saying it had conducted a study of Woodruff's charges and found them groundless. The investigation was performed, not by the department's inspector general or some independent body, but by two former directors of Energy Department laboratories, John Foster, who once headed Livermore, and George Dacy, who headed the Sandia National Laboratory.[30] Although pointing to the Foster-Dacy report as vindication of its X-ray management, the department declined to make the unclassified document public.

When Woodruff arrived back in Livermore, he found that a sign had been put on the door of his Z Division office by his newly knowledgeable colleagues. "Gorky West" it read, after the Russian city where Soviet physicist Andrei Sakharov had been sent into exile.[31]

BACK in Washington at Representative Brown's office, unsolicited letters began to arrive from current and former Livermore scientists concerning the X-ray dispute. One of the most pointed was from W. Lowell Morgan, the R Program scientist who left the effort in 1985 after the brightness setback. "I quit the program for two reasons," he wrote from the University of Colorado. "The first is that I felt that the program was going nowhere; the experiments were very difficult, yielding minuscule returns of poor quality data for a tremendous investment of effort and, in my opinion, an obscene investment of money. The second reason is that I felt that the few scientific results that we had were being grossly misrepresented in their support of the fantastic claims about the X-ray laser." The misrepresentation, Morgan concluded, "is an affront to the American public and science and does the competent and honest scientists at the Laboratory a disservice."[32]

A shorter letter was sent by Chapline, the bookish former professor who helped get the X-ray effort under way in the mid-1970s and was now a senior R Program scientist. He insisted the laser had been "undersold," not oversold. "Unfortunately," he wrote, "during the Reagan administration there has been very little expressed support for the X-ray laser program. Edward Teller and Lowell Wood have made attempts to inform officials of the Reagan administration concerning the military potential of the X-ray laser, but their efforts do not seem to have been entirely successful," a reference to the project's limited funding. In closing, Chapline insisted that the X-ray laser "has the potential to make Soviet ICBMs obsolete."[33]

AT Livermore, two auditors from the General Accounting Office (GAO), James Ohl and David L. Potter, began to conduct interviews for Representative Brown's investigation. At the top of their list was Teller. On November 24, 1987, they had a long, rambling session with the elderly physicist, who, as usual, was accompanied by his aide Budwine. Teller was familiar with at least one of the auditors, who had helped conduct the previous GAO study of the brightness flaw.

"We have progressed less than I hoped" since the last interview, Teller told the auditors. He said nothing of technical problems, however, instead pointing to limits on funding. "As a consequence," Teller said, "my worries increase. There continues to be reason to believe the Soviets know more than we do—that in their hands, the X-ray laser may have already been developed, or developing fast, into something that makes our retaliation really obsolete and our continued tardiness may be a source of great dangers."[34]

Teller joked that he desperately wanted to be investigated—not for exaggerating the X-ray laser but for not doing more to get additional funding. He then talked about the pros and cons of different antimissile defenses. Finally, the GAO auditors interrupted, saying they had "five or six" questions. Congressman Brown, they said, had asked them to compare what had been officially said by Livermore about the X-ray laser with what had come from Teller's office.

"Look," Teller protested, "I don't have an 'office.' At that time, I was a consultant here. I spoke for myself as I did for the last forty years."

Auditor Ohl quickly agreed, seeming to take sides on a delicate point in the controversy. "That's one thing that we want to impress upon him," he said, referring to Congressman Brown.

"Well," Teller huffed, "and that's how it is." The point was important since one of Woodruff's contentions was that Teller had not merely been giving his personal opinion but, by virtue of his position as director emeritus, his writing on Livermore letterhead and his constant reference to "we" in laying out X-ray laser goals and schedules, was seen as speaking on behalf of the laboratory.

Ohl said Woodruff had charged Teller with making overly optimistic and technically incorrect statements, adding that "we're trying our darndest to avoid getting in the middle of honest difference of opinion."

Teller waved his hand.

"Look," he growled, "maybe what I said was wrong. If what I said was wrong, then what I'm saying now is wrong, because I'm not saying anything different."

Teller took control of the interview, leaving the original line of questioning to zero in on his accuser.

"Since you bring up Roy Woodruff, I have to tell you that Roy Woodruff is a man in connection with whom I probably made a very serious mistake," Teller said. "I recommend him for an important job. He looked as an intelligent, energetic person. It turned out, it seems to me now, that he was very specifically not suited for a job of administrative responsibility."

The reason for this unsuitability, Teller said, was that Woodruff had shown an excess of X-ray zeal that suddenly and inexplicably reversed itself. "He seemed to be, at that time, even over optimistic about one approach, and when that over optimism, for which in itself I would not blame him, when that turned sour, he flipped into the opposite." Teller emphasized the point, saying Woodruff was "not a very steady type." Teller also stressed that his X-ray opinions were his own, never representing Woodruff or the lab or the X-ray program, although he conceded contact on the issue with lab director Roger Batzel. "I did check that opinion with the lab director to avoid confusion," Teller said. "I think you will find no essential difference, at the very most a shading of difference of opinion, I don't even know in which direction, between Roger and myself."

Auditor Ohl pressed gently onward, asking Teller what he meant in his December 1983 letter to Keyworth by saying the X-ray laser was entering the engineering phase.

"I am not quite sure what I meant," Teller replied. "My memory is not all that good. This letter is dated December 22, 1983. It is, therefore, four years old. You cannot ask me what I meant precisely at that time. You can ask me, but I cannot answer!"

"Which is understandable," said Ohl.

Teller added that in general he was "not quite clear" where to draw the line between science and engineering. "At that time," he continued, "the debate with Jay [Keyworth] was, 'Is it really a laser?' That was a scientific question. I am saying in this letter the scientific question is settled—it is a laser. That, with this principle, one can do something about defense, I fully believe now. Whether that is sufficiently significant in itself to merit a major effort, I am not quite sure. That depends on the circumstances. But what I meant here was, 'It is a laser, let's go ahead.' We did. We found some difficulties. We also found some help."

The GAO auditors also asked Teller if he was familiar with the X-ray laser "Prize of a Planet" briefing Wood had given CIA director Casey. Teller said he was not. Ohl noted that Wood's brightness figures were "misstated," as revealed by the investigation of the sensor problems.

"Right," volunteered Teller's aide, Budwine.

Gingerly, Ohl pressed a little further with Teller, saying Wood's numbers had been overstated.

"Look," Teller replied, "that I simply don't even remember."

"That's what we were talking about last time we were here," Ohl said, referring to the GAO investigation of the sensor flaws.

"Right," said Budwine.

Teller was steadfastly silent, making no comment about one of the biggest setbacks in the history of the X-ray laser program.

Ohl switched topics, saying he wanted to locate and look at copies of some of Teller's public speeches.

Teller volunteered that Ohl might buy a copy of his book, *Better a Shield Than a Sword.*

"I've got your T-shirt," said Ohl, referring to a novelty item on sale at the lab's gift shop that had "Better a Shield Than a Sword" printed across the chest. The T-shirts also bore a copy of Teller's signature, blown up large.

"Maybe that should be classified," Teller chuckled, the others joining in the laughter.

That was the formal end of the interview. But Teller took the initiative to volunteer reflections on one last point—his overall influence on the genesis of Star Wars. "I am blamed or credited entirely unduly for having persuaded the president," he said. "I did not do much, very little."

Teller insisted that his first meeting with the president had occurred in September 1982 as a result of Reagan having seen the *Firing Line* program. His statement contradicted many reports, including those of presidential adviser Karl Bendetsen and Reagan aide Martin Anderson, both of whom said the first meeting had occurred in January 1982. (Teller later softened his claim in an interview with a trusted colleague, saying the September meeting was the only one with Reagan before the Star Wars speech "in circumstances where I could talk," implying there were earlier ones in which he participated.)[35]

To the GAO, Teller also volunteered he had "probably" spoken of the X-ray laser in talking to the president's science adviser and other high federal officials. "I was strongly under the impression that here is something new, and important, and capable of development," he recalled. "I am absolutely certain that I did not say a billion, or a trillion, or a million. I said that it is new. It has this or that principle. Probably the words X-ray laser were mentioned. But as I have often said, I, in fact, did not advise the president. I advised the advisers of the president."

THE day after the interview with Teller, on November 25, 1987, the GAO auditors called on Miller, Woodruff's former deputy who had succeeded him as associate director for defense systems. Miller was asked if he agreed in general with Woodruff's charges. He replied that he had been "quite concerned" about Wood's statements. "They were having a significant effect, both externally and internally, on the program," he said, adding that they caused "significant internal tension." That tension, Miller said, was deepened by resentment over Wood's acerbic style and "resulted in tremendous difficulty in having the program go forward." Wood's lobbying in Washington "also caused me a fair amount of concern and consternation."[36]

Miller said Livermore officials had ultimately been able to correct or influence discussions in Washington so that "specific financial and programmatic decisions" were always made "on the basis of what the program was saying and not on the basis of what Lowell and Edward were saying." Of course, Teller's winning $100 million from President Reagan for Livermore's X-ray program seemed to contradict this assertion.

Miller characterized Teller's letters to presidential advisers as "generally inappropriate," given what was then known about the X-ray laser. One clear error, he added, was Teller's comment to Keyworth about the engineering phase. "That is totally inaccurate," Miller said. "Everything else I guess I would characterize as being overly optimistic."

Miller went on to say that since Woodruff's resignation, "Edward has been much more careful about what he says about the X-ray laser program." The new caution, he said, was "primarily" the result of Teller's being "better educated by the program as opposed to Lowell. Dave Nowak, who is the [R] Program leader right now, for instance, spends a fair amount of time with Edward. And so he is quite aware of all the kinds of problems that we have been having in the program, as well as the successes."

It was a rather remarkable statement. Teller's colleagues, as they had for more than a half century, were again playing an important role in helping him understand what was real and what was not about the object of his enthusiasms. They were getting him "better educated," as Miller put it. Only this time the education was occurring after an extraordinary episode in which Teller had largely cut himself off from their advice. Their role had been renewed only after great difficulties, setbacks and embarrassments to a key military program of the United States. It had taken a huge upheaval to get Teller to settle down and listen to the facts.

The GAO auditors pressed ahead with Miller, moving on to Wood's briefings. For the "Prize of a Planet" talk to CIA director Casey, in April 1985, Miller said Wood's statements had clearly been wrong, even before the detailed revelations of the brightness failure. "We knew that there were substantive corrections that had to be made," Miller said. It was "clearly incorrect" then and now, "to say we have measured weapon level output."[37]

Ohl asked whether the uncertainties had been generally known back then or only more recently.

"Well," Miller replied, "they're certainly known now and they were generally known then," noting that Maenchen had pointed to potential flaws in a series of Livermore papers. It was, Miller said, "clearly inappropriate to be making statements of that certainty to people of that level, based on the information we had a month after the shot."

When the interview was formally over, Miller volunteered that the X-ray laser program had generally been able to mitigate any misrepresentations by Teller and Wood. He said that, with the exception of President Reagan and his national security adviser McFarlane, the program had been able to give follow-up briefings that were better balanced and more sober. "I talked to Casey twice myself," Miller said, adding that he also talked to arms adviser Nitze after Woodruff resigned.

"It's important to understand that over a period of time the laboratory's view was explicitly given to most of the senior government officials that Roy was concerned about," Miller said. He did not specify the "period of time," whether months or years. A corrective briefing, Miller noted, "was not typically given in writing, which is what Roy had requested be done. He believed, as program leader, that it was important to have something documented and in writing on the guy's desk, so after you leave he'd have something to refer to."

In closing, Miller noted that the damage-repair sessions were limited to known cases of misrepresentation. "Who the hell knows of what we're not aware?" he volunteered.

MILLER'S interview was over. But he was soon forced to contradict Wood again, taking pains to correct the possibility of a false impression. Wood had testified in September 1987 before the research and development subcommittee of the House Armed Services Committee. "One of the things which is especially intriguing about X-ray lasers," Wood had said, is that a single device "can potentially destroy all Soviet objects that are presented in its field of view at any given time. To overstate the matter, you can win your war if your opponent launches all his assets at once into your field of view, even at a substantial distance." Wood added that progress on such weapons "continues at a substantial pace."[38]

Miller disputed that claim. On December 1, 1987, he wrote John M. Spratt, Jr., the South Carolina Democrat, who chaired the subcommittee. Noting he only recently became aware of Wood's testimony, Miller said he was "deeply concerned" about the risk of confusion. The X-ray laser, he said, was a basic research program— not an effort aimed at developing a weapon. As the program's head, he said, "I am cautious and mindful of the many technological hurdles we still face. Our best estimate is that it will take at least five years and an integral expenditure of a billion dollars before we can actually demonstrate whether an X-ray laser weapon can be realized and what its potential might be."[39]

WOODRUFF forged a new life for himself at Livermore even as Miller fought a rear-guard action against the forces of X-ray aggrandizement. Having won his administrative war to leave Z Division, Woodruff on December 8, 1987, began a new high-level assignment at the lab. He became head of the treaty verification program, a post that had just taken on new prominence as the United States and Soviet Union signed the Intermediate Nuclear Forces (INF) Treaty on the same day.[40] This accord was to dramatically cut nuclear arsenals in Europe and begin an innovative process of treaty policing with on-site inspectors and procedures, in contrast to the previous heavy reliance on spy satellites. The treaty verification post was both prominent and challenging. Woodruff's salary was also raised—back to $105,000, a level, the laboratory found after some research, that was consistent with past practice regarding former associate directors.[41]

Another boost for Woodruff came with the emergence of Representative Brown as a powerful friend in Congress, championing the case nationally on the House floor. The claims of Teller and Wood, Brown said on December 10, 1987, "were politically motivated exaggerations aimed at distorting national policy and funding decisions."[42]

TELLER still retained his close ties to the White House, despite the bad publicity over the Woodruff affair. As President Reagan and Soviet leader Gorbachev dined in Washington on December 8 at the state dinner celebrating the signing of the INF Treaty, Teller sat with them at the table of eight. The 79-year-old physicist was one seat away from a very popular president who was marking what would be the crowning achievement of his eight years in office.[43]

But on his way back from Washington, Teller stopped in Nevada for a scientific conference and found himself confronted by a group of reporters eager to get his reaction to Woodruff's charges. It was Teller's first public comment on the dispute. "I don't want to have anything to do with him," Teller said of Woodruff, adding that his accuser was "misinformed and misinforming."[44] Teller denied misleading the president and downplayed his role as a presidential adviser. "I have had little opportunity to talk to the president," Teller said. "I don't remember how many times I met with the president. But they were very brief meetings. They were insignificant. And they have been blown out of proportion."[45] Asked about his letter to science adviser Keyworth, Teller said, "Whether or not I said the X-ray laser was in engineering phase is not relevant. And I don't want to waste time on this subject any more."[46] Teller took the initiative to defend the X-ray laser itself, saying it was "a fundamental, new, and wonderful discovery." The device, he said, has "possible applications in defense. How effective it will be in defense, I did not know then, and I do not know now." Teller went on to call himself an "optimist" and said antimissile deployments would cost far less than critics charged.[47]

Upon reading Teller's comments in the newspapers, Woodruff wrote him a long letter, challenging his remarks. He reminded Teller of the Keyworth letter: "You admitted it was in error and asked me not to send a correcting letter because it would 'ruin your reputation,' " Woodruff wrote. He also questioned the notion that Teller had little influence with the president, recalling the Pentagon meeting in which Teller told the powerful group of defense officials that the White House had promised him $100 million. "This event did not imply to anyone involved that your interactions with President Reagan were insignificant," Woodruff wrote. In closing, Woodruff said he would be happy to discuss these issues.[48]

Teller made no response. Instead he penned a short memo to his own file, addressing a single point. Teller denied having admitted that his letter to Keyworth contained anything incorrect or embarrassing or that he said "My reputation would be ruined" if a follow-up letter were sent to the White House. "I can categorically say that no such conversation took place," he wrote. "Not only do I have no remembrance of such an interaction, but I did not believe at the time, nor do I believe now, that I wrote anything in the letter in question which could be damaging to me."[49]

As the central figures in the controversy exchanged fire, the GAO auditors probed deeper, interviewing a widening circle of scientists at Livermore. On December 23, 1987, one of them, George Maenchen, the longtime R Program scientist, wrote Ohl a letter to recap his interview. He did so because he had become worried about the GAO auditors' objectivity. "I had the feeling, very subjectively, that they were seeking to minimize the divergence of views," Maenchen told me.[50] In his letter, Maenchen called four Teller-Wood statements "totally false." These were (1) that the program had entered the engineering phase, (2) that the Romano test results were in quantitative agreement with theoretical calculations, (3) that the Cottage experiment had shown "weapon-level" performance, and (4) that with adequate funding a weapon could be fielded in a few years that was a billion or trillion times brighter than a hydrogen bomb. "You asked me," Maenchen wrote, "whether they could be characterized as merely 'unduly optimistic.' This strikes me as a very mild euphemism. These outrageous claims go far beyond the bounds of mere enthusiasm and personal optimism. They lie in the realm of pure fantasy. The problem of wildly exaggerated claims for the X-ray laser program is not a recent one. Those of us who have actually worked in the program have been painfully aware of the problem and have objected vigorously (but internally) for many years. Unfortunately, our pleas for more honest and factual reporting of the program's status and prospects have had little success. While Roy Woodruff and George Miller have reported the program properly, others like Teller and Wood have not."[51]

Maenchen said he was "amused" to find Teller's letters referring to Wood as leader of the X-ray team. "Lowell has never been in charge of, or even a member of, the X-ray laser design group," Maenchen wrote. "His contributions to the technical aspects of the program have, to my knowledge, been limited to loud, but often irrelevant, comments and criticisms in technical review meetings."

THE same day Maenchen condemned the "outrageous claims," Wood mailed a nine-page letter to Congressman Brown defending himself and Teller and charging that one and only one person at the weapons lab had exaggerated the X-ray laser's promise—Roy Woodruff. By accident or design, Wood's charge was similar to Teller's allegation that it was Woodruff and only Woodruff who was guilty of excessive optimism.

Wood's tone was quite erudite and aloof at the start, then became more personal, caustic and menacing. Research on nuclear weapons, Wood wrote, was constantly surprising. "Given the complexity and often rapidly evolving nature of the perceived truth regarding various aspects of nuclear weaponry and the central role of such weaponry in contemporary geopolitics, it would be hazardous indeed for the leadership of a superpower to depend on any single source of technical advice regarding such weaponry."[52] Diversity of opinion was a matter not only of practicality but of principle, Wood wrote. The lab, as an arm of the University of California, was devoted to free speech. "This freedom," he said, "has been exercised vigorously by many staff members, both in speaking out in public and in offering to Washingtonians their opinions on all manner of topics, ranging from the desirability of terminating the Laboratory's Weapons Program to the potential military applications of X-ray lasers. Toward elected Federal officials, this freedom-of-speech has been complete." Such facts, Wood said, contradicted the idea that there were two incompatible "channels" at work in the case of the X-ray laser—an official one and the Teller-Wood channel. "Any

Laboratory staff member can open 'a channel to Washington' any time and on any subject, simply by setting pen to paper," Wood wrote the congressman.

His position was clearly extreme, implying no hierarchy at all in the lab's dealings with Washington. Any of the 8,000 Livermore employees could speak out with equal ease, Wood seemed to be saying, their messages accorded equal weight amid the din of technical and political opinion. Nowhere did Wood address a mechanism by which the director and his aides might sift through this diversity to present an official stance, especially on intricate technical issues, something Livermore did with great regularity as it sat on federal panels and testified before Congress. His only reference to the lab director was as a guarantor of "freedom-of-speech."

Wood defended his own communications as completely honest. "I stand confidently on the documented record of what I have said to Washington on the subject of nuclear-pumped X-ray lasers, and will vigorously defend its accuracy and technical correctness against any bill-of-particulars." Wood added that his disclosures were narrowly technical, while those of Woodruff's office "tended to stress the progress made in the experimental program, the great need for stepped-up funding of the experimental program, and the early advent of militarily significant X-ray lasers, if effectively unlimited resource levels were to be provided."

Warming to the attack, Wood gave a specific instance in which he said Woodruff had oversold the X-ray laser. The occasion was the February 17, 1983, meeting of the White House Science Council just before Reagan's Star Wars speech. The overall briefing, given by Woodruff, contained "the most optimistic statements" on the quick availability and deadly power of X-ray lasers, Wood wrote. Some of the timeposts "are already in the past, and others are essentially upon us." Wood broke from his counterattack to label Woodruff's accusations and Brown's relaying them to congressional investigators "a smear." He said his own reporting of X-ray laser experiments to Washington represented "the consensus of my technical peers at these times; I stand on the record of them unhesitatingly." Unbeknown to Wood, this claim had just been contradicted by both Maenchen and Miller.

In closing, Wood tore into Congressman Brown for daring to investigate Teller, "who has been called upon by most of the Presidents during the past four decades to give trusted advice on the impact of technical developments in national security." Despite clear evidence that Woodruff's allegations had no merit, Wood wrote, "you have nonetheless chosen to give a presumption of seriousness to these dated, extensively shopped-around charges of misrepresentation and falsification of physical fact, lodged by an accuser whose formal and informal credentials pale in comparison to those of the accused, who is universally acknowledged to be one of the great physicists of this century." Wood added that Brown no doubt knew his decision to make public comments on the case "has greatly damaged my professional reputation, any more than you can be oblivious to the likelihood that you are constitutionally immunized from any legal recourse on my part."

The following day, Christmas Eve 1987, Wood mailed Brown a secret appendix to his rebuttal, some of which has been declassified. It focused on the February 1983 Science Council meeting, amplifying the charge that Woodruff was guilty of misrepresentation. At the meeting Woodruff had promised a "late-'80s militarization, production and deployment" of an X-ray laser weapon, Wood wrote, enclosing a copy of the briefing document. "Neither Professor Teller nor I have ever suggested that X-ray laser weapons could be realized on any schedules such as these, precisely contrary to Mr. Woodruff's public allegations. Who overpromised what to whom, with respect to X-ray laser weapons? Who conjured up completely fanciful, albeit highly detailed, X-ray laser weapons visions before the President—or as close to him as he could get? No letter of Professor Teller's, no briefing document of mine, no testimony ever given by either of us, no advice offered anywhere in Washington by either of us can be compared, even remotely, in the degree of optimism presented pervasively in this major briefing document on X-ray laser weaponry."[53]

Certainly, Woodruff had been an optimist in the laser's early days. But Wood's attack seemed unjustified. No evidence was ever made public, despite Wood's claims, that showed Woodruff at any time promising an X-ray laser weapon for the late 1980's. The X-ray timetable that Woodruff did promote for that period differed from Teller's in two important respects—it centered on scientific feasibility rather than deployment and it called for increased funding. Without an extra $200 million a year, Woodruff's time line moved deep into the 1990s. The point was important. All schedules in the bomb business were tied to assumptions about the availability of money, which determined the pace at which costly blasts could be conducted beneath the Nevada desert. Teller, in writing Nitze, had predicted a late 1980s "realization" for Excalibur based on a "resource-limited" program, as Livermore's effort clearly was. Finally, Wood's rebuttal made no mention of the most glaring contradictions to his thesis of all. Chief among these were Bendetsen's 1981 memo to the White House that forecast a working X-ray laser weapon in four or five years and Woodruff's late 1982 clash with Teller to keep Livermore from having to make the same kind of promise. Ironically, it was Woodruff's victory in this confrontation that made the February 1983 briefing to the White House Science Council—the briefing Wood ridiculed as "completely fanciful" —far more temperate than it would have been if Teller had prevailed.

As Wood made his counterattack, the lab took a public thrashing in early 1988 as national newsmagazines such as *Time* recounted the known details of the dispute, usually with sympathy for Woodruff. "Red Flag at a Weapons Lab," read *Time*'s headline. "Did Edward Teller oversell the President on the X-ray laser?" Toward its end, the article wondered if Livermore's reputation for technical integrity was permanently damaged. It quoted John Harvey, the lab's manager for advanced strategic systems, as saying: "When I go to Washington now, people jokingly ask me what's the next lie."[54]

The headline in *U.S. News & World Report* read: "Long Knives in the Laboratory." The magazine noted that a group of Teller loyalists at Livermore had formed an "Ad Hoc Integrity Group" to counteract the bad publicity. Among other activities, the group had gathered signatures for a petition asserting there was "no shortage of technical credibility and scientific integrity" at the lab.[55]

Director Batzel tried a more subtle approach. Writing to Congressman Brown on January 25, 1988, he explained what he saw as the root of the controversy—the positive attitude essential for success in science. "Whether in defense, energy or medicine, the researchers are generally optimistic for the outcome, even though many problems may be unresolved for many years," Batzel wrote. "Even among those optimistic for the possibilities, there are ranges of expectation. At Livermore, each of these has had its proponents. This is healthy and a natural part of scientific inquiry."[56]

TELLER took no public actions to counter the spate of bad publicity. Instead, he privately launched a veiled attack on Woodruff, much as he had done with Oppenheimer decades earlier. Teller dwelled on current issues rather than past ones, apparently seeking to raise

questions about Woodruff's suitability for his new job and implying
that he should be removed. On January 25, 1988, Teller wrote director Batzel. A lab scientist, he noted, had recently expressed "serious concern" about Woodruff's appointment to "the important job"
of treaty verification. "I do not intend to discuss the problems connected with Roy Woodruff," Teller said obliquely, "but rather the
serious questions which are tied to test verification." He said the person in the post will face "the highest demands" as "the voice of the
Laboratory" in a field with "direct effect on international affairs."
The candidate should be professional and consistent and should have
a passion for anonymity, Teller declared. "A man for this job should
best be a person whose name has never appeared in the daily papers."
Finally, Teller wrote, the candidate should be a person of even temper
and of extraordinary common sense. "I do not know whether at this
time steps can be taken to make sure that the job is rightly performed," Teller said in conclusion. "As yet no actual mistakes have
been committed" in regard to the post. "Future mistakes might be
prevented by careful thought and proper action."[57]

As Teller intrigued over Woodruff's job, he prevailed in his choice of
candidate for another—the directorship. On February 18, 1988, the
University of California Regents announced their decision. Livermore's new director was to be John H. Nuckolls, 57, a small urbane
man with silvery hair who had worked closely with Teller for decades and most recently had been associate director for physics,
where he had kept a loose rein on Wood. Nuckolls had no Ph.D. But
like Teller and Wood, he had a fertile imagination, having gained a
reputation at Livermore for inventiveness. He had worked with
Wood on a way to extract energy from black holes—collapsed stars
so dense that light cannot escape their gravitational grip. He had
labored extensively on lasers and nuclear arms, including laser fusion and the neutron bomb. He had also come up with an idea that,
in theory, could shrink an H-bomb to the size of a cocktail olive.[58]
    Nuckolls was quick to publicly state his views on the laser
dispute, telling reporters that the lab's advice to Washington was
balanced and that Woodruff had an opportunity to air his opinion
within the Reagan administration. In nearly the same breath, Nuckolls praised Teller and Wood as creative visionaries. "We need the
dreamers," he told reporters.[59]
    Behind the scenes, Nuckolls almost immediately went to work
on behalf of Teller and Wood. On March 3, 1988, he met with the

GAO auditors, Wood, and other lab officials, suggesting that all but one of the Teller-Wood statements could be viewed as similar to official laboratory comments.[60] And on April 18, the lab demonstrated its partiality in a glaring way. Paul T. Schafer, head of its office of management review, distributed a draft of the impending GAO report for comment to key employees, including former director Batzel, Nuckolls and Wood. The central figure in the investigation, Woodruff, was left off the distribution list.[61]

The bulk of the comments sought to make the report a strong vindication of Teller, showing that Woodruff's X-ray statements were similar to those of the Hungarian scientist.[62] But Miller, in his comments, rejected that thesis. "The [GAO] report distorts the fact that the integral position (i.e., sum of all statements) by the two sides during this time period are fairly different and distinct," Miller wrote. He also said the report failed to adequately note that director Batzel "agreed through this period of time with Roy's view of the program." In closing, Miller faulted a GAO survey of Livermore scientists on the X-ray issue. The GAO's selection of subjects, he said, was biased in favor of Teller. But in reality, Miller said, "I believe that the predominant opinion would agree with Roy's assessment."[63]

WOODRUFF during this period began to develop a deep sense of foreboding in regard to both the GAO report and the lab in general. It was Woodruff's impression that Nuckolls, as director, had no time to meet with him, despite numerous requests. The first meeting took place on May 18, 1988, exactly three months after Nuckolls had been named director. It was acrimonious, with Nuckolls saying Woodruff was destroying the lab. Nuckolls later defended his hesitancy to meet with Woodruff, saying that as director he had to maintain a distance lest partiality "color" any future administrative actions.[64]

As for the GAO report, Woodruff was privy to none of the lab's maneuvering. But he had nonetheless seen enough signs to worry about its fairness. On May 23, 1988, he wrote Congressman Brown, saying he feared the report would be "less than objective in many ways." A serious flaw, he said, was apparent GAO bias in the review of documents. The GAO auditors had focused only on Teller's three letters and Wood's briefing to Casey—all of which Woodruff brought to their attention. In contrast, they examined several hundred documents and letters generated by Woodruff and the weapons program. "This seems on the face of it absurd," Woodruff wrote.[65]

As it turned out, Woodruff's concerns were warranted. The 16-page GAO report, made public on July 14, 1988, found that Teller in most cases was no more optimistic than his Livermore colleagues in hailing the X-ray laser. It noted some instances in which Teller went beyond others' assessments, for the first time revealing a portion of the Nitze letter in which Teller said a single X-ray laser module could "potentially shoot down the entire Soviet land-based missile force." But the report failed to mention most of the other embellishments. And its conclusion was unambiguous. It said Livermore's "official channel, which included Mr. Woodruff, had made statements about the status and potential of the X-ray laser, which were similar to most of the statements identified by Mr. Woodruff as being 'overly optimistic and technically incorrect.' "[66]

Despite strong conclusions, the report's evidence was weak. On Excalibur, it found general agreement between Teller and Woodruff despite their battle over the 1983 Christmas letter to Keyworth. Woodruff had objected to Teller's statement about Romano results being in "essentially quantitative agreement." But the GAO found Woodruff's letter to defense and energy officials of January 13, 1984, to be essentially similar. This conclusion was reached even though Woodruff in that letter said the all-important brightness factor was only in "qualitative" agreement with predictions, implying that the scientists had failed to understand the phenomenon behind the laser's brightness. In other words, the Woodruff and Teller letters were miles apart on the point of greatest importance. Yet, incomprehensibly, the GAO cited this episode as an area of agreement.[67]

Another area of questionable equivalence centered on Teller's promise to Nitze about Excalibur being realized "in this decade." The GAO report found similarity in the 1982 and 1983 meetings of Woodruff and associates with the White House Science Council. But there Woodruff was talking about scientific feasibility, not deployment. Moreover, GAO overlooked the critical issue of money, as Wood had done. Woodruff's late 1980s time frame for the demonstration of scientific feasibility had been explicitly based on a substantial rise in funding, bringing the program to a "technology-limited pace." Another alleged similarity on this score was even more dubious. The GAO report cited a 1984 Livermore program plan asserting that the brightness goal could be achieved "in the foreseeable future," the actual date blocked out for reasons of security. As it turned out, however, this document put the predicted achievement, not in the 1980s—as Teller asserted to Nitze—but in the next decade, the 1990s.[68]

With Super Excalibur, the report was just as skewed. It ambiguously cited Woodruff's February 1985 letter in which he said the device should be developed as "rapidly as possible" but was unfit "to sell" as anything more than a concept. Inexplicably, as another point of similarity it cited Woodruff's February 1985 presentation to Senate staffers in which he used a question mark to indicate when the Super Excalibur idea might materialize—clearly emphasizing its obscure status rather than its potential as a weapon.[69]

On Wood's CIA briefing, the GAO report quoted Livermore scientists as saying the portrayed energy level had essentially been correct. It neglected the testimony of Miller and Maenchen, both of whom said Wood's assertion was clearly false.[70]

Perhaps most damning of all for Woodruff, the report said a general survey had been taken of Livermore X-ray experts for their views on the accuracy of the contested statements. It found "no uniformity of opinion," implying Teller's statements were within the range of conventional wisdom at the weapons lab.[71]

By implication, the report made Woodruff out to be a hypocrite who, while charging Teller and Wood with serious distortions of a program vital to national security, had engaged in exactly the same kind of behavior himself.

OMITTED from the GAO report was evidence that would have cast the dispute in a very different light. For instance, it made no mention of the 1981 Bendetsen memo that conveyed the most optimistic of Teller's views to the White House and committed Livermore to an X-ray weapon in as little as four or five years. Woodruff had no knowledge of this memo. In contrast, the auditors had access to a copy.[72] Perhaps most damning, the GAO auditors, by focusing on lab minutiae, missed an important part of the bigger picture. If they had spoken to William W. Hoover, who ran the Energy Department's arms programs during the period in question, they would have found that the main federal official in charge of X-ray laser research had no trouble distinguishing the antagonists from one another. "Roy was enthusiastic" about the laser, Hoover told me. "But I don't think he believed, even if all the science theory proved right, that it could be brought into the kind of operational status that Teller or Wood were suggesting."[73]

UNDERSTANDABLY, Teller and Livermore officials were delighted with the GAO report, erupting in a round of self-congratulatory statements inside and outside the laboratory. "Let me plead guilty to the great crime of optimism," Teller quipped to a reporter in responding to the report.[74]

The weekend after the report was released, on Sunday, July 17, 1988, Teller went on a radio talk show program of San Francisco station KGO to publicly celebrate his vindication. The host was Willard H. ("Bill") Wattenburg. Not the usual radio personality, Wattenburg was a former Livermore employee who retained the "Q" clearance that gave him access to secret data on nuclear arms, despite having left full-time work for Livermore in the 1960s. In addition to his talk show and other pursuits, including some minor movie roles, Wattenburg was a member of Livermore's "Ad Hoc Integrity Group" that tried to counteract bad publicity surrounding the Teller-Woodruff clash.[75]

Although the radio show often had an "open line" to discuss any topic, that night, from 10:00 P.M. until midnight, Wattenburg devoted the show to the GAO report and what he called Woodruff's false charges. Telling his listeners the X-ray affair was "a national scandal," Wattenburg said the press had been "duped into creating a story that in my opinion has bum-rapped the national defense of this nation and individuals who have served it with integrity." Going far beyond the GAO report, Wattenburg said Woodruff had "stated the same things" as Teller "in even stronger terms." Wattenburg said "It smacks of hypocrisy." He suggested that Woodruff's motive in battling Teller was simply a bid to extend his personal power.[76]

After an hour of monologues and mostly skeptical call-ins, Wattenburg devoted the show's second hour to a conversation with Teller. "I'm very happy," the scientist said. "I think the people at the General Accounting Office did a careful, conscientious, well-balanced job." Teller also lambasted Congressman Brown for making comments on the investigation before the release of the report.

"Well, Dr. Teller," Wattenburg said, "the big issue is this. How important is the X-ray laser?"

Despite the political and technical setbacks, Teller was undaunted in his optimism.

"I believe that it will have a great importance, not only in defense, but in research," Teller replied. "I am serving on the White House Science Council. I told my friends there, I told the President's science adviser, how important these things are. Roy Woodruff at that time objected to my saying all these things. I have cleared all my papers with the director of the laboratory, and Roy was quite unhappy that all the reporting did not go through him. It turned out that he was not as constructive a member of the team as I hoped he would be. And actually I had recommended him for the job that he had."

"Now that's a bit of irony," Wattenburg remarked.

"That was a case of poor judgment on my part," said Teller. "I should not have recommended him."

Three days later, on July 20, the laboratory continued the celebration by announcing that copies of the GAO report would be distributed to all its 8,000 employees, an act without known precedent.[77]

Energy Secretary Herrington, who once sympathized with Woodruff in the classified vault, joined the whirlwind of activity by holding a press conference at Livermore on July 22 in which he said the whole dispute should have been kept secret. "There should be freedom of expression within the laboratory," he said. "But I do not favor having scientists go public on opposite sides of the issue if it is going to be damaging to the laboratory. I think all this should be fought out within the structure of the laboratory." He also castigated Woodruff for becoming "personally involved" in the dispute and praised Teller. "My personal feeling as Secretary of Energy is that Dr. Edward Teller is a national asset."[78]

WOODRUFF received scores of expressions of sympathy about the GAO report, including a note from Maenchen, the R Program scientist. He called the report "pitifully inadequate" and sought to distill the essence of his own views. "I know it is not unusual for enthusiastic proponents of a project to exaggerate its benefits and to downplay the technical difficulties or costs," Maenchen wrote. "That sort of optimism is understandable and is probably automatically discounted by those who hear such briefings. What's different in the present case is the sheer magnitude of the exaggerations. In a more familiar topic such inflated claims would surely be received with the disbelief and derision they deserve. For example, I'm sure that anyone who promised to increase the horsepower of an engine by a millionfold would not be taken seriously. But in an esoteric area like the X-ray laser the most extreme claims, especially when made or endorsed by a scientist of Teller's stature, are not subjected to critical review and appear to be taken at face value."[79]

A COUNTERATTACK on the GAO report was launched August 1, 1988, by Congressmen Markey and Brown. They released copies of the Teller letters that the Energy Department had declassified at their request. The GAO had made public only tiny excerpts of them. Now much more was revealed. It was, for instance, the first time the public heard of the 100,000 independently aimable beams of Super Excalibur. "It's no wonder President Reagan bought the Star Wars concept hook, line, and sinker," said Congressman Brown.[80]

Another front was opened by Representative Fortney H. (Pete) Stark, a Democrat from California's Ninth District, which included Livermore. He investigated the accuracy of the GAO report. On September 28, the GAO briefed him on their methods, and Stark's staff carried on from there. Nearly four months later, on January 24, 1989, Stark wrote the GAO a seven-page, single-spaced letter, calling the report "inaccurate, misleading, and biased." He asked for its recall.[81]

Stark faulted the GAO for finding any similarities at all between Teller and Woodruff, saying the documentary evidence showed no such thing and that such a conclusion "defied belief." He also ripped into GAO's poll of "eight" Livermore X-ray laser experts. Three of these (Tom Weaver, Rod Hyde and George Chapline) were in Livermore's physics program, working either closely with Wood or for him. The other five (George Maenchen, George Miller, Stephen Younger, Paul Wheeler and Hank Shay) were in the "core" weapons program that actually developed the X-ray laser. These five, Stark wrote, all had testified the GAO had "misrepresented" their statements one way or another.[82] For instance, George Maenchen was cited by the GAO as having "qualified agreement" with Teller and Wood. Stark, in his rebuttal, included a letter from Maenchen saying his views had been distorted. "I believe that my views then, and now, would be more correctly characterized as 'qualified *disagreement*,'" Maenchen wrote.

On April 13, 1989, the GAO responded to Stark in a three-page letter, saying it stood by the report. "We are satisfied that our work was conducted in accordance with applicable professional standards," wrote GAO's top official, Charles A. Bowsher.[83]

THE war was not over. It turned out that one of the GAO's auditors on the disputed report, David L. Potter, a twenty-year government veteran, had been talking to Livermore about a job when the report came out. Subsequently the weapons lab hired him at a higher salary that he had at GAO. Congressman Stark, Woodruff, and others charged that the hiring was a clear conflict of interest, leaving the impression that the report was watered down in exchange for money. "It can never be proved," Hugh E. DeWitt, the Livermore dissident, wrote the new lab director, "but the appearance and suspicion is there." The episode, DeWitt said, "removes the last shred of respectability for that report."[84] Congressman Stark's office said the ethical issue was crystal clear. "It's a conflict of interest to be considering a job with someone whom you're in the process of investigating," said Bill Vaughn, Stark's top aide. "It clouds the whole report."[85]

The central issue in the episode was when Potter first learned of the job opening and started talking to Livermore about it. No information on that score was ever made public. Moreover, a related issue, when he actually applied for the job, was surrounded by some uncertainty. When first talking to reporters, Potter said he had applied for the Livermore job "toward the end" of the X-ray probe, "if not after the investigation was complete."[86] The GAO report was made public on July 14, 1988. The GAO eventually said Potter had applied for the job "in mid-July," after the report was finished. The GAO dismissed any concerns about conflict of interest. "In no case did Mr. Potter's decision to seek new employment affect the outcome of GAO audits and reports," the agency said in a statement.[87]

Potter himself downplayed the importance of his own role in the X-ray probe. "I never had primary responsibility," he recalled. "I had no conflict of interest and no way to act on it." But a once-secret document showed that both Ohl and Potter were the "assigned auditors." At the GAO, Potter held a position with an annual salary that ranged between $34,580 and $44,957. In October 1988, he began working for Livermore as a principal management analyst at a salary of $51,600.[88]

FOR Woodruff, the GAO report was a devastating blow. And it was followed by others. The laboratory redoubled its pressures, conducting a series of investigations. One involved his resume. The probe is reputed to have started when Wattenburg, the talk show host with

Livermore ties, became so worried about the lab's reputation that he launched his own investigation of Woodruff's credentials in an effort to find a flaw.[89] Wattenburg found a faulty claim in one version of Woodruff's resume that he had belonged to the Phi Beta Kappa honor society. Wattenburg brought it to the attention of lab officials. When asked about it, Woodruff denied ever having claimed the honor and said some secretary or public affairs person must have typed it in by accident. His hiring and security documents made no such claim, he noted. Lab officials pressed ahead, investigating and interviewing many lab employees to see if Woodruff had ever made the claim orally. Lab officials eventually found him guilty of "academic exaggeration," and then, when Woodruff filed a grievance to challenge the finding, withdrew the charge, only to reinstate it later in a different form.[90]

George Miller, like other lab officials, had been asked to conduct an investigation of the Phi Beta Kappa matter. Four months later, on August 16, 1988, he summed up his results saying he could "find no data" to support the charge that the credentials had been "purposefully misrepresented." He also noted that "it is clear that no personnel decisions were made on the basis of the erroneous information."[91] Unfortunately for Woodruff, the laboratory chose to ignore Miller's conclusions. Instead of dropping the matter, the laboratory embarked on a fourth investigation.

A different probe centered on Woodruff's handling of the secret letters Teller had written to various administration officials. On a tip, lab officials decided to investigate whether Woodruff had copies of the secret letters at home. Allegedly, Woodruff had his wife bring them to a laboratory meeting in January 1988 with University of California regent Stanley Sheinbaum. Although Sheinbaum and Mrs. Woodruff had the proper security clearances to view the secret letters, keeping them at home would violate federal law. In repeated meetings with lab investigators, Woodruff denied ever having the letters at home. It was not enough. Lab officials appointed yet another investigator, who was given none of the previous testimony. On May 31, 1989, Woodruff wrote lab director John H. Nuckolls to complain, saying the investigation "constitutes further reprisal actions " for having "previously disclosed improper Governmental activities."[92]

Woodruff became increasingly bitter, militant and cynical. He hired lawyers and threatened litigation. He filed grievances with the university. He battled nearly everyone in a position of authority at

the lab with waves of angry letters and threatened lawsuits. He
worked the system to try to end the harassment—to no avail.

The laboratory had clearly turned on Woodruff in the months
and years after he stepped down from his post. There was no mis-
taking the message of isolation, salary cuts, curt letters and investigations that seemed to go on without end. Moreover, given Teller's
power and outspokenness on the issue, the prospect of resolution
seemed remote. In late 1989, Woodruff began the delicate process of
negotiating a withdrawal.

The seven-year battle came to an end in May 1990 as Livermore
announced that Woodruff would leave the lab for Los Alamos, the
New Mexico rivals who had been skeptical of the X-ray laser from
the start. Woodruff was 49, having been at Livermore for 22 years.
In a terse statement, Livermore's director Nuckolls thanked Woodruff for his lab contributions. "I am pleased that Roy has been able
to work out a suitable arrangement with Los Alamos," Nuckolls
said.[93]

THE bitter clash of wills among some of the nation's most powerful
scientists was, in the end, something of a victory for both sides.
With verve, Woodruff had confronted the formidable institutional
forces arrayed against him. He had fought for honesty amid a wilderness of bureaucratic intrigues and rationalizations. He had been
true to himself and his vision of technical integrity. Perhaps most
important, he had helped bring to light the secretive workings of the
weapons labs, where concentrated power had led to a new kind of
arrogance.

But the outcome was also a victory for Teller. After all, the
Hungarian physicist had cleared his name publicly, had done his part
in having Woodruff discredited by the GAO and had eventually
succeeded in having the heretic banished from the weapons lab. For
Teller, it was all a strange reversal from the way things had been. In
the old days colleagues who struggled to keep him honest were
valued as coauthors. But that was long past. Teller now seemed to be
in a new phase of his career. His visions had grown enormously in
scope, as had his personal power. He was apparently comfortable in
its exercise and could be quite upset with those who questioned it.

In the final analysis, Teller and Livermore underwent no significant change in the wake of the biggest intellectual crisis in the
lab's history. Things remained essentially the same. First and foremost, Livermore was Teller's—a place to do with as he pleased. The

X-ray saga and clash with Woodruff produced no lessening of Teller's tendency to excitement and enthusiasm. He still had the personal drive, as well as the institutional power, to pursue whatever vision beckoned to him. The X-ray laser had lost its luster. But Teller and Wood soon found another outlet for their technical elan, embarking on the promotion of a totally new weapon for Star Wars. The episode had all the familiar features—the unearthing of an interesting idea, the formulation of amazing claims, the courting of high government officials, the wooing of the White House and, ultimately, the changing of national policy. It was a pattern Teller had used with success for a third of a century. He apparently saw no reason to change it now.

# SEVEN

# A Final
# Crusade

THE WHITE HOUSE situation room is a small, windowless, low-ceilinged area in the basement of the West Wing that is reserved for some of the nation's most sensitive discussions. It has been called the nerve center of the American government. It is secure. No spy can eavesdrop on what goes on there, no matter how sophisticated the equipment. The room is used largely for meetings of the National Security Council and secret policy talks. Filling most of it is a long oak table that can comfortably seat more than a dozen officials. If necessary, the large, polished oak panels lining the walls can open to reveal a hidden world of electronic maps and video displays. One display can quickly be linked to the Pentagon, allowing officials to see and hear each other. Among other things, the room is used to practice war games.

The place is rich in history. President Johnson often went there at night—clad in pajamas and slippers—to get the latest reports from Vietnam, sitting for hours as he heard of bombing raids and missing planes, captured villages and fresh casualties.[1] The Cabinet assembled there spontaneously after President Reagan was shot in March 1981, fearful that he might die, discussing whether the vice president should take over as head of the government, as provided for by the Twenty-fifth Amendment to the Constitution.[2]

On a summer day in July of 1988, President Reagan and some of his key aides gathered in the situation room for an important meeting. They assembled to hear about a top-secret arms project. Among those present were Vice President George Bush, national security adviser Lieutenant General Colin Powell, and William R. Graham, Jr., the president's new science adviser.

The topic of the presentation was the latest Star Wars idea from weapon scientists at the Lawrence Livermore National Laboratory—a clever refinement of "smart rocks," the devices that had replaced lasers as the centerpiece of the nation's antimissile research effort. Smart rocks were interceptor rockets meant to destroy enemy missiles by force of impact, or kinetic energy, rather than exploding warheads or deadly beams. The Livermore refinement was known as "Brilliant Pebbles." These were to be smaller, cheaper, and smarter than conventional kinetic-energy arms, being packed with fancy electronics and innovative optics. They were to be autonomous, needing no large support satellites as the conventional systems did. They were to be deployed in swarms. Up to a hundred thousand of the tiny interceptors could be lofted into space, waiting to ram and destroy enemy missiles. So many of them would orbit the earth that an aggressor would find it nearly impossible to evade them or knock them out of action. Most important, they were to be relatively cheap, a deployed system seen as costing around $10 billion.

Livermore scientists at the presentation included Teller, Wood and the new director, Nuckolls, who wanted to make it clear that the White House briefing had the lab's blessing. The scientists brought with them a full-scale model of a prototype pebble. Sitting atop the oak table, it looked impressively small, something you could comfortably hold in your arms.[3] After introductions and chitchat, Teller and Wood described how the system would work—legions of agile interceptors flying low orbits about the earth, spotting Soviet missiles as they burst through the clouds, smashing into them at high speed and destroying them. Just as important, they explained how the interceptors were to be built—simply. Many of the parts came "off the shelf," as the scientists put it. The small navigation unit was already in use. Detectors for the fish-eye lens were the same as those used in the video cameras found in millions of American homes.

Reagan loved it. Bush asked question after question. An aide later recalled that Bush was impressed with the answers.[4] Science adviser Graham, a nuclear weapons expert who had known Teller for decades, said he saw no technical barriers to the idea's perfection. The only problem, he said, would be getting enough money from Congress for exploratory work. Pleased with the cordial meeting, the group of scientists and officials posed for a picture to commemorate the occasion. The Brilliant Pebble was carefully veiled in a black drape to avoid the inadvertent release of state secrets.[5]

Over the months and years that followed, Brilliant Pebbles became one of the fastest-growing arms programs in the nation's history. The Reagan administration started the movement. The Bush administration accelerated it and singled out Brilliant Pebbles for early development in space.

IF Teller's reputation lay in ruins among many scientists in 1988, to the Republican right and White House officials it was virtually un- scathed. His continuing influence was no doubt due partly to the near-mythical status Teller had achieved over the decades. He was more icon than flesh and blood. What he represented—world-class science in the service of steely American conservatism—in many respects was seen as more important than what he sometimes said or did on specific issues. No doubt there was also an element of ratio- nalization for those who venerated the old man. Teller was seen as being so right regarding the H-bomb and other military issues that he would eventually be proven right on the X-ray laser. His heart, these people felt, was in the right place. Eager to show their support, hundreds of distinguished conservatives gathered in 1988 at a ban- quet in Washington to fete Teller and give him an award for "in- tegrity and courage in public life."[6]

In addition, Teller's recovery from the X-ray episode had been aided by secrecy. Few members of the general public knew where the laser stood technically, how precipitous had been its decline, how devastating the twin blows of false brightness and faulty focusing. If that news had been public rather than hidden in the depths of the weapons bureaucracy, there might have been a greater wariness over just how far out on a limb Teller had gone with his X-ray enthu- siasms. Even knowledgeable officials such as Nitze were ready to forgive Teller and Wood, knowing little of Maenchen's secret warn- ings about the threat of false brightness. "I don't think I was mis- led," Nitze said. "They misled themselves. They got the readings wrong."[7]

The salvaging of Teller's reputation was also helped by the favorable GAO report and a chorus of friends who claimed the only problem was what they characterized as Woodruff's trumped-up charges. For instance, an official present at the July 1988 meeting in the situation room told me that Woodruff had simply been jealous of

Teller's good access to the White House. "He decided it was an affront," the official said.[8]

Teller's defenders were quick to belittle his own wrongs even as they maligned Woodruff. For instance, this same official, though ostensibly in a position to know all the details, told me he was unaware of Teller's promise to Nitze about a single X-ray laser having a hundred thousand beams. He insisted Teller and Wood were X-ray moderates. "The conventional wisdom is that they were out selling this thing beyond its potential," he said. "But when I talked to them they went to pains to point out the problems that had yet to be solved and the potential hurdles. I thought I got an even-handed discussion."[9] This official was relatively new to his post. He was nowhere near the White House during the feverish selling of the X-ray laser in the early and mid-1980s. Therein lay a secret of Teller's success. Washington officials would come and go. There was little continuity. No high official in the Reagan administration had the slightest idea about Teller's flawed forecast to Eisenhower on clean bombs. It was Teller, and Teller alone, who on these issues had the corporate memory. The consequence of all these factors was that Teller had continuing access to the centers of American power. He advised and cajoled, his tenacity and persuasive skills as strong as ever. He could dust himself off after the X-ray incident with a quip about being guilty of optimism—and move on to the next subject.

To Teller's credit, Brilliant Pebbles was at least a nonnuclear technology. His long preoccupation with trying to extract goodness from nuclear blasts was put on hold after the collapse of the X-ray laser, at least in relation to Star Wars. But the Pebbles idea was, in one respect, very much like the other concepts Teller had championed—it was extreme. As a way to wage antimissile war, Brilliant Pebbles was as far removed from the X-ray laser as one could imagine. Pebbles was to consist of a hundred thousand weapons moving over relatively short distances. The X-ray laser was exactly the opposite, a single weapon firing up to a hundred thousand beams across vast reaches of space.

In the old days, Teller would have sought the counsel of a variety of colleagues in trying to assess the feasibility of the new antimissile idea. But not now. He had changed radically, having become increasingly reliant on his own intuition. With Brilliant Pebbles, a number of prominent experts, including ones at Livermore, pointed to serious problems. But Teller ignored them, at least in public. Most striking of all, in championing Brilliant Pebbles he contradicted one of his own antimissile tenets.

From the start of Star Wars, Teller had ridiculed the idea of basing weapons in space, saying it left them too vulnerable to enemy attack. Such logic lay behind his dismissal of the rocket interceptors of General Graham and eventually all space-based arms. It was what led him to tell Congress in April 1983 that the deployment of space weapons long before a battle was "an outlandish idea."[10] Wood had redoubled the attack with charts, graphs and mathematical rigor, writing his 1985 paper, "Concerning the Vulnerability of Objects in Space." The pair's first exception to the vulnerability rule had been Super Excalibur, which was seen as possibly being placed in geosynchronous orbit and being relatively safe because of its great distance from earth. With Brilliant Pebbles, the pair abandoned the principle altogether. The tiny interceptors had to orbit quite close to earth because of their slow speed and short range. The pebbles had to be near their targets. And no matter how great their numbers, they would always be haunted by the question of vulnerability. This was driven home as Star Wars critics suggested numerous ways the Soviets might cripple or destroy a swarm of Brilliant Pebbles.

Teller greeted the vulnerability dilemma much in the way he had dealt with the Fletcher panel and the technical collapse of the X-ray laser—silence. Wood sometimes mentioned the topic in passing, but Teller never raised the subject publicly during the idea's formative days. Skeptics charged that the plan was riddled with inconsistencies. But Teller brushed them off, switching loyalties on weapon systems with relative ease and, more important, taking the American government with him. That he did so was a final tribute to his immense powers of persuasion.

AT the start, the drive for accelerated work on kinetic-energy arms had nothing to do with advanced technology. On the contrary, the devices were seen as primitive and crude. But antimissile advocates viewed the pursuit of the technology as politically expedient since it paved the way for early deployment of Star Wars.

Teller helped lead the political agitation for kinetic-energy arms beginning in 1986 as work on lasers faltered and arms-control negotiations picked up. Antimissile advocates inside and outside the Reagan administration, sure Star Wars was losing political momentum because its research goals were too distant, struggled to make them more timely and pushed for early deployment. In October 1986, Teller and Representative Jim Courter, Republican of New Jersey, drafted a letter to President Reagan that was signed by twenty-five prominent conservatives, including Zbigniew Brzezinski and Jeane Kirkpatrick. They urged President Reagan to act quickly and decisively. "We are deeply concerned," they wrote, "that an SDI research program which has no definite consequences for defense of America and its Allies within the next ten years will not be politically sustainable."[11]

In January 1987, Defense Secretary Weinberger told an aerospace conference that "we are now seeing opportunities for earlier deployment of the first phase of strategic defense." It would be imperfect, he said, insisting that additions to the first phase would ultimately lead to more complete protection.[12] That same month, Edwin Meese, having become attorney general, boldly acknowledged the importance of political factors in the push. The system would be deployed as soon as possible, he said, "so it will be in place and not tampered with by future administrations."[13]

To achieve the goal, Pentagon planners in 1987 began a vast reordering of priorities, taking funds from exotic research on lasers and putting them into the development of large homing interceptors known as space-based kinetic kill vehicles. The Pentagon envisioned some 3,000 weapons housed in hundreds of orbiting "garages," waiting for war, guided to battle by large surveillance and battle-management satellites. The cost was seen as between $100 billion and $200 billion, with a large added expense for launching the system into space. The job was estimated to require at least 125 space shuttle flights, and perhaps twice that many. One congressional study said the deployment cost alone might eventually run as high as $1 trillion.[14]

Such gargantuan numbers and grandiose plans drove home the weakness of the whole idea. Deployment was especially tricky. After all, the January 1986 explosion of the space shuttle Challenger and an unusual number of subsequent rocket disasters had grounded nearly every type of major launch vehicle in the American inventory.[15] Virtually nothing was flying into space in 1987, much less a vast armada of very large space arms. Although the push for early deployment had strong political support from the White House, it was widely dismissed as technically flawed by many scientists, including some supporters of Star Wars.

As the early deployment stratagem began to simultaneously move forward and fall apart under its own weight, Teller and Wood in late 1986 and 1987 carefully considered ways to increase its credibility. Like many conservatives, their initial support had been purely political and pragmatic. What originally excited the pair about Star Wars was not slow-moving interceptor rockets but the prospect of laser beams shot through space at the speed of light. Even as early deployment picked up political steam, they viewed kinetic-energy arms with disdain. However, all that changed abruptly as the two scientists hit upon an interceptor idea they could call their own. The concept consumed them for the rest of the decade and eventually supplanted the Pentagon's heavy-handed plans for early deployment. As was the case with the H-bomb and the X-ray laser, the critical insight was supplied by another person, Teller seizing it and making it the heart of his new campaign.

In November 1986, Teller and Wood had breakfast in Cambridge, Massachusetts, with Gregory H. Canavan, a tall, cleanshaven former Air Force officer who worked as a physicist at Los Alamos and possessed an all-American, can-do kind of attitude.[16] All three of the physicists were board members of the Hertz Foundation, which gave fellowships to scientifically gifted college students. In part, the fellowship program was a recruitment mechanism for the weapons labs. About two thirds of Wood's O Group was composed of active Hertz fellows or alumni.[17] Hagelstein, for instance, was a Hertz fellow when he came up with the key idea for the nuclear X-ray laser. The trio was in Cambridge to interview Harvard and MIT students for Hertz fellowships. As they breakfasted at the Hyatt down the road from MIT, the conversation turned to the inherent vulnerability of space-based arms. Teller had long held that the devices were naked, just waiting to be shot down. It was one of his pet peeves. It was why he had originally wanted X-ray lasers "popped up" into space seconds before battle. Only with great reluctance had Teller made an exception to his credo and backed the idea of basing X-ray lasers in geosynchronous orbit. Canavan, on the other hand, long held that space arms could be made survivable through use of shielding, decoys, quick movement, and other techniques. Now he offered a new idea. What about making a special kind of smart rock that would be so intelligent it could operate on its own, so small it would be easy to loft into space and hard to detect, and so cheap that the Soviets would be unable to go after clouds of them?

"I argued that small satellites could be cheap and survivable," Canavan recalled. "As soon as I said 'survivable,' Teller got interested."[18]

Wood was skeptical but took copious notes. He left the breakfast meeting determined to master the world of interceptor rockets, if only to prove his friend wrong.

As Canavan later conceded, there was nothing fundamentally new in his idea. "Singlets," as they were known, had been considered during the nation's first antimissile drive in the late 1950s and early 1960s, but the electronic devices of that day were too bulky to make the weapons practical. Over the decades, however, vacuum tubes were slowly superseded by transistors, which in turn gave way to tiny but powerful computer chips. By the early 1980s, Richard L. Garwin, the IBM physicist and Star Wars skeptic, had simultaneously proposed and disparaged tiny kinetic-energy arms that he dubbed hornets. "The near-miracle of modern microelectronics," he told the National Academy of Sciences in 1983, could result in "a swarm of hornets" to attack enemy missiles. Garwin said "millions" of hornets would be needed, and these would have to be surrounded by 10 to 100 times as many decoys, creating a traffic jam of giant proportions in space.[19]

But in the early months of 1987, Teller and Wood were fairly desperate for a new Star Wars idea, especially given the collapse of the X-ray laser. Wood threw himself into exploring Canavan's idea. He found that rocket motors were no longer the $150,000 monsters he had remembered but had shrunk into $20,000 gadgets that fit in the palm of his hand. Book-sized video cameras were producing images superior to some military systems costing thousands of times as much. And one of his O Group members, Bruce McWilliams, had come up with an innovative wide-angle lens with a curved focal plane instead of a flat one. It would allow a low-orbiting vehicle to monitor an area of land the size of Virginia as well as the status of nearby interceptors—an important point for a largely autonomous system that in the midst of battle would have to know what nearby defensive arms had been lost or used. Most important, Wood knew computer chips were shrinking dramatically, allowing a small interceptor to have a very powerful "brain." To be safe, reliable and effective, the interceptor would have to have the smarts to distinguish a peaceful launching from a military attack.[20]

As he surveyed the available technology and that on the horizon, Wood felt the idea might have merit. The interceptor would be small, cheap and smart. Most important, it would have none of the vulnerabilities that came with big tracking satellites or groups of interceptors housed in orbiting garages. As Wood explained his explorations to Teller, the elderly scientist, too, became excited. In October 1987, Teller and Wood arrived in the Pentagon office of Star Wars director General Abrahamson. Word had spread that the pair had switched alliances from lasers to smart rocks. Indeed, they had a model of their device with them. Abrahamson listened for more than an hour as the two made their case. Intrigued, he said he would visit Livermore.[21] A few weeks later, Teller and Wood met again in Cambridge, almost a year after their first breakfast discussion. Wood brought two bulging briefcases with him to the hotel restaurant. From one he pulled a complete blueprint of the interceptor, as well as price lists, bids from contractors and simulations of how the interceptor might work. From the other he gingerly brought out bits and pieces of high-tech hardware—including a miniature navigation system and a fish-eye lens.

Canavan was impressed. "They had taken this idea and really done a magnificent job," he recalled.[22]

On November 25, 1987, the day before Thanksgiving, General Abrahamson and an aide toured Wood's workshops at Livermore, watching simulations, examining hardware, talking with scientists late into the night. Teller was there too, chatting and praising the work. During the day, Abrahamson dedicated a prototype imaging system based on the wide-angle lens, telling the assembled group that the laboratory's work had been a continuing "inspiration" to him. "You are the real technology base of the country," he said.[23] Abrahamson had become a believer. He told his aide to substantially raise the funding for the interceptor idea.[24]

UP to this point, the mere existence of the pebble project was a state secret. Now it went public, at least in outline. Teller and Wood did the unveiling, with President Reagan making a guest appearance in the middle of the show. There were no worries about the Soviets learning the general outlines of the idea, since America had a clear lead in the miniaturization of high technology. The occasion for the debut was a three-day conference in March 1988 at the Shoreham Hotel in Washington to celebrate the fifth anniversary of Reagan's Star Wars speech. It was sponsored by the Institute for Foreign Policy Analysis, a private group from Cambridge, Massachusetts. The conference was attended by a constellation of the SDI luminaries, including Senator J. Danforth Quayle, William R. Graham, Jr., who succeeded Keyworth as the president's science adviser, Lieutenant General James A. Abrahamson, SDI director, and Tom Clancy, author of *Cardinal of the Kremlin*, which centered on an antimissile intrigue.

Teller, who had just turned 80, gave the opening address. His part of the Brilliant Pebbles unveiling was suggestive, leaving the details to Wood. Teller said that, in conflict on earth, technology was strengthening the hand of the defender. His examples were taken from a series of conventional conflicts—Vietnam, Israel during the Yom Kippur War and more recently Afghanistan. In each case, he said, attack from the air had become unreliable because of advances in the high technology of antiaircraft arms. "In Afghanistan we see the influence of the Stinger," he said. "The Soviet military machine has been stopped by a really smart effort." That technical achievement, he said, foreshadowed strides that would shake up the antimissile field. "Accuracy, miniaturization, and cost reduction can make defense effective," he said. "Experience had begun to show, and begins to show conclusively, that contact between fast-moving objects is enough to stop anything. This is a very remarkable positive result. It came upon us slowly. It came upon me unexpectedly, to a considerable extent."[25]

Teller, on stage, applauded and smiled as President Reagan took the podium for the keynote address.

"Dr. Teller," Reagan quipped, "is proof that life begins at 80." Reagan went on to say that advances in antimissile technology had come "more rapidly than many of us ever dreamed possible." Then, for the first time, he publicly endorsed the deployment of a rudimentary antimissile system, making headlines around the world.[26]

That afternoon, Wood addressed the group, his talk filled with high energy, bold statements and sweeping historical comparisons. It was the presentation of a man filled with self-assurance and eager to share his vision with the world. "To every weapons technology, no matter how formidable it might have initially appeared to be, there has eventually risen a counter," Wood said in opening his talk. He dwelled at length on the vulnerability of offensive missiles, calling them immensely fragile. "Though they may stand as tall as modest skyscrapers, they can be killed with a child's sling-shot as they rise."[27]

The same action, he said, could be achieved by small interceptors orbiting the earth. Advances in technology allowed these weapons to be very small, weighing as little as five pounds. "Shrinking contemporary smart rocks into Brilliant Pebbles is an exercise in packaging engineering," he told the group. The interceptors, he emphasized, "are designed to be brilliant, not merely smart, and to have far better than human vision, not just crude imaging systems, so that the defensive system architecture is simply the constellation of Brilliant Pebbles, and *nothing* else. Each pebble carries so much prior knowledge and detailed battle strategy and tactics, computes so swiftly, and sees so well that it can perform its purely defensive mission adequately, with *no* external supervision or coaching." If an enemy moved his missiles around on the ground to make the defensive task more difficult, he said, success could still be achieved by simply having a hundred times as many pebbles as missiles. In round numbers, if the Soviets had one thousand missiles, a comprehensive defense would need a hundred thousand small interceptors. Small size meant that the cost of the pebbles—which was dominated by the expense of transporting them into space—would also be small, on the order of $100,000 per interceptor, including transport cost, Wood said. The total expense of a hundred thousand interceptors would be $10 billion. "Even when the usual three- to five-fold multipliers are stacked on top, you still come up with an eminently affordable strategic defense system cost of $30 billion to $50 billion," he said. In closing, Wood elaborated on Teller's comparison with the Stinger missile, supplied by the American government to Afghan rebels for shooting down Soviet aircraft and helicopters. "The Red Army has been fought to a stand-still by a rag-tag force of backward Third World guerrillas," he said. "I suggest to you that Stingers are, in virtually all pertinent respects, the Earth-bound analogs of the Brilliant Pebbles which I have sketched." The deployment of Brilliant Pebbles, he concluded, "may serve to implement Ronald Reagan's vision of a world safe from nuclear-tipped intercontinental flying machines, with comparable economy and dispatch." In their presentations, neither Teller nor Wood made any mention of the vulnerabilities that came with basing antimissile arms in space. That silence would persist.

It was a few months after the public unveiling, in July 1988, that Teller and Wood briefed Reagan on Brilliant Pebbles in the White House situation room, going into secret details of the technology. Reagan was reportedly so enthusiastic that he received a second briefing from the scientific twosome in early August.[28]

Brilliant Pebbles in orbit.

As Brilliant Pebbles became an important part of the administration's Star Wars strategy, Teller began a series of extraordinary public confessions, saying he had been too hopeful about the X-ray laser and wrong to pursue it so vigorously. It was as if, having found a new love, Teller could evaluate his former one with greater objectivity.

"I may have indeed been too optimistic," he said in late July to the editors of *Inside Energy*, a Washington newsletter. "I am dedicated not to the X-ray laser but to defense." He justified his general X-ray advocacy, however, saying all he wanted to do was make sure there was enough money to explore its technical feasibility. "It is very dangerous to stop looking in a direction that has promise," he said.[29] In August during a debate at the Heritage Foundation, the conservative think tank, Teller went further, saying he had been wrong to pursue the X-ray laser with such single-mindedness. He said the President had clearly called for the elimination of all nuclear arms, but that he and Livermore had tried to adapt the weapons to the antimissile plan. "All of the early defense efforts were based on nuclear defense," he said. "To throw that away looked to me too much." However, Teller continued, in the past two years "I got the clear conviction that I was wrong and the President was right. Nuclear defense may play eventually some role if you want to make the defense real good. The early important results are likely to come— and the inexpensive results are likely to come—from non-nuclear defense." He then hailed Brilliant Pebbles as the best nonnuclear approach.[30] The October 1988 issue of *The Washingtonian* magazine ran an interview with Teller in which he reiterated his initial skepticism about Reagan's ostensible preference for nonnuclear defense. "I thought it was too difficult," he said. "I was wrong. In the course of the years, particularly the last two years, I became convinced that non-nuclear defense will probably work. And while it is not necessarily the most complete defense, it probably is the defense that will work soonest. So the President was right and I was wrong."[31]

As Teller did his mea culpa, the Reagan administration pressed ahead with plans for early Star Wars deployment and accelerated work on Brilliant Pebbles. On November 14, 1988, *Aviation Week & Space Technology*, still a leading source of information on secret antimissile activity, reported that Brilliant Pebbles had already undergone clandestine flight testing. It quoted a defense official as saying the results had been "eminently satisfactory."[32]

TELLER'S growing confidence in Brilliant Pebbles was soon dealt a blow that left him temporarily stunned and depressed. The cause was a message from Soviet physicist Andrei Sakharov, 67, delivered in November 1988 during his first visit to the United States. Sakharov was a principal inventor of the Soviet hydrogen bomb. But he had fallen into disgrace in the Soviet Union for his outspoken views on its violation of human rights, eventually being sentenced to internal exile in the city of Gorky. Under Gorbachev, Sakharov was rehabilitated and allowed to travel.

On the evening of November 16, 1988, the Soviet and American inventors of the hydrogen bomb met for the first time. The occasion was a black-tie dinner in Washington sponsored by the Ethics and Public Policy Center, a small conservative think tank, at which Teller was to be presented an award for "integrity and courage in public life." Sakharov had been added to the agenda at the last minute. The formal dinner was one of the last big gatherings of right-wing leadership in the Reagan era, with the president due to leave office in two months. About 750 people at the Washington Hilton witnessed the encounter between the two aged giants of twentieth-century science. The audience included Robert Bork and Phyllis Schlafly, Jack Kemp and William F. Buckley, Jr.

Sakharov, graceful and stately, even with his lopsided tie and ill-fitting suit, expressed his "deepest respect" for Teller. Then he spoke his mind. Sakharov said a tragedy was unfolding with the development of the Strategic Defense Initiative, which he called a "great error" of "enormous cost." Most important, Sakharov warned, "it would destabilize the world situation." If such systems were deployed in space, he said, "there would be a temptation to destroy them, and this in itself could trigger a nuclear war."[33]

It was an ominous message, one repeated in Sakharov's private meeting with President Reagan, who "somehow managed to ignore my arguments," Sakharov recalled.[34] Here was an inventor of the Soviet H-bomb, publicly warning that deployment of Star Wars could trigger the unleashing of nuclear arms in atomic conflict. It was not quite a threat from the highest Russian circles. After all, Sakharov was renowned for his independence and forthrightness, not for carrying messages. Nevertheless, it was Gorbachev who allowed this dark prophecy to be delivered in the United States, and, as such, it carried the intimation of a high-level warning, if not a direct threat. After his public speech, Sakharov immediately departed, leaving the ceremony before Teller was presented his award.

"We honor Dr. Sakharov and wish him everything in the world," William F. Buckley, Jr., the master of ceremonies, said after Sakharov had departed. "But we don't wish to give him, as a souvenir from America to take back to Moscow, a lapsed resolution to proceed with our SDI." This declaration drew loud applause and cheers from the audience.[35]

Suddenly, the lights dimmed and Ronald Reagan materialized on a giant movie screen, hailing Teller as a "sterling example of what scientific knowledge, enlightened by moral sense and a dedication to the principles of freedom and justice, can do to help all mankind." The president called Teller a "tireless advocate" of SDI, "insisting that American citizens are entitled to protection against enemy missiles." He closed his monologue by praising Teller as "one of the giants of American science, and one of the bulwarks of American freedom."[36]

After accepting his award, Teller politely dismissed Sakharov's antimissile remarks. The Russian scientist's security clearance had been revoked twenty years ago, he said, and his technical knowledge was incomplete, since he had no recent opportunity to work on defensive arms. "It is not surprising that our points of view should differ," Teller remarked.[37]

But his public self-assurance later gave way to private doubts as Sakharov's warning hit home, according to a colleague of Teller's at Livermore.[38] Sakharov's prophecy actually had little to do with technical strides, instead focusing on the more general question of "destabilization" and the propensity of any good antimissile system to make the fighting of nuclear war thinkable—and thus a potential tool for offense and aggression. The Soviets clearly worried about this risk. American conservatives often ignored it, viewing antimissile systems only in terms of defense. But the dark side of the equation lurked in the background, as Teller and the Soviets well knew. Sakharov's warning meant there would be little chance for America to unilaterally deploy Star Wars. The Soviets were asserting their veto.

Though initially depressed by the ominous message, Teller soon bounced back. He began talking of solutions to the problem, suggesting that pebbles could be deployed by stealth in innocent-looking satellites.[39] This subterfuge was riddled with problems, not the least of which was the sheer number of deceptive launchings that would be needed. But it illustrated Teller's passionate commitment to the topic and his ability to reason his way out of nearly any corner, and take the government along with him.

TELLER traveled to the White House one last time before President Reagan left office, receiving yet another award. On January 18, 1989, Reagan gave him the Presidential Citizens' Medal, citing "exemplary deeds of service" to the country.[40] Teller reciprocated, singing Reagan's praises. Soon after receiving the award he was asked which of the presidents he had known over the decades had the best grasp of science and technology. "No competition," Teller replied,

"Ronald Reagan." Teller said Reagan's great strength was his ability to listen carefully to science advice and then act upon it. "The people who could not listen," Teller huffed, "were Ford, Kennedy, Eisenhower and above all, Jimmy Carter."[41]

TELLER'S brand of presidential guidance acquired a new object on January 20, 1989, as George Bush took up residence in the White House. Bush had a mixed record on Star Wars. He had apparently never bought the notion of a leakproof shield, although he had been careful to praise the program in public during the Reagan administration and said it was good leverage for arms-control negotiations. During the presidential campaign, he had waffled on SDI, starting out skeptical and slowly appearing to warm to the idea. His most negative comments were made in a debate with Jack Kemp on February 19, 1988, in which he rejected a rudimentary system. "Premature deployment of something that isn't totally effective," Bush said, "would do nothing but cause the Soviets to break out of the ABM treaty and overwhelm what we've got." In contrast, Kemp pledged to build and deploy even a partial shield. "It's not that simple, Jack," Bush snapped, and suggested SDI could be bargained away for a new arms-control treaty. "I want to reach out for peace and, I'm sorry, I think it's good to be doing that."[42]

Bush's comments became considerably warmer after his Brilliant Pebbles briefing by Teller in July 1988. On August 2, the candidate told a group of Chicago conservatives he was "committed to deployment of SDI, as soon as feasible, and will determine the exact architecture of the system in my first term, as the technologies are tested and proven. As president, I will not leave America defenseless against ballistic missiles."[43] Some of this was clearly posturing aimed at the Republican right. In general on the subject of SDI, Bush was quick to play to the leanings of his audience, whether right or left. For instance, his skeptical side was emphasized in a late August interview with The New York Times, Bush saying "full deployment" would be "very expensive" and that any decision would depend on further research. But in that interview he also hinted that technical breakthroughs might soon alter the equation. "There are new technologies being looked at that would make it quite economical to deploy a major SDI," he told The Times.[44]

Brilliant Pebbles quickly gained momentum during the early days of the Bush administration. First came a strong endorsement from General Abrahamson, the outgoing director of the Strategic

Defense Initiative. In an "end-of-tour" letter to Pentagon superiors, he said the tiny interceptors could be perfected in two years and their deployment begun in five. He put the bill at $10 billion for the system itself, with an added $15 billion for command and control of satellites and ground links. This was at odds with the original idea of complete autonomy for pebbles interceptors. It was a sign that Pentagon generals were uneasy with the idea of unleashing thousands of robot weapons in space to work on their own. The generals wanted positive control. "In future deployment," Abrahamson wrote, "the individual interceptors would not be activated until a human being has received adequate warning and sufficient information to ascertain that a real attack is underway. Then the human would give a release signal that would reach each interceptor by two independent communication channels."[45]

Another change tried to address Teller's old worry about the vulnerability of systems in space. Despite the swarms of Brilliant Pebbles, Pentagon experts feared the Soviets could attack them effectively. Something as simple as a large H-bomb exploded above the atmosphere might wreak much havoc. Addressing this threat, General Abrahamson wrote that "each interceptor has its own protective cocoon to help protect against Soviet ground-based lasers or other Soviet orbiting countermeasures, such as very small particles spread through a large area of space." Weapons experts, mocking Wood's penchant for flamboyant labels, sometimes called such particles "Dumb Dust." The cocoons would be jettisoned after the pebbles were ordered into battle.

In the Bush administration, the next commendation for the pebbles came from Vice President Dan Quayle, who had been briefed extensively on the idea by Teller and Wood. On March 23, 1989— the sixth anniversary of President Reagan's Star Wars speech— Quayle addressed the Navy League of the United States, calling Brilliant Pebbles "one of the most promising lines of research" and saying they could "revolutionize much of our thinking about strategic defense."[46] Quayle also promoted the idea within the government's private councils. On a Saturday morning in April 1989, President Bush met with a group of key advisers at Camp David, the presidential retreat in the Maryland mountains. They included Quayle, John Sununu, the White House chief of staff, Defense Secretary Richard Cheney, and the five members of the Joint Chiefs. The topic was Star Wars. The Joint Chiefs were at best lukewarm, worried that its escalating costs would divert funds from nuclear and conventional weapons. They said it should be pursued only as a modest research program with sharply reduced funding. Cheney objected. But the loudest voice came from Quayle. He insisted the program should be geared not toward research but toward deploying a space-based shield as quickly as possible. And he recommended Brilliant Pebbles as the way to accomplish the job.[47]

Bush moved swiftly. Later that month, he formalized a plan to make Brilliant Pebbles the centerpiece of the nation's multibillion-dollar program of antimissile research. Defense Secretary Cheney announced the change on April 23, 1989. "The emphasis," Cheney said, "will be upon the new Brilliant Pebbles concept, testing that concept over the course of the next year or two to see if we can in fact go that route. If we can, we can save a lot of money with the basic architecture of the system." The news made headlines around the country.[48] Soon after, the administration boosted the funding of Brilliant Pebbles.[49]

In short, the idea had come into its own as a central part of the government's antimissile plan. All it took was three years of determined advocacy by Teller and Wood. Moreover, the idea had weathered the transfer of power from the Reagan administration, the progenitor of Star Wars, to the far more cautious Bush administration. And it had not just survived this transfer. It had prospered.

EVEN SO, by 1989, the proposed device had changed in ways that belied much of the rhetoric that originally brought it to prominence. Most noticeably, an individual "pebble" had grown in size to the point that it now resembled a boulder. At the public unveiling in March 1988, Wood claimed a pebble might weigh five pounds. Now its advertised weight was about a hundred pounds.[50] Its length had increased from something you could hold in one hand to a three-foot-long cylinder bristling with engines and sensors. The simple "protective cocoon" referred to by General Abrahamson had grown into a heavy, high-tech shield that also provided navigation, electrical power and control of temperature and attitude.[51] And the price of an individual interceptor had soared, going from $100,000 to nearly $1.5 million, exclusive of launching costs. Most dramatically, the number of pebbles lofted into space had been dramatically cut. Originally, a hundred thousand interceptors were to be deployed, their sheer numbers making them impossible to knock out. The new figure was around 4,600. Even with these dramatic cuts, the overall cost of the first phase of an antimissile system based on Brilliant

Pebbles had grown—to $55 billion by Pentagon estimates. And government experts agreed its actual cost might be twice that when inflation, operations and maintenance were taken into account.[52]

As Brilliant Pebbles grew in size and prominence, the idea came under attack from Star Wars skeptics, including Teller's own colleagues at Livermore. Some of the criticism centered on the vulnerability issue Teller had so adroitly sidestepped. The most pointed attacks of all disparaged Brilliant Pebbles as yet another in a series of Tellerian delusions.

In June 1989, the Cambridge-based Union of Concerned Scientists, long opposed to Star Wars, made public a technical critique that found Brilliant Pebbles fatally flawed. Echoing the Fletcher report, its most pointed criticism centered on ways the Soviets could outwit the system. This task would be relatively easy, the report said, because of the interceptor's slow speed and short range. All the Soviets had to do was make their missiles faster, something they were already doing. "The effectiveness of the Brilliant Pebbles system," the report said, "would steadily fall in proportion to the booster burn time, until—faced with a true fast-burn booster—the defense destroyed few, if any, Soviet missiles." The report said that, in theory Soviet fast-burn boosters could be outwitted in three ways, but that "none is likely to be effective in practice." The first was to place the interceptors in lower orbits, closing the cap between booster and interceptor. But this move was costly, since a pebble's lower altitude meant there would be greater drag from the earth's outer atmosphere, forcing the interceptors to carry more fuel (and weight) to maintain proper orbit. The second solution was to increase the speed of the interceptors. But this, too, rapidly led to unacceptable increases in weight as engines and fuel tanks got larger. The final move was to try to attack Soviet missiles after their engines had burned out. At that stage the weapons were no longer easy to track and a host of advanced sensors would be required. According to the report, these would "add greatly to the cost and weight of each interceptor."[53]

The combination of factors meant Brilliant Pebbles would suffer "early obsolescence," the report said. In response, America would have to deploy "either a new directed-energy defense able to cope with advanced Soviet boosters or an effective midcourse defense (requiring the ability to discriminate between warheads and decoys), or both." There were no indications that either system was feasible in the foreseeable future, the report said. So, even if Brilliant Pebbles worked, its success would be temporary. "Investment in this defense scheme would merely mark the beginning of an indefinite race to stay ahead of an ever-changing Soviet offensive force," the report concluded.

Such criticism was echoed by government experts. The Jasons, a secretive group of top civil scientists who advised the Defense Department, studied the idea in June and July of 1989. They found several flaws in the areas of space vulnerability, including whether pebbles could be sufficiently "hardened" against Soviet attack or be able to outwit fast-burn boosters. John M. Cornwall, a physicist at the University of California at Los Angeles who led the Jason study, called the issues "very important." For instance, he said the pebbles might be outwitted by "brilliant" Soviet missiles and reentry vehicles. "There are problem areas which need to be considered very seriously," he told a congressional seminar.[54]

Even Livermore experts were ready to argue, albeit in obscure scientific papers, that the pebbles could easily and economically be shot out of the sky. After all, they said, the interceptors would have to be sturdy enough to operate reliably for years and possibly decades in orbit, while a weapon meant to shoot them down would have to work only for minutes, meaning it could be much simpler. Such considerations went to the issue of cost and the Nitze criteria, the main standard by which the feasibility of an antimissile system was to be judged. Roger D. Speed, a Livermore analyst, published a detailed paper that examined such tradeoffs. He concluded that the pebbles, while performing better than other space-based kinetic arms, would have no advantage over cheap, small, Soviet offensive weapons meant to knock them out. "The use of maneuver, decoys, and space-based defensive rockets to evade the Soviet threat had no merit," Speed wrote. "None of these approaches appears to be clearly economically advantageous."[55]

The most pointed criticism of all had nothing to do with technical hurdles or Soviet evasions. It focused on the idea's progenitors, Teller and Wood. "Their last major contribution to SDI's imagined arsenal, you may recall, was the X-ray laser, which hasn't quite panned out," scoffed *The New Republic*.[56] On the op-ed page of *The New York Times*, Representative Charles E. Bennett, a Florida Democrat on the House Armed Services Committee, echoed a similar theme, noting that Teller had claimed a single X-ray laser could shoot down the entire force of Soviet land-based missiles. "The problem," he wrote, "was that this claim wasn't true."[57]

AT an earlier stage of his life, Teller might have responded to such attacks with vitriol and black humor. He might have exploded in condescending rage, as he did after Three Mile Island. Or he might have dismissed it all with a snide remark. But in 1989 and 1990 as the attacks mounted against Brilliant Pebbles and his role in its promotion, Teller was an old man, his health failing. He had never been robust. In addition to his heart problems, he had digestive disorders, including severe ulcerated colitis, an inflammation of the colon. On April 12, 1989, Teller underwent surgery at the Stanford University medical center to have part of his colon removed.[58] He made a good recovery. But as he approached his eighty-second birthday, his herculean energies were beginning to fade.

Teller's followers carried on. Canavan, the Los Alamos physicist who helped get Brilliant Pebbles off the ground, wrote a paper that addressed for the first time in detail the issue of space vulnerability. Hardening, maneuverability and decoys were likely to make pebbles virtually immune from attack, it concluded. Teller was listed as a secondary author on the paper, which appeared in the prestigious British science journal *Nature*.[59]

During this period Lowell Wood began to play the role that Teller had assumed as a young man, especially in Washington. He became the visionary. And he played the part with zest. He lobbied. He cajoled. He made the rounds through congressional offices. He carried a mockup of a Brilliant Pebble on a small cart all over official Washington, reminding some observers not so much of a seasoned scientist as of a little boy. And, like Teller, his imagination soared in a host of areas. After President Bush said the nation should plan on manned voyages to the Moon and Mars, Wood proposed a way to do it that allegedly would be ten times cheaper. His idea was to use balloonlike inflatable structures to make space stations and bases on the Moon and Mars, instead of the metallic giants envisioned by the National Aeronautics and Space Administration. Many experts dismissed the notion, saying the risks were so great that American astronauts would surely die in such fragile structures.[60]

Wood's public defense of his exotic ideas became more polished, restrained and refined, removing the hint of eccentricity that had previously marked his style. He flattered his audiences. Addressing a Defense Department press conference on Brilliant Pebbles in early 1990, he was relaxed, wearing coat and tie, deflecting questions about whether the pebbles could survive a Soviet attack. The man who had written on "The Vulnerability of Objects in Space" was now ready to confidently assert the reverse. The pebbles system, he said, was "very much hardened for robust operation in the military environment."[61]

PRESIDENT BUSH pressed ahead with Brilliant Pebbles after consulting with his many advisers, including Teller and Wood. Its budget soared. The project received $18 million in 1988, $46 million in 1989 and $175 million in 1990. For fiscal year 1991, its budget more than doubled to $392 million—for the first time putting Brilliant Pebbles far ahead of the X-ray laser in federal funding. For 1992, the Bush administration called for a budget of $659 million.[62]

Bush's aim was different from that of Reagan. The political rhetoric about impenetrable shields was gone. In its place was a much humbler analysis of what an American antimissile system might do. There was no talk of "assured survival," of destroying every land-based Soviet missile or anything close to that goal—or even of protecting people. The new aim was to try to shield American missiles, even though skeptics asserted there were far easier and less costly ways for them to elude destruction, including the reduction of the Soviet threat by the political process of arms control. The Pentagon's official aim for the first SDI phase with Brilliant Pebbles was to destroy roughly 15 percent of the Soviet arsenal, allowing thousands of warheads to penetrate and detonate on American soil.[63]

In February 1990, Bush publicly proclaimed his personal commitment to the pebbles idea by touring Livermore and hailing the project. It was the first time a president had visited the California weapons lab. While addressing an auditorium filled with Livermore personnel, Bush broke from his speech to call Teller "my friend of long standing." The Hungarian scientist, then 82, sat in the audience. Bush, with a smile and a nod, praised Teller as a great pioneer in the field of national security and one of the "leading minds in science."[64] Bush went on to laud Brilliant Pebbles, saying it would strengthen deterrence by instilling doubts in an enemy's mind about the success of a preemptive strike. "If the technology I've seen today proves feasible—and I'm told it looks very promising—no war planner would be confident of the consequences of a ballistic missile attack," Bush said. An antimissile system, he added, would "also defend us against accidental launches or attacks from the many other countries that, regrettably, are acquiring ballistic missile capabilities. In the 1990s strategic defense makes much more sense than ever before."

Teller joined the enthusiastic applause.

# Epilogue

THE MAIN QUESTION this book has tried to address is how Edward Teller, a man so gifted scientifically, could repeatedly mislead the White House on critical issues of national security. That question goes primarily to the X-ray laser, which Teller promoted indefatigably to the government despite its uncertain promise. After its collapse, a similar question applies to his advocacy of Brilliant Pebbles, an antimissile idea that in some respects is even more dubious. For a man as complicated as Teller, answers to such questions can only be tentative. He is far easier to describe than explain. A review of his scientific life nonetheless suggests some answers.

As important, the saga of his misrepresentations, when viewed from a slightly wider perspective, can illuminate how the government became so vulnerable to his zeal and can perhaps suggest changes in federal procedure to limit such susceptibilities in the future. If no lessons are drawn from the costly experience, if fantasy weapons and other would-be wonders continue to distort federal planning, if science increasingly takes a back seat to politics and private agendas, then the dangers for the nation and the world will inexorably multiply, perhaps to the point of the ultimate calamity.

Most fundamentally, the trouble in Teller's life can be traced to a breakdown in relations with colleagues. His career was one long demonstration of the fact that his scientific gifts worked successfully only in a social context. Teller needed peers to give intellectual integrity to the wanderings of his extraordinarily vivid imagination. Bereft of interaction with down-to-earth colleagues, he was an undisciplined dreamer. He had little of the solitary genius of a Newton or Einstein. Over the decades, Teller's special type of social dependency was demonstrated with a range of colleagues on a host of topics—with Placzek on spectroscopy, Konopinski on fusion reactions, Bethe on atmospheric ignition, Ulam on the H-bomb, de Hoffmann on magnetohydrodynamics, Dyson on nuclear reactors. The reverse was also true. When Teller was cut off, the results could be quite embarrassing, as when Livermore's early attempts at nuclear design resulted in a series of explosive failures.

By choice, Teller lessened his reliance on colleagues as his career moved forward. The reasons are murky, probably revolving around growing confidence, a yearning for independent action and the effects of raw power. From the 1940s onward, Teller's passions played themselves out on an unusually large stage, the dimensions of which are difficult to imagine. It was the world of the bomb makers. The Manhattan Project was a state within a state, with its own airplanes and factories and cities and laws and secrets. Herbert S. Marks, the general counsel of the Atomic Energy Commission, aptly called it "a peculiar sovereignty."[1] The dimensions of this domain grew considerably during the cold war, with billions of dollars in budget authority and heady influence over the nation's leaders. Teller became the high priest of this world, ultimately accountable to no one except his own conscience. He felt the nation needed another lab for the design of nuclear weapons—and it materialized. He opposed the ending of nuclear tests—and the blasts continued. The exercise of such power was never far from the temptations of arrogance.

Another cause of Teller's isolation was his repudiation by peers upset over the Oppenheimer affair and his obsession with arms development. The loss of their friendship and professional contact hurt Teller and, as he sought to prove them wrong, probably encouraged his tendency to haughtiness. Teller's indignation over his exile was extraordinarily deep, as a reporter discovered in 1990.[2]

Toward the end of a long interview, Teller was asked how he handled the mistrust of his peers. There was no immediate response. He sat quietly with hands folded on his lap. Then his eyelids fluttered. The period of silence lasted a half minute or so.

"As best I could," Teller finally answered in a voice so soft it could barely be heard.

"Does it hurt?" the reporter asked.

Teller exploded.

"NONE OF YOUR BUSINESS!" He then paused and added in a child's singsong, "Perhaps it does, perhaps it doesn't."

There was another long pause.

"I can tell you one thing," Teller whispered. "To be very open about it, a long, long time ago, like 35 or 36 years ago, it did hurt."

Another long pause.

"I left Hungary, lost contact with my relations. Left Germany and Europe, lost contact with many friends. I retained contact and good relations with my colleagues in the United States. Now, because of political differences, I have lost many of those. Most of those. Not all. There are a few exceptions."

Another explosion.

"OF COURSE THAT HURTS! IT WAS MEANT TO HURT, AND IT DID! It was long ago, you know? In the meantime, Livermore was built. I acquired a new set of friends at an age when most people make no more friends. In the meantime, I had lots of additional problems." And with that, Teller abruptly ended the line of questioning.

The result of Teller's isolation from world-class peers, whatever its cause or causes, was clear from a scientific point of view. The overall quality of his work declined, even as his aims grew more ambitious. Starting with the Manhattan Project, Teller belittled problems that kept other physicists tossing and turning all night long and set his sights on bigger objectives ten years down the line, confidently predicting a way would be found to get there. Occasionally he was proven right, as with the Polaris warhead. More often he was off the mark. For instance, the clean bomb and the Super antimissile warhead were incipient technologies of some promise. But in Teller's hands, their potential was recklessly exaggerated. Colleagues who had the strength of character to question his convictions, who disputed his high-level salesmanship, were either unheard or ignored. In the end, their caution proved prescient. Neither idea materialized despite Teller's investment in them of extensive scientific and political resources.

Teller's frayed relations with remaining colleagues broke down completely in the case of the X-ray laser. Woodruff, the man who best understood its limitations and had the courage to challenge Teller's promotions of the would-be weapon, was first ignored and then punished. Teller's attitude was similar, if less authoritarian, with X-ray skeptics such as Kidder, Bethe and Drell. They were largely disregarded, even though it was Teller who initially courted them for aid and advice.

In dissecting the X-ray episode, it is important to remember that Teller's need for collegial aid went far beyond the realm of science. One of his main concerns was how quickly the X-ray idea could lead to a weapon—an issue that largely turned on the intricacies of bomb engineering. Teller was no expert in this area. A theoretical physicist by training, he had little of the hands-on experience that Woodruff had painstakingly acquired in the design of underground sensors and running a program of experimental blasts. Teller could see a scientific principle and its potential. But he was ill equipped to realize it or predict when others might do so.

Any analysis of Teller's relationship with peers demands special attention when it comes to Lowell Wood. Here was a youthful colleague who provided no moderation at all but seemed to goad Teller onward. Clearly, Wood was a kindred spirit, a romantic visionary who provided none of the sober analysis that Placzek, Bethe or Dyson had given Teller's early work. Most important, Wood was largely Teller's creation. The two met while Wood was a sophomore in college, the bond becoming so strong that Wood joined Livermore upon receiving his Ph.D. Wood was an extension of Teller, a protege, an intellectual devotee who pledged allegiance to the Tellerian creed and struggled to carry it forward. "Lowell," as Carl Haussmann, the Livermore veteran, observed, "is like another son to Edward."[3]

LARGELY divorced from dispassionate peers, Teller drew on the vast reservoir of his own ideas, dreams, passions and frustrations. Foremost among his frustrations was the military might of the Soviet Union. Despite America's dominance in military affairs after World War II, and despite Teller's toil over the decades to keep things that way, the Russian Communists had generally matched the military efforts of the West and in some cases exceeded them. By 1980 the Soviets had taken the lead in what was perhaps the most contentious aspect of the East-West rivalry—the building of intercontinental missiles based on land. Scattered across central Asia, the Russian missiles were topped with more than 5,000 nuclear warheads aimed at the United States, promising an unimaginable rain of destruction and death. This reversal greatly upset Teller, who had dedicated his life to making sure the United States maintained a military edge over the Soviet Union, a technical lead hinting at belligerence that could be turned into a crushing advantage during war. That was the essence of the H-bomb, which when first detonated in 1952 had an explosive force roughly a thousand times greater than any weapon then in the Soviet arsenal. Like many displaced Europeans, Teller felt Americans were children in need of protection in a dangerous world. By 1980, with the deterioration of the West's edge, Teller wanted to give the United States a new way to reassert its military superiority.[4]

Teller also had yearnings that had little or nothing to do with military utility and everything to do with personal psychology. Teller admitted as much on a *Firing Line* program, telling Buckley that "a good part, an important part, of my own psychology" was trying to negate, with antimissile arms, the horror of nuclear annihilation he had given the world.[5] The appeal of antimissile work was especially great for Teller because of its ambiguity. On one hand, the work allowed him to take the moral high ground in military debates as he renounced the evils of nuclear genocide for the ultimate good of protecting people. It humanized him. But less visibly, it also promised a new way to fight communism, in theory allowing the United States to gain the upper hand in the East-West struggle. Clearly, antimissile systems had offensive uses that were quite deadly and sure to unnerve the Soviets.

Finally, an important part of Teller's inner stirrings and strivings probably had to do with career frustration. Here was a man who had to share scientific credit nearly all the time, a man who had a long list of coauthors and collaborators. Teller's dependency on colleagues was true even of his most notable claim to fame, the H-bomb. It had been done in collaboration with key members of Oppenheimer's circle, tainting the advance in his eyes. Perhaps most painfully, Teller never won the Nobel Prize, unlike many of his peers who took a more solitary approach to the practice of science. Teller was a rare species of scientist, unquestionably world-class but having no world-class discovery to his name. Many of his achievements—helping get the A-bomb effort off the ground, founding the Livermore lab in California, defeating the drive for a nuclear test ban—were feats of persuasion rather than science. It seems likely that Teller, whether conscious of it or not, longed for a major advance to call his own.

For all these reasons, the vision of the X-ray laser had to be pure poetry for Teller, resonating throughout his being on a variety of levels, promising to end a wilderness of personal dilemmas. First, it was a scientific breakthrough of the first order that had been achieved by his loyal scientists at Livermore, with no help from the Oppenheimer crowd. The advance was also deeply personal, since perfection of the weapon would require an accumulated wisdom in the bomb business that only he possessed. Second, its projected powers were so great that the weapon might precipitate the final antimissile victory, allowing Teller to take credit for ending the nuclear nightmare and to conclude his turbulent career on a positive note. Finally, it would be a high-tech achievement sure to worry the Soviets, appearing beguilingly peaceful on the surface while quietly offering a sharp new twist to the arms race. Or so it seemed.

MODERN science is founded on a complex social system meant to winnow and sift through the contributions of individual scientists, to separate fact from fiction, to police itself, to search out error and fraud. In practice, these checks and balances work imperfectly.[6] Moreover, the quality-control problem is exacerbated in the bomb business because of its requirements for secrecy. The danger is well recognized in weapons work. To counter it, responsible program managers place special emphasis on close control within a laboratory and occasionally seek review of weapons work by teams of outside experts with the proper security clearances.

In theory, such mechanisms should have stopped Teller's wilder activities before they did any damage. In practice, Teller's ambitions for the X-ray laser repeatedly collided with this system and quickly overwhelmed it.

The first hurdle was Woodruff, the head of the secret project. His opposition to the enthusiasms of Teller and Wood began as early as 1981 when he accompanied the pair to Washington, eager to keep them from making inflated X-ray promises for which he would be held responsible. The apprehensions of Woodruff became clear to Teller as the two scientists clashed in late 1982 over the Frieman report and in 1983 over the Keyworth letter. As the pace of X-ray lobbying quickened in 1984 with the advent of Super Excalibur, and as Maenchen's fears deepened over the reliability of X-ray readings, Woodruff tried unsuccessfully to gain support from his superiors for the moderation of Teller and Wood. He wrote letters to try to correct the X-ray record but was told not to send them. He called for a special internal lab review of the X-ray laser. It never materialized. He wrote private notes to the director and his top aides, asking for help, saying he feared for the lab's reputation. Nothing happened.

The reason for the lab's inaction, explained after the fact by director Batzel, was to defend the principle of scientific freedom of expression. Teller promoted the X-ray laser with monomaniacal zeal. But Batzel's view was that such enthusiasms were acceptable, since Washington officials knew Teller was a visionary and a technical optimist. They had him calibrated.[7] This logic breaks down on two points. First, Teller was able to express his opinions far more freely than Woodruff, the head of the X-ray program whose appeal for written clarification was denied. Second, Teller's ultimate aim was not only to influence knowledgeable experts such as Keyworth and DeLauer, who knew his mixed technical record and could easily discount his excitement. It was also to sway the politicians in the White House and elsewhere who made the decisions over funding and weapons deployment. When possible, Teller went to them directly.

There are several alternate explanations for the lab's loose rein on Teller. One is simply the scientist's power. Teller got his way around Livermore—period. Another is the possibility that the lab had a vested interest in the success of the sales campaign. After all, hundreds of millions of dollars, if not billions of dollars, were at stake at a time when traditional work on nuclear weapons was starting to decline. "The lab benefited from that overselling," Ray Pollock, the National Security Council aide, told me. "Teller and Wood were good salesmen. My own feeling is that the lab used them. When necessary, it could then stand back and say that was not really the laboratory's position."[8]

Outside Livermore lay a series of intellectual checkpoints meant to ensure the validity and sobriety of ideas trying to make their way from the weapons lab to the president. Almost uniformly, these failed to slow Teller and Wood. Keyworth, the president's science adviser, had been hand-picked by Teller for his White House post and, though an X-ray skeptic, seemed to be paralyzed by divided loyalties. The Frieman panel knew the score on the X-ray laser but was ineffectual in shaping White House policy. The Fletcher panel was more successful both in analyzing the implications of the X-ray laser and in impressing these upon the middle management of the federal government. But Teller was adept at leapfrogging formal channels, writing and visiting top policy makers to argue his own unique point of view. The Fletcher panel saw the X-ray laser as potentially the downfall of Star Wars. At precisely the same time, Teller wrote President Reagan to forcefully argue just the opposite, saying his weapons "would end the MAD era and commence a period of assured survival on terms favorable to the Western alliance."[9] Teller was his own one-man apparatus for advising the government, his work finally turning into a feverish crusade between 1982 and 1985.

Late in the game, one intellectual barrier did finally arise. This was Los Alamos. Within the federal bureaucracy, the New Mexico lab advertised the existence of sensor problems on X-ray tests, saying Livermore had been tricked by false brightness. Ironically, the Los Alamos input was based on an idea that had been developed deep within Livermore. Moreover, the Los Alamos critique was largely ineffective, being narrowly bureaucratic and limited to middle managers. Unlike Teller, the Los Alamos officials had no direct access to the top. In a way, they seemed too tired to thwart Teller. As the nation's oldest weapons lab, Los Alamos often appeared to be happy with its role as the original atom architect but hesitant to shake up the weapons world.

Even after the collapse of the X-ray laser program, Teller and his aides maintained a tight grip on the public portrayal of the debacle, as demonstrated by the GAO report. This was a remarkable feat. After all, the GAO is generally a top-flight investigative agency. And its inquiry was done at the behest of the legislative branch of government, which ostensibly was a check on the executive branch and, during the period in question, was controlled by the Democrats. Earlier X-ray reviews had been initiated by the Republican-dominated executive branch. Even so, Teller ran circles around the GAO. Despite top-secret clearances, subpoena power, sworn testimony and other investigative tools, the GAO investigators only added to X-ray laser misinformation and myths.

A CENTRAL tenet of the Reagan administration was that good government was no government or, short of that, as little government as possible. This free-market philosophy resulted in the elimination of many regulatory bodies and roles. With pride, Reagan himself noted that literally thousands of pages of rules and regulations were torn up.[10] Old boundaries disappeared. Previously, lobbyists in Washington pursued their business by working the many-layered bureaucracies and members of Congress. But starting in 1981, Washington lobbyists suddenly found themselves confronted with a series of deregulated fields. The new emphasis was on personal access to high officials, preferably in the White House itself. Good contacts and connections were key—not a good grasp of federal procedure, as had previously been the case. That atmosphere helped produce the scandal at the Department of Housing and Urban Development and aided the failure of the nation's savings and loans, which could ultimately cost American taxpayers in excess of $500 billion.[11]

A laissez-faire attitude was clearly seen in the conduct of science policy. Old structures were weakened, old panels disbanded. The Reagan White House initially expressed doubts that a science adviser was needed at all. Finally, the administration said one would be appointed but would have a smaller staff and budget than his predecessor—and less access to the president.

Teller took advantage of this atmosphere to the fullest extent possible, bypassing the weakened structures of government and going directly to the people who made decisions. His plan of action relied heavily on influencing such presidential advisers as Bendetsen, Anderson, Meese, Watkins, McFarlane, and Nitze. None of these individuals was a scientist. None had the needed background to judge the technical merits of the X-ray laser. They were either conduits to the top or policy makers who could influence government plans. And, of course, Teller argued his points with President Reagan directly, both in person and in letters. The politicians visited by Teller and his cohorts heard dramatic generalizations about the X-ray laser or gazed at glossy artist's renditions of the hypothetical weapon at work in space. They had little or no idea about the feeble reality of the research, the pitfalls, the uncertainties of trying to understand what was happening a third of a mile beneath the Nevada desert during a nuclear explosion. They had no basis for judgment. Moreover, many of them, even levelheaded pragmatists, regarded Teller as something akin to a god.

The top officials of the Reagan administration were generally well disposed toward the "father" of the H-bomb, who was seen as right on many issues of military import. Most significantly, Reagan liked and respected Teller. The two resonated. Reagan, the man who cast a spell on a nation, who tended to exercise his charm more than his intellect, was eager to hear news of a way to achieve the end of possible nuclear annihilation and the onset of "assured survival," as Teller told him in the glowingly confident letters of 1982 and 1983.[12]

A clear risk of Teller's going directly to the top was his infectious sense of technical optimism. It painted a picture of scientific advance that was beguilingly simple, threatening to distort national policy in its most delicate areas. "Technical optimism unchecked can be dangerous," remarked Donald M. Kerr, director of Los Alamos during the X-ray episode. "It's dangerous because, in part, there are very few people in the government who can objectively participate in or observe and learn from a technical debate. So policies are made and decisions taken on the basis of very little information."[13]

IN the end, the emptiness of Teller's claim was demonstrated by the X-ray laser itself. No amount of salesmanship or enthusiasm could hide the fact that the weapon failed to materialize. Bendetsen's 1981 letter to the White House said Livermore would deliver a working device in as little as four years, or 1985. Teller told Nitze in 1984 that a basic weapon would be available by the late 1980s, and assured McFarlane that a second-generation device might be proven in principle in three years, or 1987.

The reality of the X-ray laser program is grim compared with Teller's glowing forecasts. Budget cuts and technical failures forced hundreds of workers from the program, adding to the small exodus of those who left voluntarily. John Nuckolls, Livermore's new director, summed up the situation in 1989 during testimony to Congress, putting a philosophical gloss on the problems. "Nature," he said, "wants its secrets unlocked slowly."[14]

Richard D. Hahn, director in the late 1980s of the Energy Department's office of weapons research, development, and testing, was more candid. "We're finding that these problems are fairly difficult," he said in a 1989 interview, adding that his assessment was "kind of a gross understatement." The program's political credibility was so low, Hahn said, that the project was unlikely to ever regain its lost funding and personnel. "You're talking about several hundred people gone from the program, never to return," he said.[15]

Today, the residue of the Excalibur program hopes to prove scientific feasibility sometime in the twenty-first century. And that is only a hope, Livermore officials being careful to offer no guarantees about a working weapon. "We're not trying to decide if we should build an X-ray laser," said David Nowak, a lab official. "We're trying to decide if we could."[16] Moreover, even if scientific feasibility can be successfully demonstrated, it might take another decade to engineer a weapon.

What all this means is that Teller's forecasts for the simplest kind of X-ray laser weapon will probably be off by a quarter century, and perhaps more. And it is worse than that. No one in a responsible position at Livermore or in the federal government so much as mentions the Super Excalibur type of weapon that Teller so excitedly described to top government officials as the salvation of Star Wars.

The intellectual fragility of Teller's claims becomes clear when the Excalibur work is compared with its close cousin, nonnuclear X-ray lasers. These peaceful devices, pioneered by Peter Hagelstein, were pursued by Livermore in parallel with the exotic weapon. Although using no bomb and far less powerful, they were seen as possibly becoming a valuable tool for science research. To date scientists in the unclassified field have failed to understand such fundamental issues as exactly why the laser works. Computer simulations predict the laser's light will have a certain set of spectral lines. But experiments show another set. In short, there is no agreement between theory and experiment, a problem that also haunted the nuclear blasts. This ignorance exists despite the conduct by the nonnuclear program of nearly 1,000 experimental "shots."[17] In the more costly, complex and difficult field of nuclear-driven X-ray lasers, the state of scientific understanding is less advanced.

All this is not to say that the nuclear X-ray laser is wholly an illusion. Something is clearly there. And little by little, it is getting stronger as the research advances, albeit in fits and starts. Absent an East-West treaty that bans or greatly restricts underground nuclear blasts, the laser might emerge sometime in the twenty-first century as a new force in the world of armament, ready, as the Fletcher panel warned, to excel at little more than the destruction of satellites and weapons in space.

A KEY question in all this is whether Teller consciously knew his claims were outside the bounds of scientific credibility or whether he was so caught up in X-ray revelry that he deluded himself into thinking the quick development schedules and astonishing weapon applications were tenable. Was he a knave or a fool, or perhaps a little of both?

Some of the scientists who fought Teller say his X-ray fervor was probably a case of self-deception. Bethe and Drell believe this to be the case, both having clashed with Teller over the X-ray laser and both having long familiarity with his passionate embrace of implausible ideas.[18] Livermore officials also lean in this direction, laying the blame to a surfeit of optimism or to the skewing of Teller's judgment by a dearth of credible information. George Miller told GAO investigators that Teller discovered X-ray sobriety after becoming "better educated."[19] And, of course, Teller himself sarcastically confessed to the "great crime" of optimism.

One can argue that Teller showed clear signs of delusion. His continuing support of the X-ray laser after its collapse bespoke an emotional commitment so deep it defied logic. His religious zeal on the antimissile issue, coupled with his long track record of greeting difficult technical endeavors with excessive optimism, supports the image of a man ready for a flight of fancy at the least opportunity.

If self-deception distorted Teller's judgment, one cause was probably his overriding sense that great things were ready to happen at any moment given an infusion of sufficient money and intellect. In part, this attitude derives from a romantic tradition that denies any limits to what can be achieved by human effort. Such optimism is also common in science, though it may be increasingly misplaced. The depressing secret that no scientist likes to admit is that, late in the twentieth century, many if not most of the easy things in science and engineering have already been accomplished. This is why some science projects are becoming so big and costly, why particle accelerators have gone from something you could literally hold in the palm of your hand to behemoths large enough to encircle the city of New York. The admission of the growing difficulty goes against the can-do ethic of science nor, as a practical matter, is it helpful in persuading federal agencies and Congress to fund new research projects. But it is the truth. For Teller—a man who lived through the science revolutions of relativity theory and quantum mechanics and who witnessed some of the century's great engineering feats—it was easy to persuade himself that the adventure could go on forever. "We must remember that what we can imagine today may be dwarfed by future realities," he told a group planning a scientific colony on the moon. "There are limits to our imagination. There are hardly any to the developments that the human mind and human activity can accomplish."[20]

Moreover, if Teller did lie to himself, he was in good company. Self-deception in science is anything but rare. Time and again, an experimenter's expectation of what he will see has shaped the data he recorded. Nor does the phenomenon affect only individuals. Sometimes a whole community of researchers falls prey to a common delusion, as when French physicists at the turn of the century thought they had discovered N-rays.[21] Such distortions of the truth occur in the realm of precise measurement and experiment. The danger is greater in the more subjective areas pursued by Teller—the feasibility of exotic weapon designs and their engineering schedules.

Even so, the thesis that Teller was totally unwitting and simply lost in an optimistic fog is contradicted by the fact that he, despite his relative isolation from world-class peers, was repeatedly confronted by remaining colleagues. Officials such as Roy Woodruff struggled for years to enlighten Teller to the complexities and failings of the laser. Woodruff says it is impossible to know Teller's state of mind but that the evidence suggests the Hungarian scientist was involved in a conscious act of exaggeration if not outright deception. First, Woodruff says, Teller knew he was pressing the bounds of credibility after the clashes in 1982 over the Frieman report and in 1983 over the Keyworth letter. Thereafter, he says, Teller consciously withdrew from further contact with him and other leaders of the X-ray program, probably fearing conflict with their more conservative goals. Woodruff notes that Teller originally sent copies of his White House letters to many laboratory officials, including him. This was the case in September 1982, when Teller called on Reagan to press ahead with exotic nuclear weaponry "at a pace commensurate with its promise for replacing Mutual Assured Destruction with assured survival." But the more technically detailed and controversial letters to Keyworth, Nitze and McFarlane had limited distribution within the lab. No official was to receive copies of the Keyworth letter. Copies of the letters to Nitze and McFarlane were to go only to Batzel and Wood, where there was little chance of X-ray opposition. "He knew what he was doing," Woodruff says.[22]

The verdict of Kidder, the X-ray skeptic at Livermore who counseled Teller, is harsher. He believes the Hungarian physicist repeatedly and consciously betrayed the scientific truth in order to further such ends as blocking arms accords and gathering money for his X-ray ambitions. "I have always known him as a clever and calculating man, rather than a starry-eyed optimist," says Kidder, who joined Livermore in 1956 and worked intimately with Teller for decades. "I never believed that his egregious exaggerations of the X-ray laser and other pet weapons were the result of an overdeveloped sense of optimism, although he enjoyed his carefully cultivated reputation for optimism and made good use of it when predicted successes failed to materialize. He understood very well the magnitude of the scientific and technological hurdles that would need to be overcome and the odds against overcoming them."[23]

Kidder says Teller was a scientific version of Lieutenant Colonel

Oliver L. North, the White House aide who lied to Congress about the administration's clandestine support of the Nicaraguan rebels. Both men, says Kidder, were right-wing ideologues who feared that knowledgeable policy makers would fail to do the "right" thing. "In North's case the 'right' thing was to support the Contras," says Kidder. "In Teller's case it was to stop the Soviets from conquering the world, as he believed they surely intended to do. Get rid of Oppenheimer, start a second weapons lab, oppose any and all restrictions on nuclear weapons testing, exaggerate the possibilities of the 'clean' bomb and the X-ray laser, but for God's sake, do the 'right' thing! If things go wrong, chalk it up to the great crime of optimism.

"Teller," Kidder continues, "was possessed with the threat of Soviet world domination. It consumed him entirely for the second half of his life. He *knew* he was right, and anybody who failed to understand the enormity and primacy of this threat was simply a fool unworthy of serious consideration.

"One could fruitfully and enjoyably talk about science with Edward—but never politics," says Kidder. "In politics there was nothing to talk about. 'The Russians were coming!' That was it."

The notion that Teller was involved in a conscious act of deception is consistent with some of his past behavior. He failed to credit Ulam for H-bomb advances. He brazenly denied that his FBI testimony led to charges against Oppenheimer, contrary to the man who drafted the charges.[24] He called for clandestine growth of the X-ray laser program and for secrecy in the lofting of Brilliant Pebbles, apparently ready to keep the public in the dark or actively misled.

Perhaps most conspicuously, he downplayed his role in the origin of Star Wars. "I am blamed or credited entirely unduly for having persuaded the President," he told GAO investigators. "I did not do much, very little."[25] This from a man who, over two long years, lobbied a host of White House advisers, labored tirelessly to sell the kitchen cabinet on the X-ray laser, battled to make a White House antimissile report more upbeat, repeatedly wrote the president in ostentatious prose, connived to get a one-on-one presidential audience, and even penned a speech in which Reagan was to announce a crash program to develop space arms.

Truth, it is said, is the first casualty in war. During the long decades of the cold war, with its threats of nuclear annihilation, its posturing and deadly bluffs, American leaders had an opportunity and rationale to practice deception on a vast new scale in pursuit of what they believed to be a greater good. Perhaps the same was true of Teller.

ANOTHER important question in all this is to what extent Teller's deception mattered. The general effects were unquestionably large. After all, his actions paved the way for Star Wars, on which more than $25 billion has so far been spent, making it the biggest and most costly program of military research in the nation's history. One can argue that many of the program's repercussions on American values and economics are quite negative. But in the curious way bad sometimes begets good, the grand deception of the X-ray laser and Star Wars also probably had some beneficial effects. These, however, must be weighed carefully against the costs and risks to the nation and the world.

Star Wars unnerved the Soviets, making them amenable to arms negotiations at a time when they were engaged in a large expansion of their nuclear arsenal. The X-ray device clearly worried them, as suggested by their unilateral moratorium on nuclear blasts. It was militarily threatening. And it exemplified the kind of subtle, high-technology achievement that the Soviet Union, with its aging infrastructure devoted to heavy industry, was unable to match, despite Teller's inflated claims to the contrary. It held out the prospect of a new kind of arms race the Soviets clearly wanted to avoid.

Star Wars and the X-ray laser may have even played a role in winning the cold war—a feat whose magnitude can hardly be exaggerated. But it would be wrong to give the laser, or even the overall Reagan military buildup, too much credit on this score. First, the X-ray laser's demise was at least partly revealed in public, lessening the shadow it cast. Second, although recent American willingness to redouble the arms race undoubtedly created competitive pressure that contributed to the ruin of the Soviet economy, a host of military and nonmilitary, technical and nontechnical factors played important, perhaps pivotal, roles in the collapse of communism. Much credit goes to the eight postwar presidents who as a loc carried out the West's policies of containment.

One recent technical factor was the West's fundamental advantage in computer chips and their numerous offspring, which have transformed Western life and industry. For the Soviet Union these devices conveyed a bitter truth—adapt to the information age or be doomed like the dinosaurs. A related factor was how the dissemination of lightweight, high-technology products eroded Soviet control over public information. In his book *Behind the Lines,* Donald R. Shanor of Columbia University showed how Soviet citizens in the 1980s increasingly relied on compact shortwave radios, television sets, and video and audio tape recorders to capture Western broadcasts and circumvent Soviet censors.[26] The walls were coming down, whether the Politburo liked it or not, long before the fall of the Berlin wall. Another factor was simply the growing hopes of repressed peoples. In *The Awakening of the Soviet Union,* Geoffrey Hosking, a historian at the University of London, argues that a large part of perestroika was triggered by the growing maturity of Soviet society.[27] Perhaps the most important single factor in communism's decline was the built-in inefficiencies of the Soviet economy, which doomed it to inferiority and perhaps to ruin. Reagan himself in his 1990 book, *An American Life,* says one of his surprises on becoming president in 1981 was intelligence and economic briefings that showed the Soviet economy was falling apart. "Communism as we knew it was approaching the brink of collapse," said Reagan in recalling the secret reports.[28] Such disclosures only bolster arguments that the East's downfall was inevitable, with or without Star Wars and the West's military buildup. Clearly, the weaknesses of communism were intrinsic, deriving from its erroneous view of human nature. A system that tries to extinguish the hope of personal reward, and most other incentives for economic and social gain, is clearly destined for decline and decay.

Although Star Wars helped make the Soviets amenable to arms negotiations, that leverage was largely wasted, since the antimissile program had just the opposite effect on the Reagan administration. In particular, the inflated promise of Super Excalibur probably played a role in making President Reagan less receptive to East-West treaties on long-range nuclear arms than he otherwise would have been. Reagan's odd performance at Reykjavik, where he refused to consider any Star Wars limitations, should keep historians pondering this possibility for some time. On the issue of arms-control hesitancy, Reagan seemed to take his cues from Teller. Any political leverage that may have accrued from Star Wars and the X-ray laser had no explicit place in Teller's agenda, as it clearly did in that of McFarlane and a few other administration officials. Teller wanted to build and deploy weapons, not use them as bargaining chips.

More narrowly, the government's technical response to the would-be weapon was also skewed, at least partly because of Teller.

The discovery that the X-ray laser was a menace to Star Wars and all objects in space, as the Fletcher panel so clearly documented, might have prompted a rational administrator to try to head off any Soviet perfection of such a weapon by negotiating an East-West ban on nuclear tests. This would have instantly relegated the embryonic threat to the scrap heap of military history. But Teller, despite all evidence to the contrary, kept insisting it would bring about an age of "assured survival." Nowhere was his continuing influence on government policy more obvious than his winning $100 million for Livermore's development of Super Excalibur after personally lobbying President Reagan.

Teller's zeal also diverted federal attention from antimissile efforts that were more tenable. One can argue that what America needed to pursue in the 1980s was ground-based defenses to catch a few missiles launched accidentally by a large nuclear power or purposefully by terrorists and small, aggressive states such as Iraq under Saddam Hussein. Antimissile systems on the ground have none of the deadly ambiguity inherent in space-based arms. Moreover, their limited goals are relatively easy to achieve. After the Gulf War and the qualified success of the Patriot missile in shooting down Iraqi Scuds, some conservatives charged that Star Wars had actually slowed work on practical antimissile programs. They noted that the Strategic Defense Initiative, eight years after its debut under President Reagan, had achieved little of practical significance even as the Army perfected the Patriot with no financial aid whatsoever from Star Wars. "We would have been farther along without SDI," said Senator Wallop, the early antimissile advocate. "It hurt more than it helped." In the months after the Gulf War a congressional move got under way to divest SDI of any responsibility for ground-based interceptors out of fear that their development would be hindered.[29]

For the nation as a whole, some of the most subtle damage resulting from Teller's influence and Star Wars was the squandering of precious intellectual resources at a critical juncture in American history, as the cold war died down and the economic wars of the 1980s heated up. Some of the nation's best technical minds were lured into military research rather than basic science or industrial development. It remains to be seen whether America, with the cold war's apparent end, can break this habit so the nation can compete against the Pacific rim and Europe in the manufacture of advanced consumer goods. At the start of the 1980s, when Reagan came into office, Japan produced a little more than 10 percent of the world's electronic goods. It followed, imitated and copied. By the start of the 1990s, Japan controlled more than 50 percent of that production and was rapidly expanding its control through innovative design.[30] While the superpowers were mired in an archaic contest, Japan was quietly taking the lead in an economic conflict that could dramatically affect Western values and dominance in the twenty-first century.

In all this, it is no small irony that Teller's zealous advocacy caused serious damage to his greatest pride and joy, Livermore. His X-ray exaggerations triggered an explosion of resentment there, with tremors still shaking the California weapons lab. Most obviously, it pushed Woodruff and a group of other talented scientists out the door, to Livermore's detriment. Most disturbing of all, the Woodruff saga sent a terrible message to scientists remaining at the lab. An Orwellian atmosphere where truthfulness is scorned and deception rewarded is sure to send any technical organization into decline, much less an elite one such as Livermore that studies some of the most subtle questions of nature and seeks to hire the most talented and creative scientists in the nation. It remains to be seen if Livermore can ever regain its reputation for nonpartisan integrity.

Least conspicuously but perhaps most dangerously, the X-ray episode undermined the process of government and, more fundamentally, of democracy. It did so through secrecy, which spread its tendrils as the X-ray laser program grew. America was founded on the proposition that government must be accountable to the people. But Teller's campaign reinforced the national-security state and the "peculiar sovereignty" of the bomb makers, both of which are fundamentally undemocratic.

The security system is necessary for some facets of military research. But its costs are high. In the case of the X-ray laser, skeptics privy to secrets had to be extraordinarily cautious about expressing reservations lest they breach security laws. Their ability to blow the whistle on bad science and dangerous policy was impaired. In this secretive atmosphere, mistakes were hidden, errors were swept under the rug, exaggerations went unchallenged. The extensive failings of the X-ray laser and the system that produced it were obscured for years. It is doubtful whether they would have come to light at all except for the historical accident of Roy Woodruff, who set in motion a series of X-ray inquiries and revelations.

The potential for another kind of damage to the democratic process undoubtedly exists as the public learns of Teller's secret maneuverings and his unusual influence, paving the way for feelings of cynicism and apathy that come with the knowledge that special interests can sway government to such an extent. But the fact of his intrigues can also become a stimulus to reform and the reassertion of democratic values.

WITH the collapse of the X-ray laser came Teller's advocacy of Brilliant Pebbles, an idea now undergoing rapid development at Livermore and other labs around the nation and still, despite the disintegration of the Soviet Union and dramatic steps to cut the world's nuclear arsenals, the heart of the Bush administration's antimissile plan. One thousand of the weapons would be lofted into space.[31] Bringing this system to life would take years, not decades. But even if successfully deployed, the pebbles would at best make a leaky shield. This is the worst possible achievement from the standpoint of East-West stability. A leaky shield works well at mopping up after a first strike but terribly at repelling a full-scale attack. Because of its limitations, a leaky shield lends itself to offensive attacks. That is probably why the Soviets voiced their deployment objections through Sakharov, rattling their nuclear saber. Today, Soviet turmoil has arguably increased the danger, or at least uncertainty. Dejected armies, yearning for some kind of role on the world stage and still possessing thousands of nuclear arms, might use Star Wars deployments and their offensive threat as a way to rationalize a coup or a war.

Teller was clearly devoted to deploying Brilliant Pebbles, for whatever mix of reasons. But the Bush administration, generally speaking, has earned a reputation for skill and sobriety. Some experts argue that its SDI actions are simply political theater aimed at keeping the Soviets on the defensive. Indeed, the project is perfect for that purpose, looking peaceful in simple political terms while threatening to accelerate the arms race. The only problem with this interpretation is that it might be wrong. President Bush, in Panama and the Persian Gulf, has shown a willingness to take political risks and offensive military action. Moreover, with striking continuity, Teller and Wood seem to have won his confidence. The signs, both public and private, all point in that direction—the White House briefings, Bush's visit to Livermore, the public lauding of Teller, the socializing with Wood. It can only be hoped that President Bush has listened as carefully to his more dispassionate advisers.

IT is easy to visualize precautions that would reduce the danger of zealous advocacy again distorting the process of government. First and foremost, existing mechanisms, review boards, laws and procedures should be exercised and strengthened. There are public laws meant to prevent bomb makers from lobbying Congress. There are executive orders that prohibit the use of federal secrecy to hide errors or to save an organization from embarrassment. There are existing Pentagon panels, such as the Jasons, meant to give top-level review to new scientific ideas. The political will must be developed to utilize these tools effectively. Most especially, secrecy must be eliminated wherever possible in order to derail the kind of false momentum that allowed the X-ray laser to get so far with so little. Openness is the only sure antidote to the abuse of power.

Further, new mechanisms must be created. To bolster the congressional analysis of science, a new agency should be founded that mirrors the General Accounting Office but has technical auditors with subpoena power, not just accountants. New mechanisms are also needed to weed out the numerous conflicts of interest evident in the antimissile debacle. High-energy physicists in the United States have a prestigious advisory panel that judges what projects have technical merit, as do many other scientific fields. No such mechanism exists for the bomb makers. Theirs is largely a free-market approach to science, with intense lobbying shrouded in secrecy. As the twin revolutions of science and technology move forward, the issues facing government are only going to become more complex, confusing, and susceptible to misjudgment and distortion. Free enterprise might be the best philosophy in the fields of business and economics. But in science, too much reliance on its impressive mechanisms can lead to tragedies that drain the public purse and endanger the nation's security, as demonstrated by the X-ray laser affair.

A REVIEW of Teller's life that focuses on shortcomings needs perspective lest sight be lost of his positive accomplishments over a long career. These were considerable. Teller understood the tyranny of communism and succeeded like no other individual in forging weapons to fight it. His decades of building bombs, of blasting boulders into the sky, of causing the planet to shudder, of doing everything in his power to frighten the Soviets, of going to the brink of war in a metaphorical sense, clearly succeeded in intimidating his foes. He played an important role in challenging Stalin's ambitions for the subjugation of Europe. His tireless militancy, occurring over a large part of the twentieth century, made pivotal contributions to peace and freedom in the Western world. In all this, moreover, he was a man of principle. He did what he believed in, regardless of whether or not it made him a pariah. Perhaps Teller was even correct, as Sakharov contends, to have undermined Oppenheimer's influence in favor of a more vigorous pursuit of American military power.[32] While the merit of Teller's specific anticommunist acts will long be debated, it is indisputable that he railed against the injustices of the Soviet system at a time when many in the West were content to pursue creature comforts and to forget the gulags, the suffering and the spiritual repression of a significant part of humanity. He was the ultimate cold warrior, giving that often strident posture an aura of respectability.

In the end, however, Teller was undone in no small part by the thing that made him—his hatred of communism. The Reagan administration, by its own admission, came to office determined to regain military *superiority* over the Russians by embarking on a vast buildup of missiles, ships, satellites, bombers and nuclear warfighting machinery.[33] Teller eagerly joined the fray. The collapse of communism should have been Teller's moment of glory, vindicating his vision. Instead it was a time of embarrassment. The X-ray saga revealed that Teller and his associates had taken on some of the worst attributes of their Russian foes. The disintegration of the Communist bloc showed that much of its economic and military might had been a ruse. So, too, the X-ray laser in many respects was a lie.

Teller's agenda went beyond politics. His posturing over the X-ray laser was meant to do much more than secure funds to further its development or frighten the Soviets. As was the case with so many cold war politicians, his agenda also furthered ends that were uniquely personal, helping promote his lab, his friends, his vision of how to use the atom. Ultimately, by threatening to raise the risk of nuclear war, Teller's personal goals seemed to be ready to triumph over the interests of the people he ostensibly served.

A review of Teller's scientific life can lend a false impression about his influence. His energies were so extensive, his technological appetite so large, and his political power so great, that it would seem his impact on society was nothing short of overwhelming. That was not the case. His influence, while large in some respects, was greatly diminished from what it might have been by virtue of an unexpected source of resistance. Time and again, society itself proved to be a moderating factor, ultimately assuming the role once played by sympathetic colleagues, winnowing and sifting through the ideas of Teller's that emerged from the world of military secrecy, rejecting many that he wanted to materialize.

The world we live in bears little resemblance to the one envisioned by Teller. There are no antimissile arms defending whole continents, no limited nuclear wars, no fallout shelters behind every home. The nation rejected the continuation of atmospheric nuclear tests, which Teller lobbied for so feverishly. It embraced the Antiballistic Missile Treaty, which barred the deployment of extensive systems of defensive arms. It's a MAD world—the thing Teller helped create, the thing he deplored, the thing he tried so tirelessly to overturn.

Mankind is still wrestling with Teller's legacy, still trying to sort through the projects and ideas he championed. Star Wars is politically beleaguered as public fear of the Soviet military fades. It may be dead. On the other hand, this is a time of extraordinary change in the world, with new possibilities and new technologies and new alliances emerging all about us. Star Wars may survive simply by virtue of its promise of a reversal in the field of nuclear armament. Moreover, Teller, his heirs and his laboratory would have it prosper. Behind the barbed wire fences of Livermore, they are doing everything in their power to arm the heavens. Perhaps an understanding of Teller's career—including his rare genius, his deep frustrations and his troubled relations with colleagues—can help resolve the issue in a way that lessens the risk of nuclear war.

# X-RAY LASER TESTS

| CODE NAME | LAB | DATE | RESULT |
|-----------|-----|------|--------|
| Diablo Hawk | LLNL | September 13, 1978 | Test apparatus fails |
| Dauphin | LLNL | November 14, 1980 | First probable X-ray laser, though some experts say evidence is sketchy |
| Cabra | LLNL | March 26, 1983 | Sensors fail |
| Romano | LLNL | December 16, 1983 | First hard X-ray laser evidence |
| Correo | LANL | August 2, 1984 | Laser fails |
| Cottage | LLNL | March 23, 1985 | First focusing attempt |
| Goldstone | LLNL | December 28, 1985 | First good measure of brightness shows basic laser is dimmer than previously believed |
| Labquark | LLNL | September 30, 1986 | More focusing tests |
| Delamar | LLNL | April 18, 1987 | First fear that focusing has failed |
| Kernville | LLNL | February 15, 1988 | First high-quality data on basic laser |

LLNL = Lawrence Livermore National Laboratory
LANL = Los Alamos National Laboratory

# Acknowledgments

THIS BOOK was made possible by many people, some of whom I cannot thank by name because their assistance was rendered on the condition of anonymity. It was they who lifted the barrier of secrecy surrounding the X-ray laser so I could better understand its rudimentary nature. Without them, there would be no public basis for judging the extent of Teller's exaggeration. To them I extend my heartfelt gratitude for their trust and my admiration for their courage. My guides did what they did in the conviction that X-ray disclosures would do no harm to national security and would in fact help repair its foundations—that serious distortions in the public record would be corrected, that the arcane process of turning ideas into armaments would be demythologized and, ultimately, that democracy would be strengthened and would become more resistant to distorting influences in the future.

To federal authorities, I would like to state that Roy Woodruff and I took every precaution in our interviews to stay away from topics that might be considered sensitive. Roy and Mary Woodruff did, however, address what must have seemed like endless questions about their experiences at Livermore and the politics and personalities of the weapons labs. To them, many thanks for a remarkable show of kindness and candor.

Edward Teller, perhaps understandably given the nature of the book and the X-ray laser saga, did nothing to aid my work and, I suspect, some things to hinder it. Although I have interviewed him several times in the past decade, for stories appearing in *Science* and *The New York Times* and for my book *Star Warriors*, he turned down all interview requests for this work. His most memorable response came in a letter typed on Hoover

Institution stationery. Other than the date, my name and address and his signature, it contained a single word: "No!" Some of Teller's colleagues, including Lowell Wood and Roger Batzel, also avoided my questions. Such silence poses a problem for an author intent on balance. In response, I have combed the record for their comments and have quoted them. I have also tried to bring the fairness issue close to home by mentally substituting my own name for theirs while reading the manuscript.

Many individuals at Livermore and Los Alamos, formerly at the weapons labs or in government, or associated with Teller and his colleagues in some other way took time to share their thoughts, either for this book or for earlier X-ray projects. Many thanks to Martin Anderson, Karl R. Bendetsen, Hans A. Bethe, John T. Bosma, Gregory H. Canavan, Ashton B. Carter, George F. Chapline, Jr., Angelo M. Codevilla, Richard D. DeLauer, Hugh E. DeWitt, Sidney D. Drell, Gerald R. Ford, Richard L. Garwin, Peter Glazer, John W. Gofman, Daniel O. Graham, Carl Haussmann, William W. Hoover, R. Norris Keeler, Donald M. Kerr, George A. Keyworth 2nd, Ray E. Kidder, William A. Lokke, George Maenchen, Gerald E. Marsh, Robert C. McFarlane, W. Lowell Morgan, Paul H. Nitze, David Nowak, John H. Nuckolls, Ray Pollock, Theodore A. Postol, David L. Potter, John Rather, Victor H. Reis, Gilbert D. Rye, Gottfried T. Schappert, Harrison H. Schmitt, Robert W. Selden, Stanley K. Sheinbaum, H. Guyford Stever, Charles J. Taylor, Theodore Taylor, Edwin W. Thomas, Mary E. Tuszka, Edward W. Walbridge, Malcolm Wallop, Willard H. Wattenburg, Alvin M. Weinberg, William G. Wells, Jr., Barbara L. Whitten, Sandy Woodruff, Gerold Yonas, and Stephen M. Younger. Thanks as well to individuals who spoke but requested anonymity for political reasons, including Teller colleagues at Livermore, former White House officials, members of the White House Science Council and participants in the Frieman study for the White House Office of Science and Technology Policy.

A special thanks to Mrs. Karl R. Bendetsen, who opened the files of her late husband to me, and to the administrators and staff of the Hoover Institution in California, where the Bendetsen papers are kept.

The documents made public by such congressmen as George E. Brown, Jr., Edward J. Markey and Pete Stark were critical to the completion of this book. Many thanks to these men and their aides. My gratitude also extends to the staffers at the Energy Department who declassified and left largely intact a number of formerly secret documents, including Teller's letters to the White House. These federal servants, by interpreting their mandate liberally amid pressure to do otherwise, have aided their nation in a significant way.

A number of other individuals supplied copies of Livermore documents, reports and letters, greatly expanding upon those already made public. These donors wish to remain anonymous, so I will not thank them by name. But my debt, and gratitude, are great.

Four historians were generous with their time and materials. Many thanks to Gregg Herken of the Smithsonian Air and Space Museum, who shared manuscripts, notes and insights; to Robert S. Norris of the National Resources Defense Council, who helped clarify H-bomb history and many other matters; to Chuck Hansen, who lent his knowledge of nuclear lore and dug through his voluminous files to check important items; and to Donald R. Baucom, former historian of the Strategic Defense Initiative Organization, who provided his draft manuscript, *Origins of the Strategic Defense Initiative: Ballistic Missile Defense, 1944–1983*. It was a valuable guide to early Star Wars history, including the work of the Bendetsen committee.

Three journalists took time to discuss their X-ray laser experiences. Thanks to Bill Moseley, a free-lancer, to Clarence A. Robinson, Jr., formerly of *Aviation Week & Space Technology*; and to Keith Rogers, formerly of *The Valley Times* of California, whose enterprising coverage of the Livermore lab was a great help.

The public-affairs offices of the Lawrence Livermore National Laboratory, the Los Alamos National Laboratory and the Energy Department were generally prompt and courteous in tracking down articles and checking facts. So were Mike Doble and William J. O'Connell, spokesmen of the Strategic Defense Initiative Organization, who provided transcripts, articles, budget numbers and other assistance. The White House furnished copies of various speeches.

The librarians and libraries of *The New York Times*, *The Washington Post*, *The Washington Times*, *The Los Angeles Times*, *The Sacramento Bee* and *The Valley Times* were indispensable.

For materials and assistance, many thanks to Bruce R. Abell of the Hudson Institute, to Steven Aftergood and John E. Pike of the Federation of American Scientists, to Jean Baron of *The Washingtonian*, to Lesta Cordil of *Reader's Digest*, to Mark D. W. Edington of the Institute for Foreign Policy Analysis, to Patricia G. Garfinkel of the House Science Committee, to John Horgan of *Scientific American*, to Scott McMahon of High Frontier, to Bradley Miller of the Heritage Foundation, to Scott Peters of the U.S. Council for Energy Awareness, to Herbert M. Ryan of Dresser Industries, to Dan Snodderly of the Ethics and Public Policy Center, to Bob Tarver of the Committee on the Present Danger and to Robert Zirkle of the Union of Concerned Scientists.

At *The New York Times*, my colleague Nicholas Wade read an early draft of the manuscript and made a number of perceptive comments. Holcomb B. Noble read a late draft; his abundant insights and careful line-by-line editing were of major assistance. Thomas B. Cochran and Robert S. Norris of the Natural Resources Defense Council made many good suggestions, as did Gregg Herken of the Smithsonian Air and Space Museum. Many thanks as well to several manuscript readers familiar with the technical side of the X-ray laser story, who shall remain anonymous. It goes without saying that any errors of fact or interpretation are my own.

For able assistance in research, my gratitude goes to Gabriella Blanco and Julia Rothwax.

For encouragement throughout the ups and downs of writing this book, many thanks to Walter and Ingrid Blanco, Margaret Brennman-Gibson, Paul and Jody Gallo, Gina Kolata, Mary Jean Maier, Fabienne Marsh, Colin Norman, R. Jeffrey Smith, Josephine A. Stein, my parents in Milwaukee, my midwestern family and my wife's family.

At Simon & Schuster, Alice E. Mayhew performed the magic of turning a rambling manuscript into a book, aided by Eric Steel. Thanks also to Eric Rayman, Marcia Peterson, and Marcia B. Paul. Free-lance artist Jana Brenning drew the wonderful line drawings. My agent, Peter Matson of Sterling Lord Literistic, was the source of generous encouragement.

Lastly, I would like to thank my wife, Tanya, to whom this book is dedicated, for her wise counsel and unfailing support throughout the three-year project. Reading this kind of manuscript is no small accomplishment with small children around. Yet Tanya did that and much, much more. Her high standards were an inspiration to me from start to finish.

William J. Broad
Larchmont, New York
October 1991

# Notes

## PROLOGUE

1. The war-crimes episode is recounted in Stanley A. Blumberg and Gwinn Owens, *Energy and Conflict: The Life and Times of Edward Teller* (Putnam, New York, 1976), pp. 441–446. The other Teller details are found in standard biographical works.
2. Eugene P. Wigner, "An Appreciation of the 80th Birthday of Edward Teller," in Hans Mark and Lowell Wood, eds., *Energy in Physics, War and Peace: A Festschrift Celebrating Edward Teller's 80th Birthday* (Kluwer Academic Publishers, Boston, 1988), pp. 1, 12.
3. Quoted in Blumberg and Owens, p. 1.

### CHAPTER ONE

## ATOM VISIONARY

1. Interview, Alvin M. Weinberg, April 12, 1990.
2. Hans A. Bethe, "Comments on the History of the H-bomb," *Los Alamos Science*, Fall 1982, p. 49.
3. Quoted in Robert Coughlan, "Dr. Edward Teller's Magnificent Obsession," *Life*, September 6, 1954, p. 61.
4. Freeman Dyson, *Disturbing the Universe* (Harper & Row, New York, 1979), p. 98.
5. Quoted in Coughlan, p. 61.
6. Quoted in Norman Moss, *Men Who Play God: The Story of the H-Bomb and How the World Came to Live with It* (Harper & Row, New York, 1968), p. 68.
7. Blumberg and Owens, p. 6.
8. *Ibid.*, pp. 2, 8.
9. Edward Teller and Allen Brown, *The Legacy of Hiroshima* (Doubleday, Garden City, New York, 1962), p. 81.
10. Blumberg and Owens, p. 24.
11. Richard Rhodes, *The Making of the Atomic Bomb* (Simon & Schuster, New York, 1986), p. 106.
12. *Ibid.*, p. 104.
13. Quoted by Francis Crick, *Life Itself* (Simon & Schuster, New York, 1981), pp. 13–14.
14. Blumberg and Owens, p. 21.
15. *Ibid.*, pp. 25–26.
16. *Ibid.*, pp. 16–20.
17. *Ibid.*, p. 34.
18. *Ibid.*, p. 35.
19. Quoted in John Newhouse, *War and Peace in the Nuclear Age* (Knopf, New York, 1989), p. 38.

20. Wigner, p. 8.
21. *Ibid.*
22. Blumberg and Owens, p. 48.
23. Quoted in interview, Hans A. Bethe, December 7, 1989. Bethe witnessed this interaction as he worked beside Teller and Placzek in Rome at Fermi's laboratory where they had gone for a seminar. See Blumberg and Owens, pp. 46–48.
24. Wigner, p. 9.
25. Blumberg and Owens, p. 59.
26. This episode is recounted in Moss, *Men Who Play God*, pp. 67–68.
27. Blumberg and Owens, pp. 60–63.
28. Quoted in *ibid.*, p. 67.
29. Interview, Hans A. Bethe, December 7, 1989.
30. Wigner, p. 9.
31. Rhodes, pp. 269–271.
32. Blumberg and Owens, p. 83.
33. Quoted in *ibid.*, p. 87.
34. Rhodes, pp. 417, 538–547. For Teller's own description of his implosion work, see Blumberg and Owens, pp. 455–456.
35. Jeremy Bernstein, *Hans Bethe: Prophet of Energy* (Basic Books, New York, 1979), pp. 45–54.
36. Blumberg and Owens, p. 109; Edward Teller, *Better a Shield Than a Sword* (The Free Press, New York, 1987), p. 68.
37. Teller, *Better a Shield*, p. 68.
38. Blumberg and Owens, p. 116.
39. The episode was recounted in an interview with Hans A. Bethe, December 7, 1989; also see Rhodes, p. 418.
40. Arthur Holly Compton, *Atomic Quest* (Oxford University Press, New York, 1956), p. 127.
41. Interview, Hans A. Bethe, December 7, 1989; also see Rhodes, p. 419.
42. Nuel Pharr Davis, *Lawrence and Oppenheimer* (Simon & Schuster, New York, 1969), p. 131.
43. Teller, *Better a Shield*, p. 70.
44. Norman Moss, *Klaus Fuchs: The Man Who Stole the Atom Bomb* (St. Martin's Press, New York, 1987), p. 71.
45. Rudolf Peierls, *Bird of Passage: Recollections of a Physicist* (Princeton University Press, Princeton, 1985), pp. 199–200.
46. Dyson, p. 88.
47. Coughlan, p. 62.
48. Quoted in Strobe Talbott, *The Master of the Game: Paul Nitze and the Nuclear Peace* (Knopf, New York, 1988), p. 49.
49. Rhodes, pp. 771–772.
50. Bethe, "Comments on the History of the H-bomb," p. 47.
51. Quoted in John McPhee, *The Curve of Binding Energy* (Ballantine, New York, 1975), p. 64.
52. For an overview of the new H-bomb history see William J. Broad, "Spy's Role in Soviet H-bomb Now Discounted," *The New York Times*, January 3, 1990, p. A1.
53. Quoted in Stanley A. Blumberg and Louis G. Panos, *Edward Teller: Giant of the Golden Age of Physics* (Scribners, New York, 1990), p. 124.
54. Thomas B. Cochran and Robert S. Norris, "Nuclear Weapons," *Encyclopedia Britannica*, 15th edition, 1990, Vol. 29, p. 579.
55. Blumberg and Owens, p. 280.

56. Edward Teller, "The Work of Many People," *Science*, February 25, 1955, p. 267.

57. Blumberg and Panos, pp. 124–125.

58. "H-Mystery Man: He Hurried the H-bomb," *Newsweek*, August 2, 1954, p. 23.

59. James Shepley and Clay Blair Jr., *The Hydrogen Bomb* (McKay, New York, 1954).

60. Chuck Hansen, *U.S. Nuclear Weapons: The Secret History* (Crown, New York, 1988), p. 56.

61. Quoted in Moss, *Men Who Play God*, p. 78.

62. Quoted in "Knowledge Is Power," *Time*, November 18, 1957, p. 21.

63. Herbert York, *The Advisors: Oppenheimer, Teller and the Superbomb* (W.H. Freeman, San Francisco, 1976), p. 133.

64. Hansen, p. 39.

65. Teller and Brown, p. 64.

66. Interview, Hans A. Bethe, December 7, 1989.

67. Letter, Joseph E. St. Sauver to author, January 9, 1983. A different explanation for the failure is found in Hansen, p. 67.

68. Hansen, pp. 67, 70–73.

69. York, p. 134.

70. Quoted in Richard Rhodes, "Teller's Charges Discredited Oppenheimer," *The New York Times*, April 7, 1990, p. A24.

71. Blumberg and Owens, pp. 358–360.

72. *In the Matter of J. Robert Oppenheimer: Transcript of Hearing before Personnel Security Board and Texts of Principal Documents and Letters* (MIT Press, Cambridge, 1971), p. 726.

73. This episode is recounted in Duane C. Sewell, "The Branch Laboratory at Livermore during the 1950's," in Hans Mark and Lowell Wood, eds., *Energy in Physics, War and Peace: A Festschrift Celebrating Edward Teller's 80th Birthday* (Kluwer Academic Publishers, Boston, 1988), p. 323.

74. "Thirty Years of Technical Excellence, 1952–1982," Lawrence Livermore National Laboratory, 1982, pp. 2, 5.

75. Glenn T. Seaborg, *Kennedy, Khrushchev and the Test Ban* (University of California Press, Berkeley, 1981), p. 8.

76. Quoted in Stephen E. Ambrose, *Eisenhower the President* (Simon & Schuster, New York, 1984), p. 399.

77. John W. Finney, "U.S. Eliminates 95 Percent of Fall-Out From the H-bomb," *The New York Times*, June 25, 1957, p. 1.

78. Ambrose, p. 399.

79. James Reston, "Eisenhower Wary of Atom Test Ban," *The New York Times*, June 27, 1957, p. 1.

80. These three government documents are quoted in Chuck Hansen, "Operation Hardtack and the 'Clean Bomb,' " 1989, unpublished manuscript. For a description of this work, see William J. Broad, "From Cold War to Nuclear Nostalgia," *The New York Times*, December 12, 1989, p. 1.

81. Edward Teller and Albert L. Latter, *Our Nuclear Future* (Criterion, New York, 1958), p. 85.

82. The project is described in detail by Dan O'Neill, "Project Chariot: How Alaska Escaped Nuclear Excavation," *The Bulletin of the Atomic Scientists*, December 1989, p. 28.

83. Quoted in *ibid.*, p. 33.

84. Edward Teller, "We're Going to Work Miracles," *Popular Mechanics*, March 1960, p. 97.

85. Quoted in O'Neill, p. 34.

86. *Ibid.*, pp. 34–35.

87. Interview, Theodore Taylor, May 31, 1989.

88. Joan Lisa Bromberg, *Fusion: Science, Politics, and the Invention of a New Energy Source* (MIT Press, Cambridge, 1982), p. 18.

89. Quoted in "Magnetic Bottle," *Time*, June 18, 1956, p. 71.

90. Edward Teller, "Can We Harness Nuclear Fusion in the 70's?" *Popular Science*, May 1972, p. 88.

91. Quoted in Richard McCormack, "Teller Speaks on Greenhouse, SDI, Nuclear Power, Presidents and More," *New Technology Week*, March 20, 1989, p. 6.

92. Teller and Brown, p. 128.

93. *Ibid.*, pp. 233–235.

94. *Ibid.*, p. 236.

95. *Ibid.*, p. 128.

96. For an overview of the test and its effects, see William J. Broad, "Nuclear Pulse: Awakening to the Chaos Factor," *Science*, May 29, 1981, p. 1009.

97. The Senate testimony is reprinted in Teller, *Better a Shield*, pp. 106–113.

98. Quoted in "Man with a Mission," *Newsweek*, September 2, 1963, p. 22.

99. Seaborg, pp. 269, 272.

100. Blumberg and Owens, p. 414.

101. Quoted in "Dollars vs. Lives—A U.S. Choice," *U.S. News & World Report*, May 29, 1967, p. 45.

102. William R. Kintner, ed., *Safeguard: Why the ABM Makes Sense* (Hawthorn, New York, 1969), p. 101.

103. "Cannikin: Cold Days in Alaska," *LLL 25 Years in Pictures*, Lawrence Livermore Laboratory, 1977, p. 18.

104. "Not Only Humane, But Truly Effective," *U.S. News & World Report*, May 26, 1969, p. 87.

105. Wallace Turner, "Aleutian H-Bomb Is Fired Without Setting Off Quake," *The New York Times*, October 3, 1969, p. 1.

106. "The Amchitka Affair . . . ," *The New York Times*, July 4, 1971, section 4, p. 10.

107. "Cannikin," Livermore, pp. 18–19; Anthony Ripley, "After 3 Nuclear Explosions, A.E.C. Is Leaving Amchitka to Wind and Fog," *The New York Times*, August 5, 1973, p. 37.

108. Thomas B. Cochran, William M. Arkin, Milton M. Hoenig, *Nuclear Weapons Databook: Volume One, U.S. Nuclear Forces and Capabilities* (Ballinger, Cambridge, 1984), pp. 163–165.

109. Interview, weapon expert.

110. Lowell Wood and John Nuckolls, "The Development of Nuclear Explosives," in Hans Mark and Lowell Wood, eds., *Energy in Physics, War and Peace: A Festschrift Celebrating Edward Teller's 80th Birthday* (Kluwer Academic Publishers, Boston, 1988), p. 317.

111. Blumberg and Owens, p. 379.

112. Michael Kramer and Sam Roberts, *I Never Wanted to Be Vice-President of Anything: An Investigative Biography of Nelson Rockefeller* (Basic Books, New York, 1976), pp. 219–220.

113. Blumberg and Owens, p. 1.

114. Interview, weapon expert.

115. Interview, Charles J. Taylor, December 18, 1989.

116. Quoted in *ibid.*

117. Interview, Charles J. Taylor, January 14, 1990.

118. For examples of such considerations see William J. Broad, "A Fatal Flaw in

the Concept of Space War," *Science*, March 12, 1982, p. 1372; William J. Broad, "Star Wars: Pentagon Lunacy," *The New York Times*, May 13, 1982, p. A27.

119. Interview, weapon expert. General Starbird is dead and William A. Lokke declined comment, saying, "It's not time to talk" about the clash, interview, December 15, 1989.

120. David Binder, "U.S., Soviet Agree on Size of A-Tests for Peaceful Use," *The New York Times*, April 10, 1976, p. 1.

121. Cochran *et al.*, *Nuclear Weapons Databook, Volume One*, p. 164.

122. Blumberg and Owens, p. 435.

123. Daniel Ford, *Cult of the Atom* (Simon & Schuster, New York, 1982), p. 230.

124. Aljean Harmetz, "When Nuclear Crisis Imitates a Film," *The New York Times*, April 4, 1979, section 3, p. 18.

125. Teller, *Better a Shield*, p. 159. For a review of his work there, see Joseph G. Morone and Edward J. Woodhouse, *The Demise of Nuclear Energy? Lessons for Democratic Control of Technology* (Yale, New Haven, 1989), pp. 67–70.

126. Edward Teller, *Energy from Heaven and Earth* (W. H. Freeman & Company, San Francisco, 1979).

127. "Playboy Interview, Edward Teller," *Playboy*, August 1979, p. 59.

128. "Teller," Associated Press, May 7, 1979.

129. "People in the News," Associated Press, April 16, 1979; *Playboy*, p. 194.

130. Quoted in Walter Pincus, "Reactors Safer Than Alternatives, Scientists Say," *The Washington Post*, May 8, 1979, p. A15; Jim Luther, "Energy Future," Associated Press, May 8, 1979.

131. Edward Teller, "I WAS THE ONLY VICTIM OF THREE MILE ISLAND," *The Wall Street Journal*, July 31, 1979.

132. "Propaganda," *The New York Times*, August 17, 1979, p. 24.

133. Quoted in R. M. Campbell, "Freedom Power," *The New York Times*, December 12, 1979, p. A30. See also prepared notes, "Remarks of Dr. Edward Teller," 1979, annual conference of the Atomic Industrial Forum.

CHAPTER TWO

## A REBELLIOUS AIDE

1. R. D. Woodruff, "Nuclear Weapons and American Defense Policy," *Defense Science 2001*, December 1983, p. 45.

2. Interview, Roy D. Woodruff, January 13, 1984.

3. William J. Broad, "Some Atomic Tests Being Kept Secret by Administration," *The New York Times*, January 29, 1984, p. A1.

4. Interview, Roy D. Woodruff, July 16, 1989. Much of this biographical section is based on this interview.

5. Interview, Roy D. Woodruff, July 21, 1989.

6. *Ibid.*

7. *Ibid.*

8. Roy D. Woodruff, Application for Employment, University of California Lawrence Radiation Laboratory, February 15, 1968.

9. Interview, Roy D. Woodruff, July 16, 1989.

10. James P. Sterba, "Atom-Test Blast Set in Colorado," *The New York Times*, May 13, 1973, p. 26.

11. Quoted in Edward C. Burks, "Republican Governors Assured of 'More Open' Administration," *The New York Times*, May 11, 1973, p. 17.

12. Interview, Roy D. Woodruff, July 16, 1989.

13. Quoted in James P. Sterba, "A-Blast in Colorado Does Less Damage Than Was Expected," *The New York Times*, May 18, 1973, p. 1.

14. Interview, Roy D. Woodruff, July 16, 1989.

15. *Ibid.*

16. *Ibid.*

17. William J. Broad, "Bomb Tests: Technology Advances Against Backdrop of Wide Debate," *The New York Times*, April 15, 1986, p. C1.

18. *Ibid.*

19. William J. Broad, *Star Warriors* (Simon & Schuster, New York, 1985), p. 107.

20. Bill Moseley, "Interview: Star Warrior Peter Hagelstein," *Omni*, May 1989, p. 91.

21. Interview, Roy D. Woodruff, July 16, 1989.

22. Broad, *Star Warriors*, pp. 109–110.

23. *Ibid.*; interview, Roy D. Woodruff, November 18, 1990.

24. Broad, *Star Warriors*, p. 111; interview, Roy D. Woodruff, November 18, 1990.

25. Interview, Roy D. Woodruff, July 16, 1989.

26. Interview, weapon expert.

27. Broad, *Star Warriors*, pp. 20–46.

28. Interview, Carl Haussmann, May 9, 1984.

29. Broad, *Star Warriors*, pp. 178–180.

30. *Ibid.*, p. 181.

31. Letter, Lowell Wood to Joe Nilsen, January 23, 1985.

32. Broad, *Star Warriors*, pp. 96–107.

33. Moseley, p. 78.

34. *Ibid.*, p. 91.

35. Broad, *Star Warriors*, p. 113.

36. Moseley, p. 91.

37. Interview, weapon expert.

38. Broad, *Star Warriors*, p. 114.

39. *Ibid.*, p. 116.

40. Interviews, weapon experts.

41. Ashton B. Carter, "Directed Energy Missile Defense in Space," Congressional Office of Technology Assessment, April 1984, p. 25.

42. Interviews, weapon experts.

43. *Ibid.*

44. Interview, George F. Chapline, Jr., October 31, 1990.

45. Moseley, p. 91.

46. Broad, "Bomb Tests."

47. Interview, George F. Chapline, Jr., October 31, 1990.

48. *Ibid.*

49. Broad, *Star Warriors*, pp. 116–117.

50. *Ibid.*, pp. 118–119.

51. Interviews, weapon experts. A joule is an extremely small unit of energy— about one watt over a period of one second. A 100-watt light bulb uses 6,000 joules of energy a minute.

52. *Ibid.*

53. *Ibid.*

54. *Ibid.*

55. Interview, Roy D. Woodruff, July 18, 1989.

56. This exchange is based on interviews, William W. Hoover, September 25, 1991, and Roy D. Woodruff, July 18, 1989.

57. Interview, Roy D. Woodruff, July 18, 1989; the congressional trip is also mentioned in Gregg Herken, *Counsels of War* (Oxford University Press, New York, 1987), p. 338.

58. Clarence A. Robinson, Jr., "Advance Made on High-Energy Laser," *Aviation Week & Space Technology*, February 23, 1981, p. 25.

59. Interview, Richard D. DeLauer, December 5, 1989.

*CHAPTER THREE*

## THE SELLING OF STAR WARS

1. For a description of the seminar and its location, see Mary McGory, "Seminar: 'Ain't Gonna Study War No More,' " *The Washington Post*, September 18, 1983, p. C1.

2. Proceedings of the "International Seminar on the World-Wide Implications of a Nuclear War," E. Majorana Center for Scientific Culture, Erice, August 14–19, 1981. My thanks to Richard Garwin for a copy of this document.

3. Ronald Reagan with Richard G. Hubler, *Where's the Rest of Me?* (Karz, New York, 1981), p. 17.

4. Dialogue Transcript, *Murder in the Air*, New York State Archives, January 29, 1940; also see Philip M. Boffey *et al.*, *Claiming the Heavens* (Times Books, New York, 1988), pp. 3–6.

5. Ronald Reagan, *An American Life* (Simon & Schuster, New York, 1990), pp. 126–131; see also Lou Cannon, *President Reagan: The Role of a Lifetime* (Simon & Schuster, New York, 1991), pp. 88–89, 321.

6. Boffey *et al.*, p. 7; James Chace and Caleb Carr, *America Invulnerable* (Summit, New York, 1988), p. 294.

7. Interview, Edward Teller, February 26, 1985, quoted in William J. Broad, "Reagan's Star Wars Bid: Many Ideas Converging," *The New York Times*, March 4, 1985, p. A1.

8. Chace and Carr, p. 294; Teller, *Better a Shield*, p. 38.

9. Edward Teller, "SDI: The Last, Best Hope," *Insight* magazine (*Washington Times*), October 28, 1985, p. 75.

10. Chace and Carr, pp. 294–295.

11. Quoted in "Reagan, Top Scientists Air Issues," *Sacramento Bee*, June 4, 1971, p. A5.

12. Cannon, pp. 288–291, 319, 326.

13. Quoted in Martin Anderson, *Revolution* (Harcourt, Brace, Jovanovich, New York, 1988), pp. 63–72.

14. Quoted in Ronnie Drugger, *On Reagan: The Man & His Presidency* (McGraw-Hill, New York, 1983), p. 423.

15. Interview, Martin Anderson, August 8, 1986.

16. Robert Scheer, *With Enough Shovels: Reagan, Bush & Nuclear War* (Random House, New York, 1982), pp. 232–233.

17. Martin Anderson, "Policy Memorandum No. 3, Reagan for President, Foreign Policy and National Security," August 1979. My thanks to Anderson for a copy of this document.

18. *Ibid.*

19. James Canan, *War in Space* (Harper & Row, New York, 1982), pp. 153, 158.

20. Interview transcript, Daniel O. Graham, July 7, 1987, interviewed by Lieutenant Colonel Donald R. Baucom, historian, Strategic Defense Initiative Organization, p. 3. For B Team history, see Talbott, pp. 144–147.

21. "Project Defender," Congressional Research Service, July 1987.

22. Interview, Graham, SDIO, p. 5.
23. Interview, Angelo M. Codevilla, Wallop's aide, August 19, 1986.
24. Malcolm Wallop, "Opportunities and Imperatives of Ballistic Missile Defense," *Strategic Review*, Fall 1979, p. 13.
25. Interview, Angelo M. Codevilla, August 19, 1986.
26. Interview, Martin Anderson, August 8, 1986.
27. "1980 Republican Platform Text," *Congressional Quarterly Almanac*, 1980, p. 58-B.
28. Interview, Harrison H. Schmitt, February 26, 1985.
29. Interview, Martin Anderson, August 8, 1986.
30. Robert Reinhold, "Los Alamos Physicist May Get Post As Science Adviser in White House," *The New York Times*, May 8, 1981, p. A20.
31. Quoted in Herken, *Counsels*, p. 397.
32. Robert Reinhold, "13 Experts Named to Counsel Reagan's Adviser for Science," *The New York Times*, February 18, 1982, p. A12.
33. Quoted in Gregg Herken, "The Earthly Origins of Star Wars," *Bulletin of the Atomic Scientists*, October 1987, p. 23.
34. Interview, Karl R. Bendetsen, February 21, 1985. Bendetsen died of a heart attack in June 1989. For biographical background see "Karl R. Bendetsen, 81, Executive and High-Ranking U.S. Official," *The New York Times*, June 30, 1989, section 1, p. 16, and *Current Biography* (W.H. Wilson, New York, 1952), pp. 47-48. For Bendetsen's link to the Committee on the Present Danger, interview, Bob Tarver, research associate for the committee, April 30, 1991.
35. Lieutenant Colonel Donald R. Baucom, historian, Strategic Defense Initiative Organization, "Origins of the Strategic Defense Initiative: Ballistic Missile Defense, 1944–1983," draft manuscript, December 1989, p. 276.
36. Interview, Karl R. Bendetsen, February 21, 1985.
37. Baucom, "Origins," p. 273.
38. Agenda, High Frontier Panel Meeting, September 5, 1981. This document is in the Karl Bendetsen collection, Hoover Institution archives, Stanford University (hereafter "Bendetsen collection").
39. Letter, Karl R. Bendetsen, "Some Ground Rules for Participants," August 26, 1981. Bendetsen collection.
40. Anderson, p. 90.
41. *Ibid.*, p. 91.
42. *Ibid.*, p. 94; Letter, Karl Bendetsen to Edward Teller, August 26, 1981. Bendetsen collection.
43. Anderson, pp. 94–95.
44. "Summary of remarks by Edward Teller," addendum to a memorandum by Karl R. Bendetsen to the Secretary of Defense [Caspar Weinberger], September 14, 1981. The letter described the White House meeting to Weinberger. Bendetsen collection.
45. Teller was not the only antimissile advocate to use the term "assured survival." But he appears to have been among the first and clearly was central in giving the notion currency high in the Reagan administration, starting in 1981. General Graham in his 1982 High Frontier report adopted the phrase, although his goals were far less ambitious than Teller's and his use of the phrase thus more ambiguous (Lieut. Gen. Daniel O. Graham, *High Frontier: A New National Strategy*, Heritage Foundation, Washington). In 1983, after the Star Wars speech, Teller used the phrase in print to describe Reagan's antimissile goals (Edward Teller, "Reagan's Courage," *The New York Times*, March 30, 1983, p. A30). By 1984 the idea was so popular that it became a book title, *Mutual Assured Survival* (Baen Books, Simon & Schuster, New York). Although this antimissile paean was authored by Jerry

Pournelle and Dean Ing, it is notable that two technical contributors were Lowell Wood and Rod Hyde, both protégés of Teller.

46. Interview, Graham, SDIO, p. 9.

47. *Ibid.*

48. Interview, Daniel O. Graham, February 18, 1985, quoted in William J. Broad, "Reagan's Star Wars Bid: Many Ideas Converging," *The New York Times*, March 4, 1985, p. A1.

49. Quoted in William J. Broad, "Space Weapon Idea Now Being Weighed Was Assailed in '82," *The New York Times*, May 4, 1987, p. A1.

50. Anderson, p. 95.

51. Letter, Karl Bendetsen to Edwin Meese, October 20, 1981. Bendetsen collection. A copy of this letter is also contained in Livermore's files, under Teller's classification code, suggesting he had a hand in its preparation. Moreover, the letter's format is conspicuously different from all others in the Bendetsen collection, its style being that of a Livermore interdepartmental memorandum. Such facts, considered in light of the letter's precise technical language, argue that it was a Livermore memo to which Bendetsen lent his name.

52. Interview, Graham, SDIO, p. 9.

53. Interview, Roy D. Woodruff, December 16, 1989.

54. Angelo Codevilla, *While Others Build* (Free Press, New York, 1988), p. 71.

55. Interview, Victor H. Reis, December 9, 1989.

56. Codevilla, p. 83.

57. William J. Broad, "Laser Wars on Capitol Hill," *Science*, June 4, 1982, p. 1082.

58. Agenda and Attendees for High Frontier Panel, "Classified Briefing by Dr. Teller on Nuclear Options," Dr. Keyworth's facilities, November 2, 1981. The Bendetsen collection.

59. Interview, Peter Glazer of Arthur D. Little, participant in High Frontier briefing, January 30, 1990.

60. The split is covered in detail in Baucom, "Origins," pp. 296–317.

61. Seth S. King, "New Layoffs Push U.S. Jobless Rate to 8.9% From 8.4%," *The New York Times*, January 9, 1982, p. 1.

62. Anderson, p. 95.

63. *Ibid.*, pp. 95–97.

64. Evidence of whether Teller participated in the White House meeting of January 8, 1982, is mixed. Long before he died, Bendetsen told me Teller was there (interview, Karl R. Bendetsen, February 21, 1985). So, too, Anderson in *Revolution* says Teller was there (p. 95). Anderson later told me he looked up Teller's schedule at the Hoover Institution for his whereabouts on that date, finding he was in Washington. Anderson concluded Teller was definitely at the meeting (interview, Martin Anderson, September 7, 1990). Edwin W. Thomas, a White House aide who helped set up the meeting, initially said Teller was there but later changed his mind (interviews, Edwin W. Thomas, September 14, 1990). Keyworth said his "recollection" was that Teller was absent (letter, Bruce Abell, Keyworth's assistant, to author, September 24, 1990). Bendetsen's correspondence to panel members the day after the meeting lists Hume and Coors as his companions but makes no mention of Teller (letter, Karl [R. Bendetsen], "Report to Members of the High Frontier Project Panel," January 9, 1982; Bendetsen collection). One interpretation of the evidence is that Teller was there but his presence downplayed to minimize friction with General Graham, who, though excluded from the meeting, was still being pressed by the Bendetsen panel to keep his report private. General Graham believes this might be the case (interview, General Graham, January 25, 1990). Indeed, on January 9, the day after the meeting, Teller wrote General Graham from

the Cosmos Club in Washington to urge him to keep the High Frontier report private, implying he did not attend the Bendetsen meeting with the president (letter, Edward Teller to General Daniel O. Graham, January 9, 1982; Bendetsen collection). In general, Teller has been vague on when he first met with the president. He told auditors from the General Accounting Office that the first time he "saw" the president was in September 1982 after his appeal on *Firing Line* (transcript, GAO Interview with Edward Teller, November 24, 1987, p. 10). Later, he told a trusted colleague that the September meeting was the only one with Reagan before the Star Wars speech "in circumstances where I could talk," implying there were other ones (Ken Adelman, interview with Edward Teller, "Washington Is a Mystery," *The Washingtonian*, October 1988, p. 96).

65. Interview, Karl R. Bendetsen, February 21, 1985.

66. "Final Report to the President by the High Frontier Panel," January 8, 1982. Bendetsen collection.

67. Anderson, p. 96.

68. Interview, Karl R. Bendetsen, February 21, 1985.

69. Letter, Ron [Ronald Reagan] to Karl R. Bendetsen, on White House stationery, January 20, 1982. Bendetsen collection.

70. Interview, Graham, SDIO, p. 11.

71. Lieut. Gen. Daniel O. Graham, *High Frontier: A New National Strategy* (Heritage Foundation, Washington, 1982), p. x.

72. Letter, G. [George] A. Keyworth to The Honorable Karl Bendetsen, November 10, 1981.

73. Letter, Karl Bendetsen, "Report to the Members of the High Frontier Project Panel," January 9, 1982. Bendetsen collection.

74. Martin Anderson, "Minutes of Management Meeting," White House, January 11, 1982. My thanks to Anderson for a copy of these handwritten notes.

75. Interview, Victor H. Reis, December 9, 1989.

76. Interview, member of White House Science Council, January 22, 1990.

77. *Ibid.*

78. Interview, former White House official, June 10, 1990.

79. Transcript, *Firing Line*, Southern Educational Communications Association, June 15, 1982.

80. Interview, Edward Teller, February 26, 1985.

81. Blumberg and Panos, p. 7.

82. Quoted in interview, Ray Pollock, January 19, 1990. Pollock was a staff member of the National Security Council present at the White House meeting.

83. *Ibid.*

84. Teller recalled this part of his White House visit on a *Firing Line* program. Transcript, Southern Educational Communications Association, October 19, 1987, p. 8.

85. Blumberg and Panos, p. 8.

86. Interview, Ray Pollock, January 19, 1990.

87. Quoted in Blumberg and Panos, p. 8.

88. Interview, Ray Pollock, January 19, 1990.

89. "Laser Talks," *Aviation Week & Space Technology*, September 20, 1982, p. 15.

90. Letter, Edward Teller to The Honorable Ronald Reagan, President, September 25, 1982, declassified with deletions.

91. Letter, Edward Teller to Karl R. Bendetsen, December 29, 1982, on Hoover Institution letterhead, with attachment, "Proposal for Inclusion in the President's State of the Union Address." Bendetsen collection.

92. Letter, Karl R. Bendetsen to Teller and other members of the High Frontier

Panel, December 27, 1982, with attachment, "Proposal for Inclusion in the President's State of the Union Address." Bendetsen collection.

93. Paul L. Montgomery, "Throngs Fill Manhattan to Protest Nuclear Weapons," *The New York Times*, June 13, 1982, p. 1.

94. Jonathan Schell, *The Fate of the Earth* (Knopf, New York, 1982).

95. Quoted in Robert C. Williams and Philip L. Cantelon, eds., *The American Atom* (University of Pennsylvania Press, Philadelphia, 1984), p. 282.

96. Hedrick Smith, *The Power Game* (Random House, New York, 1988), p. 605; see also Reagan, *An American Life*, p. 560.

97. Quoted in Anderson, p. 97.

98. *Ibid.*

99. Quoted in Richard Halloran, "Navy's Chief Discusses Morality and Weapons," *The New York Times*, May 6, 1983, p. A32.

100. Donald R. Baucom, "Hail to the Chiefs," *Policy Review* (Heritage Foundation), Summer 1990, p. 71; Baucom, "Origins," p. 365.

101. Quoted in Blumberg and Panos, p. 8.

102. Smith, *The Power Game*, p. 607; Blumberg and Panos, p. 9; Baucom, "Hail," pp. 71–72; Baucom, "Origins," pp. 369–371.

103. Transcript, *Firing Line*, October 19, 1987, p. 9.

104. Quoted by Teller in *ibid.*

105. Interview, Robert C. McFarlane, December 5, 1989.

106. Letter, Robert C. McFarlane to author, November 15, 1989.

107. For the president's reason for striking no bargains see Reagan, *An American Life*, p. 548.

108. Baucom, "Hail," p. 72.

109. Baucom, "Origins," p. 376; Smith, *The Power Game*, p. 608. The White House discussion that follows is based on Smith.

110. Quoted in *ibid.*

111. *Ibid.*

112. *Ibid.*

113. Quoted in Caspar Weinberger, *Fighting for Peace: Seven Critical Years in the Pentagon* (Warner, New York, 1990), p. 304.

114. *Ibid.*

115. Baucom, "Hail," p. 72.

116. Smith, *The Power Game*, p. 613.

117. "The President's View," *Newsweek*, March 18, 1985, p. 21; also see Reagan, *An American Life*, pp. 547–548.

118. Smith, *The Power Game*, pp. 609–610.

119. Interview, Ray Pollock, January 19, 1990.

120. Broad, *Star Warriors*, pp. 123–124.

121. Interview, Roy D. Woodruff, July 18, 1989. This description of the La Jolla meeting is based primarily on the Woodruff interview, corroborated in parts by the Reis interview, December 9, 1989, and by an interview with a member of the White House Science Council, January 22, 1990.

122. *Ibid.*

123. Interview, weapon expert.

124. Thomas B. Cochran, William M. Arkin, Robert S. Norris, Milton M. Hoenig, *Nuclear Weapons Databook: Volume Two, U.S. Nuclear Warhead Production* (Ballinger, Cambridge, 1987), pp. 12–13.

125. Interview, member of the White House Science Council, January 22, 1990.

126. Quoted in Robert Scheer, "Teller's Obsession Became Reality in 'Star Wars' Plan," *The Los Angeles Times*, July 10, 1983, section 6, p. 6.

127. Interview, member of the White House Science Council, January 22, 1990.

128. Interview, Roy D. Woodruff, December 16, 1989. The confrontation between Woodruff and Teller is based on this interview.

129. *Ibid.*; interview, Sandy Woodruff, January 20, 1990.

130. Interviews, Roy D. Woodruff, July 18, December 16, 1989.

131. *Ibid.*; see also "Briefing to Congressmen George Brown and Pete Stark on GAO's report on the accuracy of statements concerning DOE's X-ray laser research program," General Accounting Office, September 28, 1988, p. 12.

132. "System Concept Study," Martin Marietta Denver Aerospace, February 1983.

133. Interview, Frieman study participant, August 21, 1986.

134. Janne E. Nolan, *Guardians of the Arsenal* (Basic Books, New York, 1989), p. 13.

135. Quoted in Herken, *Counsels*, p. 342.

136. Interview, Gilbert D. Rye, February 6, 1990.

137. Letter, Victor H. Reis to author, September 14, 1986.

138. For more on Keyworth's conversion see Herken, "The Earthly Origins," pp. 25–26; Smith, *The Power Game*, pp. 610–612.

139. For more on quick-deployment pressures see Frank Greve, "How Reagan's Plan Caught Many Administration Insiders by Surprise," *San Jose Mercury News*, November 17, 1985, p. 1.

140. Blumberg and Panos, pp. 2–3.

141. "President's Speech on Military Spending and a New Defense," *The New York Times*, March 24, 1983, p. A20.

142. *Ibid.*

143. Teller, "SDI: The Last, Best Hope," p. 77.

144. Herken, "The Earthly Origins," p. 27.

145. Quoted in R. Jeffrey Smith, "Reagan Plans New ABM Effort," *Science*, April 8, 1983, p. 170.

146. "President's Speech," *The New York Times*.

147. Edward Teller, "Reagan's Courage," *The New York Times*, March 30, 1983, p. A30.

148. Letter, Victor H. Reis to author, September 14, 1986.

149. "Star Wars," *Newsweek*, April 4, 1983.

150. Reagan, *An American Life*, p. 547.

151. Interview, William W. Hoover, September 25, 1991.

152. Letter, Robert C. McFarlane to author, November 15, 1989; interview, December 5, 1989.

153. Reagan, *An American Life*, p. 550.

*CHAPTER FOUR*

## CRACKS IN THE SHIELD

1. Boffey *et al.*, pp. 82–84; William J. Broad, "Anti-Missile Laser Project Is Delayed Nearly 2 Years," *The New York Times*, April 17, 1988, section 1, p. 36.

2. William J. Broad, "Critics Say 'Star Wars' Test May Be a Treaty Violation," *The New York Times*, May 12, 1990, section 1, p. 9.

3. Wayne Biddle, " 'Star Wars' Technology: It's More Than a Fantasy," *The New York Times*, March 5, 1985, p. A1; Boffey *et al.*, p. 93.

4. The explosion of the space shuttle Challenger in January 1986 threw this antimissile program, and many others that were dependent on the shuttle, into disarray. See William J. Broad, "Reverberations of the Space Crisis: A Troubled Future for 'Star Wars.' " *The New York Times*, June 15, 1986, section 1, p. 1.

5. William J. Broad, "Allies in Europe Are Apprehensive About Benefits of 'Star Wars' Plan," *The New York Times*, May 13, 1985, p. A1.

6. *Ibid.*

7. "Strategic Defense Initiative Program: Extent of Foreign Participation," General Accounting Office, GAO/NSIAD 90-2, February 1990.

8. Handwritten notes, Bendetsen panel meeting, September 11, 1984. Bendetsen collection.

9. Quoted in Smith, *The Power Game*, p. 612; this interaction was first reported in Robert Scheer, "Flaws Peril Pivotal 'Star Wars' Laser," *Los Angeles Times*, September 23, 1985, p. 1. It was confirmed by DeLauer in an interview, December 5, 1989.

10. Interview, Gilbert D. Rye, February 6, 1990.

11. "Nuke," United Press International, March 23, 1983.

12. "Underground Nuclear Test Postponed at Least One Day," Associated Press, March 24, 1983; "National Briefs," Associated Press, March 26, 1983.

13. Interview, weapon expert.

14. Interview, Roy D. Woodruff, July 18, 1989.

15. Interview, weapon expert.

16. Interview, Roy D. Woodruff, July 18, 1989.

17. Testimony, Edward Teller, April 28, 1983. *Defense Department Authorization and Oversight Hearings*, Committee on Armed Services, House of Representatives, Ninety-eighth Congress, first session. Part 5 of 8 parts. Research, Development, Test, and Evaluation—Title II, pp. 1353–1371.

18. *Ibid.*, p. 1357.

19. "Memorandum for the President," May 23, 1983. Bendetsen collection.

20. *Public Papers of the Presidents*, National Medal of Science, Remarks at the Awards Presentation Ceremony, Presidential Document 769, May 24, 1983.

21. "Defensive Technologies Study Sets Funding Profile Options," *Aviation Week & Space Technology*, October 24, 1983, p. 50.

22. Interview, Gerold Yonas, February 23, 1985.

23. Quoted in letter, R. D. Woodruff to Distribution, February 4, 1985, on Livermore letterhead, declassified with deletions. This point is also made in United States General Accounting Office, "SDI Program: Evaluation of DOE's Answers to Questions on X-ray Laser Experiment," GAO/NSIAD-86-140BR, June 1986, p. 5.

24. Quoted in Gerold Yonas, "The Strategic Defense Initiative," *Daedalus*, Spring 1985, p. 75.

25. Interview, Fletcher panel member, February 23, 1985; also quoted in William J. Broad, "Reagan's Star Wars Bid: Many Ideas Converging," *The New York Times*, March 4, 1985, p. A1.

26. Quoted in Sanford Lakoff and Herbert F. York, *A Shield in Space?* (University of California Press, Berkeley, 1989), p. 14.

27. Quoted in Tina Rosenberg, "The Authorized Version," *The Atlantic*, February 1986, p. 26.

28. Quoted in Jerome B. Wiesner and Kosta Tsipis, "Put Star Wars Before a Panel," *The New York Times*, November 11, 1986, p. A25.

29. Interview, weapon expert.

30. "Energy Weapons," *Aviation Week & Space Technology*, September 5, 1983, p. 17.

31. Clarence A. Robinson, Jr., "Study Urges Exploiting of Technologies," *Aviation Week & Space Technology*, October 24, 1983, p. 50.

32. Charles Mohr, "Reagan Is Urged to Increase Research on Exotic Defenses Against Missiles," *The New York Times*, November 5, 1983, p. A32.

33. Quoted in Rosenberg, p. 28.

34. Interviews, Ray E. Kidder, December 13, 1989, June 13, 1990.

35. "Underground Test Conducted After Wind Delays," Associated Press, December 16, 1983.

36. Interviews, weapon experts.

37. Interview, Roy D. Woodruff, July 16, 1989.

38. Edward Teller, "A Gleam in the Eye of SDI," *The Washington Times*, February 23, 1988, p. F1.

39. Letter, Edward Teller to George A. Keyworth, December 22, 1983. A declassified version of Teller's letter containing numerous deletions was prepared by the Energy Department at the request of Congressmen George E. Brown of California and Edward J. Markey of Massachusetts, who released it and other documents on August 1, 1988. (Other documents in this group are hereafter referred to as coming from the "Brown-Markey collection.")

40. This and other formerly secret parts of the Keyworth letter are detailed in "Accuracy of Statements Concerning DOE's X-ray Laser Research Program," General Accounting Office, June 1988, GAO/NSIAD-88-181BR, p. 4.

41. Letter, Teller to Keyworth.

42. *Ibid.*

43. Cochran *et al.*, *Nuclear Weapons Databook, Volume Two*, p. 13.

44. Letter, Teller to Keyworth.

45. *Ibid.*

46. Quoted in interview, Roy D. Woodruff, July 18, 1989.

47. Interview, Roy D. Woodruff, July 18, 1989.

48. Quoted in *ibid.*; Teller has denied he said this to Woodruff, see Chapter Six, p. 229.

49. Draft letter, Roy D. Woodruff to George Keyworth, December 28, 1983, declassified with deletions. Brown-Markey collection.

50. Interview, Roy D. Woodruff, July 31, 1988.

51. *Ibid.*

52. Letter, R. D. Woodruff to Distribution, January 13, 1984, declassified with deletions. This letter is discussed in, "Accuracy of Statements," 1988 GAO report, p. 5.

53. *Ibid.*

54. Interview, Roy D. Woodruff, July 18, 1989.

55. Talk, George Maenchen, "XRL Design," Lawrence Livermore National Laboratory, February 15, 1984.

56. Interview, George Maenchen, December 14, 1989. In this interview Maenchen was careful to give no technical details. These were gathered from other weapon experts.

57. Interview, Lowell L. Wood, Jr., November 6, 1983.

58. The article was William J. Broad, "X-ray Laser Weapon Gains Favor," *The New York Times*, November 15, 1983, p. C1.

59. Broad, *Star Warriors*, p. 13.

60. Interview, Edward Teller, May 7, 1984.

61. Carter, p. 48.

62. *Ibid.*, p. 26.

63. Ray E. Kidder, "A Successful X-Ray Laser Will Doom President Reagan's 'Star Wars' Program for Ballistic Missile Defense," July 19, 1984. Unpublished manuscript.

64. Transcript, "The Real Star Wars," NBC News, September 8, 1984, p. 50.

65. E. Walbridge, "Angle Constraint for Nuclear-Pumped X-ray Laser Weapons," *Nature*, July 19, 1984, p. 180.

66. Weapon expert quoting George Maenchen, Livermore report COPD 84-92, April 6, 1984.

67. George Maenchen, Livermore report COPD 84-193, August 14, 1984, distribution list, p. 76.

68. Interviews, weapon experts.

69. Interview, Edward W. Walbridge, February 2, 1990.

70. Robert Jastrow, *How to Make Nuclear Weapons Obsolete* (Little, Brown, Boston, 1983).

71. Robert Jastrow, "Technical Feasibility of the President's Proposal for Defense Against Soviet Missiles," Prepared Testimony for the House Republican Study Committee, August 9, 1984, p. 8.

72. Interviews, weapon experts.

73. Broad, *Star Warriors*, pp. 162–163.

74. The genesis of the idea is given in letter, George Chapline to Representative John D. Dingell, April 11, 1989.

75. Letter, Rod Hyde and Lowell Wood to Edward Teller, September 9, 1984, listed in a compilation of Livermore documents for 1988 GAO study (hereafter "Livermore GAO compilation").

76. This episode is recounted by Susan Cohen, "The Man Who Made Reagan a Space Warrior," *West* magazine (*San Jose Mercury News*), May 19, 1985, p. 7.

77. Steven R. Weisman, "Reagan, at U.N., Asks Soviet for Long-term 'Framework' to Press for Arms Control," *The New York Times*, September 25, 1984, p. A1.

78. Letter, Edward Teller to Paul Nitze, U.S. Department of State, December 28, 1984, declassified with deletions. Brown-Markey collection.

79. *Ibid.*

80. Talbott, p. 217.

81. Gerald E. Marsh, "SDI: The Stability Question," *Bulletin of the Atomic Scientists*, October 1985, p. 23.

82. " 'Star Wars' Report Sees Launching Cost of Up to $1 Trillion," *The New York Times*, August 2, 1987, p. 23.

83. Letter, Edward Teller to Robert C. McFarlane, December 28, 1984, declassified with deletions. Brown-Markey collection.

84. Interview, Roy D. Woodruff, July 19, 1989.

85. Draft letter, Roy D. Woodruff to Paul H. Nitze, January 31, 1985, declassified with deletions. Brown-Markey collection.

86. See, "Accuracy of Statements," 1988 GAO report, p. 7. This report paraphrases parts of the Nitze letter and Woodruff's response that were deleted in declassified versions.

87. Interview, Roy D. Woodruff, July 19, 1989.

88. "Accuracy of Statements," 1988 GAO report, p. 8.

89. Batzel's logic was recounted in interview, Roy D. Woodruff, July 19, 1989.

90. "State of the Union: 'Second American Revolution,' " Transcript of President's State of the Union Address to Congress, *The New York Times*, February 7, 1985, p. B8.

91. Interviews, Paul H. Nitze, October 2, 1991, and Roy D. Woodruff, July 19, 1989.

CHAPTER FIVE

THE COLLAPSE

1. Leon Festinger, Henry W. Riecken, and Stanley Schachter, *When Prophecy Fails* (Harper & Row, New York, 1956).

2. *Ibid.*, p. 12.

3. Memo, Lowell Wood to Fritz Rittmann, January 24, 1985, on Livermore interdepartmental letterhead.

4. This episode is based on interview, Roy D. Woodruff and Mary E. Tuszka, July 19, 1989; Kerr in interview, February 17, 1990, declined to share his recollections, saying, "There are some conversations I consider private."

5. Viewgraph, Lowell L. Wood, "Recommendations," Lawrence Livermore National Laboratory, January 30, 1985, declassified with deletions.

6. Ibid.

7. Notes, Physics Program Review, Lawrence Livermore National Laboratory, January 30, 1985, p. 3.

8. Interview, Roy D. Woodruff, July 19, 1989.

9. Ibid.

10. Ibid.

11. Quoted in notes, Physics Program Review, p. 5.

12. Ibid.

13. Ibid., p. 6.

14. Interview, Mary E. Tuszka, July 19, 1989.

15. Letter, R. [Roy] D. Woodruff to Distribution, Lawrence Livermore National Laboratory, February 4, 1985, declassified with deletions.

16. Letter, R. [Roy] D. Woodruff to Major General G. Kenneth Withers, Director, Office of Military Applications, U.S. Department of Energy, February 6, 1985, declassified with deletions. Brown-Markey collection.

17. Viewgraph, Roy D. Woodruff, presented to Senate staff, February 13, 1985.

18. Memo, Roy Woodruff to Roger Batzel, Carl Haussmann, Robert Hollingsworth and Mike May, February 19, 1985.

19. Quoted in "Staff Memorandum" to Representative Edward J. Markey, April 15, 1986.

20. "Policy for Nuclear Research in the Strategic Defense Initiative," Caspar W. Weinberger and John S. Herrington, signed, respectively, February 21, 1985, and February 27, 1985.

21. Interview, Ray E. Kidder, December 13, 1989.

22. Agenda, X-ray Laser Program Review for Hans Bethe and Sidney Drell, Lawrence Livermore National Laboratory, March 21, 1985.

23. Quoted in interview, Sidney D. Drell, December 14, 1989.

24. Interview, weapon expert.

25. Interviews, weapon experts.

26. Letter, Hugh E. DeWitt to author, May 14, 1985. DeWitt is a Livermore scientist and X-ray skeptic.

27. Interviews, weapon experts; Mike Ross, "Cottage Nuclear Test Detonated by the Lab," Livermore Newsline, March 27, 1985; Livermore GAO compilation.

28. Interview, Roy D. Woodruff, July 19, 1989.

29. Ibid.

30. Quoted in Liz Mullen, "Physicist Teller Speaks at UCI on Space Arms Race," Los Angeles Times, Orange County edition, April 4, 1985, part 2, p. 6.

31. Note, Lowell L. Wood to author, April 15, 1985. Attached to this note was a copy of the invitation.

32. William J. Broad, "Gains Reported on Use of Laser for Space Arms," The New York Times, May 15, 1985, p. A1.

33. William J. Broad, "Science Showmanship: A Deep 'Star Wars' Rift," The New York Times, December 16, 1985, p. A1.

34. Lowell Wood, "Pillars of Fire in the Valley of the Giant Mushrooms," A Briefing Presented to James Abrahamson, Director, Strategic Defense Initiative Organization, April 19, 1985, declassified with deletions.

35. Lowell Wood, "Soviet and American X-ray Laser Efforts: A Technological Race for the Prize of a Planet," A Briefing Presented to William Casey, Director of Central Intelligence, April 23, 1985, declassified with deletions.

36. Quoted in transcript, GAO interview with George H. Miller, November 25, 1987, declassified with deletions, p. 14. This interview recounts some of the formerly secret contents of Wood's briefing to Casey.

37. Interviews, Roy D. Woodruff, July 19, 1989, and February 18, 1990.

38. Memo, George Miller to Roy Woodruff, "Lowell Wood and R Program," undated.

39. R. Jeffrey Smith, "Lab Officials Squabble Over X-ray Laser," Science, November 22, 1985, p. 923.

40. Interview, Robert C. McFarlane, December 5, 1989; letter, Robert C. McFarlane to author, November 15, 1989.

41. The figures are noted in Markey "Staff Memorandum," Attachment II.

42. Brochure, "The Nuclear Directed-Energy Research Facility and the Nuclear Test Technology Complex," Lawrence Livermore National Laboratory, undated.

43. Interview, Donald M. Kerr, February 17, 1990.

44. Interviews, weapon experts.

45. Ibid.

46. Ibid.

47. Ibid.

48. Ibid.

49. Ibid.; see also Robert Scheer, "Scientists Dispute Test of X-ray Laser Weapon, The Los Angeles Times, November 12, 1985, p. 1; "Briefing to Congressmen George Brown and Pete Stark," GAO, 1988, p. 18.

50. "Birthday Blowout," Scientific American, July 1985, p. 58.

51. Seth Mydans, "Soviet to Stop Atomic Tests; It Bids U.S. Do Same," The New York Times, July 30, 1985, p. A6.

52. "U.S. Officials Say 2 Key Projects Require More Atomic Tests," The New York Times, July 30, 1985, p. A6.

53. This episode was first reported in Smith, "Lab Officials Squabble," and expanded in Robert Scheer, "The Man Who Blew the Whistle on Star Wars," Los Angeles Times Magazine, July 17, 1988, p. 6. This version is based on these two articles and interview, Roy D. Woodruff, July 20, 1989.

54. Quoted in Smith, "Lab Officials Squabble."

55. Interview, Roy D. Woodruff, July 20, 1989.

56. Ibid.

57. Memo, G. [George] H. Miller to Distribution, "Sandia SDI Discussions," September 23, 1985.

58. Interview, W. Lowell Morgan, June 5, 1989.

59. Scheer, "Flaws."

60. Interview, Stephen M. Younger, February 7, 1990. Parts of this interview are quoted in William J. Broad, "Crown Jewel of 'Star Wars' Has Lost Its Luster," The New York Times, February 13, 1990, p. C1.

61. Lowell Wood, "Concerning the Vulnerability of Objects in Space to Attack by Ground-Based Laser Systems," Lawrence Livermore National Laboratory, undated.

62. Quoted in interview, Roy D. Woodruff, July 20, 1989.

63. Vincent Kiernan, "In a lab not very far away . . . ," The Tri-Valley Herald (of California), October 19, 1985, p. 1.

64. Letter, Roy D. Woodruff to Roger Batzel, October 19, 1985, declassified with deletions.

65. Interview, Roy D. Woodruff, February 18, 1990.

66. Interviews, Roy D. Woodruff and Mary E. Tuszka, July 20, 1989.
67. Jack C. Comly *et al.*, "Modeling of Diagnostics Foil Behavior with a Non-LTE Atomic Kinetics Code," Los Alamos National Laboratory, October 1985.
68. Interview, Roy D. Woodruff, July 20, 1989.
69. *Ibid.*
70. Letter, Roy D. Woodruff to Roger E. Batzel, October 29, 1985, on Livermore letterhead.
71. Interview, Roy D. Woodruff, December 16, 1989.
72. "National Lab Official Quits," Associated Press, November 1, 1985.
73. Interview, George F. Chapline, Jr., January 11, 1988.
74. Interview, Stephen M. Younger, February 7, 1990.
75. Note, Christopher Hendrickson to Roy Woodruff, November 4, 1985.
76. R. Jeffrey Smith, "Experts Cast Doubts on X-ray Laser," *Science*, November 8, 1985, p. 646.
77. Scheer, "Scientists Dispute Test."
78. Quoted in Keith Rogers, "Weapons Test Set Despite 'Flaw,' " *The Valley Times* (of California), November 13, 1985, p. 1.
79. Teller, *Better a Shield*, p. 37.
80. Quoted in "Looking at SDI," Lawrence Livermore *Weekly Bulletin*, December 18, 1985, p. 3. Keyworth subsequently denied having said this, according to Bruce Abell, his assistant at the Hudson Institute, where he later worked. Letter, Bruce Abell to author, September 24, 1990. At my request, Abell sent me a copy of the speech, "Proposed Remarks of Dr. G. A. Keyworth, II, to the Laser '85 Conference." It contains no statement like the one attributed to Keyworth by the Livermore publication.
81. Representative Edward J. Markey, "Goldstone X-ray Laser Test Should Be Delayed," *Congressional Record*, December 5, 1985, p. E5406.
82. William J. Broad, "30 Lawmakers Urge Delay in Laser Weapon Test," *The New York Times*, December 7, 1985, p. A7.
83. Interview, weapon expert. For lack of notification, interview, congressional aide, September 23, 1991.
84. Interview, Roy D. Woodruff, July 20, 1989. Nitze in interview, October 2, 1991, could not remember asking for Woodruff. "But it sounds probable," he said. "It's the sort of thing I would have done because I seriously took his reservations and I thought he was a bright guy."
85. Interviews, weapon experts.
86. "SDI Program: Evaluation of DOE's Answers," 1986 GAO report.
87. Quoted in William J. Broad, "U.S. Researchers Foresee a Big Rise in Nuclear Tests," *The New York Times*, April 21, 1986, p. A1.
88. Quoted in Moseley, p. 74.
89. Quoted in "Accuracy of Statements," 1988 GAO report, p. 11.
90. Charles B. Stevens, "Teller Confirms X-ray Laser Breakthrough," *Fusion*, September–October 1986, p. 45.
91. *Ibid.*
92. Interviews, weapon experts.
93. *Ibid.*
94. "Nuclear Directed Energy Weapons Research, Historical Funding," Department of Energy response to author's query, October 1989.
95. William J. Broad, "Congress Deals Near-Fatal Blow to 'Star' of 'Star Wars' Plan," *The New York Times*, October 21, 1990, section 1, p. 30.
96. Troy E. Wade II, testimony before the Energy and Water Development subcommittee of House Committee on Appropriations, March 12, 1988, "Energy and Water Development Appropriations for 1989," Part 6, p. 787.

97. Teller, "SDI: The Last, Best Hope," p. 75.

98. Edward Teller, "Progress Made in Protective-Defense Research," *The New York Times*, December 29, 1985, section 4, p. 14.

99. Tape recording, Teller talk at University of Colorado at Boulder, October 13, 1986.

100. Teller, *Better a Shield*, pp. XI, 27, 241.

101. Transcript, "Better a Shield Than a Sword," *Firing Line*, taped October 19, 1987, pp. 6–10.

102. Quoted in Keith Rogers, "Teller: 'Star Wars' Will Combat Cheating," *Valley Times* (of California), December 10, 1987, p. 1.

103. Quoted in Keith Rogers, "Teller to Reagan: Invite Sakharov," *Valley Times* (of California), December 16, 1987, p. 1A.

*CHAPTER SIX*
## ASSIGNATION OF BLAME

1. Blumberg and Panos, p. 218.

2. Interview, weapon expert.

3. Memo, Edward Teller to Michael M. May, May 14, 1970.

4. Interview, Hugh E. DeWitt, February 23, 1990.

5. Quoted in *ibid.*

6. Quoted in Dan Stober, "Teller Denies 'Star Wars' Charge," *San Jose Mercury News*, December 10, 1987, p. 1B.

7. Transcript, "Bill Wattenburg Show," station KGO, July 17, 1988, 11–12 P.M., Audio-Video Service of San Francisco, p. 5.

8. Videotape, *60 Minutes*, CBS, November 13, 1988.

9. Interview, Roy D. Woodruff, July 20, 1989.

10. Letter, Roger E. Batzel to David Pierpont Gardner, President, University of California, February 5, 1986.

11. Quoted in Deborah Blum, "Weird Science: Livermore's X-Ray Laser Flap," *Bulletin of the Atomic Scientists*, July/August 1988, p. 12.

12. Letter, Roy D. Woodruff to Roger E. Batzel, March 20, 1986.

13. Interview, Roy D. Woodruff, July 20, 1989.

14. *Ibid.*

15. Talbott, pp. 304–326.

16. Quoted in William J. Broad, "Who's Ahead Now in Nuclear Arms?" *The New York Times*, March 1, 1987, section 4, p. 3.

17. Interview, Roy D. Woodruff, July 20, 1989.

18. Memo, Roger E. Batzel to Roy D. Woodruff, "Your Position Within the Laboratory," February 2, 1987.

19. Letter, Roy D. Woodruff to Roger E. Batzel, February 4, 1987.

20. Interview, Hugh E. DeWitt, September 23, 1991. Press release, "Laboratory Director Roger Batzel Announces Retirement Plans," Lawrence Livermore National Laboratory, March 2, 1987.

21. "In the Matter of a Grievance Proceeding Between Roy Woodruff, Grievant, and George Miller, Associate Director for Defense Systems, Lawrence Livermore National Laboratory," September 17, 1987.

22. Letter, David Pierpont Gardner to Roy D. Woodruff, October 20, 1987.

23. Written statement, Robert M. Nelson, cochairman of the Southern California Federation of Scientists, Los Angeles Press Club, October 21, 1987.

24. Dan Morain and Richard E. Meyer, "Teller Gave Flawed Data on X-ray Laser," *The Los Angeles Times*, October 21, 1987, p. 1.

25. William J. Broad, "Dispute on Star Wars Device Erupts," *The New York Times*, October 22, 1987, p. A31.

26. Interview, Roy D. Woodruff, July 21, 1989.

27. *Ibid.*

28. "A Call for GAO Probe of Livermore Laser," *The San Francisco Chronicle*, October 24, 1987, p. A8.

29. Written statement, Roger E. Batzel, Lawrence Livermore National Laboratory, October 23, 1987.

30. Keith Rogers, "Livermore Lab Director Disputes Teller Allegations," *Valley Times* (of California), October 24, 1987, p. A3.

31. Interview, Roy D. Woodruff, July 21, 1989.

32. Letter, W. Lowell Morgan to Congressman George E. Brown, Jr., November 3, 1987.

33. Letter, George Chapline to The Honorable George Brown, November 10, 1987.

34. Transcript, GAO interview with Edward Teller, November 24, 1987, declassified with deletions, p. 2. The rest of this episode is based on interview transcript.

35. Quoted in Adelman, p. 96.

36. Transcript, GAO interview with George H. Miller, November 25, 1987, declassified with deletions, pp. 1–2. The rest of this episode is based on interview transcript.

37. *Ibid.*, p. 14.

38. Transcript, hearings before the Research and Development Subcommittee of the House Armed Services Committee, September 15, 1987.

39. Letter, George H. Miller to The Honorable John M. Spratt, Jr., December 1, 1987.

40. William J. Broad, "In From the Cold at a Top Nuclear Lab," *The New York Times*, December 27, 1987, section 4, p. 14.

41. Memo, George H. Miller to Helga Christopherson, "Salary Approval for Mr. Roy D. Woodruff," Lawrence Livermore National Laboratory, December 4, 1987.

42. George E. Brown, Jr., "Questions of Integrity at Livermore Laboratory," *Congressional Record*, December 10, 1987, p. E4745.

43. Rogers, "Teller to Reagan: Invite Sakharov."

44. Stober, "Teller Denies 'Star Wars' Charge."

45. "Physicist Denies Misinforming President on Laser," *The Herald* (of California), December 10, 1987, p. 16.

46. Deborah Blum, "Father of H-bomb: X-ray Laser Unproven," *The Sacramento Bee*, December 10, 1987, p. A1.

47. Keith Rogers, "Teller: 'Star Wars' Will Combat Cheating," *Valley Times* (of California), December 10, 1987, p. 1A.

48. Letter, Roy D. Woodruff to Dr. Edward Teller, December 10, 1987.

49. Memo, Edward Teller to file, January 8, 1988. Note that although Teller in the memo said he had "no remembrance of such an interaction," he later told Wattenburg, the radio talk show host, that "Roy Woodruff at that time objected to my saying all these things." See p. 239.

50. Interview, George Maenchen, December 14, 1989.

51. Letter, George Maenchen to James Ohl, December 23, 1987.

52. Letter, Lowell Wood to The Honorable George E. Brown, Jr., December 23, 1987.

53. Lowell Wood, "Classified Reply to Woodruff Allegations," December 24, 1987, declassified with deletions.

54. Michael D. Lemonick, "Red Flag at a Weapons Lab," *Time*, January 18, 1988, p. 52.

55. Peter Dworkin, "Long Knives in the Laboratory," *U.S. News & World Report*, February 29, 1988, p. 16.

56. Letter, Roger E. Batzel to The Honorable George E. Brown, Jr., January 25, 1988.

57. Memo, Edward Teller to Roger Batzel, January 25, 1988.

58. Broad, *Star Warriors*, pp. 62, 181.

59. Quoted in Dan Stober, "Physicist Named Livermore Lab Chief," *San Jose Mercury News*, February 19, 1988, p. 1B.

60. Memo, Lowell Wood to Ron Rocker, March 4, 1988.

61. Memo, Paul T. Schafer to Distribution, April 18, 1988.

62. Memo, "Specific Comments on Draft GAO X-Ray Laser Report," Lawrence Livermore National Laboratory, undated.

63. Memo, G. [George] H. Miller to J. [James] I. Davis, April 28, 1988.

64. Interviews, John H. Nuckolls, September 29, 1991, and Roy D. Woodruff, July 31, 1988.

65. Letter, Roy D. Woodruff to The Honorable George E. Brown, Jr., May 23, 1988.

66. "Accuracy of Statements," 1988 GAO report, p. 3; William J. Broad, "Atom Laser Had Early Fans Besides Teller, Study Finds," *The New York Times*, July 15, 1988, p. B5.

67. "Accuracy of Statements," 1988 GAO report, pp. 4–5; Letter, Congressman Pete Stark to The Honorable Charles A. Bowsher, General Accounting Office, January 24, 1989, p. 4.

68. "Accuracy of Statements," 1988 GAO report, pp. 9–10; "Briefing to Congressmen George Brown and Pete Stark," GAO, 1988, p. 12.

69. "Accuracy of Statements," 1988 GAO report, p. 10.

70. *Ibid.*, pp. 12–13.

71. *Ibid.*, p. 6.

72. Letter, [Karl] Bendetsen to Edwin Meese, "X-Ray Lasers for Space Defense," October 20, 1981, as listed in Livermore GAO compilation. In the compilation this letter is listed as having a document number of PHYS-81-4. The PHYS code was consistently used by Teller in originating classified documents, suggesting that he or his office was the Bendetsen letter's source.

73. Interview, William W. Hoover, September 25, 1991.

74. Lee Siegel, "Teller Claimed X-ray Laser Could Destroy All Land-Based Soviet Missiles," Associated Press, July 16, 1988.

75. Interview, Willard H. Wattenburg, June 8, 1989.

76. Transcript, "Bill Wattenburg Show," station KGO, July 17, 1988, 10–12 P.M., Audio-Video Service of San Francisco, pp. 1–6.

77. "GAO Report to Be Available," *Newsline*, Lawrence Livermore National Laboratory, July 20, 1988.

78. Transcript, Press Conference with Energy Secretary John S. Herrington, Lawrence Livermore National Laboratory, July 22, 1988.

79. Letter, George Maenchen to Roy D. Woodruff, September 7, 1988.

80. Quoted in William J. Broad, "Scientist's View of Lasers Helped 'Star Wars,' " *The New York Times*, August 1, 1988, p. A13.

81. Letter, Stark to Bowsher, p. 1.

82. *Ibid.*, p. 2.

83. Letter, Charles A. Bowsher, Comptroller General of the United States, to Fortney H. Stark, April 13, 1989.

84. Letter, Hugh E. DeWitt to John Nuckolls, Director, Lawrence Livermore National Laboratory, May 3, 1989; Keith Rogers, "GAO Accountant's Hiring Criticized by Lab Physicist," *Valley Times* (of California), May 6, 1989, p. 1A.

85. Quoted in Keith Rogers, "Lab Conflict Alleged in Hiring Prober in Laser Study," *Valley Times* (of California), April 19, 1989, p. 1A.

86. *Ibid.*

87. Keith Rogers, "Lab Duties of GAO Auditor Questioned," *Valley Times* (of California), April 26, 1989, p. 1A.

88. Interview, David L. Potter, September 23, 1991; Keith Rogers, "GAO to Examine How Auditor Got Livermore Lab Job," *Valley Times* (of California), April 22, 1989, p. 1A.

89. Interview, Willard H. Wattenburg, June 8, 1989.

90. Interview, Roy D. Woodruff, July 21, 1988.

91. Letter, George H. Miller to Roy D. Woodruff, August 16, 1988.

92. Letter, Roy D. Woodruff to John H. Nuckolls, May 31, 1989; William J. Broad, "Weapon Scientist Says Harassment Is Renewed," *The New York Times*, June 6, 1989, p. C7.

93. Quoted in William J. Broad, "Dispute Settled at Weapons Lab," *The New York Times*, May 23, 1990, p. A18; Press Release, "Roy Woodruff to Join Los Alamos National Laboratory," Lawrence Livermore National Laboratory, May 1990.

CHAPTER SEVEN

A FINAL CRUSADE

1. Richard N. Goodwin, "President Lyndon Johnson: The War Within," *The New York Times Magazine*, August 21, 1988, p. 34.

2. Anderson, p. 314.

3. Interview, participant at White House meeting, August 14, 1989.

4. Fred Barnes, "Pebbles Go Bam-Bam," *The New Republic*, April 17, 1989, p. 12.

5. Interview, participant at White House meeting, August 14, 1989.

6. Transcript, Edward Teller and Andrei Sakharov Address the Seventh Annual Ethics and Public Policy Dinner, "Science, Technology, and Freedom," Ethics and Public Policy Center, November 16, 1988.

7. Interview, Paul H. Nitze, October 2, 1991.

8. Interview, participant in White House meeting, August 14, 1989.

9. *Ibid.*

10. Testimony, Edward Teller, April 28, 1983, House Committee on Armed Services, p. 1357.

11. Quoted in John H. Cushman, Jr., "Conservatives Urge Quick U.S. Action on Missile Defense," *The New York Times*, October 3, 1986, Section A, p. 13.

12. R. Jeffrey Smith, "SDI Decision 'May Be Nearing'; Weinberger Tells of 'Opportunities for Earlier Deployment,' " *The Washington Post*, January 23, 1987, p. A17.

13. "Meese Calls for Speedup in Deploying 1st Stage of 'Star Wars' Defense," *The Washington Post*, January 15, 1987, p. A18.

14. John H. Cushman, Jr., "Partial Antimissile Deployment Weighed," *The New York Times*, January 16, 1987, p. A3; David E. Sanger, "Many Experts Doubt 'Star Wars' Could Be Effective by the Mid-90's," *The New York Times*, February 11, 1987, p. A1; "Soviet Defenses Could Boost 'Star Wars' Deployment Cost to $1 Trillion," Associated Press, August 3, 1987.

15. For a recounting of some of the launcher problems, see William J. Broad, "2

Years of Failure End As U.S. Lofts Big Titan Rocket," *The New York Times*, October 27, 1987, p. A1.

16. This breakfast meeting episode is based on an interview with Gregory H. Canavan, December 5, 1989, and on Ralph Kinney Bennett, "Brilliant Pebbles," *Reader's Digest*, September 1989, p. 128.

17. Broad, *Star Warriors*, p. 40.

18. Interview with Gregory H. Canavan, December 5, 1989.

19. Richard L. Garwin, "Hornet History," unpublished manuscript, April 19, 1989.

20. Bennett, "Brilliant Pebbles," p. 130.

21. *Ibid.*, p. 131.

22. Interview with Gregory H. Canavan, December 5, 1989.

23. Quoted in "SDIO director dedicates wide-angle lens system," *Newsline*, Lawrence Livermore National Laboratory, December 2, 1987, p 3.

24. Bennett, "Brilliant Pebbles," p. 132.

25. Transcript, Edward Teller, Opening Address, "SDI: The First Five Years," Institute for Foreign Policy Analysis, Inc., March 14, 1988.

26. James Gerstenzang, "Reagan Backs Action on 'Star Wars,' " *Los Angeles Times*, March 15, 1988, p. 1; Transcript, Ronald Reagan, Keynote Address, "SDI: The First Five Years," Institute for Foreign Policy Analysis, Inc., March 14, 1988.

27. Lowell Wood, "Concerning Advanced Architectures for Strategic Defense," Invited paper to conference on The Strategic Defense Initiative: The First Five Years, March 13–15, 1988, Washington, D.C., Livermore preprint of speech, UCRL-98434. A reprint of most of this talk appears in " 'Brilliant Pebbles' Missile Defense Concept Advocated by Livermore Scientist," *Aviation Week & Space Technology*, June 13, 1988, p. 151.

28. "Washington Roundup," *Aviation Week & Space Technology*, August 22, 1988, p. 15.

29. "Teller Rebuts Criticism of His SDI Role," *Inside Energy*, July 25, 1988, p. 1.

30. Transcript, Edward Teller and Albert Carnesale, "The Technological Feasibility of SDI," Heritage Foundation, August 30, 1988.

31. Quoted in Adelman.

32. Theresa M. Foley, "Brilliant Pebbles Testing Proceeds at Rapid Pace," *Aviation Week & Space Technology*, November 14, 1988, p.32.

33. Transcript, Teller and Sakharov, p. 2.

34. Andrei Sakharov, *Moscow and Beyond* (Knopf, New York, 1991), p. 69.

35. Transcript, Teller and Sakharov, p. 3; Sidney Blumenthal, "When Giants Meet; H-Bomb Fathers Sakharov & Teller's SDI Dialogue," *The Washington Post*, November 17, 1988, C1.

36. Transcript, Teller and Sakharov, p. 5.

37. *Ibid.*, p. 6.

38. Interview, Teller colleague, April 25, 1989.

39. Interview, Teller colleague, February 26, 1990.

40. "Reagan Fetes Teller for Exemplary Service," *Valley Times* (of California), February 2, 1989, p. 6A.

41. Quoted in McCormack, p. 8.

42. Quoted in Barnes, "Pebbles Go Bam-Bam," p. 14.

43. Quoted in *ibid.*

44. Gerald M. Boyd, "Bush Is Cautious About Deploying a Missile Defense," *The New York Times*, August 26, 1988, p. A1; "Bush Transcript on 'Star Wars,' " *The New York Times*, August 26, 1988, p. D17.

45. James A. Abrahamson, "End of Tour" Report, *SDI Monitor*, March 20, 1989, p. 83.

46. Transcript, Remarks by the Vice President to the Navy League of the United States, March 23, 1989.

47. Fred Barnes, "Danny Gets His Gun," *The New Republic*, June 26, 1989, p. 10.

48. "Cheney 'Not Comfortable' With B-2, Presses 'Brilliant Pebbles,' " *Aerospace Daily*, April 25, 1989; Michael R. Gordon, "Bush Plans to Cut Reagan Requests for Key Weapons," *The New York Times*, April 24, 1989, p. A1.

49. Theresa M. Foley, "Sharp Rise in Brilliant Pebbles Interceptor Funding Accompanied by New Questions About Technical Feasibility," *Aviation Week & Space Technology*, May 22, 1989, p. 20.

50. Transcript, Remarks by the Vice President to the Navy League of the United States, March 23, 1989.

51. Strategic Defense Initiative Organization, "1989 Report to Congress," March 13, 1989, p. 5.3-4.

52. Transcript, Defense Department press conference, General George Monahan, Director, SDI, and Lowell Wood, February 9, 1990; R. Jeffrey Smith, "Pentagon Increases SDI Push," *The Washington Post*, February 18, 1990, p. A1.

53. "Issue Backgrounder: Brilliant Pebbles," Union of Concerned Scientists, Cambridge, Mass., June 1989.

54. Audio tape, "The Future of Strategic Defenses and Antisatellite Weapons," congressional seminar series, American Association for the Advancement of Science, September 27, 1989; "Are Brilliant Pebbles on the Shelf?" *Military Space*, October 9, 1989, p. 1.

55. Roger D. Speed, "ASAT's vs. Brilliant Pebbles," Lawrence Livermore National Laboratory, UCRL-ID-103669, March 1990.

56. "Too Brilliant by Half," *The New Republic*, May 29, 1989, p. 7.

57. Charles Bennett, " 'Brilliant Pebbles'? No, Loose Marbles," *The New York Times*, June 17, 1989, section 1, p. 23.

58. "Teller Recuperating from Colon Surgery," *Valley Times* (of California), April 25, 1989, p. 3A.

59. Gregory Canavan and Edward Teller, "Strategic Defense for the 1990's," *Nature*, April 19, 1990, p. 699.

60. William J. Broad, "Lab Offers to Develop an Inflatable Space Base," *The New York Times*, November 14, 1989, p. C5; William J. Broad, "NASA Losing 30-Year Monopoly in Planning for Moon and Mars," *The New York Times*, January 15, 1990, p. A1.

61. Transcript, Defense Department press conference, February 9, 1990.

62. Interview, Mike Doble, public affairs, Strategic Defense Initiative, May 29, 1991; Broad, "Crown Jewel."

63. Smith, "Pentagon Increases."

64. Transcript, "The Bush Speech," *Valley Times* (of California), February 8, 1990, p. 4A. Videotape, "President Bush's Visit," Lawrence Livermore National Laboratory, February 7, 1990.

## EPILOGUE

1. Quoted in Rhodes, p. 277.

2. Steven H. Heimoff, "A Conversation with Edward Teller," *Express* (of East San Francisco Bay), August 31, 1990, p. 1.

3. Interview, Carl Haussmann, May 9, 1984. For more on Wood's relationship with Teller see Broad, *Star Warriors*, pp. 179–188.

4. Teller's brooding about the Soviet arms buildup is seen in a magazine piece he wrote just before the Star Wars speech, Edward Teller, "Dangerous Myths About Nuclear Arms," *Reader's Digest*, November 1982, p. 139. Also see a liberal's response, Frank von Hippel, "The Myths of Edward Teller," *The Bulletin of the Atomic Scientists*, March 1983, p. 6.

5. Transcript, *Firing Line*, Southern Educational Communications Association, June 15, 1982, p. 7.

6. William Broad and Nicholas Wade, *Betrayers of the Truth: Fraud and Deceit in the Halls of Science* (Simon & Schuster, New York, 1982).

7. "Accuracy of Statements," 1988 GAO report, p. 5.

8. Interview, Ray Pollock, January 19, 1990.

9. Quoted in Yonas, p. 75.

10. Reagan, *An American Life*, p. 298.

11. For an example of how personal access became more important than procedure, see Jeff Gerth, "A Onetime Aide to Bush Shows a Lobbyist's Magic," *The New York Times*, July 15, 1990, section 1, p. 1.

12. Letters, Teller to Reagan, September 25, 1982, and July 23, 1983, the latter quoted in Yonas, p. 75.

13. Interview, Donald M. Kerr, February 17, 1990.

14. Testimony, John Nuckolls, before the House Committee on Armed Services, "Hearings on National Defense Authorization Act for Fiscal Year 1990—H.R. 2461. Department of Energy Modernization Study and Department of Energy Defense Programs," March 13, 1989, p. 788.

15. Quoted in Vincent Kiernan, "Excess Hype of X-ray Laser Causes Funding Gap of Weapons Research," *Space News*, October 9, 1989, p. 1.

16. Interview, David Nowak, R Program leader, Lawrence Livermore National Laboratory, February 5, 1990; Vincent Kiernan, "Budget Cuts Stymie X-ray Laser Tests," *Space News*, November 13, 1989, p. 32.

17. Barbara L. Whitten, "Neon-Like Soft X-ray Lasers," Lawrence Livermore *Energy and Technology Review*, February-March 1989, p. 22.

18. Interview, Hans A. Bethe, December 7, 1989. Interview, Sidney D. Drell, December 14, 1989.

19. Transcript, GAO interview with George H. Miller.

20. Teller, *Better a Shield*, p. 188.

21. Broad and Wade, pp. 107–114.

22. Interviews, Roy D. Woodruff, July 31, 1988, and December 16, 1989.

23. Letter, Ray E. Kidder to author, October 31, 1990, and interview, September 29, 1991.

24. Richard Rhodes, "H-bomb Dreams," *The New York Times*, February 11, 1990, book review, p. 3; Edward Teller, "H-Bombs to 'Star Wars': An Insider's View," *The New York Times*, March 21, 1990, p. A26; Richard Rhodes, "Teller's Charges Discredited Oppenheimer," *The New York Times*, April 7, 1990, p. A24.

25. Transcript, GAO interview with Edward Teller, November 24, 1987, declassified with deletions, p. 10.

26. Donald R. Shanor, *Behind the Lines: The Private War Against Soviet Censorship* (St. Martin's Press, New York, 1985).

27. Geoffrey Hosking, *The Awakening of the Soviet Union* (Harvard, Cambridge, 1990).

28. Reagan, *An American Life*, pp. 237–238.

29. Interview, Malcolm Wallop, February 6, 1991, quoted in William J. Broad, "The Patriot's Success: Because of 'Star Wars' or In Spite of It?" *The New York Times*, February 10, 1991, p. E5. Also see Malcolm Wallop, " 'Patriots' Point the Way," *The New York Times*, January 31, 1991, p. A23. For the move to take ground-

based work out of Star Wars, see Bruce Schoenfeld, "Support Seen Growing for Moving Tactical Missile Defense From SDI," *Defense Week*, May 6, 1991, p. 6.

30. Peter De Selding, "Thompson's Alain Gomez: Japan Bashing at Its Very Best . . . Or Worst," *New Technology Week*, December 4, 1989, p. 1.

31. William J. Broad, "New Course for 'Star Wars,' From Full to a Limited Defense," *The New York Times*, January 31, 1991, p. A18; Andrew Rosenthal, "U.S. Offers to Negotiate on 'Star Wars,' " *The New York Times*, October 16, 1991, p. A3.

32. Andrei Sakharov, *Memoirs* (Knopf, New York, 1990), pp. 98–100.

33. Reagan, *An American Life*, p. 294.

# Bibliography

Abrahamson, James A. "End of Tour" Report, *SDI Monitor*, March 20, 1989.

Adelman, Ken. "Washington Is a Mystery," *The Washingtonian*, October 1988.

Ambrose, Stephen E. *Eisenhower the President* (Simon & Schuster, New York, 1984).

Anderson, Martin. *Revolution* (Harcourt, Brace, Jovanovich, New York, 1988).

Associated Press, "People in the News," April 16, 1979.

———. "Teller," May 7, 1979.

———. "Underground Nuclear Test Postponed at Least One Day," March 24, 1983.

———. "National Briefs," March 26, 1983.

———. "Underground Test Conducted After Wind Delays," December 16, 1983.

———. "National Lab Official Quits," November 1, 1985.

———. "Soviet Defenses Could Boost 'Star Wars' Deployment Cost to $1 Trillion," August 3, 1987.

*Aviation Week & Space Technology.* "Laser Talks," September 20, 1982.

———. "Energy Weapons," September 5, 1983.

———. "Defensive Technologies Study Sets Funding Profile Options," October 24, 1983.

———. "Washington Roundup," August 22, 1988.

Barnes, Fred. "Pebbles Go Bam-Bam," *The New Republic*, April 17, 1989.

———. "Danny Gets His Gun," *The New Republic*, June 26, 1989.

Baucom, Donald R. "Origins of the Strategic Defense Initiative: Ballistic Missile Defense, 1944–1983," draft manuscript, December 1989.

———. "Hail to the Chiefs," *Policy Review* (Heritage Foundation), Summer 1990.

Bennett, Charles. " 'Brilliant Pebbles'? No, Loose Marbles," *The New York Times*, June 17, 1989.

Bennett, Ralph Kinney. "Brilliant Pebbles," *Reader's Digest*, September 1989.

Bernstein, Jeremy. *Hans Bethe: Prophet of Energy* (Basic Books, New York, 1979).

Bethe, Hans A. "Comments on the History of the H-bomb," *Los Alamos Science*, Fall 1982.

Biddle, Wayne. " 'Star Wars' Technology: It's More Than a Fantasy," *The New York Times*, March 5, 1985.

Binder, David. "U.S., Soviet Agree on Size of A-Tests for Peaceful Use," *The New York Times*, April 10, 1976.

Blum, Deborah. "Father of H-bomb: X-ray Laser Unproven," *The Sacramento Bee*, December 10, 1987.

———. "Weird Science: Livermore's X-Ray Laser Flap," *Bulletin of the Atomic Scientists*, July/August 1988.

Blumberg, Stanley A., and Gwinn Owens. *Energy and Conflict: The Life and Times of Edward Teller* (Putnam, New York, 1976).

Blumberg, Stanley A., and Louis G. Panos. *Edward Teller: Giant of the Golden Age of Physics* (Scribners, New York, 1990).

Blumenthal, Sidney. "When Giants Meet; H-Bomb Fathers Sakharov & Teller's SDI Dialogue," *The Washington Post*, November 17, 1988.

Boffey, Philip M., *et al. Claiming the Heavens* (Times Books, New York, 1988).

Boyd, Gerald M. "Bush Is Cautious About Deploying a Missile Defense," *The New York Times*, August 26, 1988.

Broad, William J. "Nuclear Pulse: Awakening to the Chaos Factor," *Science*, May 29, 1981.

———. "A Fatal Flaw in the Concept of Space War," *Science*, March 12, 1982.

———. "Star Wars: Pentagon Lunacy," *The New York Times*, May 13, 1982.

———. "Laser Wars on Capitol Hill," *Science*, June 4, 1982.

———. "X-ray Laser Weapon Gains Favor," *The New York Times*, November 15, 1983.

———. "Some Atomic Tests Being Kept Secret by Administration," *The New York Times*, January 29, 1984.

———. *Star Warriors* (Simon & Schuster, New York, 1985).

———. "Reagan's Star Wars Bid: Many Ideas Converging," *The New York Times*, March 4, 1985.

———. "Allies in Europe Are Apprehensive About Benefits of 'Star Wars' Plan," *The New York Times*, May 13, 1985.

———. "Gains Reported on Use of Laser for Space Arms," *The New York Times*, May 15, 1985.

———. "30 Lawmakers Urge Delay in Laser Weapon Test," *The New York Times*, December 7, 1985.

———. "Science Showmanship: A Deep 'Star Wars' Rift," *The New York Times*, December 16, 1985.

———. "Bomb Tests: Technology Advances Against Backdrop of Wide Debate," *The New York Times*, April 15, 1986.

———. "U.S. Researchers Foresee a Big Rise in Nuclear Tests," *The New York Times*, April 21, 1986.

———. "Reverberations of the Space Crisis: A Troubled Future for 'Star Wars,' " *The New York Times*, June 15, 1986.

———. "Who's Ahead Now in Nuclear Arms?" *The New York Times*, March 1, 1987.

———. "Space Weapon Idea Now Being Weighed Was Assailed in '82," *The New York Times*, May 4, 1987.

———. "Dispute on Star Wars Device Erupts," *The New York Times*, October 22, 1987.

———. "2 Years of Failure End as U.S. Lofts Big Titan Rocket," *The New York Times*, October 27, 1987.

———. "In From the Cold at a Top Nuclear Lab," *The New York Times*, December 27, 1987.

———. "Anti-Missile Laser Project Is Delayed Nearly 2 Years," *The New York Times*, April 17, 1988.

———. "Atom Laser Had Early Fans Besides Teller, Study Finds," *The New York Times*, July 15, 1988.

———. "Scientist's View of Lasers Helped 'Star Wars,' " *The New York Times*, August 1, 1988.

———. "Weapon Scientist Says Harassment Is Renewed," *The New York Times*, June 6, 1989.

———. "Lab Offers to Develop an Inflatable Space Base," *The New York Times*, November 14, 1989.

———. "Spy's Role in Soviet H-bomb Now Discounted," *The New York Times*, January 3, 1990.

———. "NASA Losing 30-Year Monopoly in Planning for Moon and Mars," *The New York Times*, January 15, 1990.

———. "Crown Jewel of 'Star Wars' Has Lost Its Luster," *The New York Times*, February 13, 1990.

———. "Critics Say 'Star Wars' Test May Be a Treaty Violation," *The New York Times*, May 12, 1990.

———. "Dispute Settled at Weapons Lab," *The New York Times*, May 23, 1990.

———. "Congress Deals Near-Fatal Blow to 'Star' of 'Star Wars' Plan," *The New York Times*, October 21, 1990.

———. "New Course for 'Star Wars,' From Full to a Limited Defense," *The New York Times*, January 31, 1991.

———. "The Patriot's Success: Because of 'Star Wars' or in Spite of It?" *The New York Times*, February 10, 1991.

———, and Nicholas Wade. *Betrayers of the Truth: Fraud and Deceit in the Halls of Science* (Simon & Schuster, New York, 1982).

Bromberg, Joan Lisa. *Fusion: Science, Politics, and the Invention of a New Energy Source* (MIT Press, Cambridge, 1982).

Brown, George E., Jr. "Questions of Integrity at Livermore Laboratory," *Congressional Record*, December 10, 1987.

Burks, Edward C. "Republican Governors Assured of 'More Open' Administration," *The New York Times*, May 11, 1973.

Campbell, R. M. "Freedom Power," *The New York Times*, December 12, 1979.

Canan, James. *War in Space* (Harper & Row, New York, 1982).

Canavan, Gregory, and Edward Teller. "Strategic Defence for the 1990's," *Nature*, April 19, 1990.

Cannon, Lou. *President Reagan: The Role of a Lifetime* (Simon & Schuster, New York, 1991).

Carter, Ashton B. "Directed Energy Missile Defense In Space," Congressional Office of Technology Assessment, April 1984.

Chace, James, and Caleb Carr. *America Invulnerable* (Summit, New York, 1988).

Cochran, Thomas B., William M. Arkin, Milton M. Hoenig. *Nuclear Weapons Databook: Volume One, U.S. Nuclear Forces and Capabilities* (Ballinger, Cambridge, 1984).

Cochran, Thomas B., William M. Arkin, Robert S. Norris, Milton M. Hoenig. *Nuclear Weapons Databook: Volume Two, U.S. Nuclear Warhead Production* (Ballinger, Cambridge, 1987).

Cochran, Thomas B., and Robert S. Norris. "Nuclear Weapons," *Encyclopaedia Britannica*, 15th edition, 1990, Vol. XX.

Codevilla, Angelo. *While Others Build* (Free Press, New York, 1988).

Cohen, Susan. "The Man Who Made Reagan a Space Warrior," *West* magazine (*San Jose Mercury News*), May 19, 1985.

Comly, Jack C., *et al.* "Modeling of Diagnostics Foil Behavior with a Non-LTE Atomic Kinetics Code," Los Alamos National Laboratory, undated.

Compton, Arthur Holly. *Atomic Quest* (Oxford University Press, New York, 1956).

*Congressional Quarterly Almanac.* "1980 Republican Platform Text," 1980.

Congressional Research Service. "Project Defender," July 1987.

Coughlan, Robert. "Dr. Edward Teller's Magnificent Obsession," *Life*, September 6, 1954.

Crick, Francis. *Life Itself* (Simon & Schuster, New York, 1981).

Cushman, John H., Jr. "Conservatives Urge Quick U.S. Action on Missile Defense," *The New York Times*, October 3, 1986.

———. "Partial Antimissile Deployment Weighed," *The New York Times*, January 16, 1987.

Davis, Nuel Pharr. *Lawrence and Oppenheimer* (Simon & Schuster, New York, 1969).

De Selding, Peter. "Thompson's Alain Gomez: Japan Bashing at Its Very Best . . . Or Worst," *New Technology Week*, December 4, 1989.

Drugger, Ronnie. *On Reagan: The Man & His Presidency* (McGraw-Hill, New York, 1983).

Dworkin, Peter. "Long Knives in the Laboratory," *U.S. News & World Report*, February 29, 1988.

Dyson, Freeman. *Disturbing the Universe* (Harper & Row, New York, 1979).

E. Majorana Center for Scientific Culture. Proceedings of the "International Seminar on the World-Wide Implications of a Nuclear War," Erice, August 14–19, 1981.

Festinger, Leon, Henry W. Riecken, and Stanley Schachter. *When Prophecy Fails* (Harper & Row, New York, 1956).

Finney, John W. "U.S. Eliminates 95 percent of Fall-Out From the H-bomb," *The New York Times*, June 25, 1957.

*Firing Line.* Transcript, Southern Educational Communications Association, June 15, 1982.

———. Transcript, Southern Educational Communications Association, October 19, 1987.

Foley, Theresa M. "Brilliant Pebbles Testing Proceeds at Rapid Pace," *Aviation Week & Space Technology*, November 14, 1988.

———. "Sharp Rise in Brilliant Pebbles Interceptor Funding Accompanied by New Questions About Technical Feasibility," *Aviation Week & Space Technology*, May 22, 1989.

Ford, Daniel. *Cult of the Atom* (Simon & Schuster, New York, 1982).

General Accounting Office. "SDI Program: Evaluation of DOE's Answers to Questions on X-ray Laser Experiment," GAO/NSIAD-86-140BR, June 1986.

———. "Accuracy of Statements Concerning DOE's X-ray Laser Research Program," GAO/NSIAD-88-181BR, June 1988.

———. "Briefing to Congressmen George Brown and Pete Stark on GAO's report on the accuracy of statements concerning DOE's X-ray Laser Research Program," September 28, 1988.

———. "Strategic Defense Initiative Program: Extent of Foreign Participation," GAO/NSIAD-90-2, February 1990.

Gerstenzang, James. "Reagan Backs Action on 'Star Wars,' " *Los Angeles Times*, March 15, 1988.

Gerth, Jeff. "A Onetime Aide to Bush Shows a Lobbyist's Magic," *The New York Times*, July 15, 1990.

Goodwin, Richard N. "President Lyndon Johnson: The War Within," *The New York Times Magazine*, August 21, 1988.

Gordon, Michael R. "Bush Plans to Cut Reagan Requests for Key Weapons," *The New York Times*, April 24, 1989.

Graham, Daniel O. *High Frontier: A New National Strategy* (Heritage Foundation, Washington, 1982).

Greve, Frank. "How Reagan's Plan Caught Many Administration Insiders by Surprise," *San Jose Mercury News*, November 17, 1985.

Halloran, Richard. "Navy's Chief Discusses Morality and Weapons," *The New York Times*, May 6, 1983.

Hansen, Chuck. U.S. *Nuclear Weapons: The Secret History* (Crown, New York, 1988).

———. "Operation Hardtack and the 'Clean Bomb,' " 1989, unpublished manuscript.

Harmetz, Aljean. "When Nuclear Crisis Imitates a Film," *The New York Times*, April 4, 1979.

Heimoff, Steven H. "A Conversation with Edward Teller," *Express* (of East San Francisco Bay), August 31, 1990.

Herken, Gregg. *Counsels of War* (Oxford University Press, New York, 1987).

———. "The Earthly Origins of Star Wars," *Bulletin of the Atomic Scientists*, October 1987.

Hosking, Geoffrey. *The Awakening of the Soviet Union* (Harvard, Cambridge, 1990).

*Inside Energy.* "Teller Rebuts Criticism of his SDI Role," July 25, 1988.

Jastrow, Robert, *How to Make Nuclear Weapons Obsolete* (Little, Brown, Boston, 1983).

———. "Technical Feasibility of the President's Proposal for Defense Against Soviet Missiles," Prepared Testimony for the House Republican Study Committee, August 9, 1984.

Kidder, Ray E. "A Successful X-Ray Laser Will Doom President Reagan's 'Star Wars' Program for Ballistic Missile Defense," unpublished manuscript, July 19, 1984.

Kiernan, Vincent. "In a lab not very far away . . . ," *The Tri-Valley Herald* (of California), October 19, 1985.

———. "Excess Hype of X-ray Laser Causes Funding Gap of Weapons Research," *Space News*, October 9, 1989.

———. "Budget Cuts Stymie X-ray Laser Tests," *Space News*, November 13, 1989.

King, Seth S. "New Layoffs Push U.S. Jobless Rate to 8.9% from 8.4%," *The New York Times*, January 9, 1982.

Kintner, William R., ed. *Safeguard: Why the ABM Makes Sense* (Hawthorn, New York, 1969).

Kramer, Michael, and Sam Roberts. *I Never Wanted to Be Vice-President of Anything: An Investigative Biography of Nelson Rockefeller* (Basic Books, New York, 1976).

Lakoff, Sanford, and Herbert F. York. *A Shield in Space?* (University of California Press, Berkeley, 1989).

Lawrence Livermore National Laboratory. "Cannikin: Cold Days in Alaska," *LLL 25 Years in Pictures*, 1977.

———. "Thirty Years of Technical Excellence, 1952–1982," 1982.

———. "Looking at SDI," *Weekly Bulletin*, December 18, 1985.

———. "SDIO director dedicates wide-angle lens system," *Newsline*, December 2, 1987.

———. "GAO Report to Be Available," *Newsline*, July 20, 1988.

Lemonick, Michael D. "Red Flag at a Weapons Lab," *Time*, January 18, 1988.

Luther, Jim. "Energy Future," Associated Press, May 8, 1979.

Maenchen, George. COPD 84-92, Lawrence Livermore National Laboratory, April 6, 1984.

———. COPD 84-193, Lawrence Livermore National Laboratory, August 14, 1984.

Markey, Edward J. "Goldstone X-ray Laser Test Should Be Delayed," *Congressional Record*, December 4, 1985.

Marsh, Gerald E. "SDI: The Stability Question," *Bulletin of the Atomic Scientists*, October 1985.

Martin Marietta Denver Aerospace. "System Concept Study," February 1983.

McCormack, Richard. "Teller Speaks on Greenhouse, SDI, Nuclear Power, Presidents and More," *New Technology Week*, March 20, 1989.

McGory, Mary. "Seminar: 'Ain't Gonna Study War No More,' " *The Washington Post*, September 18, 1983.

McPhee, John. *The Curve of Binding Energy* (Ballantine, New York, 1975).

*Military Space*. "Are Brilliant Pebbles on the Shelf?" October 9, 1989.

Mohr, Charles. "Reagan Is Urged to Increase Research on Exotic Defenses Against Missiles," *The New York Times*, November 5, 1983.

Montgomery, Paul L. "Throngs Fill Manhattan to Protest Nuclear Weapons," *The New York Times*, June 13, 1982.

Morain, Dan, and Richard E. Meyer. "Teller Gave Flawed Data on X-ray Laser," *The Los Angeles Times*, October 21, 1987.

Morone, Joseph G., and Edward J. Woodhouse. *The Demise of Nuclear Energy? Lessons for Democratic Control of Technology* (Yale, New Haven, 1989).

Moseley, Bill. "Interview: Star Warrior Peter Hagelstein," *Omni*, May 1989.

Moss, Norman. *Men Who Play God: The Story of the H-Bomb and How the World Came to Live with It* (Harper & Row, New York, 1968).

———. *Klaus Fuchs: The Man Who Stole the Atom Bomb* (St. Martin's Press, New York, 1987).

Mullen, Liz. "Physicist Teller Speaks at UCI on Space Arms Race," *Los Angeles Times*, Orange County Edition, April 4, 1985.

*Murder in the Air*. Dialogue Transcript of Reagan's 1940 movie, New York State Archives, January 29, 1940.

Mydans, Seth. "Soviet to Stop Atomic Tests; It Bids U.S. Do Same," *The New York Times*, July 30, 1985.

NBC News. "The Real Star Wars," transcript, September 8, 1984.

Newhouse, John. *War and Peace in the Nuclear Age* (Knopf, New York, 1989).

*New Republic*. "Too Brilliant by Half," May 29, 1989.

*Newsweek*. "H-Mystery Man: He Hurried the H-bomb," August 2, 1954.

———. "Man with a Mission," September 2, 1963.

———. "Star Wars," April 4, 1983.

———. "The President's View," March 18, 1985.

*New York Times*. "The Amchitka Affair . . . ," July 4, 1971.

———. "Propaganda," August 17, 1979.

———. "President's Speech on Military Spending and a New Defense," March 24, 1983.

———. "State of the Union: 'Second American Revolution,' " Transcript of President's State of the Union Address to Congress, February 7, 1985.

———. "U.S. Officials say 2 Key Projects Require More Atomic Tests," July 30, 1985.

———. " 'Star Wars' Report Sees Launching Cost of Up to $1 Trillion," August 2, 1987.

———. "Karl R. Bendetsen, 81, Executive and High-Ranking U.S. Official," June 30, 1989.

Nolan, Janne E. *Guardians of the Arsenal* (Basic Books, New York, 1989).

O'Neill, Dan. "Project Chariot: How Alaska Escaped Nuclear Excavation," *The Bulletin of the Atomic Scientists*, December 1989.

Oppenheimer, J. Robert. *In the Matter of J. Robert Oppenheimer: Transcript of Hearing Before Personnel Security Board and Texts of Principal Documents and Letters* (MIT Press, Cambridge, 1971).

Peierls, Rudolf. *Bird of Passage: Recollections of a Physicist* (Princeton University Press, Princeton, 1985).

Pincus, Walter. "Reactors Safer Than Alternatives, Scientists Say," *The Washington Post*, May 8, 1979.

*Playboy.* "Playboy Interview, Edward Teller," August 1979.

Reagan, Ronald. *An American Life* (Simon & Schuster, New York, 1990).

————, with Richard G. Hubler, *Where's the Rest of Me?* (Karz, New York, 1981).

Reinhold, Robert. "Los Alamos Physicist May Get Post as Science Adviser in White House," *The New York Times*, May 8, 1981.

————. "13 Experts Named to Counsel Reagan's Adviser for Science," *The New York Times*, February 18, 1982.

Reston, James. "Eisenhower Wary of Atom Test Ban," *The New York Times*, June 27, 1957.

Rhodes, Richard. *The Making of the Atomic Bomb* (Simon & Schuster, New York, 1986).

————. "H-bomb Dreams," *The New York Times*, February 11, 1990, book review.

————. "Teller's Charges Discredited Oppenheimer," *The New York Times*, April 7, 1990.

Ripley, Anthony. "After 3 Nuclear Explosions, A.E.C. Is Leaving Amchitka to Wind and Fog," *The New York Times*, August 5, 1973.

Robinson, Clarence A., Jr. "Advance Made on High-Energy Laser," *Aviation Week & Space Technology*, February 23, 1981.

————. "Study Urges Exploiting of Technologies," *Aviation Week & Space Technology*, October 24, 1983.

Rogers, Keith. "Weapons Test Set Despite 'Flaw,' " *Valley Times* (of California), November 13, 1985.

————. "Livermore Lab Director Disputes Teller Allegations," *Valley Times*, October 24, 1987.

————. "Teller: 'Star Wars' Will Combat Cheating," *Valley Times*, December 10, 1987.

————. "Teller to Reagan: Invite Sakharov," *Valley Times*, December 16, 1987.

————. "Lab Conflict Alleged in Hiring Prober in Laser Study," *Valley Times*, April 19, 1989.

————. "GAO to Examine How Auditor Got Livermore Lab Job," *Valley Times*, April 22, 1989.

————. "Lab Duties of GAO Auditor Questioned," *Valley Times*, April 26, 1989.

Rosenberg, Tina. "The Authorized Version," *The Atlantic*, February 1986.

Rosenthal, Andrew. "U.S. Offers to Negotiate on 'Star Wars,' " *The New York Times*, October 16, 1991.

Ross, Mike. "Cottage Nuclear Test Detonated by the Lab," Lawrence Livermore National Laboratory, *Newsline*, March 27, 1985.

Sakharov, Andrei. *Memoirs* (Knopf, New York, 1990).

————. *Moscow and Beyond* (Knopf, New York, 1991).

*San Francisco Chronicle.* "A Call for GAO Probe of Livermore Laser," October 24, 1987.

Sanger, David E. "Many Experts Doubt 'Star Wars' Could Be Effective by the Mid-90's," *The New York Times*, February 11, 1987.

Scheer, Robert. *With Enough Shovels: Reagan, Bush & Nuclear War* (Random House, New York, 1982).

———. "Teller's Obsession Became Reality in 'Star Wars' Plan," *The Los Angeles Times*, July 10, 1983.

———. "Flaws Peril Pivotal 'Star Wars' Laser," *The Los Angeles Times*, September 23, 1985.

———. "Scientists Dispute Test of X-ray Laser Weapon, *The Los Angeles Times*, November 12, 1985.

———. "The Man Who Blew the Whistle on Star Wars," *The Los Angeles Times Magazine*, July 17, 1988.

Schell, Jonathan. *The Fate of the Earth* (Knopf, New York, 1982).

Schoenfeld, Bruce. "Support Seen Growing for Moving Tactical Missile Defense From SDI," *Defense Week*, May 6, 1991.

*Scientific American*. "Birthday Blowout," July 1985.

Seaborg, Glenn T. *Kennedy, Khrushchev and the Test Ban* (University of California Press, Berkeley, 1981).

Sewell, Duane C. "The Branch Laboratory at Livermore During the 1950's," in Hans Mark and Lowell Wood, eds., *Energy in Physics, War and Peace: A Festschrift Celebrating Edward Teller's 80th Birthday* (Kluwer Academic Publishers, Boston, 1988).

Shanor, Donald R. *Behind the Lines: The Private War Against Soviet Censorship* (St. Martin's Press, New York, 1985).

Shepley, James, and Clay Blair, Jr. *The Hydrogen Bomb* (McKay, New York, 1954).

Siegel, Lee. "Teller Claimed X-ray Laser Could Destroy All Land-Based Soviet Missiles," Associated Press, July 16, 1988.

Smith, Hedrick. *The Power Game* (Random House, New York, 1988).

Smith, R. Jeffrey. "Reagan Plans New ABM Effort," *Science*, April 8, 1983.

———. "Experts Cast Doubts on X-ray Laser," *Science*, November 8, 1985.

———. "Lab Officials Squabble Over X-ray Laser," *Science*, November 22, 1985.

———. "SDI Decision 'May Be Nearing'; Weinberger Tells of 'Opportunities for Earlier Deployment,' " *The Washington Post*, January 23, 1987.

———. "Pentagon Increases SDI Push," *The Washington Post*, February 18, 1990.

Speed, Roger D. "ASAT's vs. Brilliant Pebbles," Lawrence Livermore National Laboratory, UCRL-ID-103669, March 1990.

Sterba, James P. "Atom-Test Blast Set in Colorado," *The New York Times*, May 13, 1973.

———. "A-Blast in Colorado Does Less Damage Than Was Expected," *The New York Times*, May 18, 1973.

Stevens, Charles B. "Teller Confirms X-ray Laser Breakthrough," *Fusion*, September-October 1986.

Stober, Dan. "Teller Denies 'Star Wars' Charge," *San Jose Mercury News*, December 10, 1987.

———. "Physicist Named Livermore Lab Chief," *San Jose Mercury News*, February 19, 1988.

Strategic Defense Initiative Organization. "1989 Report to Congress," March 13, 1989.

Talbott, Strobe. *The Master of the Game: Paul Nitze and the Nuclear Peace* (Knopf, New York, 1988).

Teller, Edward. "The Work of Many People," *Science*, February 25, 1955.

———. "We're Going to Work Miracles," *Popular Mechanics*, March 1960.

———. "Can We Harness Nuclear Fusion in the 70's?" *Popular Science*, May 1972.

———. *Energy from Heaven and Earth* (W. H. Freeman & Company, San Francisco, 1979).

———. "I WAS THE ONLY VICTIM OF THREE-MILE ISLAND," *The Wall Street Journal*, July 31, 1979.

———. "Dangerous Myths About Nuclear Arms," *Reader's Digest*, November 1982.

———. "Reagan's Courage," *The New York Times*, March 30, 1983.

———. Testimony, April 28, 1983. *Defense Department Authorization and Oversight Hearings*, Committee on Armed Services, House of Representatives, Ninety-eighth Congress, first session. Part 5 of 8 parts. Research, Development, Test, and Evaluation—Title II.

———. "SDI: The Last, Best Hope," *Insight* magazine (*Washington Times*), October 28, 1985.

———. "Progress Made in Protective-Defense Research," *The New York Times*, December 29, 1985.

———. *Better a Shield Than a Sword* (The Free Press, New York, 1987).

———. "A Gleam in the Eye of SDI," *The Washington Times*, February 23, 1988.

———. "H-Bombs to 'Star Wars': An Insider's View," *The New York Times*, March 21, 1990.

Teller, Edward, and Albert L. Latter, *Our Nuclear Future* (Criterion, New York, 1958).

———, and Allen Brown. *The Legacy of Hiroshima* (Doubleday, Garden City, New York, 1962).

*Time*. "Magnetic Bottle," June 18, 1956.

———. "Knowledge Is Power," November 18, 1957.

Turner, Wallace. "Aleutian H-Bomb Is Fired Without Setting Off Quake," *The New York Times*, October 3, 1969.

Union of Concerned Scientists. "Issue Backgrounder: Brilliant Pebbles," Cambridge, Mass., June 1989.

United Press International. "Nuke," March 23, 1983.

*U.S. News & World Report*. "Dollars vs. Lives—A U.S. Choice," May 29, 1967.

———. "Not Only Humane, But Truly Effective," May 26, 1969.

*Valley Times* (of California). "Reagan Fetes Teller for Exemplary Service," February 2, 1989.

———. "Teller Recuperating from Colon Surgery," April 25, 1989.

von Hippel, Frank. "The Myths of Edward Teller," *The Bulletin of the Atomic Scientists*, March 1983.

Wade, Troy E., 2nd. Testimony Before Energy and Water Development Subcommittee of House Committee on Appropriations, March 12, 1988, "Energy and Water Development Appropriations for 1989," Part 6.

Walbridge, E. "Angle Constraint for Nuclear-Pumped X-ray Laser Weapons," *Nature*, July 19, 1984.

Wallop, Malcolm. "Opportunities and Imperatives of Ballistic Missile Defense," *Strategic Review*, Fall 1979.

———. " 'Patriots' Point the Way," *The New York Times*, January 31, 1991.

*Washington Post*. "Meese Calls for Speedup in Deploying 1st Stage of 'Star Wars' Defense," January 15, 1987.

Weinberger, Caspar. *Fighting for Peace: Seven Critical Years in the Pentagon* (Warner, New York, 1990).

Weisman, Steven R. "Reagan, at U.N., Asks Soviet for Long-term 'Framework' to Press for Arms Control," *The New York Times*, September 25, 1984.

Whitten, Barbara L. "Neon-Like Soft X-ray Lasers," *Lawrence Livermore Energy and Technology Review*, February-March 1989.

Wiesner, Jerome B., and Kosta Tsipis. "Put Star Wars Before a Panel," *The New York Times*, November 11, 1986.

Wigner, Eugene P. "An Appreciation of the 80th Birthday of Edward Teller," in Hans Mark and Lowell Wood, eds., *Energy in Physics, War and Peace: A Festschrift Celebrating Edward Teller's 80th Birthday* (Kluwer Academic Publishers, Boston, 1988).

Williams, Robert C., and Philip L. Cantelon, eds. *The American Atom* (University of Pennsylvania, Philadelphia, 1984).

Wood, Lowell. "Pillars of Fire in the Valley of the Giant Mushrooms," A Briefing Presented to James Abrahamson, Director, Strategic Defense Initiative Organization, April 19, 1985.

―――. "Soviet and American X-ray Laser Efforts: A Technological Race for the Prize of a Planet," A Briefing Presented to William Casey, Director of Central Intelligence, April 23, 1985.

―――. " 'Brilliant Pebbles' Missile Defense Concept Advocated by Livermore Scientist," *Aviation Week & Space Technology*, June 13, 1988.

―――. "Concerning the Vulnerability of Objects in Space to Attack by Ground-Based Laser Systems," Lawrence Livermore National Laboratory, undated.

―――, and John Nuckolls. "The development of nuclear explosives," in Hans Mark and Lowell Wood, eds., *Energy in Physics, War and Peace: A Festschrift Celebrating Edward Teller's 80th Birthday* (Kluwer Academic Publishers, Boston, 1988).

Woodruff, Roy D. "Nuclear Weapons and American Defense Policy," *Defense Science 2001*, December 1983.

Yonas, Gerold. "The Strategic Defense Initiative," *Daedalus*, Spring 1985.

York, Herbert. *The Advisors: Oppenheimer, Teller and the Superbomb* (W. H. Freeman, San Francisco, 1976).

# Index